RUTH BENEDICT

RUTH BENEDICT
Patterns of a Life

Judith Schachter Modell

UNIVERSITY OF PENNSYLVANIA PRESS
Philadelphia • 1983

This work was published with the support
of the Haney Foundation.

Library of Congress Cataloging in Publication Data

Modell, Judith, 1941-
   Ruth Benedict, patterns of a life.

   Bibliography: p.
   Includes index.
      1. Benedict, Ruth, 1887-1948.   2. Anthropologists—
United States—Biography.   I. Title.
GN21.B45M63   1983   306'.092'4   [B]   82-21989
ISBN 0-8122-7874-7

Printed in the United States of America

To Mollie Schachter

Contents

Preface

MY BIOGRAPHY OF Ruth Benedict has been a long quest and steady company for over ten years. Curiosity about the woman who sought to understand herself through writing, in poetry and biography, and through the traditional roles of wife, schoolteacher, and charity worker soon turned to absorption in and profound respect for her "discovery" of anthropology. I traced Ruth Benedict's path, caught up, intrigued, and influenced by her choices while yet maintaining my distance and preserving—as she might say—my own course. There is, I hope, a fair balance of dispassion and empathy, of judgment and of admiration, in the chapters of my book.

Ruth Benedict helped to determine the history of her discipline, in the United States and in the world. Her books *Patterns of Culture* and *The Chrysanthemum and the Sword* are classics in anthropology and reference points of humanistic thought in the twentieth century. In my account, I unravel the threads connecting Ruth Benedict's extraordinary professional achievements to her private struggles and personal dilemmas. I have respected her deep discretion while portraying the "passionate experience" behind an intellectual contribution of strength, vigor, and severity. The words Ruth Benedict used about Mary Wollstonecraft's life are appropriate to her own.

I could not have accomplished my task without the help of many people. Margaret Mead immediately encouraged my project, appreciating the need for a full-length biographical study of her teacher, colleague, and friend. As in all her endeavors, Mead supported the work of another scholar with time, information, and enthusiasm. Among colleagues and friends of Ruth Benedict who gave me their time and thought were the late Ruth Sawtelle Wallis, and Theodora Kroeber, as well as Leonard Doob, E. Adamson Hoebel, Ruth Landes, Sidney Mintz, and Leo Rosten. I am indebted to librarians and archivists at the Columbiana Collection (Columbia University), the American Philosophical Society, the Smithsonian, and most especially the Vassar College Special Collections librarians, Frances Goudy and Lisa Browar.

My colleagues and friends provided guidance and help on various issues of substance, as well as reminding me that although a biographer's life necessarily intertwines with her subject's, a biography must be kept fully distinct from an autobiography. I would like to thank Dan Ben-Amos, William Davenport, Larry Frank, Elsa Greene, Clyde Griffen, Elvin Hatch, Robert Kiste, John Modell, Charles Rosenberg, and George Stocking for reading, editing, and talking over the manuscript. At the University of Pennsylvania Press, John McGuigan has been a surpassingly fine editor, friend, and support.

To others who participated as I sought to interpret Ruth Benedict's pattern of life, I express gratitude and appreciation.

1
A Life of Ruth Benedict

"IT IS CURIOUS TO SEE how the basic patterns of our lives hold from baby-hood to decrepitude. All the tale could be told if we could set down the simple theme at the more and more significant times in which we work it out in our different stages of growth."[1]

My biography of Ruth Fulton Benedict is an attempt to "set down the simple theme" in order to illuminate the far-from-simple life of a woman whose contribution to anthropology drew sustenance and energy from an aware self-development. Not "all the tale" has been told, but a first and necessary step has been taken toward its fuller unfolding in the future.

Pattern is crucial. The word represents Ruth Benedict's view of a life: her own, other people's, another society's. Pattern also summarizes the content and approach of her anthropology; she left the word to generations of anthropologists and common readers. Because pattern represented, for Ruth, the character and the continuity in a life, I have used her concept to organize my story of her life.

Two points are significant. A pattern takes shape around a basic theme; when we discover the one, we begin to perceive the other. A pattern, too, is "worked out" by a subject; the word implies process as well as shape.

Ruth "worked out" her pattern along a theme that was essentially a contrast: life and death, experience and intellect, female and male. These were her phrasings; her life became a search for accommodation between two poles. "I come out always on a special cross roads," she wrote in her journal in July 1930. The phrases refer to a specific moment, her father dead and her mother weeping, and Ruth made the vision essential in her "design for living."[2]

I have emphasized her statement "We work it [theme] out in different stages of growth." Ruth considered life a creative process and meant the working and reworking of a theme. I have talked about composing, narrating, and revising to suggest her "working out" of theme, a process evident in gestures and moods and not only (sometimes not at all) in words.

In her life and in her writings, pattern referred to making and seeing order. Pattern simultaneously referred to understanding and communicating a "unique" way of life. Expressing and perceiving a pattern constituted a single process for person and for culture, but only and always in glimpses. To realize a whole pattern—to tell the complete tale —was the task of an observer, biographer, ethnographer, or second self.

Throughout her life, Ruth observed and compared "designs for living." For her, a life that lacked order must collapse; "some degree of consistency is necessary or the whole scheme falls to pieces."[3] These phrases from her study of Japanese culture can be applied to her biography. The effort to work out a significant pattern lay behind Ruth Benedict's diaries, her biographical essays, her ethnographies, and her public activities. The presentation of patterns so that others might comprehend was her achievement, as a woman and as an anthropologist.

Every biography is constrained by chronology, by the beginning, middle, and end of a life. And biographers move through time differently: a linear progression from birth to death; a back-and-forth movement of retrospection and anticipation; a thematic arrangement of significant moments. Many biographers also face the difficulty of relating individual to social time. I have handled the first problem—beginning, middle, and end—by a thematic emphasis within a general chronological structure. I have handled the second by viewing historical developments somewhat through Ruth Benedict's eyes.

In saying I view external events through her eyes, I do not mean simply taking Ruth Benedict at her word—or accepting her assessments of a particular episode, in contemporary affairs or in anthropology. I have, rather, juxtaposed her emphases against my judgment of the significance of historical and personal events. The juxtaposition revealed her characteristic mode of seeing, the "values of existence" that are a life for the biographer and ethnographer. I have not, then, written the biography of a woman to exemplify a culture and an era, of a thinker to indicate an intellectual atmosphere, or of an anthropologist to present the history of a discipline. These are all part of my account. Mainly I have followed through an individual woman's choices, noting her selection of items from her context, her intellectual background, and her profession. I have focused on Ruth's re-creation of circumstances, an effort parallel and necessary to her creation of an identity.

As did Ruth Benedict herself, I regard her life as the unfolding of a theme. I use "theme" for repeated and ramifying elements, expressed in thought, feeling, and event: the strains that persistently recur. A theme, known or not, articulated and unconscious, unifies disparate, disconnected details into a coherent shape. Resonating and changing over time, theme stretches the boundaries of a pattern without destroying its basic lines.

A theme unfolds with help from the actor, and a biographer must acknowledge this creativity in representing a life. Over the years, Ruth attained a surer, more perceptive "charting of her course";[4] her perceptions provided me with a structure for distinct chronological episodes. I have tried, too, to preserve her sense of timing, in terms a poet would recognize. I have reproduced the rhythms and the stresses in her life, around the theme she formulated, movingly, in 1935. Life and death, her mother and her father, outburst and calm—the phrases varied, their meaning and relationship changed in response to events, but the contrast never disappeared entirely.

Ruth realized, and revised, much of the pattern of her life. Had she completed the design, the biographer would have a small task. But she had not; no one knew better the difficulty of seeing life "whole" and of putting together the fragments of an "adventure."

APPROACH

In 1959 Margaret Mead published *An Anthropologist at Work*.[5] Throughout the book, between "the writings of Ruth Benedict," she interspersed biographical sections based on personal contact and on documents. The resulting collection provides several perspectives on the anthropologist: a life story in anthology form. Ruth appreciated the value of multiple perspectives; she also emphasized the importance of a whole, integrated, and evocative portrait.

Mead did not consider her volume a complete biography, and the 1974 version less than the 1959;[6] neither book contained the full account her friend and colleague deserved. *An Anthropologist at Work* does have unity, a set of drawings of the same person in different attitudes and moods. It lacks the broad-scale and deliberate assessment Mead was too close to Ruth Benedict to provide. Margaret Mead not only knew many of the people in Ruth's story, she also shared many of the incidents. In her accounts Mead exercised both tact and discretion. Clearly, too, Margaret Mead did not aim for a distanced overview of life-and-works or for a strict and penetrating analysis of Ruth's character. Mead does sketch the dominant motives in her friend's life, leaving material for a reader to organize into a meaningful "whole." She also described a friendship.

The friendship flourished between 1923 and World War II, a guidepost in each woman's course. Ten years after Ruth's death in 1948, Margaret may not have been the ideal person to look appraisingly or analytically at Ruth Benedict. Their intimacy, intense around interruptions, imposed restraints on Mead as literary executor, but even more, constrained her public interpretations of Ruth's struggles to unify love, work, marriage, and career. The two women discussed everything from love affairs to international peace negotiations; these discussions laid the foundation for lifetime habits of mind and emotion and, as well, for a significant anthropology. Not all could be told and, Mead admitted, even given the perpetual conversations there were still things about Ruth she did not know or, knowing, did not understand. Margaret could not, for instance, compare her relationship to Ruth's other attachments: some "passions" Ruth never mentioned.[7] Too, Ruth's marriage to Stanley Benedict remained a problem. Margaret openly expressed her perplexity at that relationship.

Margaret Mead, like Stanley Benedict, completed a portion of Ruth's story, fitting into an intricate pattern of intimacies whose design is best seen by an outside observer. At times Margaret indicated her place in Ruth's emotional constellation mainly by judicious elisions, omitted phrases suggesting much. At other times she provided unique insight into the quality of Ruth's encounters, interactions she saw and heard about. *An Anthropologist at Work* contains the invaluable knowledge given by a close friendship, a knowledge that was, however, consequently shaded and subdued. One can read between the lines of *An Anthropologist at Work*, as Mead surely intended. She published an "anthological" biography, and she expected readers to participate imaginatively in the unfolding of a life.

An Anthropologist at Work inspired my undertaking. Margaret Mead encouraged my project, knowing that not all the documents had been used and that not all the points had been made. Her collection served as a major source for me, containing otherwise unavailable materials (e.g., Edward Sapir's letters, Ruth's presumably having been lost in a fire),[8] information a close woman friend would have, and an awareness of Benedict's professionalization special to a fellow anthropologist.

In 1972 I added to the account of *An Anthropologist at Work* an extended interview with Margaret Mead. She had just published *Blackberry Winter*, and memories crowded her mind; she talked eagerly, vividly, and lovingly about Ruth. Margaret Mead left me with much to think about, a certain amount to suppress (or not announce), and a great deal of support for my interpretations. Her support of my biography lasted until her death in November 1978.

Ultimate justification for writing a full-length biography of Ruth Benedict lies in what Ruth in her writings and Mead in her conversation advocated: understanding of another life gains immeasurably from accumulated perspectives.

My own point of view comes from an involvement with Ruth Benedict that, though not firsthand, was intense. I did not have to manage the constraints of friendship; I did have to struggle with the demands of a continual self-exploration. A question about Ruth Benedict's life often prompted one about my own. This set up a process of reciprocal insight, and I learned more about Ruth as a woman and anthropologist while exploring my own responses to those roles.

Few biographers these days deny the element of autobiography, or personal involvement, in a biography. Most admit the personal in initial choice of subject. What happens next depends on each biographer, who alone faces the task of distinguishing an autobiographical from a biographical insight, in research and in presentation. I began writing a biography of Ruth Benedict because I was intrigued by the woman who emerged from Mead's pages. In the course of investigations, interviews, and hours in the library, I occasionally experienced sharp irritation, even boredom, that alternated with a too-close identification. These responses, though different, reminded me of biographical strictures. Helpful readers of the manuscript pointed out my too obvious presence.

I was also alert to temperamental and contextual differences. Ruth Benedict and I were not alike and not contemporaries, but we did share certain situations. I recognized the Vassar that Ruth Benedict went to from 1905 to 1909, surprisingly like the Vassar I attended half a century later. The Columbia University neighborhood had changed in fifty years, but I "knew" her office, classrooms, Low Library, and nearby restaurants. Situational similarities had life-course parallels: I, too, shifted from literature to anthropology after a nonacademic interruption. These similarities supported my decision to compare her statements to instances in my life. I opted for a kind of judgment entailing a large but (I hope) proportioned dose of speculation.

I took my responses as partial standard and as "granite" for the "rainbow" of speculation that completes a biography;[9] then I discovered how well my approach suited Ruth Benedict. In doing the research, I realized any a priori scheme violated her notion of understanding and communicating a life. According to Ruth, procedures came from an active encounter between observer and observed; each discovery demanded a new engagement with material. What sounded simple turned out to be, as her students also learned, difficult and challenging. Self-reflection became a guide to responsible inquiry. I took a similar attitude in my biography of her.

I tried, too, to honor her conviction that this seeming intricacy represented an ordinary way of understanding. Ruth Benedict created a common-sense comparative method and deliberately incorporated the method into her discipline. I have tried to be equally attentive to the elements of my biographical approach. In the following chapters I distinguish speculation from critical analyses of Ruth's various statements, and each of these from her own explicitly explanatory remarks.

A consistency emerged from the statements she made about her life, echoed in the reports about her by friends, colleagues, and students. I treated interviews like texts, listening, questioning—essentially reading between the lines of a remembered contact. For interviews I had to judge the relationship between my informant and Ruth, calculating the degree of personal and professional association.

The interviews provided further perspectives more often than distinct facts. "Every intelligent step ahead seems to me just that highly necessary step, not a CLUE or a SOLUTION"[10]—to become, however, a CLUE when delved and interpreted. I checked memories against other information, questioning why a person might tell a particular anecdote, criticize an issue, assume an event in Ruth Benedict's life. Informants talked about her as a woman, a teacher, and an anthropologist, rarely separating one from the other.

The interviews did not yield a wide range of opinions. Responses generally fell into two categories. Some people deeply admired Ruth and used words like "awe," "adulation," and once or twice "crush" to describe their feelings. Others were put off and used words like "vague," "wispy," and "incomprehensible." Those who liked her personally took on her anthropology; those who disliked her abstracted, "affected" manner called her work "nonmethodological" and "poetic"; the last, an ambiguous designation, did not always imply rejection of her anthropology.

Interviews accomplished another purpose. I had constantly to defend myself. People who knew Ruth challenged my views, and interviews turned into lively debates. Talking, usually for five or six hours, forced me to examine my impressions and conclusions, an examination that lasted well after the interview ended.

Several informants asked not to be identified. Although a few, including Margaret Mead, have since died, I continue to respect wishes for anonymity, citing "personal interview" and date where necessary.

The material Ruth Benedict saved substantiated my view of a searching, restless, and discreet woman. She kept few personal papers;

aside from the journals and small diaries, she saved drafts of short stories, poems, and literary pieces. I found little personal correspondence, though I assume such letters are in the closed boxes at Vassar College. The Ruth Benedict Collection at Vassar contained ten open and full file boxes; two boxes were closed until 1999, a restriction iterated in Mead's will in 1978.

Ruth did save letters about her work and the profession: the future of anthropology, the place of folklore in anthropology, and the bearing of selected disciplines on cross-cultural research. A foresightful academic, she also saved letters about research money and publications, written for herself and by the 1930s for her students. These letters testify to the intertwining of her professional life and her private life. Ruth rarely spoke about her work in a neutral voice, and she wasted no time, breath, or paper on issues she considered trivial or people she deemed inconsequential.

The American Philosophical Society houses the Franz Boas correspondence, including letters to and from Ruth Benedict. In these I observed the student become close friend and colleague; the friendship between Ruth and Franz Boas grew out of and then determined the contours of anthropology. The American Folk-Lore Society letters (1927–1940) show a harassed editor arguing against uncooperative and wordy contributors, bemoaning clumsy style, and pleading for money to support the *Journal of American Folklore*. Again, a sarcastic phrase, a candid plea for help and advice, an unstinted appreciation of effort revealed the woman's character.

I read these materials as I think Ruth Benedict would have, waiting for the sudden realization of pattern that comes from constant reinterpretation of data. Throughout my aim has been to gather "those impressions and turns of phrase which more than any statement of fact shape life in biographies as they do in reality."[11]

Inevitably there will be gaps. I have not filled these with background material or with information gained by applying psychoanalytic techniques. I mentioned elsewhere my treatment of background, but the point about psychoanalysis deserves a few sentences. I avoided a psychoanalytic approach because of my own lack of expertise and because Ruth disliked that mode of describing character. Actually she expressed an ambivalent anti-Freudianism. Truth, for her, lay *in* not beneath the surface, but "surface" shifted with traumatic events. Nevertheless, certain incidents and statements in her life lent themselves to psychoanalytic interpretation, and I have presented these with special care. Her preoccupation with death and her partial deafness are examples; each distanced her from surroundings and isolated her in ways she noted.

My book does not tell the story of unconscious and hidden impulses.

Instead I am concerned with the interaction between unconscious motives and surface manifestations. Ruth herself was thoroughly, often painfully, aware of the delicate passage from formative event to articulated idea. She learned to preserve the energy while rearranging the content of her impulses for an audience.

Ruth Benedict, I think, had a poet's view of the unconscious and conscious, and I used literary analysis to accomplish goals somewhat similar to psychoanalysis. In verse, Ruth objectified her dilemmas and pinpointed the compelling fantasies. Behind a pseudonym, she developed a rhetoric that put an abstract and frequently spiritual view of the human condition into earthy and tangible images. The metaphysical tradition, yoking emotion to intellect, suited the poet. But yet, while she acknowledged the often unconscious origin of an intellectual preoccupation, she steadfastly guarded against the exposure of her emotions. To tell her truth I have honored her principles, ones she worked hard to formulate precisely, elegantly, and in a personal voice.

Autobiographical Statements

An existing autobiography poses a problem for any biographer. The subject has told a story, and the biographer must deal with a deliberate self-presentation. In my interpretation of Ruth Benedict, autobiography posed a particular problem. Throughout I have emphasized her inclination to revise and her awareness of self-conceptualizations. I could not treat "The Story of My Life"[12] as simply a factual account. It *is* a truthful account, of the way she formulated her life.

"The Story of My Life" revises the past and draws a self for the future. Ruth turned her artistry to moments in childhood and adolescence partly to anticipate the woman she might become. In the autobiographical fragment she reviewed early episodes, reimagining herself through a series of dramatic vignettes: hidden in a damp haymow, running from an uncle's kiss, wearing the wrong dress at a school party. The images accumulated resoundingly, and Ruth revealed the sensuous side of a temperament whose other side was a determined intellectuality. By intention or not, Ruth's autobiography recalled the considered, sensual core of her poems, her conversations, and her anthropology. Her personality emerged, sharply drawn against figures—real and imaginary— who drifted across her variegated landscapes.

I read the autobiography for insight into a perspective that evolved from an original simple contrast: death and life. In 1935 Ruth returned to the start of her "spiritual journey" (a phrase from a biography of Beethoven she admired[13]) and drew out her "attitude toward existence,"

the theme of her pattern. The autobiography described a self caught by
surroundings and conveyed the tension between individual and custom
Ruth developed into an anthropology. The "fact" in her narrative is the
bond between spontaneous impulse and persistent idea, between private
dilemma and a professional achievement. In "The Story of My Life"
Ruth set out a "way of seeing" that for me, and for her, represented a
"way of living."

Ruth Benedict wrote for herself, to compose episodes into a design
and to assure herself of a consistency of purpose. She exaggerated a few,
omitted several, and dramatized many incidents, in an attempt to revive
the several personae composing her identity and to explain her pattern.
But she had a practical motive, too, and a quite real audience to check
on rampant imaginings and uncensored self-description. Margaret Mead
had encouraged self-analysis, and Ruth, responding to the request, displayed her trust in the friendship. Simultaneously she justified a mode of
describing character common to all her writings. Ruth wrote the "Story"
right after completing *Patterns of Culture*.

Freud, she told Mead in 1932 (while working on *Patterns of Culture*), "lost" the person; Virginia Woolf, on the other hand, conveyed
personality, in a poetic unity superior to analytic "disunity."[14] Yet Ruth
did not ignore psychoanalysis, notably in first drafts of the "Story" and
possibly in concluding her narrative at adolescence. The "end at a beginning" (of adulthood), however, primarily invoked a notion of recur-
rence, echo of being born when her father died.

Ruth Benedict invariably had an audience in mind when she wrote,
including a severe second self, and she disciplined her writings accord-
ingly (she even revised diary entries). The autobiography, no exception,
was carefully arranged for presentation. Ruth did several drafts before
putting her "Story" aside, satisfied with a version of the tale.

She had tried other versions, less direct and equally autobiographical. I considered her sonnets an autobiographical source; similarly significant were her biographical studies of three "restless women"—Mary
Wollstonecraft, Margaret Fuller, and Olive Schreiner.[15] Ruth finished
the "Mary Wollstonecraft" essay and through her heroine grappled with
issues of motherhood, love, sexual passion, recognized achievement, and
ideological principles. In writing about the eighteenth-century feminist,
Ruth discovered she had to order these issues in her own life and work
out her own understandings of the balance between self-fulfillment and
public demands. She turned from biography to sonnets, in some ways a
more elaborate mask but in many ways a far more revealing statement.
Ruth claimed a greater ease in verse. "My prose beats with the rhythm
of verse," she once wrote.[16]

Screened by metaphor, by the "beat," and by a pseudonym, Ruth

Benedict posed questions about human existence that, her phrases revealed, touched her own experience closely and intimately. The poetry convinced me of the significance of image and fantasy in Ruth's view of the world. I found it not enough, then, to say that she cared about style (she certainly did) or that she wanted her ideas to be effectively conveyed; I realized that creating images for her constituted an argument. Envisioning a setting was the beginning, means, and end of inquiry. "Envision" is a central concept in my interpretations of Ruth Benedict. She put her vision into poems and constructed an ideal world representing yet distinct from private turmoils and wishes.

For me, too, Ruth's poetry possessed an urgency the "Story" did not. For nearly two decades the poet worked to grasp her "contraries" and in the process prepared her anthropological perspective. She learned that an artfully presented design could be a persuasive plan of action, and in applying this lesson she influenced her discipline's history and her country's outlook. As an anthropologist, Ruth Benedict drew on the world, not just the self, for provocative images, and she rearranged these for a general public.

"But man is a species which can create his way of life—his culture. . . . His social life has developed, for good or evil, within a human framework which he has himself invented and espoused."[17] She considered "arrangement" man's glory and his necessity. To this she added the element of artistry.

THE CHOICE OF RUTH BENEDICT: FEMINISM AND ANTHROPOLOGY

I read Margaret Mead's *An Anthropologist at Work* ten years ago while studying processes of "translation" from private to public statement, my focus on women. Mead's collection of Ruth Benedict writings, selectively arranged around her memories of a friend and colleague, caught my attention, the juxtaposition of private and public startlingly apt. My initial attraction to Ruth had not been to an important anthropologist or to a feminist.

My decision to supplement Mead's account with a full-length biography, however, presumed a judgment of Ruth Benedict's importance. Her distinct style of translating private expression into public text had importance because "public" became an influential anthropology and a position on contemporary events. Ruth's anthropological approaches and her political attitudes shared roots, I discovered, with her understanding of feminism, what she called the "woman issue."

I had focused on women in analyzing modes of expression. My focus reflected a suspicion that for women the constraints on expression were stringent partly because self-definition was problematic and partly because public expression often obeyed "male" standards. I realized eventually that Ruth Benedict had suspected much the same. She displayed a tension between private and public in her writings, her activities, her gestures of friendship. I came to appreciate, too, her conclusion that women's expressions must be grounded in women's experiences, and to realize the extent to which she unknowingly anticipated a 1970s and 1980s feminism.

My own experiences, following a first reading of *An Anthropologist at Work,* clarified my feminism. "Vicarious participation" in another woman's life (as Ruth described her biographical approach) led me to reconsider the source of my perspective and the meaning of feminism for me and for my subject. Unconsciously at first, I was following Ruth's prescription, combining the questioning of myself with the questioning of another for mutual clarification. The process revealed the quality of my feminism and that of Ruth Benedict.

Ruth Benedict anticipated current feminist thought precisely in her perception of links between self and other in the conduct of an inquiry. In order to specify the features of and the constraints on her life as a woman, she imagined herself in another woman's life, in another place, of another temperament entirely. She learned, too, that a vividly evoked scene mirrored self as much as did varied personae. Through her "figures"—settings and heroines—Ruth constructed and changed a conceptualization of herself as a woman. Hers was not a political feminism, but an engaged intellectual approach first to the lives of women and then to the life of any individual. My feminism appears to be much of a piece with hers.

Ruth carried the attempt to relate "woman's nature" to conventional demands into her cross-cultural research. Her feminism—her concern with women—influenced the content of an anthropology focused on the individual-in-culture and the attitude of an anthropologist determined to widen the parameters of individual choice. As a woman and an anthropologist, Ruth Benedict adopted a viewpoint that sometimes baffled and frustrated her. The effort to respect diverse designs did not rest easily with a need to maintain—and occasionally preach—long-held principles. The result was a continual compromise, characteristic of her outlook on the woman issue, of her anthropological assessment of cultures and of her political activism in World War II.

Yet Ruth clung to a belief in individuality and in the importance of individual vision. She persuaded herself, and others, to attend to the promptings of nature and of dreams; these fit into and revitalized the existing design. Through individual vision, a society was invigorated and could recompose its pattern. Ruth's view of culture creating, then being created by, each individual formed both her particular feminism and her innovative anthropology.

She had briefly introduced elements of popular feminist ideology into her personal debates. Mainly she was too cautious a thinker to embrace doctrine. Ruth never took up a feminist banner; she admired those who did, and behind her admiration stirred a yearning for certainties. Above all, she distrusted categories and permanent "pigeonholes" and would not refer to herself as a feminist or, later, a culture-and-personality anthropologist. By the 1950s she was given the second designation and in the 1970s was accepted into the feminist canon.

Off and on I tried to pinpoint her feminism and settle the issue she never (I believe) settled. Her fixing of ideas to experiences made any classification impossible. Eventually I decided on a description adequate to my understanding and accurate to her statements. I describe a set of mind, an attitude about creation of self that she formulated in a feminist context and refined in an anthropological one. For me Ruth's feminism was one aspect of her encounter with experiences.

The daydreams and fantasies of her childhood, dissatisfaction with jobs and with acquaintances, a "barren" marriage, "her own bewildered struggles"[18]—all stretched feminism into a broader political outlook, ultimately a philosophical position. Throughout her life, her writings, and her career she searched for ways of channeling restless energies into proper and effective form. In the end this quest led to an anthropology at once original and obedient to disciplinary rules.

In 1919 Ruth Benedict enrolled in her first anthropology course, almost at the same moment writing in her journal: "Nature lays a compelling and very distressing hand upon women."[19] That year, too, she drafted an essay on the "woman issue." Unknowingly she had by then the building blocks of her discipline: a perception of conflict between self-fulfillment and custom, and a rhetoric that embedded "cold dry logic" in evocative imagery. Consistent with the rest of her life, Ruth's anthropology acknowledged the stress of individuality, the push of the particular against conventions and absolutes. And her anthropology illustrated the delicate balance entailed when attention is paid to the human and to the creativeness that, with constraint, constitutes the human condition. Ruth Benedict incorporated the balance into professional work that was powerfully popular in appeal.

I became a Benedictian anthropologist. This involved, to some extent, recognizing the affinities between a biographical and an anthropological approach. Becoming an anthropologist involved, for me as for

Ruth Benedict, charting a way through the observer-observed problem. Like my subject, I believed an inquiry included the observer and could finally be justified because the observer claimed a commitment to the "observed." I also shared Ruth's view that self-awareness both sharpened inquiry and provided some guard against plodding thoughtlessly through the life of another. Curiosity inspires the task; a sense of one's self can channel the curiosity, preserving integrity of observer and observed. Ruth convinced me of the connection between personal engagement and a researcher's responsibility.

My generation of anthropologists has little interest in "salvage ethnography" and increasing doubts about traditional categories of cultural description. Current efforts to redefine goals and methods bring us back to Ruth Benedict. Absorbed in her life story, I realized how inevitably social scientists today must acknowledge her point of view. Those who, like me, adopt her approach do so because she suits a contemporary world-society and because she incorporated into passionately committed statements the historically proven precepts of her discipline.

Through her living and her writings, Ruth Benedict contributed to the intellectual milieu which we—anthropologists, feminists, both or neither—still inhabit. She argued for "individualized wisdom" and ideas tested in experience. This fostered a humility and a justice in her inquiries we would do well to attend to, whatever our positions.

A Note on Ethics

Ruth Benedict regarded the panorama of designs for living with awe. She also had confidence in her ability to recreate and to represent these designs so they would be effective and useful. "Useful" raises problems; Ruth did not discuss the ethics of cross-cultural research, but a viewpoint is implied in her notion of pattern.

Pattern represented the particular, individual spirit, to be treated on its own terms. Ruth took enormous pleasure in differences and would not relinquish them by establishing hierarchy or paradigm for human behavior. Added to this respect for uniqueness was an optimism about the ability of a person and a society to see its own way to improvement. She was optimistic about voluntary social engineering, sometimes more than about personal change. The two, however, were closely related.

A culture pattern was unique and, for Ruth Benedict, had a unique dynamic from the personalities and the creativeness of members of the society. Change could not, therefore, be imposed, but must recognize the existing structure and its distinct motivating "visions."

The other component of her ethical position had to do with reference of data to self. In her biographical studies Ruth questioned herself; in her cross-cultural studies she questioned American society. She did not spare herself, and she did not spare her culture the sharp eye of appraisal. She neither accepted nor dismissed out of hand any of the various accommodations to "this wonderful power, a voltage with which the universe is believed to be charged."[20]

Ruth Benedict concentrated on specifics and on self-generated change—the core of her ethical position. She refused to fix principles and undertook (and urged others) to chart a course for each new adventure. There was bravery in this, part and parcel of her disciplinary approach. Ruth staunchly included the unpredictable, human element and humbly doubted the impact of unadorned scientific findings. She shunned generalization in order to argue for the infinite possibilities of human life. Ruth Benedict did not minimize the importance of self-determined change, even when the need for change was desperate.

Her anthropology was not about laws. Her anthropology *was* about effort and continuity and creativity, and about the role of human imagination in the construct of a viable design for living. Ruth demonstrated, unforgettably, the enormous differences from culture to culture and tried to show the enormous individual difference possible within one culture. For her the force of custom and the interdependency of traits did not restrict but provided opportunity for dream to become reality and—she hoped—for individuals to find fulfillment. As a woman and an anthropologist, Ruth Benedict accepted responsibility for displaying diversity to "common readers." Ordinary people, their wishes and ideals informed by an anthropological perspective, could alter the world.

PATTERN IN ANTHROPOLOGY

Ruth Benedict was lucky: the beginnings of academic anthropology in America suited her, allowing her to legitimize a private style of interpretation. In the biography, I describe a coincidence between personal and disciplinary history and convey the history of anthropology through one practitioner, through her responses to and reception by the discipline. Ruth would have understood this approach; for her, intellectual history *was* the story of individual commitments. Anthropology, especially, seemed to Ruth to be wrapped in the experience of individual anthropologists.

Her own contribution had to do with an ability to transfer personal tensions into structured inquiries. She thought much about "uniqueness," about the opportunities for creating self within conventions, and about the manifestations of individuality in a person and a society. Ruth maintained, too, a belief that wisdom stemmed from experience and from dreaming: vision stretched the boundaries of reality. After World War I, in her first anthropology courses, the alternatives she had envisioned and the possibilities she imagined appeared in societies she studied.

Ruth brought a passion (her "gemlike flame") to anthropology and found a "vessel" for her unfocused ambitions. She eventually chose the word pattern to represent means and end of an inquiry whose impulse was personal and whose implications were vast. The word referred to the content and the method of her anthropology and, inextricably, to her perspective on "the swift, whirling facts of her own life."[21] Ruth chose the word carefully and did not offer a simple definition. To an audience of poets, scientists, and general readers she gave a word at once attractive and indefinite, useful and tantalizingly vague. She picked a plain word on purpose, assuming a common-sense understanding that eliminated the need for exactness and avoided the danger of jargon. Pattern was not a mysterious word, and Ruth Benedict did not consider hers a mystifying science. She did demand work, the work of perceiving and conveying pattern.

This trust in individual engagement made life hard for students, colleagues, friends, and commentators. In classes she taught a frame of mind, and in writings she displayed a conviction about the rightness of certain outlooks. People who admired her appreciated the leeway to create their own approach. Those who wanted method, laws, and "cold dry logic" minded the note of startled revelation in her anthropology. Ruth claimed, without apology, that cross-cultural understanding, like interpersonal understanding, demanded a "leap of faith." She meant that after collecting, viewing, and reviewing data, the observer waited for pattern to emerge, the underlying spirit to appear. Then he had to *describe*, actively, effectively, and with respect for the subject's presentation of pattern.

The word, pattern, carefully chosen, incorporated a good deal: Ruth's view of the composition of a life and of the way of understanding and describing a life. Nor, ultimately, was pattern without definition or specific meaning. The word acquired definition in Ruth's life stories, referring to the processes of selection essential to self-portrait. Ruth also used pattern to emphasize the selectivity in social science method and to suggest the coherence characteristic of culture and of person—necessary to the survival of both.

Pattern represented at once a method of inquiry and the subject, the entity being studied. Pattern might, in fact, be defined as a "way of seeing," a familiar definition of anthropology which, however, acquired multiple connotations in Ruth's writings. From "way of seeing" she developed an approach and, incidentally, a response to the "who sees, who makes pattern" question. The following paragraphs on pattern should be read, as well, as a paraphrase of my biographical approach.

To say the observer "sees" and the individual (person, society) "lives by" pattern simplifies a complex interrelationship. The individual at once experiences and creates pattern, realizing an underlying coherence in behaviors and attitudes ranging from the ordinary to the extraordinary, from mundane greetings to a crisis-induced ritual. Ruth added another significant point when she suggested that the individual does not perceive whole or constantly a lived pattern. Statements and gestures provided partial, temporary clues. But such glimpses were necessary: Pattern must appear from time to time, to be confirmed and valued, altered and reimagined. Ruth simply added to this the idea that no one can survive in the full steady glare of a known pattern, a completed tale. "Light the more given is the more denied." She was wary, and she saw dangers in full illumination, in the "ecstasy" of total comprehension. Words and phrases from her poems bear directly on an understanding of her "patterns of culture."

The observer, distanced in whatever way, can see pattern "whole." Above the immediacies, the observer gained an edge on perceptiveness and, unenmeshed, realized the pattern another lived by. Whether ethnographer, biographer, or second self, the task was to extract and represent pattern accurately and effectively.

Given these assumptions, Ruth Benedict could not but turn her anthropology into a supremely descriptive science. And like a biographer she had to come to terms with the artifice required for accurate portrayal. She faced the problem of presenting an account that would inspire response and yet not distort the original design—the subject's presentation. Ruth set a still valid goal: to convey the spirit of another life without exposing secrets or deadening the imagination in "logical" prose.

Ruth made a further point about pattern that influenced my biographical approach. She claimed that patterns emerged sharply through contrast and that self-other constituted a primary contrast. From her experiences she knew a private pattern could only be drawn clearly against the outline of an "exotic" and therefore visible pattern. She had set her course against Mary Wollstonecraft's, and she had recognized the dominant colors of her own by the lights and shadows of distant landscapes. The process of observing became equally, and simultaneously, a process of self-awareness and readiness to change. Ruth used her comparative method to confront the compulsions of the known.

A sequence of episodes, like places and selves, set up contrasts. Through the "different stages of growth" moments stood out, distinct and yet continuous with a past—and a future. Time presented contrasting images; the movement of a life from one phase to another brought increased clarity. Ruth applied these lessons from her life to her public statements. In everything she stressed the play of contrast against similarity, and the balance of stability against an inspired, invigorating adventure. Pattern did not mean stasis, a cover for unconscious impulses and an end to change. Pattern, rather, reflected ongoing accommodations between spontaneous impulse and necessary order. Pattern was a flexible composition of chaotic strivings.

Just before their marriage, Stanley Benedict remarked on "your mask, Ruth."[22] Temporarily distressed by his view, she eventually came back to her own. The "presented" face and arranged features were the truth of a person and, as well, of a culture. The threat lay in "thickening";[23] the mask must not rigidify and fail to respond to shifting dreams. Pattern referred to a unique and ongoing story, to the sequence of episodes as well as to the coherence of elements. Human beings created order, Ruth Benedict believed, and over time, sometimes clumsily and sometimes beautifully. The composite of individual designs made up a culture-pattern because, in her grandest assumption, cultures like people craved order.

Ruth Benedict added a judgment, lightly disguised under her semi-aesthetic vocabulary. She praised the well-integrated, the carefully-formed pattern. She also praised an open-endedness in patterns: the capacity of a design to incorporate inconsistencies and "swirling facts." The thought of endlessness in pattern comforted a woman who began her story with a death. For me, the nonclosure of a pattern confirmed the links between her life story and her disciplinary perspective.

Pattern was Ruth's most significant contribution to anthropology because the word told what a culture was, for its members and for observers, for those subjected to and chafing against custom and for those who, to be instructed, observed custom from a distance. Pattern was also her most significant contribution because the word reminded people that scientific method resonated to personal experience; on thought, "pattern" perfectly represented the living as well as the knowing of a life. None of it, after all, seemed so strange. Like her "culture," Ruth Benedict's "pattern" belongs to and illuminates common-sense ways of viewing the world.

CONCLUSION

Friends remember Ruth Benedict as a formal and composed woman. I have tried to capture this in the biography and to speculate about origins and effects. She *was* composed, but with an effort. The placidity and self-containment visible in public covered a restless nature, a woman committed to a dreaming whose consequences she regarded warily and whose realization she hoped for. In careful compositions she worked to reconcile competing desires, arranging incidents and moods. These efforts to structure the episodes of her life by an otherwise guarded woman proved invaluable. I was able to compare various texts, looking for the continuities and the discontinuities in a self-conscious rhetoric. Textual analysis gave me a picture of the woman and a configuration of the anthropologist.

Ruth was equally at home with a sensuous metaphor and an axiomatic phrase, a conversational tone and a poetic cadence. Her style was purposeful, reflecting a stamina not always apparent to those who met her and a sensitivity to visual and tactile impressions that quickened her ideas. The continuities and the changes in her style influenced my interpretation of the woman, wife, poet, and anthropologist. Ruth remained "at work" in her several roles, and she worked to reconcile their demands in phrases that bore directly on her life. Through modes of expression she balanced the demands of nature and of convention, poetry and anthropology, humanities and science. Rhetorical continuities manifested a lived consistency which Ruth did not always recognize but which she thoroughly depended on for each new adventure.

In one sense my book is a story of compositions: my narrative rearranges her deliberate creations of a "way of seeing." Ruth Benedict left a record in various texts. Her works are autobiographical not by plan but by urgency, the urgency of defining her ambitions and channeling her pressing curiosities. "All her writings mirror her life," Ruth wrote about Mary Wollstonecraft. The statement applies to her own life, as long as one considers the mirror prismatic.

The "figures" of childhood fantasies, adolescent fiction, and amateur poetry wove through Ruth Benedict's accounts of the Pueblos, Japan, Eastern Europe, and her society. In preserving images and phrases, Ruth expressed her purpose without confessing its origins—without, ever, "opening her mouth too wide."[24] She also maintained an intensity of expression from childhood until death. Nearly every word she wrote reflected the energy of a search for coherence.

My book is the biography of a writer, a woman who moved through compositions toward a reconciliation in life. "Compose" is especially apt. Ruth Benedict aimed for balance, being composed in readiness for change. Her poems talk of "running brooks" picking up reflections from the surroundings without "freezing" into place. She did not, in my understanding, ever achieve a final version, a completed composition. She left us with questions and with the materials for creating our own, provisionary answers. She warned, too, against abstractions and reminded us that answers mean little freed from experiencing.

Did anthropology satisfy the longings and ambitiousness Ruth described in herself? The question runs through my book, and I am convinced that variations of the question dominated her several self-assessments. She came to anthropology with doubts, pulled between the poles of a ramifying contrast, and with vaguely formed solutions embedded in a distinct style of viewing. Anthropology did discipline her self-inquiries and, to a remarkable extent, legitimized the questioning of a woman "always on some cross-roads." Anyone who reads her monographs the way she wanted will respond to the debate behind elegantly wrought portraits and will respond personally.

Without the hope that her writings and statements would alter people's lives, Ruth Benedict could not have persisted. Anthropology disciplined but did not completely satisfy her longings. She went on, not just to "endure" (her mother's word), but because of a faith that stemmed back to the individualism espoused by her religion, her society, and her teachers. Ruth Benedict added a notion of educating and meant by the word an expansion of the parameters of individual choice. She also gained a comfortable confidence in herself as an educator. At her best, out loud and on paper, Ruth persuaded people to change—in free will and from personal wisdom.

As I portray her in the following chapters, a thread of confidence sparkles beside the darker one of melancholy and despair. Ruth Benedict was proud of her compositions and of her impact on an eventually attentive world—even while she suspected that

> Frail dreams
> Are for the old, whose mirth blasphemes
> All perpetuities save death.[25]

How would Ruth Benedict have responded to my account of her life? She combined a probing curiosity about other lives with a discretion about her own. She also spent a lifetime envisioning alternative designs for herself, a more congenial place and a more contented temperament. I offer yet another design, an attempt to tell the truth of Ruth's life through a thematic sketch of the total pattern. She created and expressed, over the years, a distinct attitude toward existence; that attitude formed her anthropology and is our best lesson from her life.

I have described the attitude: a respect for individuality and a confidence in the power of individual imaginations to remake reality; a

belief in the importance of comparison; a trust in the beneficial transmission of "visions" from one person to another, one society to another.
In these views, Ruth provided the sturdiest justification for her own
biography I could want.

Yet she *was* a private woman, and she expected secrets to be kept
or at least offered up with great care by each possessor.[26] Recognizing
her own privacies monitored her curiosity about others. She respected
the masks, the ritualized expressions of emotion, and the display of order
presented by a person and by a society. She also pried, gently and cautiously, searching for hints of a central impelling motive—the "theme"
in a pattern. She rarely demanded or appreciated uncensored exposure,
and knew she knew enough when she glimpsed, in a flash of insight, the
total shape.

Ruth Benedict inevitably included the observer, the second self, the
biographer, and ethnographer, who with special privilege and special
responsibility saw and communicated patterns. In her notion of the observer, Ruth again, unknowingly, justified my undertaking: rewriting her
life story. As observer, I have rearranged the insights of a consciously
perceptive, self-interpreting woman. I have rearranged her versions of
the story around a theme she formulated in adulthood, then realized had
guided her life before and without a purposeful formulation.

I have not written the biography of a "remarkable woman" or an
"anthropological genius." Rather, I write of the ongoing combination of
those two in Ruth's experiences and in her perspectives. In the following
chapters I have outlined, for her, the parameters of a "search for truth."[27]

The life of Ruth Benedict seems to me one of extraordinary, enduring, and often fierce commitment. She made a commitment to exploring
and conveying the terms of living, to specifying the unfolding theme in
any individual pattern. She began with herself, straining to realize the
motives in her own life, and never entirely banished herself from inquiries. Fantasies and daydreams, fiction and sonnets gave way to ethnographies, theories of folklore, public speeches, and propaganda, but
Ruth kept the quest and the energy of her belief in educating, in visions,
and in changes. I detect an urgency in her living, from the earliest, private drafts of a story to the public writings of her last years. The voice
is consistent.

Her contribution extends beyond anthropology, beyond feminism
and broader political statements. Ruth's contribution has to do with a
resolution of private debates in a public encounter and a thoughtful professionalism. Her impulses and the modes of resolution remained rooted
in her interpretation of the "woman issue" in American culture.

Contribution seems finally too small a word to cover the significance of Ruth Benedict to a contemporary world. Her significance comes from her construct of a design for living in an effort she did not separate from the construction of an anthropology. Ruth never forgot that her personal struggles and movements toward understanding characterized the human condition. Out of this came an anthropological perspective and, unshakably, an attention to the "ordinary person" wherever that person lived and however she or he "recast the universe."[28]

Ruth Benedict believed that each one of us can create the terms of an existence, can individually take the initiative of imagining a better world. I hope in my biography to have conveyed her vision of human potential and its sources in a lived experience.

2

The Early Years

*"Certainly from my earliest childhood
I recognized two worlds"*

"THE STORY OF MY LIFE begins when I was twenty-one months old, at the time my father died," Ruth Benedict began an autobiography in 1935. Her first memory appropriately begins her biography. The incident initiated an unfolding rather than a chronology. Ruth linked her birth to her father's death; she perceived in the juxtaposition not the first of a series of events but the focal point of an endlessly elaborated pattern. She saw her life guided less by time than by theme, and the form she consequently gave an autobiography determines the form I give her biography. When Ruth wrote the fragment of her "story" for her friend and colleague Margaret Mead, psychoanalysis intrigued them both. Ruth rejected Freudian "free association" and chose instead to reconstruct her story, a deliberate design of crucial pieces.

Ruth Benedict appreciated the importance of a "primal scene" as long as a literary interpretation qualified the psychoanalytic meaning. She believed in destiny not as effect following cause but as an aspect of human character. To some extent, too, she had a poet's vision. She did not portray life as linear progression; she saw, rather, the drawing together of elements into an increasingly coherent pattern. The poet replaced movement toward a goal with a coming-full-circle. In this view, the life course becomes a process of arranging and rearranging, of fitting new elements to recurring themes. In a larger sense, not newness but emerging is important: Aspects of life come to light and are given place. As the poet reworks her sonnet, so the woman revised the pieces of her life.

Let me rephrase for a moment, to get closer to Ruth's understanding of the story of an individual life and, later, of a cultural life. Ruth saw the "story" less as narrative than as an arrangement, a composition of key elements. Distinct pieces came together and formed a unique design, a bounded and comprehensible configuration. I am using her words. "Design," "configuration"—these are words she tried before settling on "pattern."

Ruth Benedict never felt completely happy with "pattern," though she chose it for the title of her 1934 book and considered calling her 1946 book *Patterns of Japanese Culture.* In the end she needed a word and gave up struggling to find an exact rendering of her sense that pieces compose themselves and life is not random, whether of person or group. I will adopt her word to convey the consistency in her life.

I use the word "pattern" in the way Ruth Benedict did, to incorporate several related notions. One notion had to do with order, by which she meant harmony of interchangeable components. On the analogy of a sonnet, her favored poetic form, Ruth emphasized the structure rather than the specificity of parts. Order, the sonnet still her reference, implied the existence of dominant and guiding themes. Elements took their places according to an emphasis, an orientation initiated by a crucial contrast, as her own life had been. Finally, order meant full circle and a completed design.

Ruth Benedict's life came full circle: Her pattern found closure and consistency along the theme of birth and death. Ruth died on the anniversary of her father's birth. She attached her birth to the death of her father. The subject has given the biographer a beginning of her life and the vocabulary for writing that life.

The beginning is tied to a death, though almost two years actually separated Ruth's birth from Frederick Fulton's death. Ruth Fulton was born on June 5, 1887, in New York City. Her father, Frederick Fulton, had finished medical school in 1885; her mother, Bertrice Shattuck Fulton, had graduated five years earlier from Vassar College. Dr. Fulton practiced surgery and began to explore cancer research. Bertrice Fulton's job did not seem less worthwhile than her husband's, for she had learned at college that bringing up children was a worthy and socially useful activity. Frederick Fulton was thirty and his wife twenty-six years old when Ruth was born.

A year and a half later Bertrice Fulton had another child. A second daughter, Margery, was born the day after Christmas, December 26, 1888. By then the family lived in Norwich, New York, fifteen miles northeast of Binghamton. The Fultons had moved back to the central New York town hoping that there Frederick Fulton might recover from his debilitating, undiagnosed fever. Frederick Fulton and Bertrice Shattuck had both grown up in the Norwich area, and though they lived with the Shattucks, in 1888 they essentially moved back into an extended family.

Fever continued to weaken Frederick Fulton, leaving him without the energy to be husband and father. By the time Ruth was old enough to form an impression, her father appeared pale, gaunt, and sickly. The deathlike image frightened the little girl into a memory not represented in the photos adults showed her: "Certainly these glimmerings have nothing to do with his pictures, which were taken in full health and with the round beard and whiskers that were the fashion of the times. My memories have to do, instead, with a worn face illuminated with the translucence of illness, and very beautiful."[1] Through November and December 1888, Bertrice Fulton had been busy nursing her husband and one baby while waiting for another. Ruth did not write about how her mother looked during that winter. Bertrice Fulton, caught between eager anticipation of a baby's birth and dreadful foreboding of her husband's death, appeared neither placid nor completely fearful; instead her face displayed an array of conflicting emotions. And she was not in close contact with her first baby, who had then the attention of her grandparents. Certainly Ruth did not take from this time as clear-cut a picture of Bertrice as of Frederick Fulton.

On March 26, 1889, Frederick Fulton died. Ruth had not turned two; she may have been talking and quite likely was already walking, exploring the upstairs and downstairs of the farmhouse, venturing out onto the vine-covered front porch and even into the sweet-smelling hollyhock bushes around the house. That March day someone put an end to Ruth's toddling adventures. Perhaps an aunt or a grandparent dressed her in black and brought her into the family gathering. Ruth next remembered her mother, who "wanted desperately to have me remember my father. She took me into the room where he lay in his coffin, and in an hysteria of weeping implored me to remember."[2]

There lay her father, calm and beautiful and still young. Alongside the utter quiet of death came the racking sobs of her mother, an unforgettable, and unforgivable, contrast.

> Certainly from my earliest childhood I recognized two worlds, whether or not my knowledge was born at that tragic scene at my father's coffin—the world of my father, which was the world of death and which was beautiful, and the world of confusion and explosive weeping which I repudiated.

She rejected her mother's world and yearned to join her father's: "I identified him with everything calm and beautiful that came my way."[3]

The scene would have affected any child. To an inevitably indelible impression Ruth added a special sensitivity to visual detail and a tendency to extend difference into stark contrast. Her mother occupied one world, her father another. Ruth spent her waking hours in the world of her mother, and the hours of her privacy and her freedom in the world she associated with her father. The contrast involved rejecting one world for the other, yet realizing she could never fully occupy the dreamed-of world.

Ruth formed her first outward perceptions in visions of death and of grief, and she carried the image of faces with her for the rest of her life. Behind faces, for the child and then the adult, lay the spirit of a life, and Ruth read character out of the set of a head and the look in an eye. Behind character she created whole contexts, as she had that March day in the Shattuck farmhouse. She grew up and added words to pictures, becoming constructor as well as viewer; she used words in order to pull out the significance of pictures she saw. Much later Ruth learned that words themselves could make the pictures and could communicate the private vision to others.

At two years old, however, all this lay in the future. The child knew the shock of seeing a father in his coffin and a mother who wept without control. It might have seemed to the young child that a familiar pattern had been irretrievably torn. She could not imagine the next weeks and months would establish new patterns, ones she had a large part in making.

"The unparalleled beauty of the country over the hill"

With two babies and no husband, Bertrice Fulton needed the support of her parents, Joanna and John Samuel Shattuck. She needed, almost certainly, their economic help (Frederick Fulton had barely begun his medical practice), and also their emotional support. Her husband had died at the beginning of his career and, thirty-one years old, at the peak of physical vitality. Frederick Fulton's devotion to work led to his final illness, and for his daughter fever displayed a sacrifice to research.

Years after this childhood vision of her dead father, Ruth Fulton Benedict took Bertrice Fulton to the Boston Fine Arts Museum. She wrote of her mother's reaction:

> She knows little of painting, and an El Greco I liked meant nothing to her. But when we went into the large gallery where it hangs she went at once to the portrait, not knowing

it was "mine." I could not understand. Finally she turned to me and said, "It is your father. It is your father just before he died. There are no pictures of him as he looked then, but now you know what he looked like."[4]

Fray Paravacino, in the portrait, has a thin and shadowed face, and his dark eyes focus intensely on the book in his lap. Frederick Fulton bequeathed to his daughter the image of a questing, devoted, humanitarian, and near-tragic scientist.

For Bertrice Fulton the spring and summer months of 1889 must have been a time of sorting out emotions, making plans, and adjusting to a widowhood which came close upon motherhood. The presence of her parents helped, as did the soothing surroundings of Shattuck Farm. The green fields and low hills of Chenango County seemed peaceful, especially after the noise and activity of an 1880s New York City.

Norwich itself, county seat of Chenango, had the busy air of a central town for neighboring farms. The town had grown over the century to nearly 6,000 inhabitants when Bertrice Fulton and the children moved there in 1888. The population changed in size but not in composition, remaining as homogeneous as at its founding a century before. Settled by people like the Shattucks and the Fultons, Yankee families moving west from New England villages, Norwich housed a small proportion of immigrants and a smaller number of nonwhite individuals. (Of 38,000 in Chenango County in 1890, 37,474 were white, 297 were "colored," and 5 were "civilized Indians," according to the 1890 census.)

Like the Shattucks and the Fultons, too, most Norwich residents were Baptists, and many attended church with the Shattucks and the Fultons. Bertrice's father, John Samuel Shattuck, was a deacon of the church, and Frederick's uncle, Justin Fulton, was a pastor. Bertrice Shattuck Fulton spent the first years of her widowhood within the comfort of a large and settled family.

The Shattucks had migrated to New York State from Massachusetts. Ruth's family embodied the stereotypical American ancestry: Mayflower arrivals in search of religious freedom; six of her ancestors fought in the Revolutionary War. (Years later when she was asked to join the Daughters of the American Revolution, Ruth abruptly refused. She did respect her family origins, if not its place in American society, and she helped an Ohio relative trace genealogy more readily than she supported the DAR.[5]) The original settlers were John and David Shattuck, who traveled west until they found a suitable stopping place along the banks of the Chenango River. There they established a hundred-acre farm, and the land was passed down to Ruth's grandfather John Samuel Shattuck (and eventually to Ruth herself).

Sometime, too, early in the nineteenth century, the Fultons left their New England towns for newer communities in New York State. The Fultons settled in small villages near Norwich, and like the Shattucks they supplied the local Baptist churches with pastors and deacons.[6] One Fulton, Samuel J., gave up the church for medicine. He studied at the Cleveland Homeopathy Hospital, practiced in Norwich, and joined the Homeopathic Society of the County of Chenango in 1887.[7] Two years earlier his son Frederick Samuel Fulton had graduated from the New York Homeopathic Hospital.

The town of Norwich and the county of Chenango prospered in the 1880s and 1890s. Dairy farms like the Shattucks' did well, and Norwich Pharmacal Company provided jobs and income for the nonfarmers of the community. The farmers marketed milk, butter, hay, and potatoes; the drug company shipped goods to distant places, and the community bustled along in comfortable harmony.

For Ruth, commerce and prosperity mattered little. The beauty of the landscape counted. Behind John Samuel Shattuck's property lay the foothills, a gradual decline from the farther northeast Catskill range. "The surface consists of two high rolling ridges, separated by the valley of the Chenango. The highest summits are about five hundred feet above the valleys."[8] Such gentle hills invited exploration, and Ruth Fulton spent much of her childhood wandering over the ridges in search of her "undiscovered country."[9] The next ridge over became home for each new daydream.

Settled in the farmhouse, Bertrice Fulton took care of the little babies. Ruth and Margery were close enough in age to be treated like twins, first doubling and then easing Bertrice Fulton's responsibility. Joanna Shattuck helped out, but mainly she seems to have managed the housework while her daughter devoted herself to her daughters. Both women did full-time jobs inside the house while Grandfather Shattuck did and directed the outside farmwork. Managing a farmhouse in the late nineteenth century was not easy; laborsaving devices were few and adults drew children into tasks as soon as possible. Inside, the women spent time cooking, cleaning, and sewing clothes for the three-generation family.

Child care became a full-time occupation for Bertrice Fulton partly because she chose such an accommodation to early widowhood. "My mother was crushed by my father's death."[10] Turning to the "two babies" eased her grief and absorbed her energies. Taking care of children also suited Bertrice Fulton's college training. She had learned, during four years at Vassar (1878–82) that instructing children, including one's own, could be a perfectly worthwhile activity for a woman of her social standing.

Furthermore, Norwich offered few distractions to a twenty-nine-year-old widow. Bertrice Fulton may or may not have considered remarriage; a majority of widows her age, in the nineteenth century, did marry again. Bertrice Fulton either chose not to or let circumstances dictate the choice for her. She did choose to dramatize her widowhood well beyond the demands of ordinary mourning, at least according to her older daughter.

> She made a cult of grief out of my father's death, and every March she wept in church and in bed at night. It always had the same effect on me, an excruciating misery with physical trembling of a peculiar involuntary kind which culminated periodically in rigidity like an orgasm. It was not an expression of love for my mother.[11]

Ruth may have minded, resented, and repudiated her mother's grief so severely because she suspected an exaggeration. Bertrice Fulton demonstrated despair while competently managing her life. She was not "crushed" by Frederick Fulton's death—saddened, yes, but not defeated, and with a wonderful mechanism for coping in her conscientious, constant instruction of Ruth and Margery. Ruth perceived another uncomfortable disjunction: her mother taught the girls to be mannerly, honest, and disciplined; how could the young child fit this lesson with the example of an apparently undisciplined sentimentalism?

Bertrice Fulton puzzled Ruth for the whole of the two women's lives. (Bertrice Fulton, dying at ninety-three, outlived her daughter by five years.) Ruth minded her mother's displays of feeling so much that one suspects a strong attraction to these vivid ritual enactments. Bertrice Fulton's grief was the outward show of inner passion, a passion whose direct expression Mrs. Fulton apparently denied herself after Frederick Fulton's death but, equally apparently, transferred into indirect, effusive, ceremonial expression. Ruth, somewhat older than Margery, reacted differently, always troubled by the sources and the consequences of passionate commitment to another person and the vulnerabilities attached to telling of love. Bertrice Fulton grieved at regular intervals and taught her daughters about endurance and the pressures of "reality." Ruth remained troubled, as well, by this lesson in hardship and never completely embraced such pragmatic self-discipline that made of "four walls reality." The phrase is from a poem, and in later years Ruth expressed her ambivalence in the measured metaphors of her verse. Sometime after she had left her mother's household she wrote a poem to her mother and talked of love and passion and relinquishing one's will to another:

She took his hands and laid them to her breasts,
Laughing to know again the swoon she'd known
Till then on far hill pastures all alone,
Or fingering the cloudy palimpsests
Of a bright wintry heaven.
All her quests
Had sailed but for this prize, this one note blown
To lead her captive, and white flesh and bone
Yielded to strangeness and to sweet unrest.[12]

Through her mother (an often unclear model), Ruth grappled with issues central to her own life. She put these in terms of passion versus planned self-determination.

Bertrice Fulton could be called a "transitional woman." She moved toward twentieth-century independence and self-sufficiency without discarding nineteenth-century conventions for female roles. She spent four years away at college, but the choice of Vassar kept her within cultural norms for women of her general social and economic class. At Vassar she remained within patterns she had learned at home, and in a Baptist home. Bertrice Fulton belonged to the small group of daughters whose parents supported "advanced education."[13] These women, like Bertrice Fulton, came from middle-class business and clerical families. The Baptists stressed education: "The young women of our Baptist families have not gone to women's colleges in the proportion which our numbers would suggest," bemoaned the *Baptist Quarterly*, which then advised, "The way to remedy an evil is to remedy it"—an obscure way of saying, "Send the girls to school."[14]

Women's colleges, like Vassar, in the late nineteenth century did not train women out of wifehood and motherhood or destroy their religious pieties. Intellectual stimulation had to be kept within bounds; few women who finished college when Bertrice Fulton did rejected marriage and children. Their education reached fulfillment in the making of a better home and the raising of a better family.

In Ruth's eyes, however, her mother's acceptance of domesticity appeared vastly different from her grandmother's. Bertrice Fulton learned a motherhood, instructed her daughters, and suppressed impulses and gentle embraces. By contrast, or as Ruth made the contrast, Grandmother Shattuck seemed naturally gentle and loving. Ruth Fulton put her responses to the women into two portraits, each equally faithful and equally fanciful. She placed these pictures next to one another, and the contrast stood out sharply and significantly. The little girl filled in details of character and of interpretation. Persistently she could make of "faces" the revelation of lifetime concerns.

So Ruth added to the image of Bertrice Fulton a woman over-whelmed by "her worry and concern about little things."[15] She portrayed her grandmother as spiritually transcendent, rising above the petty de-tails of day-to-day life. Joanna Shattuck seemed to her granddaughter at once the ideal Victorian wife and a delicately romantic being. Joanna Shattuck's life on one level revolved around that of her husband and four children: Hettie, Bertrice, Myra, and Mary Shattuck. On another level she existed beyond the social and historical era that shaped her life as a different era shaped her daughter's (and granddaughter's) life.

Ruth claimed she did not love her mother.[16] She was enraptured by her grandmother. Joanna Shattuck remained outside conventions, not be-cause she overthrew these conventions but because society's demands did not touch the inner core of her being. Had Ruth Fulton named anyone a saint, it would have been her grandmother. Ruth did not use that word. Instead she wrote a poem to Joanna Shattuck titled "Of Graves":

> She always laughed a little laugh
> And nodded down to me:
> "The rabbit nibbled at the grass
> Will someday cover me."
>
> And days I shiver swift and strange
> This still is what I see:
> Sunlight and rabbit in the grass.
> And peace possesses me.[17]

Neither her mother nor her grandmother knew what went on in Ruth's mind; neither could object to her private view of them. "That day [in the haymow] it came to me with a brilliant flash of illumination that I could always without fail have myself for company, and that if I didn't talk to anybody about the things that mattered to me no one could ever take them away."[18]

Another world existed, the other half of the division Ruth Benedict recreated in 1935. Inside there was a world of women, dutifully busy with household chores. Outside was a world of farmwork and fields, dominated by John Samuel Shattuck. Ruth associated the idea of peace, calm, and purpose with Grandfather Shattuck, in contrast to the busy-ness and confused sounds inside the house. Ruth escaped from conver-sations and domestic demands by running down the front-porch steps into the garden. The house might be filled with relatives, too much talk-ing, and too much touching; outside, all stretched open, quiet, and un-peopled, except as Ruth chose to find her people. "The transition back into the mundane world and all its confusions was likely to be stormy."[19]

Ruth associated the world of her grandfather with her special moments, "my pearls of great price." She associated his world with fantasies and daydreams, and with death.

> I had gone out into the barn to jump in the hay, but instead I went to a retreat of mine in the haymow. Under a big beam one could make a cavern in the hay completely concealed in the dark. It was a hiding place we used in hide-and-seek in the haymows, but I used to go there alone and lie in the hot dark, the hayseeds sticking to my wet skin. The family could always understand jumping in the hay, but they could never have understood lying in the dark in the hay if there wasn't a hide-and-seek game going on. (I suppose I liked my hiding place because it was my "grave," and they certainly would have disapproved if they'd known that.)[20]

There seems to be, unacknowledged, a sexual connotation in the acknowledged death-wish. Ruth Fulton told no one of her preoccupation with death and suspected that if she had told, Bertrice Fulton would scold her for morbidness and self-absorption. The attraction to death, on one hand a pull toward peace and stillness, was also inextricably bound to passion, more than Ruth Benedict admitted. In her hot and dark haymow grave, the child's wet skin responded to the touch of seeds. This was a private, untold, unadmitted sensuality, associated with darkness and "graves." Ruth, similarly, compared her involvement with her mother's grief to "an orgasm," a response of pain, trembling, and rigidity. A violent distaste for "daylight," her term for expressed and exposed emotion, lasted throughout Ruth's life. Extreme feelings of any sort threatened her sense of self and remained a vivid memory from childhood. As a child, too, she had imposed upon herself stern "tabus," one against weeping in front of anyone, the other against revealing pain.[21] Not until she was nearly thirty did Ruth try out the ways in which ecstasy might fit her "worlds."

The wished-for world of death, of quiet and isolation, could never be secure. Ruth Fulton created fantasies and daydreams of countries over the hill, always fearing the intrusion of everyday reality. Too often she was right, and the intruder was her mother. Bertrice Fulton supervised her daughter and unsuspectingly destroyed the "precious pearls" Ruth collected. Bertrice Fulton had inserted sobs into the stillness of death; she told Ruth not to spend too much time outside in the farmfields but to come in and help shell peas for lunch. Ruth mentions peashelling twice in her autobiography, disliking the chore and the gathered family of fourteen who demanded so much food.[22]

One afternoon Bertrice Fulton walked with Ruth into the Chenango hills.

About the time I was five my mother thought I was old
enough to stand the climb up the west hill, and one day I
went up with her and my aunts. I had been promised that
we'd go up to the top and look over. It was a long climb for
my legs, and I was very hot and tired when at last we came
to the edge of the pasture and looked down into the rolling
hills beyond—and *Uncle George's farm* [hers]. Instead of the
wonderland I'd pictured it was all familiar and anything-but
romantic territory. . . . I never played again with my little
playmate over the hill.[23]

From then on Ruth at once yearned for and was properly wary about the
"beautiful country on the other side of the west hill."

When she did not go outside with her daughter, Bertrice Fulton
wanted to know where Ruth was going by herself. Ruth appeared so
absentminded; she did not tell her mother where she was and did not
answer when her mother called. Frequently, too, Bertrice found Ruth
not miles away but well within hearing distance. Most often Ruth had
discovered her place to play near her grandfather.

Bertrice Fulton made rules. Neither Ruth nor Margery was to wander
far from the farmhouse without reporting her whereabouts. As long as
Ruth stubbornly refused to answer calls the rule had to be enforced, and
for the more obedient younger sister as well. Even amid family farms
Bertrice Fulton did not feel perfectly confident; there was the Chenango
River to make fears concrete.

Ruth tried to stay within range, but running away "figured as my
family crime," she wrote later.

Mother had gone away for a few days' visit when I was three
or four, and had asked for my promise that I wouldn't run
away while she was gone. But I did. When she got back she
questioned me about my promise, and I refused to answer.
She ruled that I should stay in the house till I'd told her.

Day after day Ruth stayed inside, absolutely refusing to let her mother
into "my other world." "The whole family were hard put to it, and after
I'd experimentally turned on the spigot of the kerosene can in the wood-
house and let out the whole contents on the floor, Mother decided to
change her ruling." Bertrice Fulton tried another punishment.

So one morning Mother took me into the downstairs bedroom
and said that I must stay there without anything to eat till I'd
told. I remember very well my efforts all that day. The family

ate dinner at noon, and the afternoon wore on. They ate supper and the lights were lighted. Mother sat with me most of the day waiting. At last I got it out. My relief was like physical drunkenness.[24]

She gives the incident many sentences in her autobiographical fragment. But this "crime" preceded a worse one, this punishment anticipated a harder one.

Bertrice Fulton did not invariably discover Ruth's transgressions. As often as not, the haymow, the barn, and Grandpa Shattuck himself sheltered the little girl. She did not have to say where she was, and she did not have to answer demands. Yet the world she knew "by herself"—the "only world I was happy in"—continually lay open to risk. Someone might come in, someone might ask her about it; it might be ruined by tantrums, "sins," and lies. Piety and truth-telling, Ruth remembered afterward, dominated the household, and the child did not take her "sins" lightly.

One day she told her mother she was going to the elder patch, "which was allowed," but went across the railroad tracks instead

That day on the flat Grandfather welcomed me royally. . . . When they came up for milking I rode up on the empty wagons. But here was a difficulty, and I had to tell Grandfather that Mother didn't know I'd gone to the flat. He smiled down at me and said, "Well, if she doesn't ask, we won't tell her."

The secret was to be theirs—except that Bertrice Fulton did ask Ruth where she had been all day.

But that evening after milking, when Grandfather came in for supper, he lifted me up to his face and whispered to me, "Did Mother ask?" What could I do? I said no, and he smiled at me again. But I ate no supper. I had lied to my grandfather, and that was a different matter. My grandfather, I suppose, belonged to "my" life; anyway he was one of my self-elected loyalties, and I'd been false to it.[25]

This time Bertrice Fulton realized there was no need for punishment. Ruth had transgressed her own rules about integrity and consistency of motive. She felt the full weight of having sinned, a severe guilt at violating her deeply held principles.

Margery rarely needed similar disciplining. The two girls might be close in age, but they were different in temperament, and increasingly over the years. Ruth claimed, "It is curious how small a part in my real life my sister played." Yet Ruth constantly compared herself to Margery, and would do so throughout her life. To Ruth, Margery seemed content from childhood on: she was a "cherubically beautiful child with no behavior problems."

In the "pious" household, dominated by the "grand old man with strong, calm movements" and ruled by the strictures Bertrice Fulton learned from popular books like L. Emmett Holt's *The Care and Feeding of Children,* having a "clean slate" was a supreme virtue. Margery had such, and Ruth did not. "Margery and I said the Lord's prayer every night at Mother's knee, and the phrase that bothered me was the 'Forgive us our debts.' I understood it very literally as meaning that everything I had done would be wiped out as if it had not been." The prayer offered Ruth a chance to be as "sinless" as Margery. Before Ruth turned six she decided not to take the easy chance for a "clean slate." She stopped saying the bothersome phrase and was at least twelve before she said the words again. "I had no Puritan load on my conscience about my unforgiven sins, and no obsession about them. It was merely that by not saying the prayer I made myself responsible for them."[26]

She did not tell of the omission, or of her satisfaction. She had learned to keep her accommodations secret, and the compromise with religion made no break in her pattern.

Baptist faith is not a Sunday religion; its principles dominate day-to-day activities. Besides going to the local church every Sunday, the Shattucks and the Fultons gathered daily for prayer. Often Grandfather Shattuck officiated: He "led us all in family prayers on our knees every morning around the breakfast table." The phrase he used then echoed through Ruth Fulton's poetry: The Lord should lead us toward "the light that shineth more and more unto the perfect day." John Samuel Shattuck represented, for Ruth, the clarity and integrity of Baptist faith.

Sometimes Justin Fulton ran the family prayer meetings. Frederick's uncle Justin was a familiar presence in the house, and as a pastor he conducted far stricter services than did Grandfather Shattuck. Baptists claimed all worshipers were equal in the sight of God while incorporating "skilled" prayer leaders into the otherwise democratic faith.[27] Justin directed prayers, preaching passionately from the heart, in sharp contrast to the somber dignity of Grandfather Shattuck's manner. Ruth detected further disconcerting elements in Justin's behavior.

Justin did not visit only for prayers. He came as uncle, and he acted his avuncular role to the hilt. Ruth could barely tolerate his loving joviality—suddenly Justin might come bounding up the front steps, demanding kisses and hugs from his two nieces. At first both girls ran away, into the kitchen and upstairs. A game for Margery and Justin represented for Ruth a serious urge to escape.

> The big scene of the kind I remember [her reluctance to be touched] was with Uncle Justin. Uncle Justin was my father's uncle and a Fundamentalist, Tremont Temple, Baptist parson. He was a big, cock-sure man. . . . He gave Margery a fifty cent piece on one visit for kissing him, and then tried to to give me mine. But I ran in terror from room to room, and finally hid on the treadle under the sewing machine.[28]

She was approximately four years old.

Ruth later wrote of her extreme physical aloofness. She may have been "considered very 'touchy' about physical contacts," but her "touchiness" fit into a household where the hows and whys of giving way to feeling were never quite clear to a child. An emphasis on passionate, wholehearted devotion seemed hard to reconcile with self-control and sense of proportion; prayer meetings were not quite right when led by a man who roughhoused a resisting child; mourning ceremonies spoiled the perfect stillness that belonged to death.

The Baptist religion itself confused a little girl thoughtful beyond her age. Baptists combined a literal and strict interpretation of the Bible with an emphasis on the personal experience of conversion. "We are people of the Book," Baptists claimed, guided by the written word. "An individual must feel in his heart a bond to Christ," the Baptists also claimed, stressing an idiosyncratic embracing of religious doctrine; the Baptist knows "soul liberty."[29]

Ruth, who thrived on contrasts, saw only confusion and the crisscrossing of boundaries in these various pronouncements. Where difference was absolute and characteristics clearly distinct, Ruth was content. When one world invaded the other—when her mother intruded into her imaginary "countries" or the Shattucks regulated her personal "piety"— then Ruth had once again to rebuild a private place no one could enter or touch.

> Ever since I had stopped playing with my little playmate who lived over the hill, "my" world had been one I made up mostly of my Bible. . . . The story of Jesus was "my" world. I liked that part of my Bible better than any other book I had. I can't disentangle now how much or how little I understood, but it was a way of life that made sense to me—that I "recognized" in a way I did not recognize my mother's world.[30]

The world Ruth Fulton constructed before she was ten contained elements from the Bible, from poems of William Blake, and from her own vivid fantasies. The people there had a "strange dignity and grace" and did not walk but skimmed the ground "in one unbroken line."[31]

Walls did not stand firm, and Ruth could not keep her world separate and pristine. Ruth compared, and she began to measure carefully and painfully the relative merits of "my" world and "their" world. Was it wrong, she asked when she was three years old, to see Christ in her father? Was it wrong to insist upon a world in which Frederick Fulton and Christ might be envisioned as one figure?

> One of the first scenes I remember in detail was in the living room at my grandfather's with all the family about. I had just said that the Christ on the wall—the big "Christ before Pilate"—was my father, and my mother's face was set for the scene of grief any mention of my father always called up, and my grandparents' faces were shocked with the blasphemy, or perhaps only the naivete, of my illusion.[32]

There seemed to Ruth to be no clear way of bringing religion into daily thoughts. The world she created out of the Bible had to be guarded, first when she dreamed it up and later when she wrote it down in poetry. Nor was there one clear way to respond to death. Her mother's grief overwhelmed the child, and filled her with a suspicion about sincerity she insistently conveyed between the lines of her autobiographical fragment. Another, undoubtedly more frightening, thought had to do with the possibility of a desirable death, a death that made the perfect and proper end to a kind of life.

> When I was four, my grandmother took me . . . to a tenant house on the hill where the baby had just died, and we saw the dead child as a matter of course. She was laid out in the stiff parlor, and I remember vividly her transparent beauty. She seemed to me the loveliest thing I had ever seen, and I remember contrasting her with the ragmuffin brothers and sisters and the bedraggled mother.[33]

Around this same time her grandmother condemned bitterly the suicide of a neighboring servant girl.[34] Choosing to die offered a provocative and problematic alternative to the relentlessness of living.

When Ruth was in her twenties she wrote of "A god that kinder, being death, / Set limit to this folly, breath."[35] From 1888 until 1892

Ruth framed these thoughts in private, in a world she desperately tried to sort out from familialism, Baptist teachings, Uncle Justin's kisses and her mother's weeping, and her own childhood "crimes." She took her chances of escaping from family and piety, wisdom and severity, in the surrounding fields and hills, in the Bible, and in the ever-available world of imagination. Then, in 1892, Ruth Fulton turned five; she was ready to go to the local elementary school.

"The world was all a very strange place"

Ruth celebrated her fifth birthday on June 5, 1892. That September her mother brought her to a local elementary school, one of several Norwich Free Public Schools. One can imagine Ruth's uncertainties about the first day of school. She had not before ventured far from the Shattuck household or had many contacts with children not part of her family. Her imaginary playmates did what she told them, acted the way she wanted them to, and had personalities she admired—and created. Occasionally the world of fantasy had given way, and Ruth met a child living on the far side of the hill. But these were rare encounters; Ruth lived in a sheltered world before she went to school.

One day that fall Bertrice Fulton heard some startling news. Ruth Fulton, her mother was told, had a hearing impairment. Tests indicated that the five-year-old was partially deaf, and probably had been since infancy. No one in the Shattuck or the Fulton family suspected that Ruth's bout with measles in infancy had left such severe permanent damage. If Ruth herself wondered why voices merged into one another, why she couldn't distinguish her mother's calls from other people's, and why too much talking drove her into a near frenzy, she had never spoken her fears out loud.

And no one thought it odd that the child chose to spend those preschool, free hours with her grandfather. Ruth had been, as a toddler, considered the adventurous child. But it also seems likely that Ruth could hear Grandfather Shattuck better than she could hear anyone else. He had preached, and his voice had a different tenor from other voices in the family. Furthermore, the grandchild and grandfather visited outside, where random noises of a household did not interfere with talk.

With two babies at home to instruct, Bertrice Fulton had often found herself growing irritated at the one's lack of attention. Even a two-year-old child can be expected to answer; Ruth, apparently absorbed in her own thoughts, ignored her mother's calls. Before the school diagnosis Ruth's silences had been treated as those of a shy, timid, and willfully disobedient child. Margery set the contrast: quick and eager, chatty and cheerful at her tasks. The mother may have wondered, without saying, why the older could not take a lesson from the younger sister.

Once or twice, too, during the preschool years, Bertrice Fulton had lost her patience. Ruth had refused to answer once too often, and Bertrice Fulton decided to take the child in hand. She offered a penny for every time the child answered at the first word. "And I usually earned the penny. But my hearing was pretty bad at this time [c. 1890], and doctors began taking out my tonsils and trying by various means to help keep my eardrums intact."[36] It may have been less a strain to accept the characterization of timidity and obstinacy. "The theory was that I didn't choose to answer—which was true, too."[37]

Deafness added a dimension to another childhood pattern. Ruth had learned to flee from demands and pennies and unspoken comparisons into the fields and hills around Shattuck Farm. A world existed there, spun from daydreams and literature. From her private world Ruth banished voices and confusion, people who urged her to answer and to "join us." Her private world was silent, orderly, and sedate, a place she perfectly fit. Sound gave way to color and form; dignified figures skimmed by, and nothing disrupted the gentle harmony—a rhythm of visual detail not of sound. "Happiness was in a world I lived in all by myself, and for precious moments."[38]

Yet there were moments throughout these early years when Ruth felt troubled over her lack of fit to the Norwich community. In a town the size of Norwich she seemed alone in her "imperfection," and she, too, would have been relieved at the official diagnosis. Deafness explained Ruth's inattention and at least partly explained her own strangeness to the child. Ruth's deafness was not total, though exactly how deaf she was is not known. In the late nineteenth century audiologists did not have precise measures of hearing loss. Degree did not matter, however, to either Ruth or her mother. Both accommodated to a new fact of life.

Learning that the fault lay with hearing and not sheer obstinacy helped Bertrice Fulton keep her temper when Ruth did not answer. Bertrice Fulton accepted the dictum of her era, to be a conscientious, intelligent, and not impulsive parent. She took her child-rearing principles from available texts and must have read about deafness and the manuals for treating a deaf child like a normal child. Exercising the patience she preached, Bertrice learned to talk slowly and form her words clearly. Facial expressions became crucial in that household; communicating became a matter of sight as much as of sound.

Deafness explained some things, but the diagnosis did not transform Ruth into a sociable child. She continued to suffer from her "difference" and may at this time—in the Norwich school playground—have developed the stammer characteristic of her later speech. In her eagerness to talk, Ruth's words stumbled out on top of one another, or failed to come at all. Sometimes, especially in adulthood, Ruth's friends offered to find for her the word tantalizingly and visibly on the tip of her tongue. Giving Ruth the first blocked word often released her and, once launched, she spoke fluently. Fluency also depended on how at home Ruth felt, how many people were nearby, and how clearly she could see the faces of her listeners. She watched closely for changing expression, and practiced interpreting point of view from visual signals. Seeing her listeners concentrate on her words, Ruth relaxed and her sentences came unobstructed. But in moments of anxiety she still waited for words with coughs, hums, and silences.

Over the years she learned to cope. As a child, at home and at school, Ruth found the effort to hear enormous, tiring, and stressful. Talking left her and frequently her listener exhausted. Conversations between Ruth and Bertrice Fulton, particularly, left both on the edge of anger and ended in outbursts of temper. Ruth may, in fact, have needed these outbursts and the pure relief of direct and comprehensible communication.[39] She did not have to lip-read fury; later she became adept at supplementing hearing with lipreading.

Ruth and her mother managed better when Ruth gave her mother "pieces" to read. From time to time in frustration at the buzzing confusion of sounds, Ruth constructed her "perfect place" beyond the hill, but gradually she learned how to occupy imaginary worlds without antagonizing her family and especially her mother. Ruth increasingly wrote out her daydreams. Her mother rewarded written compositions with praise and with pleasure.

Ruth discovered another advantage: writing released her from tedious household chores like shelling peas. Margery had become "handy" at domestic tasks. The younger sister spent time with Bertrice Fulton and Joanna Shattuck, in the kitchen learning to cook and in the parlor learning to sew. Ruth wrote her stories, read Dickens, Scott, the Bible. The division of tasks, at first a relief, had a painful side. Ruth felt herself pulled away from and simultaneously drawn toward the sounds of the three women working together. The women in her family demonstrated a kind of harmony in housework, an understanding of one another's movements which lasted into adulthood. As a little girl, Ruth veered between enjoying the release from work and minding the exclusion.

Possibly Bertrice Fulton encouraged her older daughter to develop talents that were not domestic. Perhaps she thought of Ruth in terms of strong inner purpose and motivation; perhaps more than she acknowledged, Bertrice Fulton liked to think of her older daughter in the image of Frederick Fulton. Ruth resembled her father, and Margery her mother. Such an alignment is often made in families.

Ruth wanted to be like her father. Throughout childhood and early adulthood the desire to resemble him formed the stuff of her ambitions. She patterned her life on Frederick Fulton's devotion to lofty purpose, in her case implemented by writing stories rather than by inquiring into disease and health. Another side of the girl yearned to be like her mother. She harbored this wish with much uncertainty and ultimately found a way of being like Bertrice Fulton that was hardly a deliberate imitation. Ruth resembled her mother in one striking respect.

From infancy until adolescence Ruth Fulton threw violent temper tantrums. "They came on for no reason the family could fathom, and they swept on thereafter without my feeling that I had any participation in them. I was violent either to myself or to anyone else within reach."[40] The screaming and kicking acceptable for a two-year-old became incredible and incomprehensible in a five-year-old, then in a ten-year-old. Ruth raged and wept and didn't know why. She named her furies the "blue devils," a name that stuck and provided a convenient representation for moods Ruth could not or would not fathom.

No one understood what drove Ruth into anger. It may have been partly a panic at not hearing. Deaf or partially deaf children frequently succumb to uncontrollable outbursts.[41] As she grew older Ruth added to frustration a guilt at disrupting the rhythms of her own private world. "Of course, I was always punished and wept over, but I can't remember any guilt about the tantrums. What I was guilty about was the spoiling of my moments, my bogging myself down in violence so that they didn't come again."[42]

Her tears gained attention and resembled the mourning performances of Bertrice Fulton. Ruth had a model for her emotional outbursts, though she does not suggest this in her autobiographical account. The pattern for violent outbursts had been set by her mother and repeated every year. Ruth watched her mother weep, a view she despised and had to witness. She was drawn to the emotion her mother displayed in grief and almost only in grief. She took, then, an image of a woman overwhelmed by a passion that swept her beyond the controls she ordinarily and severely applied to herself and to others. Bertrice Fulton's mourning represented ecstasy for Ruth and became engrained in her memory and developed in her poetry.

Ruth despised the unseemly side of tears. She wanted to participate, yet condemned these signs of losing self in emotion: "There is a certain amount of evidence of this [withdrawal from emotion] in the vividness with which I remember early scenes of my mother's pain. . . . My feeling at these times was nearest to humiliation—and repudiation."[43] She similarly succumbed to and condemned her own angry tantrums.

Ruth, essentially, accommodated to an ambivalence about emotion evident in the Shattuck-Fulton household. She lived by rigid and self-imposed tabus:

> I had two deeply felt tabus that are among my earliest memories and have continued through most of my life; certainly they were established before we left the farm the fall that I was six. One of these was against crying before anyone. It was a final humiliation which was devastating to me. It never occurred except in the terrible aftermaths of my tantrums when the sin of violence to "my" world overwhelmed all other tabus.[44]

She also satisfied the urgent need to cry out in these tantrums, knowing the outbursts brought punishment from herself and from those around her. Ruth Fulton developed a kind of ingenuity at deciding how much she could justifiably (to herself) express of inner turmoil, in what form, and on what occasions. One way to establish a pattern for herself was to copy people in her family.

Bertrice Fulton condemned the outbursts that uncannily echoed her own. One after another, however, her efforts to stop Ruth's tantrums proved futile. Ruth celebrated her outbursts as regularly as Bertrice Fulton observed her March rituals.

When Ruth was eleven years old and still having tantrums, Bertrice Fulton tried another remedy. Away from the presence but not the influence of her parents, Bertrice Fulton brought the Bible to help. One night, after Ruth had cried herself into exhaustion, her mother sat down and had a solemn talk with Ruth. She talked about control and self-discipline, about calm and proper behavior. Then she "dictated a promise, which I repeated after her, never to have another tantrum. She went out of the room and brought back a Bible and a candle, and gave it to me to read at a verse which invoked the aid of Jehovah."[45]

The temper tantrums went away. The "blue devils" tormenting Ruth did not. The eleven-year-old continued to suffer from stomachaches. "For years and years they descended upon me about every six weeks."[46] She asked for sympathy and pampering, an unfocused and simple response to pain. Someone took care of her, and no one asked questions;

"bilious attacks" were an acceptable nineteenth-century ailment. When she expressed her furies and terrors in physiological disguise the near-adolescent girl did not have to talk. Both mother and daughter attended to the torturous vomiting, and bed worked a wonderful cure. "The third day, when I sat up in bed for my first poached egg, was always a high watermark of felicity, a day I think of with greater pleasure than any of the days when I was well."[47]

Ruth had stomachaches once every six weeks. At thirteen the stomachaches went away and Ruth began to menstruate. Every six weeks she had a period, and every six weeks she had severe cramps. Ruth had moved from being a child to being an adult in one sense, but clearly retaining a pattern from childhood in the rhythmic imitation of stomachaches in her monthly periods. To be debilitated and out-of-the-ordinary at regular intervals surprised no one in the Shattuck household and, as well, suited an image of Victorian womanhood still influential in late-nineteenth-century American society. Ruth took advantage, unconsciously expressing continuing anxieties in the new way and adding to the difficulties she already felt a need now to come to terms with female sexuality. Whatever Ruth guessed about her mother's nighttime outbursts of weeping, she revealed only partially in the association with orgasm and in reenacting at age thirteen her own schedule of childish outbursts for a woman's experience.

For Ruth the years from age eleven to age eighteen brought changes, of which menstruation was especially dramatic. Things had begun to change in 1892, when she left the Shattuck household to go to the Norwich school. Two years later, in 1894, her "life story" took another turn.

"In Owatonna I was very much the leader; in Buffalo, not at all"

Bertrice Fulton found herself, in 1892, without a great deal to do. Her daughters spent the day in school, and Joanna Shattuck handled household chores. Domesticity demanded little time and less attention, and the woman who had determined to go to college in 1878 was not satisfied drifting through life on a farm. An 1894 photograph shows an intense woman. Bertrice Fulton is sitting on the front porch of the farmhouse, a favorite spot for Shattuck photos, holding two girls in her lap. Like her older daughter, she expresses only the glimmer of a smile. The stiffness on her face seems deliberate, not just discomfort at slow-moving photography. Bertrice Fulton's severity of expression complements her severity of dress. She wears a high-collared white blouse, a dark skirt, and her hair pulled back behind her ears. The dress is conventional; she has added an expression appropriate to widowhood. Ruth and Margery look younger than their respective seven and six years, and each looks like a proper Victorian daughter. Their dresses are white, lacy, and long.

Around the time this photo was taken, Bertrice Fulton accepted a job in St. Joseph, Missouri. (Perhaps the photo celebrated her departure from the family home.) She prepared Ruth and Margery for the train ride across country, from rural New York into the Midwest.

The state of Missouri, like others, spent money on education in the last decades of the nineteenth century. Education had been neglected before the Civil War and totally forgotten during it. By the end of the century, education became a first priority for Missouri's leaders. This involved spending money, expanding the school system, and hiring new teachers.[48] Planned innovations would prove the state's concern.

An income and the possibilities for innovative teaching attracted Bertrice Fulton, but accepting the job and the journey west had more complex reasons. Seven years had passed since her husband's death, and the nature of her widowhood changed. Her children needed less care and instruction, and Bertrice began to consider a life in which Ruth and Margery did not absorb all her energies. She may also have wanted to test her skills at bringing up children with children other than her own. As long as she remained at home, and a daughter, she limited her explorations as a mother. Surrounded by family, too, she may have felt constricted in opportunities to fulfill her own desires, whether or not these involved remarriage. Teaching in the Norwich elementary school, as she did for one year, hardly removed her from the supervision of the Shattucks and the Fultons.

If Bertrice Fulton experienced doubts and confusions about the move west, she seems not to have let her daughters know. To her older daughter, Bertrice Fulton was a woman who "fit" her setting and her times, who did not chafe against the demands of her society. Ruth saw her mother make a satisfactory compromise between domesticity and a career. From one perspective Bertrice Fulton presented a fine image of a strong and purposeful woman, deciding her fate. With this image Ruth had to reconcile the weeping and the uncontrolled gestures of mourning. Ruth set a high standard for her mother, who was a brave and unselfish woman, in the process working out standards for herself.

Bertrice Fulton may have taken on excessive trappings of widowhood to balance her ambitions and her migrations across the country. She accepted a conventional role as widow in order to act independently. The dramatic demonstrations of grief Ruth Fulton never tolerated suited her mother's acceptance of society's stereotype of the young widow, an acceptance that also allowed her some freedom of action. Ruth did not understand this part of widowhood much better than she understood the intense passion behind her mother's marriage. Two decades later Ruth would understand the force of conventional roles; she copied her own sensitivity to social images from the mother she convinced herself she did not resemble. The knowledge of passion remained elusive.

But Bertrice Fulton did not totally accept the role of widow. She would not stay at home in Norwich, taking care of her parents, teaching elementary and Sunday school. Whatever drove her to choose Vassar and to believe she could raise two babies when her husband had barely finished medical school sustained Bertrice Fulton after Frederick Fulton's death in 1888. In 1894, the same spirit impelled her to travel nearly 2,000 miles from Norwich to St. Joe.

Bertrice Fulton went to St. Joe planning to bring the children back to the Shattuck farm every summer, and she carried out the plan. She also brought her older sister Hettie Shattuck along to help care for the girls. Aunt Hettie came perilously close to another stereotype for the American woman, the unmarried aunt helping others in the family. Ruth does not say much about Hettie; she probably added this image of a typical nineteenth-century female role to her growing gallery. In reconstructing the figure of maiden aunt, Ruth adjusted a conventional drawing to her own compelling fantasies. She now built up her self-image with pieces borrowed from the pattern of Aunt Hettie's life, as she had earlier borrowed from the lives of Joanna Shattuck and Bertrice Fulton.

Beneath the pictures Ruth set out of the women she knew, she sensed a contentment with choices made and options accepted. Joanna Shattuck lived her life for others, without torment; Hettie took on the care of her nieces without protesting against the cloistered, all-female domesticity. Bertrice Fulton left for work every morning, confident about her daughters' well-being.

When the four arrived in 1895, St. Joe was a growing and prospering city. Located on a major East-West route, the city attracted travelers, migrants, and, by the end of the century, local farmers in need of city income. With 60,000 people St. Joe seemed enormous compared to Norwich, and noisy and smelly beyond anything Ruth had known before. When she looked away from the city, she saw a landscape quite different from Chenango County. Flat prairie lands replaced the low hills of her childhood. Farms stretched out beneath the open midwestern sky; Ruth's search for an "undiscovered country" had no perceptible limits.

The people themselves looked different from those she had known in Norwich. Ruth had moved from family, from people like the Shattucks and the Fultons—white, middle-class, New England Baptists and Protestants—into a heterogeneous population. Class mixed with race, and St. Joe had a kind of rough-and-ready atmosphere the New York State town lacked. Ruth met blacks in the streets of the city, families of "free Negroes" and emancipated slaves. She would only have seen this part of St. Joe's population, not known the children in school. Educational innovation in late-nineteenth-century Missouri did not include integration.

Within the city the population established diverse family and household arrangements. This was not Norwich, where families had lived stably for generations, but a western city where various groups arrived, stayed, moved on. Ruth's schoolmates, like Ruth, may have had unattached people—aunts, uncles, boarders—living with them. Nevertheless, a new city and new school touched off feelings Ruth recognized: She was "different" from everyone else. The partial deafness did not help, and neither did Margery's gregariousness.

Margery may also have reacted differently to being without a father. She did not share Ruth's awkwardness. Nor did she maintain a self-image of apartness and isolation to which fatherlessness contributed, as Ruth did. Ruth could explain to friends the presence of Aunt Hettie —her mother needed help—but she could not talk about the vision of death she carried in her memory. The view of her father's face in his coffin had become part of the pattern of her life, as it had not in Margery's life. Ruth dramatized the "primal scene" her sister had been too young to witness. The scene dominated her private world, and she jealously guarded this world from the intrusion of others. Not letting anyone in, Ruth denied herself the comforts her mother or Aunt Hettie might have been able to provide to soften the pains of adjusting to strange places and unfamiliar people.

Ruth had only two years to get to know Missouri. She had barely grown familiar with the midwestern city when her mother took another job. In 1897, Bertrice Fulton once again packed up her family to move, this time to Owatonna, a small city in southeastern Minnesota. The girls and Aunt Hettie prepared for another train trip, as Bertrice Fulton pursued her career. The Minnesota job offered financial security and higher status. Bertrice Fulton would be "Lady Principal" of Pillsbury Academy. A further thought may have crossed her mind: If she were principal, her daughters could go to classes in an elite private academy.

Bertrice Fulton pursued a career not only to satisfy her own ambitions and utilize her "training." She also had proud plans for her daughters, and these included providing Ruth and Margery with the best education possible on a single woman's income.

Ruth liked Owatonna. The little city sat amid hayfields and solidly built farmhouses. Even without the Catskill foothills and the Chenango River, Owatonna echoed Norwich more faithfully than St. Joe could. The stretch of land and flat, cloudless sky of the Midwest begins to break up in the southeastern part of Minnesota. This part of the state is close to the border between Minnesota and the almost-eastern landscape of Wisconsin, and near the Mississippi River.

Ruth undoubtedly read Mark Twain and appreciated the romance of this perfectly American river. She liked living seventy-five miles away from a scene that dominated American literary imagination, and she may even have liked knowing her search for an "undiscovered country" had parallel in her nation's history. Owatonna was comfortable, and a private academy provided an easier welcome than did a Missouri public school:

> For the first time people began to play some real part in my life—not very real, but at least occupying. At school I was the leader of the little group of the elite, and curiously all the professors' children were girls and those we took in were also girls. Boys did not figure at all.[49]

Pillsbury Academy represented refinement and intellectual endeavor to parents, a midwestern version of an eastern school. And, as if to emphasize the distance of school from worldly affairs, the red brick buildings took possession of Owatonna's one hill. A block or two away were the white clapboard houses of middle-class townspeople, and elm-lined streets dropping into the town square. In the center, dominating the square, stood a building equal in dignity to the academy. A Louis Sullivan bank sat pompously on the northwest corner, representing worldly affairs and an optimistic prosperity.

In Owatonna, Ruth met people she found more congenial than any she had known before. These daughters of professors resembled her, and in comfort with them she heard more easily, spoke more fluently. The little girl did not even seem to mind, in 1897 and 1898, that her mother oversaw the classes she attended and the teachers she met. She also, as always, had the outdoors, a constant and kindly refuge: "I still have a notebook chiefly concerned with the scenery, like: 'The sun came up over the Mississippi like this: △ ,' with red chalk painting in the sun."[50]

This was a good time, but again a short time. The family had weathered two Minnesota winters, spending the summers in Norwich, when Bertrice Fulton accepted another job. In 1899 Bertrice Fulton decided to move back to New York State, to the city of Buffalo. Two years before, in 1897, Buffalo incorporated the library, making the private institution into a public facility. The city needed a head librarian, and Bertrice Fulton took the position. In the job she gained permanence, if a smaller salary than from previous teaching jobs. Buffalo was closer to the Norwich farm, and train lines through Binghamton made visits to the Shattucks easier than they had been from Missouri and Minnesota.

In 1899 the family took another train, through Chicago, along Lake Erie, and into Buffalo. Ruth turned twelve in June, and that year, by her own report, "was unusually unaccountable." Her tantrums increased, a discomfort not helped by moving to a new place. Margery, not quite eleven, kept her cheerful spirits; her temperament and her age made moving easier. The two sisters were uneasy allies at best. In 1900, too, Aunt Hettie died, a disruption of family patterns somewhat softened by the arrival of Bertrice's younger unmarried sister, Myra. The people changed, but the tone of the all-female household remained the same. Ruth grew fonder of Auntie My than she had been of Aunt Hettie and added to her constellation another vision of the "maiden aunt."

Buffalo residents called their city the "Queen City" and demonstrated the chauvinism characteristic of a "second city." Through the 1890s Buffalo had become an important commercial and industrial center, attaining a population of 400,000 in 1900. Located at the eastern tip of Lake Erie, the west end of the Erie Canal, and between the United States and Canada, Buffalo became an active port of exchange. Businesses, banks, and hotels flourished along Main Street. Had Ruth Fulton cared, she would have noticed another Louis Sullivan bank, equally pompous and commanding but serving a clientele different from the Owatonna citizenry. Window-shoppers in downtown Buffalo strolled by elegant department stores and fancy restaurants, distant from the noisome warehouses lining the Niagara River front:

> This fashionable part of Buffalo, where one knew practically everyone one met on the street, was only a small portion of it, but it seemed to us to be the only real Buffalo. On the other side of Main Street where all the stores were, it was just an outer wilderness.[51]

Developments throughout the nineteenth century added to Buffalo's geographical advantage. In 1825 the Erie Canal was completed, and ten years later the railroads ensured Buffalo's position. By 1900, between 500 and 700 miles of track ran within the city limits, besides those going to Chicago and the East Coast.[52] Ships continued to cross back and forth from Canada, carrying migrants and tourists.

In 1896 engineers turned Niagara Falls into electric power. Buffalo "lit up," called itself the "Electric City," and boasted of its infinite energy supply. Steel and iron industries took advantage of the endless energy, and these large industries brought smaller ones, and workers, into the city. Immigrants arrived by rail and boat from East Coast cities and across the river from Canada. Buffalo's old settlers extended a mixed welcome to the newcomers. Poles, Italians, and Ukranians from the East Coast seemed different from the Anglo-Canadians and German immigrants of the 1850s and 1860s. The immigrant arrivals settled in firmly bounded areas and did not cross the streets into unknown neighborhoods.

From center city north stretched Delaware Avenue; here Buffalo's original inhabitants lived, sons and daughters of New England families who had traveled west in the late eighteenth century. Delaware Avenue looked elegant: "Nearly all Buffalo houses were covered with ampelopsis, a rapidly growing, small-leaved vine."[53]

Delaware Avenue also protected its elegance, and the writer of the quoted sentences detected the claustrophobia that accompanied Buffalo's stratification: "In 1880 Buffalo was a cozy town. At least it was for those who formed the nucleus in the center of it, that central part made up of Delaware Avenue and the avenues parallel to it and the cross streets that intersected the privileged area."[54]

The people who lived on Delaware Avenue knew little about the Hungarians and Slovaks to their north, or the large Polish community in the southeast section of the city. Nor did they have dealings with the Italians and Irish who lived between the lakeshore and Buffalo Creek. Residents of Delaware Avenue got on the trolley car, two blocks away, and went downtown to shop, to have tea in a hotel, to visit the city art museum.

Bertrice Fulton, Ruth and Margery, and Aunt My moved near Delaware Avenue, taking an apartment above the household of another of Bertrice's sisters, Mary Shattuck Ellis. Aunt Mary and Uncle Will showed the new residents the city and provided steady comfort and company for the four women. Typically, Bertrice Fulton depended on family, the supporting context for her own ambitions. Her career did anything but cut her off from family.

Buffalo must have been lovely in September, especially where the

Fultons lived. The Buffalo Chamber of Commerce proudly publicized the city's "stately homes" and luxurious open green spaces. Two decades before, in the 1870s, the city had commissioned Frederick Law Olmsted to design an extensive park system, and when Ruth and Margery arrived the city contained 1,200 acres of pure park land. Over the years of the twentieth century, trees and grass made disappointingly little relief from the smoke and stench of the "Electric City."

Bertrice Fulton went off to the Main Library on Lafayette Square. The library, like Olmsted's park system, was a source of civic pride. Chamber of Commerce brochures, however, did not mention the role of the library in Buffalo's growing social reform movement. By incorporating the library and turning it into a public institution, Buffalo's elite soothed some troubled consciences. Reading and learning might lift the immigrants from a condition of poverty into prosperity and appreciation of the "American way of life," a hope Buffalonians shared with other urban residents. Branch libraries supplemented the Main Library, and in 1899 Buffalo hired a Polish librarian.[55] But no one went so far as to put Polish books in the library; such a collection might hinder "assimilation."

The library in effect belonged to Buffalo's first families. In her job Bertrice Fulton confronted the knotty dilemmas of a social reform movement and met the leisured women who dominated the movement. Whatever difficulties she encountered with reformism, Bertrice Fulton also took advantage of her contacts with Buffalo's upper classes. Once more her determination to provide the girls with the best available education surfaced, and she enrolled Ruth and Margery with the daughters of the library's supporters. Ruth and Margery started high school in Masten Park High School, a public school. (At some time Bertrice had enrolled the girls in the same grade at school, perhaps for convenience, and perhaps when they moved from Norwich to Missouri.) A year after arriving in Buffalo the two girls went off to St. Margaret's Episcopal Academy for Girls, a transfer Bertrice Fulton had somehow managed, maybe with the help of Mary and Will Ellis.

Ruth had few fond memories of St. Margaret's. She shared this opinion with Mabel Dodge, who did not have to contend with being new and different. Mabel Dodge belonged to one of Buffalo's upper-class families and took her place in the elite circles of the growing city. But she also had a fine critical wit and a yearning for independence, bordering on the outrageous. By the time she was an adult, Mabel Dodge had a reputation as a Bohemian, a liberal, devoted to "good causes." She managed her background well, neglecting neither the charms nor the "civil liberties" of those from different backgrounds.

Ruth met her at St. Margaret's first, and years later knew her as the wife of a Taos Indian and a firm advocate of Indian rights. For the while, however, the two adolescents—otherwise unlike—had St. Margaret's in common to complain about. "I do not remember learning a single thing at St. Margaret's where I went to school until I was sixteen years old," Mabel Dodge wrote. Prayers were regular—9:00 A.M. in the yellow and white assembly hall—and the principal was stern, severe, and upright. The school's motto did not inspire Mabel Dodge, who quoted it sarcastically: "He also serves who learns to stand and wait."[56]

Ruth Fulton appreciated the sarcasm and she especially admired the writer, with awe bordering on a crush: "The first person I ever saw who, I knew, belonged somewhere else than in the world I stood so aloof from was, amusingly enough, Mabel Dodge"—amusing because twenty years later the two women built a friendship on shared love of the Southwest Pueblos. Ruth stood "aloof," but not quite happily. She envied her sister's sociability and watched Margery slip easily into new groups of friends. She also envied someone like Mabel Dodge, who had the certainty to distance herself deliberately from Buffalo, its petty snobberies and looming social evils.

Ruth reached a peak of self-consciousness from 1900 to 1905 at St. Margaret's. She felt keenly her deafness and her stammer and added to these distinguishing characteristics a sensitivity to being poor and fatherless. In a 1948 letter, Douglas Haring remembered his Aunt Grace and Ruth Fulton running through their Buffalo house, "screeching with laughter."[57] His account suggests the giggling unease that was the other side of an adolescent girl's tragic self-image. Ruth kept a view of herself as isolated and odd, testing and elaborating this image through fictional figures of various traits and capabilities. The people she made up became, as in Norwich, Ruth's favored companions and the touchstones for a self-characterization she even more intensely engaged in during the Buffalo years.

Circumstances as well as age made a difference. "In Owatonna we had everything" and in Buffalo they seemed to have nothing. Whatever Auntie My prepared did not compare to the provisions in neighboring Delaware Avenue houses. Ruth could not trade stories with her classmates about family trips and large dinner parties. Ruth had no father who went "downtown" every morning and who brought dignified visitors home at night. She could not talk of mysterious transactions in the "city." Nor did her private and persistent attraction to death and the image of her father in his coffin seem a proper thing to tell her friends. Ruth's father was best left for her fantasies. At thirteen and fourteen many girls daydream; Ruth's dreams continued to have a somber cast, referring back to scenes in the Shattuck farmhouse and to associations formed in childhood.

Ruth thought about these things later. Meanwhile, in Buffalo, she experienced her oddity and uncongeniality in direct ways. Not only did she have trouble hearing what people said and lack the conversational facility to compensate for shyness, she also suffered from the family's poverty. "In Buffalo, we were very poor," she wrote. Partly a comparison to others, their poverty was also quite real. Bertrice did not receive a high salary.

> Mother elected to take the position of librarian in charge of the large staff because of its greater security as compared with the teaching jobs she had had in the Middle West. Library salaries could be depended upon to advance at a regular amount each year, and the job was permanent until retirement age. She went on a salary of sixty dollars a month— fifteen dollars a week for a family of four. I remember the momentous occasion of spending one dollar and fifty cents for a hat. Every year in rotation one of us could have a new coat.[58]

The girls at St. Margaret's who dressed up, had new coats, and took "lessons" reminded Ruth in more than words of economic distinctions. Ruth's world consisted of upper-class, white Anglo-Saxon Protestants, at school and in her neighborhood. No one from the "wrong side" of the tracks or from the riverfront came into the Buffalo Ruth knew as an adolescent.

Margery tried to accommodate, to smooth over the economic differences. She realized the importance of "wardrobe" and worked hard to make this aspect of the Fulton sisters' lives match everyone else's:

> By the time we went to Buffalo we were making some of our own clothes, and the process of learning to use paper patterns and making "simulated box plaits" was terribly trying to me. Margery had learned by making doll's dresses, but I'd never cared how my dolls were dressed. Margery had even made my doll a dress once because she had been distressed about her, but it wasn't a distress I could appreciate.[59]

In those years, Ruth learned to ignore the way she looked, to consider clothes a minor bother at best and irrelevant to the serious purposes of life. Certainly she could not sew as well as Margery—"Margery was the 'handy' one" is a repeated theme in her autobiographical fragment. And though she did not want to be as sensitive to others' opinions as "fashion" demanded, typical adolescent concerns impinged. "Much, much later when we graduated from high school I remember being humiliated because I hadn't known enough to select the proper dress for an afternoon party and had worn a white one—white wasn't a daytime color then."[60]

In Buffalo, Ruth turned back to writing with a seriousness prompted by adolescent turmoil and by ongoing competition with Margery. Ruth needed a fantasy world as she had in childhood, but by the time she was fourteen or fifteen her imaginary people changed. Ruth replaced the romantic and transcendent figures of her childish daydreams with concrete personages who walked the ground literally and figuratively. Ruth Fulton imagined women less of great beauty than of perfect integrity, who struggled for purpose in life. These heroines embodied the writer's budding dilemmas and the girl's sense of developing options, alternatives for a woman's life. Events for Ruth's fictional heroines became a series of challenges, rarely eventuating in a "happily ever after" ending.

During her adolescence Ruth learned that she could test her own character with the characters she created. Her stories are less chronological narratives than a series of personifications. She had learned the intense importance of studying portraits, and from visual impressions she extracted elements to make up the "precious pearls" of her private world. With words she became more than a perceiver; she became a participant as well, remaking herself in the image of others. Ruth used writing to explore and pull out the constituents of her own being.

Once, too, her imaginary figures had depended on the actual figures in her life. Ruth had found in her father the image of hero, an ambitious and tragic man. Through her mother and grandmother first, then aunts and teachers, she worked out possibilities for women, who had to find a balance between selfless ecstasy and a passionate, true engagement of self. In Buffalo, Ruth depended less on family and friends for inspiration and model. Ruth broadened her scope and drew characteristics from a wider range than she had known in Norwich. But the Bible remained her favored source: "No book even at this time [in Buffalo] ever competed with the Bible. The story of Ruth was better than *Ramona*."[61] The story of Ruth and of devotion was *her* story; Sir Walter Scott's romantic heroines did not suit so well.

In fiction Ruth manipulated the world of women and men she looked out upon. She also began to let the world of fiction impinge upon the world of reality; she began to let the people she lived with see the figures she felt she belonged with. Gradually members of her family saw the people she recognized as her "own." In the process Ruth adjusted to her liking the world of Auntie My and Bertrice Fulton, her sister, and her aunt and uncle Ellis.

Ruth made then an important discovery about writing. Although her handwriting was "execrable" compared to Margery's "neat round hand," her stories impressed people. Her mother, true to training, increasingly guided her daughter's developing talent. And so while Margery went off to art school every Saturday morning, "I stayed home and wrote pieces for Mother to correct." Bertrice Fulton did not praise effusively, but she did pay full attention to Ruth's compositions. "Mother, I know, thought it wasn't a good idea to give the child an inflated sense of what her scribblings were worth, but I think it was only fair to counterbalance for the moment my abiding sense of Margery's 'handiness.' "[62]

Ruth widened her audience. She showed her pieces to Uncle Will, as years earlier she had let her grandfather into her private world. Uncle Will offered a response Grandfather Shattuck had not: "He offered me a dollar if I would copy ten 'pieces' into a notebook for him, and I guess he still has it," she wrote in 1935.[63]

The reward pleased Ruth: "It gave me a great sense of pride and responsibility."[64] Ruth's attitudes about her writing, established in 1900–1905, became part of the emerging pattern. She learned that writing opened up self without exposing secrets. She learned, too, how to construct a satisfactory, if never final, life story. There was another lesson, equally important—writing was rewarded in various ways, by an audience she chose. Ruth began to realize that her choices did not have to be those of Joanna Shattuck or Bertrice Fulton or Margery in order to be valid choices. To some extent it was Uncle Will, and the monetary reward, that made this last point for Ruth.

Being rewarded with a dollar instead of a conscientious editorial remark or a loving kiss in Ruth's view gave composing a legitimate sanction. Her uncle represented the "outside" world to Ruth, a world of men and of public activities, of ambitions and conventional criteria for judgment. Uncle Will stood for something quite different from the household world of Bertrice, Auntie My—and Margery. To the women in her life, Ruth responded with distinct ambivalence; she regarded their approval always with a grain of doubt. Ruth needed an Uncle Will at that moment to balance the world of women at home and at school.

Writing also provided escape. When the real world closed in, with random noises and confusing standards for behavior, Ruth ran off to a world she fit. She made this world, and lived in it, with the closed-off self-absorption her mother had found impossibly irritating ten years before. Ruth did not think Margery's trips to art school every Saturday accomplished some of the same escape—Margery seemed so accommodating. Life in Buffalo was not easy for either girl, constantly reminded at St. Margaret's of their stringent circumstances. Neither wardrobe nor lessons nor skills provided the Fultons with the amenities their schoolmates and neighbors conspicuously displayed. Yet the two never formed an alliance. Ruth struggled to find her own way without the help of a younger sister.

Bertrice Fulton worked hard. She tried to give the mechanisms of conformity to two daughters, each uncertain of how much she wanted to conform. Nor was Bertrice Fulton certain; she did not want to push her daughters into situations where they would be completely at a disadvantage, suffering a social handicap because their futures would not resemble that of Buffalo's upper-class women.[65] St. Margaret's girls were expected to go to good colleges, another problem for the Fultons, and one solved fortuitously by a Buffalo resident and, coincidentally, a loyal Vassar graduate—a woman remembered only as "Mrs. Thompson." "During the girls' senior year at St. Margaret's, Bertrice Fulton received a letter from Mrs. Thompson's secretary, which read [Margery later recalled], 'Mrs. Thompson has been pleased to place your two daughters, Ruth and Margery Fulton, on her list of Vassar Scholarships for September, 1905.' Only that, and nothing more."[66]

3

Explorations

"The world of thought and ideals"

BERTRICE FULTON'S AMBITIONS for her daughters did not end with St. Margaret's and Buffalo life. She determined that her daughters choose college, as she had chosen college three decades earlier. Whatever awkwardnesses Ruth and Margery suffered from socially, both did well in school. Homework, in fact, might have been a useful distraction from conventional student activities. In 1905, their last year at St. Margaret's, both girls won scholarships to Vassar College, Bertrice Fulton's alma mater. That the money came from an alumna suited college policy and sentiment; too, Vassar readily accepted the daughters of an early student. Vassar College trained generations of women in the same family, much as contemporary male colleges did.

The Vassar plan came as no surprise to Ruth and Margery. During their childhood and adolescence, each had been directed to develop her own talents and to grasp available opportunities. When Bertrice Fulton moved from job to job in the 1890s, she had her children in mind as much as any ambitions of her own. What she did not say, she showed in her actions. Bertrice was not daunted by the apparent stringencies of her life. She would show her daughters the possibilities for women, even in widowhood and in what Ruth called "extreme poverty." Their mother's staunchness made a sometimes difficult lesson for the two girls. Ruth, especially, responded to the model, the more intensely the more she suspected she might never attain a like accommodation.

After graduation from St. Margaret's (and Ruth's mistaken "white dress"), the household took their summer trip to Norwich. In September 1905 Ruth and Margery went together to Poughkeepsie, New York—a train ride and a carriage ride from station to campus.

Vassar had been chartered nearly a half-century earlier, in 1861, and opened in 1865. The college had the further distinction, which Vassar girls did not forget, of being founded by a brewer—one Matthew Vassar. Matthew Vassar believed women should have an education equal to though not the same as the education of the men they would marry. For Vassar girls would marry, and be better wives and mothers for having attended college. At first the brewer called his school Vassar Female College, a "finishing academy" for girls of the middle classes.

Matthew Vassar also believed that women, or their fathers, should pay for an education. His plans did not involve turning Vassar into a charity school, for working girls from poor families. Tuition gifts, like Ruth's and Margery's, did not violate his intentions since these were from private individuals and did not demand either school philanthropy—breeding dependence—or student jobs, a distraction from proper intellectual pursuits. For extra money, Vassar girls might do a bit of work: shelving books in the library, tutoring fellow students, tidying the dormitory parlor. The founder told his policy to the faculty, and the faculty told it to the public. In 1880 Dr. Maria Mitchell, professor of astronomy, commented on the scholarship student: "She learns to expect to be held up, and she ceases to stand upright. I believe a girl loses her nicety of morals who looks around to see who is coming to her rescue."[1]

The prosperous brewer voiced generally strong opinions. If Vassar was not to resemble certain charitable women's colleges then being established, no more was his seminary to overemphasize "intellectuality." At Vassar the development of the "brain" would not result in diminishment of the "bosom."[2] Physical hygiene would be as important as mental exercise. Vassar girls graduated healthy and flourishing, as well as bright and well-read.

Matthew Vassar's philosophy of female education dominated the years Bertrice Fulton attended college, 1878–82. The philosophy was still evident when Ruth and Margery arrived, though the presidency and personnel had changed. In 1884 James Monroe Taylor began a thirty-year term as president. A preacher replaced two preceding male educators only to clothe the original message in clerical phrase. Taylor perpetuated his predecessor's principles; exhortations for a balance between mental and physical health alternated with biblical parables in his speeches to the student body.

The campus itself, in early fall of 1905, provided a glorious autumnal welcome. Main Hall, pompous behind its portico, Jewett dormitory, the astronomy building, and the chapel sat uncrowded amid grassy spaces and pine trees. A new student easily forgot the bustling Hudson River town where the train had stopped. She could ignore the ware-houses and shops of downtown Poughkeepsie, and if tempted to venture out, passed the brick wall which, surrounding the campus, marked a separation between town and gown. Students had all they needed within the walls and rarely walked into Poughkeepsie.

Beyond the dorms and classroom buildings, the "cultivated" part of Vassar, lay the "uncultivated" part. A short stroll through fields and trees brought the walker to a marsh around a small, brackish lake. At Sunset Lake, students could carry on intimate conversations or sit alone in private study of the universe. One can picture, and the *Vassar Quarterly* did, two students in straight dark skirts, topped by white blouses, circling the lake deep in conversation about the French Revolution, Christina Rossetti, or the Milky Way. One can also picture, though there is no existing photograph of such a scene, Ruth Fulton sitting by the lake, a book in her lap, her mind half on that, half in some other country.

When Ruth and Margery entered, Vassar had one thousand students. A solid curriculum provided these students with Matthew Vassar's carefully designed "well-rounded" background. Lucy M. Salmon taught history, and her classes set a pattern for courses at Vassar and later at colleges throughout the country. Dr. Salmon argued that disciplines be directed toward practical ends; history, for example, did not end in documents or secondary sources. History, Dr. Salmon said, concerned itself not with some "vague life of the mind," but with "real events." She went on to specify: Each student must know American politics and policies—because of the "grave political problems yet unsettled and demanding the serious attention of every mature mind."[3]

Over in her own building, the Vassar Observatory, Dr. Maria Mitchell taught astronomy. Her course, too, set an example, of science for female students. She taught students how to adjust the telescope and calculate the movements of stars. Girls at Vassar learned a scientific method, firmly. They learned to test evidence and look for proof, not to depend upon approximations and the ladylike "just about right."[4] Ruth Fulton added portraits to her collection of female "lives": the lady historian, active, determined, bold, and outspoken; the lady astronomer, devoted to scientific method and research, less actively involved in the "practical" ends of her science.

Ruth Fulton took the required set of courses, a curriculum established in 1903 and "virtually unchanged for nearly 20 years." English, Math, Latin, or Greek were required in the freshman year. A modern language, history, and physics or chemistry were taken in the freshman or sophomore year. Juniors had to take one semester of philosophy or psychology, and no girl could graduate without "Ethics."[5] Ruth's transcript records Phi Beta Kappa and honors, along with As and Bs in English, history, and ancient languages. In the fall of her sophomore year she got a D in German and that same spring a D in music—two understandable failings, given her deafness, in an otherwise respectable record. According to the brewer and the first three presidents, the curriculum prepared Vassar graduates for undertaking "enlightened tasks" in the service of their own development and the betterment of humankind. Vassar girls were not always sure how they would accomplish their tasks, but that for the moment did not seem to matter.

At Vassar, Ruth found an "undiscovered country." Within the campus walls lay worlds to be explored. Ruth eagerly read through the small catalog of courses, looking forward to new books and exciting conversations. Both by plan and by physical arrangement, Vassar encouraged the exchange of ideas among students. Just inside the front door of each dormitory was a parlor, with nineteenth-century landscapes and portraits to look at, Victorian couches to settle down on, and bookcases to explore. (A less explicit but equally persistent function of these parlors was to serve as waiting room for male suitors. Vassar girls learned to converse, after all, in order to "improve their chances.") Student companionship supplemented classroom encounters: "The influence of hundreds of mentally eager girls upon the characters of one another, when they live for four years in the closest daily companionship, is most interesting to see. . . . No more healthy, generous, democratic, beauty-loving, serviceable society of people exists than the girls' college community affords."[6]

Ruth's choice of an English major turned out to be supremely satisfying. She recalled, ten years later, sitting in a windowseat and experiencing a "revelation" at the end of Walter Pater's *Renaissance*:

> And then came Pater. Every instant of the late afternoon is vivid to me. I even know that I had to creep to the windowseat to catch the last dim light in that bare tower room of my Freshman days. The book fell shut in my hands at the end, and it was as if my soul had been given back to me, its eyes wide and eager with new understanding.[7]

She could have read Pater on her own, and may have; Ruth realized at Vassar that learning did not have to be a private, even secret, matter. She recognized, as the founder of Vassar had intended her to, that learning came from shared experiences. With people whose interests and backgrounds matched hers Ruth did not need a lot of talk and chatter to know herself "congenial" in the community. Her deafness seemed manageable then, and in the all-women environment she communicated comfortably and confidently, at least with those who shared her passions and detected the sources of her initial shyness and awkwardness.

That students fit so well together in the Vassar community was not fortuitous. The founder and his successors saw to it that Vassar's student body had few rough edges. Neither Ruth nor Margery had reason to mind that at Vassar, as at Pillsbury Academy and St. Margaret's, their spending money and their wardrobes did not equal everyone else's. These were minor differences compared to the designed likenesses among the students. Vassar girls wanted the same things out of life: self-fulfillment in marriage or in a career, the chance to improve society by teaching one's own and other people's children, the opportunity to make a mark on the world.

At least almost all Vassar students shared these goals. Ruth's friends did. Agnes Benedict, Katherine Norton, Elizabeth Atsatt, Harriet Taylor —these women, like Ruth, did not plan to go to professional school, though they did consider extra training in education and in social work. Graduates like these left Poughkeepsie, confident they could be good wives and mothers if life offered that alternative, competent career women if that were the alternative. Ruth and her friends counted on a satisfying future and one free of conflict and confusion.

Such optimistic women made up the majority of college women in early twentieth-century America. There existed, also, a minority, another sort of female student. These women spoke out in protest, arguing that American women had gained education and no rights in American society. They claimed, and traveled the country to do so, that American society oppressed half its population. From their protests came heated debates at suffrage leagues, political rallies, socialist meetings—but few on campus itself. If Ruth and students like her worried about the conditions under which women had to make a future, they did so in private diaries not public speeches.

Activist students at Vassar struggled largely without success to win support from fellow students. Behind the indifference lay the firm proclamation of President Taylor and of Vassar trustees against meetings. Neither the president nor alumnae demonstrated sympathy for soapbox speeches and women's movements. Asked to give a talk on campus, Harriet Stanton Blatch, class of 1878, replied:

> For several reasons I have lost my interest in Vassar College. 1st because of its narrow sectarianism . . . 2nd the last chair endowed was on the condition that no women should fill it.

3rd I sent a copy of "The History of Woman Suffrage" as a gift to the Library, which was rejected without thanks. Hence I feel no interest in the success of an institution that can thus insult womanhood collectively and individually.[8]

In Ruth's class Inez Milholland also tried to convince Vassar women they should not put up with "insults." Just outside the campus gates, Milholland held meetings and gave speeches. She was dramatic, and she was safe, as long as she did not come closer than the nearby cemetery where she held meetings. (Six years later Vassar students brought the meetings inside, organizing gatherings of the College Equal Suffrage League; the League, established in 1900, reached Poughkeepsie in 1915.) Ruth Fulton may have admired her classmate's drama and conviction; she evidently did not attend Milholland's rallies.

Nor did most of Ruth's fellow students, who, like her, were daughters of conservative business and clerical families. Yet they all knew what was going on. In their shock at student activities Vassar publications described these "radical" events in vivid detail, listing names of those who did attend. The Vassar alumnae magazine noted that President Taylor had in 1908 sternly forbidden all suffragette meetings; nevertheless, the magazine reported, "Inez Milholland is holding meetings just the same over in the grave-yard near the campus."[9] On a June day in 1909 her meeting consisted of about forty undergraduates, ten alumnae, two male "visitors" (the men are not identified), and "the warrior for women's legal rights" Harriet Stanton Blatch, along with Charlotte Perkins Gilman, Rose Schneiderman, and Helen Hoy. In spite of the reprimands of Taylor and the shock of some alumnae, students and faculty attending the well-publicized rally came through unharmed. (Lucy Salmon participated, protected by her recognized value on the Vassar campus.)

These few Vassar radicals of the prewar period went on to fight for women's rights in the streets and in the courts of cities and state capitals, and in their professions. In 1915, Inez Milholland, a lawyer, but having lost none of her dramatic flair, rode down Fifth Avenue on a horse, wearing a white banner reading "Votes for Women." By then Vassar students and alumnae regarded her as more a heroine than a villain. Her classmate, Ruth Fulton Benedict, too, voiced sympathy for claims of oppression that had seemed revolutionary ten years before.

Meanwhile, a student at Vassar, Ruth Fulton extended her particular perceptions and tested her relationships with other people. She made friends here, and her memory of Owatonna might serve again: "For the first time people began to play some real part in my life."[10] Ruth's friends from Vassar remained friends for the rest of her life, thus enacting one of Matthew Vassar's dreams of a lasting community of Vassar graduates. (In 1979, talking of Ruth Benedict's anthropology, Ruth Underhill remarked with pleasure that she and Ruth had both been "Vassar girls." Underhill graduated in 1901, eight years before Ruth Benedict.)

Ruth Fulton made her way apart not only from Inez Milholland and her companions but—more significantly—apart from Margery Fulton. Ruth formed a small and intimate group of friends; Margery, as outgoing and cheerful as ever, had a larger circle of friends and was better remembered by classmates. Both were active in student clubs, and their names appear in the yearbook under associations like the drama club, the literary club, Deutsche Verein. But Margery was the popular sister, Ruth still the intellectual one; Margery was the sociable sister and Ruth still the scholar. In their senior year Margery was elected class president.

At Vassar, Ruth did not so stringently compare herself to Margery as she once had. With her own friends, and the intimacy combined with intellectuality fostered by her environment, Ruth did not have to measure her successes and failures against Margery's. She also put aside for a while that other important contrast, between the "world of my father" and the "world of my mother." She was in her mother's world in a sense and in a world of infinite possibilities in another sense. Powerful impressions of women at work, of diverse modes of living, of various arrangements for human relationships filled her mind and stirred her imagination. Ruth moved from the picture of her father in death and her mother in mourning to a consideration of human potential and the workings of imagination in general.

In their senior year, while Margery presided Ruth Fulton wrote an exceptional paper on symbolism and added a copy to the growing collection of "pieces" she kept stored away. She threw together (and always would) a miscellaneous collection of old envelopes, notecards, shopping lists, and drafts of papers. The messiness of storage belied the significance of what she saved.

> Man is always reaching out beyond the world he sees and hears. In every age since history began, he has tried to express, even amid the confusion of his thought and the crudities of his language, something of that other world he only feels and does not touch or see—the world of thought and ideals. . . . He has looked at Nature and seen in its bountiful sky, in its life-giving sun, and in its majestic storms, the embodiment, the symbol of his aspirations.[11]

Ruth did not save "The Sense of Symbolism" because others praised it. She had received As and rewards for writing throughout her college years, and now these rewards came from women who had achieved something notable in the world—not just from Uncle Will and occasionally her mother. It was certainly important to Ruth to have acknowledgment of her worth, but she also recognized in "The Sense of Symbolism" an important beginning for a persistent thread in her pattern.

In her senior year Ruth won first prize for another essay. This piece, called "Literature and Democracy" and published in the *Vassar Miscellany*, brought its author the college composition award. She wrote about public libraries, art, and "the reading mob."[12] Meanwhile Margery rehearsed for Vassar College's traditional daisy chain ceremony. Wearing long white dresses and carrying a chain of yellow flowers, a select group of girls would lead the graduating class of 1909 through their solemn ceremony. Ruth accepted her literary prize, and Margery accepted her honor as class president.

The four years had given Ruth a sense of her own accomplishments. She began to see worth in her purposes, a worth confirmed by friends and teachers. The women at Vassar replaced Uncle Will, grades and comments replaced the "dollar," but the effect was similar: "It gave me a great sense of pride and responsibility."[13] On that June day in 1909 one can imagine Bertrice Fulton proudly watching her two different daughters finish the school she had left nearly thirty years earlier. Not long after graduation the two girls made typical—and equally conventional— choices. Margery married Robert Freeman, a Presbyterian minister trained at Princeton. The Freemans moved to Pasadena, California. Ruth made another choice.

"Dresden and Rome seem very far in the distance"

Ruth Fulton's postgraduation plans included travel through Europe for the year, with two Vassar friends. She, Elizabeth Atsatt, and Katherine Norton would spend 1909–10 abroad, a trip completely paid for by Mr. C. M. Pratt of Glen Cove, Long Island, an old friend of Norton's father and dean of Pomona College. A photograph shows the three young women dressed and seated formally in preparation for the "grand tour."

Someone gave Ruth as a going-away present a small black notebook in which to record impressions of her journeys. Her first entry is dated August 12–28 and titled "Chicago." Ruth, Elizabeth, and Katherine stopped in Chicago to visit with another classmate, Harriet Taylor. Taylor belonged to a settlement house family, and one event of the Chicago stay was a visit to Hull House. Ruth did not show much interest: "Saw Hul House," she wrote, more excited by another event. On that

Chicago visit Ruth Fulton met Harriet Monroe, poet and publisher of *Poetry*, a small avant-garde magazine. (A decade later Harriet Monroe would print several of Ruth's poems under the name "Anne Singleton.")

The black notebook contains practically nothing about Europe. It is stuffed with old envelopes, scraps of paper, and index cards jammed with lines of verse. The one or two descriptions of things she saw in Europe, like the paragraphs Ruth wrote in Buffalo, "had a beat like verse —the whole description had—but I didn't know how else to say it."[14]

There are other notes in the book, suggesting an unfamiliar exploration on Ruth's part. On shipboard she wrote, "Jack Hooker, brother Carolyn. Pretty bad!" and on another page, "Arthur Bundy, 2nd cabin!" Ruth, Elizabeth, and Katherine may have laughed and teased in critical comment, more than Ruth recorded. Ruth, with her two friends, fit herself into an image of the young American woman; the woman had been well described by contemporary writers, and Ruth had details to choose from:

> They are almost always pretty and conscious of the fact from the tip of their highest feather on their flamboyant hat to the tips of their sometimes shabby kid gloves. They prattle unceasingly, and use a great deal of slang. In passing them, you hear words like "kid," "corker," "stuck on himself," "in the push" falling from the prettiest lips.[15]

The rarely used black notebook suggests Ruth's attempt to test herself against the model of a "typical American girl." She simultaneously turned away from words, the formal patterning of experience, to experience itself. In Europe, Ruth visited a first "really important undiscovered country," and she determined not to let phrases intervene between herself and "the rich processes of living."[16] For one year Ruth Fulton considered writing less the true "stuff" of her world than a screen between personal responses and external circumstances. She threw herself as never before into the nitty-gritty of daily activities. Her experiences included sore feet, tired eyes, crowds of people, strange foods and smells, and the awesomely wonderful objects of an ancient civilization. Nor was conversation demanded; she and her companions filled the role of American *jeune fille* and could be forgiven a silent lack of comprehension. For once Ruth's confusion in the midst of chatter matched someone else's.

The three girls went from Rome to Paris to London, apparently unchaperoned and independent. They went in quest of adventure and culture, and at least found the latter. Ruth ignored the one demand put on her, to prove the "worth" of her trip by writing it down. She refused to be driven by principle into foregoing pleasure; there would be principle enough when she returned to familiar country. Moreover, the views were striking in and of themselves, and Ruth did not have to recreate the beauties and the contrasts in literary language. The sights of that year in Europe persisted in memories stronger than the phrases and habits learned from literature. She needed all her energies to see the Uffizi Palace, the Louvre, the National Portrait Gallery in London; words were not (for a time) necessary.

In the spring of 1910 Ruth sailed home. She arrived in the United States without a clear idea of what she wanted to do. A background in literature had, as Vassar intended, provided a basis for self-development. Less certainly, Ruth found out, did her training provide a basis for a public achievement or a salary. She was not alone in feeling at loose ends; many women left college only to wonder about the value of their education in a day-to-day world. Ruth moved back to Buffalo and into her mother's house. Bertrice Fulton had her job in the library; economic need did not push Ruth into decisions, and a woman in her early twenties still had a few years of leeway. Ruth did not show special concern about her future, yet.

"Life was a labyrinth of petty turns"

Buffalo had changed in the five years since Ruth lived there; the urban conditions she knew had intensified. The city of "infinite electric power" had grown smellier, more polluted, and more populated. People crowded into housing that the city fathers with some justification refused to call tenements. As long as Buffalo's poor lived in individual dwellings, the city felt free of the worst urban blight. Delaware Avenue and downtown Buffalo reflected the prosperous side of the city, and a young woman did not have to walk near the river or in the enlarging immigrant neighborhoods.

But young women *did* walk through these streets. The American social reform movement had expanded in the years Ruth spent at Vassar and in Europe. Cities across the country confronted social problems with welfare policies, night-school courses, urban gardens. Chicago boasted of its settlement house movement, and Buffalo of the first Charity Organization Society (C.O.S.). Ruth had rejected the Jane Addams image and could not imagine herself living in Hull House. She did volunteer for the Charity Organization Society, to "visit" the poor.

In 1877 an Englishman, the Reverend S. H. Gurteen, brought the idea of a charity society to Buffalo. The C.O.S. was established as a mechanism for coordinating existing public and private agencies. Industrial growth created a need for charity, but before Gurteen arrived charity in Buffalo had been individualized and haphazard. The C.O.S. heralded the upsurge of "scientific" charity and professional social work. Personal almsgiving, Gurteen had claimed, must be replaced by careful inquiry into the merits of every client and the worth of any case. Churches gave way to official agencies as the centers of charity; goodhearted individuals, increasingly into the twentieth century, gave way before ranks of trained investigators.

Ruth had come at a good time for women and nonprofessionals. To accomplish its purposes the C.O.S. required a large pool of workers and began by drawing on the number of ready and willing humanitarians in Buffalo at the turn of the century. For years prominent clergymen had encouraged their congregations to attend to the problems of the poor, and when almsgiving lost favor the same clergymen encouraged people to learn how to prepare reports on individual cases. Women who had given money in the 1890s by the early 1900s made inquiries and evaluated "willingness to work," recorded number in household, and noted extent of disease and attendance of children at school.

These eager, generous, and leisured individuals participated in another change of attitude as the twentieth century matured. Less and less did social workers, humanitarians, and reformers attribute poverty to innate individual flaws. More and more, people involved in social causes came to believe that environment, not character, created poverty.

The poor person was not immoral, just out of a job. The C.O.S. shifted its attitudes and continued to function energetically through the pre–World War I period. Operating with the philosophy that to change circumstances would change people's lives, the C.O.S. valiantly strove against the poverty spreading through Buffalo's immigrant neighborhoods. Those volunteers who managed to see above the piles of paperwork the C.O.S. required might also share the ideal of instructed improvement. The ideal reflected the dominance of American liberalism and the influence of Social Darwinism.[17]

The C.O.S. provided a set of activities for "raising of the poor" from the lower class into at least the middle class. A C.O.S. worker could teach in night schools, helping Polish and Italian adults master the language their children learned in school—if their children went to school; C.O.S. workers had to deal daily with what they called "truancy" and with parents who sent children to work instead of to classes. The Polish population, particularly, seemed to the C.O.S. to cling stubbornly to a belief that sixteen-year-old girls and boys should contribute to household income and not spend time in schools.

A C.O.S. worker could also work at neighborhood clinics, treating the apparently endless cases of tuberculosis. And there was the public library, the main branch on Lafayette Square, and local branches scattered through the west and south sides of the city where Poles and Italians lived. Bertrice Fulton's contacts with C.O.S. workers in the library may have propelled her daughter into taking the job she did. The library belonged, too, to social reform movements.

Ruth Fulton became a "friendly visitor" for the C.O.S. in 1910. She visited poor families, bringing moral and material comforts. The former, less expensive, was more encouraged. Help came with precepts, and the best precept was the visitor's own careful and "American" behavior. Each "friendly visitor" set an example; her way of life, speech, and habits would encourage clients to copy and to change their lives.

The visitor also noted specific problems and probable causes. If she suspected illness, she called the city physician, who came to check her diagnosis before recommending treatment or medicines. If she suspected simple lack of a job, the visitor's course of action was not so promising. By 1910 tuberculosis clinics and hospital wards existed; unemployment services did not fully operate until World War I. Recent child labor legislation had the unforeseen effect of plunging families deeper into poverty with loss of working members. So the friendly visitor noted the unemployment, reported the case to an appropriate agency, and hoped something would turn up.

Ruth Fulton carried out her friendly visits in the Polish neighborhoods of Buffalo. She spent much of the day walking from house to house, on streets she hardly knew. Polish pride about living in separate houses only made Ruth's work harder, at least in terms of the ground she had to cover. Every morning the twenty-four-year-old woman set out to walk through her assigned neighborhood, into houses where Buffalo's boasted electricity did not reach and lack of plumbing did.

Ruth did not visit "tenements," nor did she see people "in the depths" of poverty and despair. The Polish population, over all, puzzled Buffalo's well-intentioned middle class. The Poles presented a different picture from a group like the Italians. The Poles represented the "respectable poor" and should have been less of a problem to the city than colorful accounts in the *Buffalo Express* suggested.[18] Buffalo's Poles worked hard, struggling to buy their one-family houses. Italians, in a contrast the *Express* leaned upon heavily, occupied abandoned warehouses along the riverfront. No one could tell who was family inside these buildings; a hodgepodge of people crowded into buildings not planned for residency in the first place. Haphazard living arrangements added terror to the already infamous Canal Street area, where Buffalo's good citizens only went (or said they went) on charitable missions. To Buffalo, the Italians not the Poles stood for the worst of urban conditions before World War I.[19] Italians and not Poles constituted Buffalo's "slum population." The houses Poles lived in looked respectable on the outside, whatever the poverty behind front doors.

Poles seemed, in general, to be succeeding as an ethnic group. For the numbers out of work, lacking food and clothing—the people Ruth visited—there were numbers at work, in steel mills and iron foundries. Poles had become active and increasingly powerful in city politics; besides holding good jobs, they ran for office and won. In power, these people fought to preserve Polish identity through public gestures, statements, and ceremonies. No citizens, Ruth included, could misunderstand the impulse. The Polish population of Buffalo did not want totally to merge, Ruth learned along with other Buffalo reformers who were baffled at the sturdy refusal to Americanize. Instead Poles demanded that Polish be spoken in the public schools or they would, they threatened, keep their children in parochial schools. They demanded, too, that Polish priests preach in neighborhood churches, and they rejected the Irish Catholic hierarchy. If Catholicism sat uneasily with Buffalo's Protestant elite, a mass in Polish was even more strange.[20]

Ruth visited not a defeated population but the unfortunate segment of a generally successful and politically active ethnic group. She went into small houses to see mothers who had too many children at home, some too young and others too frail to go outside. She saw men out of jobs and without the optimism or skills for getting a job. Mentioning that Polish families lived in "private dwellings," the Chamber of Commerce did not count the families who lived in fear of losing their dwellings.[21] Disease and joblessness wore away at the environmental explanation with demonstration of sheer human misery. For Poles, unfamiliarity with English enormously complicated their problems.

The difficulty and near impossibility of communicating with her clients drove Ruth into despair, prompting anger at the situation and at herself. Often she must have suppressed a sense of futility in face of the muttered, half-heard, and barely comprehended complaints of the individuals she saw. She could not talk easily and could hardly hear what an often frightened and embarrassed person said to her. Anxiety rendered Ruth's lipreading skills useless. Nor could the "visitor" ask a woman holding a crying baby to stop, slow down, form her words more carefully and visibly. Ruth's main and urgent task was to let an individual know where and how to get medical help, how to enroll children in school, and the possibilities for finding a job. She had to show that the city of Buffalo did offer aid to the poor. She also fought off gloom, depression, and hopelessness when confronting the men, women, and children behind her conscientiously prepared reports.

Deafness and details plagued her, tempting Ruth into her childhood "crime" of running away. At hand lay Buffalo's generous open park system, a relief from despairing questions. What could she, one woman on the bottom (unpaid and untrained) of a large bureaucratic organization do to get jobs, hospitalization, and schooling for hundreds of people? There seemed to be a flood of applications that even the efficient C.O.S. could not hope to answer.

Ruth needed an energy, a stamina, a purposefulness she suspected she did not have and never would have. The thought of Jane Addams, by 1910 the model lady philanthropist, only convinced Ruth of her own incompetence and lack of "fit" to the C.O.S. But Ruth stuck to her job. She had powers of endurance, and the job suited an emphasis on doing "good" she had learned at college and at home. She lived out one ideal for women, giving to others, even if with a struggle. Besides, Ruth must have asked herself often what else she could do to gain satisfaction and fulfillment. Perhaps she convinced herself, too, that she followed in her father's footsteps, turning scientific inquiry to humanitarian purposes. Certainly she knew she followed her mother's principle that "life is not all cake." A silent inner command grew stronger the more Ruth chafed at circumstances.

At home in the evenings Ruth wrote stories. Long ago she had found writing a relief from chores and from comparisons to Margery. In that winter of 1910, stories became a lifeline for Ruth. She escaped from the hopelessness of her days, and maybe from the limited contentment of a household shared by Bertrice and her sister Myra, into a world tailored to her liking. Ruth no longer dreamt of perfect worlds where individuals realized glorious self-fulfillment and complete intimacy. She created new characters, drawing less on the Bible and on stately patriarchal figures than on the scenes she confronted in day-to-day walks on the streets of Buffalo.

During this year Ruth turned her attention to female goals and personalities. Women dominated the Buffalo stories, by force of character and through their roles in plot. Ruth did not draw women of romantic beauty and ethereal goodness; her women strove for integrity, purpose, and absolute devotion to a cause. These women replaced the "little playmate over the hill,"[22] except that more than ever Ruth created not companions but a version of herself. Into her fictional heroines she put desired traits and began to build a "self" she could live with as long as she had to.

For background Ruth used the details of C.O.S. work, and Buffalo's

urban environment—the sidewalks and squalor along with the poverty
and desperation. Her women confronted personal dilemmas in a society
where prosperity did not extend to all members. In one story, Emily
tries to save two frail Kominsky women from the tuberculosis that killed
the rest of the family. "There's nothing left but the cruelty and the waste
and a death in the dark like Anna's," she tells the doctor. "Dr. Joe raised
his head; his eyes were dark with the joy of battle. He drew a full
breath. . . ."[23] The medical man takes over, and the battle may be won.

Ruth Fulton called this and companion stories "The Emily Stories."
She may have been remembering another woman writer, of a century
earlier, Emily Brontë. Ruth never chose names lightly, and "Emily" remained her fictional heroine for several years. The nineteenth-century
English writer echoed themes in Ruth's life story. Like Ruth, Emily
Brontë grew up in a "pious household," and like Ruth, Emily found release by "running away" outside. A likeness of motive and a dramatic
unlikeness of place pleased Ruth; Emily's "wild moors" contrasted to the
gentle Norwich hills in look but not in function. The passion Brontë described in *Wuthering Heights* must also have attracted Ruth. Few
readers can resist the power of the Heathcliff-Cathy love, sweeping all
before it. "Is life no more than this? that always I should come / Un-
marked from passion, unbranded from despair?" She wrote the lines as
Anne Singleton, ten years later. In 1934 Ruth again put *Wuthering
Heights* on her "Reading List."

Ruth wrote herself into the "Emily Stories," maybe more than she
intended. Besides creating a heroine who tried out the dreams she cautiously nurtured, Ruth also returned to her ambivalences about her relationship with Margery. Several stories tell of two sisters, and one, called
"The Chance for Life," tells of an older sister threatened by tuberculosis.
The younger sister stays healthy, grows chubby and cheerful. The older
sister turns pale, weak, melancholy, and eventually dies. The sisters do
not have a father. He died when both girls were infants.

Tuberculosis reached epidemic proportions in 1909, prompting the
New York State legislature to require that cities build special hospitals
and special wards in existing hospitals.[24] The tuberculosis that weakened
and killed her clients had other connotations as well. Absorbed in an
English literary tradition, Ruth linked the disease to the "fate" that
struck writers of genius in their prime. She knew the clichés and undoubtedly knew the tragic story of John Keats, dead at the peak of his
creativity. Ruth added the reality of deaths among Buffalo's poor to
sharpen the picture she constructed from reading. In the person of the
older sister in one "Emily story" she too became tubercular; she too became tragic. In these stories, Ruth not only explored the ways in which

a woman met life, she also explored the ways in which poets had died. To be the dying poet might suit her as well as becoming the woman of purpose.

Ruth Fulton struggled to fight off another image connected with sickness, weakness, and death. If tuberculosis fit the tradition of romantic poetry, a different frailty belonged to femininity in a tradition Ruth also knew. Debilitating illness recalled the figures of women a generation before her own. Ruth emphasized the contrast: in dying, artists "saved their souls alive"[25] while women lost their "souls" in succumbing to frail bodies. Joanna Shattuck represented a Victorian woman, a model at once attractive and distressing to Ruth:

> My grandmother was slim and white,
> And idle as can be,
> And sometimes in the bright sunlight
> She'd shiver suddenly.[26]

The tubercular artist offered a vivid image to Ruth Fulton, and not just as a figure of tragedy. On the face of a tubercular patient appeared symptoms of a striking clarity, the pale white of fatigue alternating with the rosy flush of fever. At age twenty-four, in Buffalo, Ruth rarely referred to how she looked, even implicitly in describing her heroines; these women were always more brave than beautiful, more purposeful than sexual. Ruth was drawn to the symbolic disease first because of its association with individuals of genius doomed to die. But the tubercular patient also displayed a set of physical traits attractive to Ruth—a visible contrast between pale calmness and the redness of coursing blood. These responses she incorporated into fiction and into daydreams. Most of the time, however, Ruth had to handle efficiently and coolly a horrifyingly real disease and a group of people who had little to hope for in their situation.

Altogether Ruth found life in Buffalo more and more an endurance, less and less a worthwhile experience. Her work seemed futile and endless, and she was not paid. She lived with her mother and had constantly before her Bertrice Fulton's recognized achievements. The evening "Emily stories" provided only limited outlet and eventually contributed to the mask of isolation Ruth Fulton created for herself. She grew impatient with her work and with writing for herself as sole audience. In depression, rather than turning outward and searching for distractions, Ruth turned inward and closed off the world. Her life took place within the four walls of the apartment near Delaware Avenue, in the southwest section of the city, and in the scenes she imagined for Emily.

Whatever the immediate precipitating factors, sometime in 1911 Ruth Fulton decided to move to Pasadena, California. She planned to live with Margery and her family. She boarded the train in Buffalo, to ride through Chicago and farther west than she had yet been.

"The chance to fulfill our one potentiality—the power of loving"

Bertrice Fulton watched Ruth go off to Pasadena, understanding her decision. Ruth after all had a model in Aunt Hettie and in Auntie My, the unmarried woman prepared to help her sister with children and household.

Ruth had qualms about her plans, and time to think about these on the five-day train ride from Buffalo to the West Coast. She did not share the optimism of conventional California-bound travelers or their "Sunday picnic" moods.[27] Moreover, her dislike of Buffalo and of volunteer work had not stilled doubts about the wisdom of Margery's marriage to Robert Freeman. Margery knew of her sister's unspoken disapproval of her marriage and wrote once, years later, "At that point [marriage] I seemed to fail her utterly, for she believed I had become but the witless reflection of my dominant husband."[28]

The decision to go to Pasadena was complicated by Ruth's inclination to compare herself with other women, primarily her sister and her mother. (Joanna Shattuck died in 1909, the year Ruth finished college.) For Ruth, going from Buffalo to Pasadena represented at some level a desire once more to test herself against Margery, now married and with two babies at home. Simultaneously Ruth decided she could no longer be just a daughter, though what role would replace this she did not know. She planned to help Margery, as Hettie and Myra had helped Bertrice, without ever stating exactly her responses to this maiden-aunt role. Bertrice Fulton was an extraordinarily powerful model to live with; she had managed widowhood, taken up a career, moved around, and succeeded where (and when) it was still difficult for women to succeed. She must have had moments of deep loneliness; she may have depended on Ruth for emotional satisfactions a child could not provide a parent— or could not provide and also follow her own course. Ruth needed to chart her way, and to do this she had to escape the small Buffalo household. That Margery wanted her help subdued remaining ambivalences about leaving Bertrice, though not the gnawing anxieties about her own future.

Once in Southern California, Ruth lost some of her anxiety. Los Angeles stirred her as it had generations of Americans, a fantasy come to life. Startled by the unexpected and unfamiliar beauty, Ruth fell prey to the dreams of paradise other travelers had brought with them on their westward pilgrimages. "One reads of tomato vines nineteen feet high; of cabbage plants that grew twenty feet in the air . . . of a Gold of Ophir rosebush in Pasadena with 200,000 blossoms. . . ."[29] Thirteen years later, Ruth Benedict would discover another "dreamland" made real on earth. In 1924 Ruth saw the Southwest Pueblos for the first time, and she wrote in a poem, "Beauty has blown her fever through me."[30]

Pasadena had its own glories, apart from the city of Los Angeles. Known as the "Crown of the Valley," Pasadena boasted the most glorious orange groves in the region.

> The orange tree is the living symbol of richness, luxury, and elegance. With its rich black-green shade, its evergreen foliage, and its romantic fragrance, it is the millionaire of all the trees of America, the "golden apple" of the fabled Gardens of the Hesperides. . . . It is not by chance that millionaire row in Pasadena should be called Orange Grove Avenue.[31]

When Ruth Fulton moved into the Freeman house at 675 Magnolia Avenue, she moved into a distinct social as well as geographical neighborhood. The citrus belt created a class as much as a natural barrier, and Ruth added a dislike of elitism to her lingering discomfort at Margery's chosen way of life. Pasadena was an upper-class white and homogeneous community; Robert Freeman conducted church services for Pasadena's "first" families. The homogeneity and the consequent claustrophobia recalled the Delaware Avenue neighborhood, though in Buffalo "no trespass" was figurative and in Pasadena quite literal: a sign on every orange grove.

Ruth thought of Norwich, too. By the time she arrived in Pasadena, families had been settled for several decades. Pasadena residents had "old" money and represented the aristocracy of the Southern California region.[32] If not Mayflower descendants, they retained, even exaggerated, the piety and puritanism of the people Ruth had known in New York State. Californians tried hard to recapture the "spirit of village fellowship, of suburban respectability" they had left "at home."[33] Ruth recognized the imitation of a style left behind.

She entered Freeman family life, determined to carry out the task she had now undertaken. She would do what she set out to do; this aspect of Bertrice Fulton's life never disappeared from Ruth's calculations. The Freemans welcomed her, and Ruth apparently enjoyed the presence of the "babies," as she referred to her nieces and nephews. (Margery and Robert had five children: Robert, Bertrice, Margaret,

Fulton, and David.) But Ruth's fondness for the babies—just Robert
and Bertrice when she arrived—did not keep her contentedly at home.
In the fall of 1911 Ruth accepted a teaching job, perhaps for a sense
of accomplishment and perhaps to contribute to the Freeman household
income. Margery stayed home with the children, Robert attended to
pastoral duties in the Pasadena Presbyterian Church, and Ruth traveled
to West Los Angeles.

During 1911–12 she taught at Westlake School for Girls and, not
yet a driver, may have commuted on the Los Angeles Pacific Electric
Interurban transit system.[34] Ruth recognized and felt at home in the all-
female environment. In 1911, however, she taught rather than learned
the advantages of being well read, well rounded, and enlightened. That
year for the first time Ruth had to stand in front of a roomful of faces,
addressing people whose expressions sometimes puzzled her and whose
voices sometimes faded away. Teaching California adolescent girls
could not have been easy, but there were occasional moments of gratification. "I am glad to put my effort into my English classes—glad to
have the girls like their work and like me."[35] The characteristic stammer,
from shyness and deafness, came and went depending upon her self-
confidence.

Ruth stuck it out. She endured the difficulties and the embarrass-
ments in order to keep her devils at bay, and in 1912 she moved to a
school closer to home, in Pasadena. The atmosphere of Miss Orton's
School for Girls recalled St. Margaret's and, different versions, Vassar
College and Pillsbury Academy—schools for carefully selected pupils.
Like the other private schools Ruth had known, the Orton School satisfied ambitious parents: their daughters were getting an education and
a "finishing" equal to that of an Eastern academy. Ruth's students were
fresh, eager, middle-class girls, and if they reminded her of the classmates at St. Margaret's, they did seem to appreciate their education
more than did (at least some) students in the Buffalo school. Asking
for money for an annuity for Miss Orton in 1934, a group of alumnae
remembered the "loving and intelligently planned training with which
our Miss Orton started us out in life."[36]

Sometime in 1912 Bertrice Fulton moved into the Freeman household with her daughters. Her own mother had died three years before,
and Myra had gone to Norwich to care for John Samuel Shattuck, who
died the following year, in 1913. Rather than be alone in Buffalo, Bertrice
Fulton came to California to help out. She thrived in the grandmother
role, and people who saw her then—she was in her fifties—describe "new
life" on her face. Photographs show her holding Margery's babies in
her lap and looking unusually contented. Bertrice Fulton was still

mother-teacher-nurturer, as she had been and would be all the years Ruth knew her. She liked family life, and the sense of give-and-take in the Freeman household echoed back to the years in Norwich. Pasadena contrasted pleasantly with Buffalo for mother, as it had for daughter one year earlier.

For Ruth, the presence of her mother reactivated a strong and compelling image of one woman's choices. In 1912 Ruth had once more to grapple with the living model, not just her reconstructed understandings of her mother's pattern. The situation did echo Norwich, in detail as well as in tone: a three-generation family lived together, the women taking care of children and household chores. And again Ruth found herself on the fringes. Like Robert Freeman she left the house for a paying job; like her mother and her sister, when she came home at night she was drawn to the babies and to domesticity.

Ruth also had taken her mother's career. She followed Bertrice Fulton into teaching, searching in that role for a satisfaction she missed in her charity-organization work. Bertrice Fulton undoubtedly set a stern model, complicated by the outbursts in grief that seemed to her eldest daughter an odd and unforgivable aberration in a life otherwise marked by discipline and purposefulness. Ruth used the word "purposeful" with ambivalence and wondered over her mother's combination of endurance and passion, stamina and profound mourning. Puzzling about her mother remained a necessary way of discovering for herself the balance between passion and logic, love and duty.

> Lovers have only bitterness of death.
> To all beside there is some channelled silence
> In deep grief that still keeps faith with breath;
> From loss and loveliness some sudden incense
> Drifts voluptuous down their sorrow.[37]

Ruth wanted, she said in 1915, to "chart" her own life—to resist the pull of her mother, of Vassar, and of twentieth-century conventions for women. She tried to take her bearings on the decision to come to Pasadena: "A day in the mountains, a good-night time with the babies can almost frighten me with happiness. But then it is gone and I cannot see what holds it all together. What is worth while? What is the purpose? What do I *want*?"[38]

Along with these went other, familiar questions about how like and how different she was from other people. During the Pasadena years, Ruth again depended upon her dexterity with words to uncover and clarify vague longings. As in Buffalo, too, she searched her surroundings not her books for figures upon which to embroider a personal debate. The literary models, the writers and their answers, gave less aid than did the "ordinary" people with whom Ruth Fulton spent her days. Heroes gave way, temporarily, not to heroines but to the women she met every day. Against their lives Ruth balanced her account of ecstasy and achievement, and the sources of each for a woman. In a reticent family, Ruth might only guess whether Margery had moments of ecstasy and a sense of purpose.

Ruth was twenty-four years old when she arrived in Pasadena, but age did not raise worries about love, ecstasy, and commitment. Her society gave her time; women of her generation and class did not marry right after college, if marriage was their choice. Increasing single-ness, and single-mindedness, in America and among American women concerned contemporary journalists and commentators. Ruth, mean-while, did not dread spinsterhood; she admired Aunt Hettie and Auntie My. She dreaded rather a life without passion:

> And down the burnt-out air shall come
> No hurt upon the night, no cry
> Our hearts must stir to satisfy,
> No portent of delirium. . . .[39]

Ruth's "blue devils" burst through their boundaries in Pasadena. Verse could not hold them, neither could prose-fiction nor teaching nor someone else's babies. And Ruth did not talk: "But until I was thirty-five I believed that the things that mattered must always hurt other people to know or make them interfere, and the point was to avoid this."[40]

Surrounded by women, Ruth found it impossible to turn to them for support and a perspective on her own difficulties. While she por-trayed private dilemmas within the fictional lives of women, she shied away from real women who might guide her through the puzzles in her own life story.

Various versions of feminism presented themselves to Ruth Fulton in the pre–World War I years. To understand her responses to early-twentieth-century feminist movements, one has to consider her a writer and a maker of images. Ruth linked the feminist issue to problems she broached in fiction and in sonnets, of dreaming more than one could realize and of following "unicorns" when real solutions existed. Ruth's feminism, over the years, became another version of the contrast she elaborated and substantiated from her earliest vision of the "world of my father" and, opposed to that, the "world of my mother."

At Vassar, from 1905 to 1909, Inez Milholland offered a practical remedy. At rallies she pleaded with students to confront directly the limitations on their lives as women. Ruth avoided the rallies, suspecting that political activism was not her way. To find her way she compared herself to the Vassar students she knew: suffragettes and militant feminists; her mother and her sister, whose lives seemed alike; friends who chose devotion to work over marriage. Ruth made her life by testing herself against these figures, no less when she turned to the problem of women in society than when she had turned to problems of growing up in Buffalo.

A tension persisted between her inclination to write an essay, a fortress of words to enclose herself in, and her unmediated responses to external, vivid details, whether of landscape, face, or fantasy. Ruth knew well how to use words. She also knew the power of words to shut her off from an "ecstatic realization."

In Pasadena, Ruth Fulton tried on too many "masks." She found during the fall of 1912 a scattering of images that confused rather than clarified her personal choices. Ruth decided for the first time to keep a journal. The decision had a momentous quality: "I want it [she says about the journal] to help me to shake myself to rights during the next few months. . . . I have not dared to be honest, not even with myself."[41] She went back, at age twenty-five, to an inquiry she had begun in different guise twenty years before. No one else read the entries in a diary; it was as secret as the haymow.

Ruth wrote to absorb and to contain reactions to the circumstances of her life. When circumstances closed in, she could—or thought she could—build a private place where no one else would come. In Norwich, Ruth first constructed her other worlds, escaping from the uncongenial into the imaginary—the latter fiercely guarded. In Owatonna, "people were important" and writings were few. In Buffalo in 1900–1905, Ruth tested her dreams against reality, and an audience of her mother and Uncle Will acknowledged her accomplishment. At Vassar and after college (1910–11) Ruth took seriously the role of writer. Tangible rewards legitimized a personal engagement with words; she wanted to publish her pieces.

By the time Ruth got to Pasadena, she had lost her ambition to publish. Writing became private again, a refuge she took in the black notebook left over from Europe. "The faithfulness of this old notebook is touching. It has travelled across half of Europe and all of America without once learning the object of its existence. . . . I want it now for a very different purpose," she wrote on October 12, 1912.[42]

Ruth did not write much in 1912–13. She did, however, revise extensively. Hers was a diary not of brief, passionate entries, spur-of-the-moment thoughts but of purposive near-essays. She completely rewrote the first October entry, and then in July tied her "ending" entry to her beginning one. Journal entries for her year, a school year, form a completed piece. She intended this and often left out individual dates.

Ruth turned her journal into a heuristic monologue. The subject was not new, but style and approach were—a difference the writer knew altered content. She planned this time to be utterly honest with herself, to take herself on as she had never dared before. She took "pen in hand," now to probe the old vulnerabilities and exorcise the "blue devils." Ruth set about discovering herself with the deliberation and discipline she had learned in the Shattuck household.

At age twenty-five Ruth decided to tear down disguises that had earlier controlled her inquiries. In daydreams, fiction, and poems Ruth worked hard to mask personal dilemmas. And she remained dissatisfied; characters she created seemed strangely distant from her "real" world and, more disturbingly, distant from her "real" self. "I've just come through a year in which I have not dared to think; I seemed to keep my grip only by setting my teeth and playing up to the mask I had chosen. I have not dared to be honest, not even with myself."[43] The heroic and noble "character" gone, Ruth experienced a terror that is evident in the intensity of her prose:

> I tried, oh very hard, to believe that our own characters are the justification of it all. Bob believes it, and I think Margery would if she ever felt it mattered. But the boredom had gone too deep; I had no flicker of interest in my character. What was my character anyway? My real *me* was a creature I dared not look upon—it was terrorized by loneliness, frozen by a sense of futility, obsessed by a longing to *stop*. No one had ever heard of that Me.[44]

Ruth began to face the possibility that, stripped bare of the "tightly adjusted" mask, the vulnerable "Me" would have no defenses. Yet, with mask tightly on, the "Me" risked being strangled, a future Ruth anticipated not uneagerly: "I longed to be old—sixty or seventy—when I fancied the Me might have been strangled by the long-continued tight-lacing of the mask. I only wanted my feelings dulled."[45] She started the journal to banish such thoughts and to force the masks off.

It all might have been easier had Ruth not doubted what lay behind masks. Perhaps the "real Me" was inextricably connected to the "presented Me." Without the face made for and by the world, what was a self? This was not a new question for Ruth. The woman who habitually depended on visual images to give information about character and, in a practical sense, to tell her what people were saying, constantly questioned the relationship between portrait and "real self." Suppose she tore off the fine outer coloring and found nothing—or dullness?

Ruth's notions of dullness and boredom connected to two other words, "achievement" and "fulfillment." To not be bored a person had to *do* something—not a simple prescription for a woman uneasy with her society, with her own capabilities, and with her own passions. She had not, either, come to any conclusion about how much of the problem was hers alone, how much due to her "soul," and how much due to upbringing, conventions, and gender.

Ruth asked about the sources of restlessness and dissatisfaction and about the possibilities for achievement. She asked, also, about the connection between achievement and the phrase her society reserved for women: "self-fulfillment." Ruth came to see the latter—fulfillment—as female, private, removed from a world of "true worth." She made "validation" another important word; the public world "validated" male achievement and smiled kindly upon female fulfillment—or so it seemed in the winter of 1912–13. "My aspirations this year have been so many agony points."[46]

The biographer ends up distilling into short phrases a wave of chilling confusions. Ruth couldn't find her solution. She wondered endlessly about the person who failed to find fulfillment. Did the fault lie in character or in circumstances? Further, if there could be no self without "public image," how then judge the suppression or fulfillment of self?

Such questions constituted the core of Ruth Fulton's feminism and later, altered, were central to her anthropological inquiries. Ruth's feminism on the one hand diffused, becoming a version of the larger issue of individuality and custom, of creativeness and order—for any person any time; on the other hand, her feminism narrowed into a quite specific debate. Ruth put the matter bluntly: marriage and babies versus a career.

> So much of the trouble is because I am a woman. To me it seems a very terrible thing to be a woman. There is one crown which perhaps is worth it all—a great love, a quiet home, and children. We all know that is all that is worth while, and yet we must peg away, showing off our wares on the market, if we have money, or manufacturing careers for ourselves if we haven't.[47]

She had models through which to pursue the pros and cons of her ongoing, silent debate. At home Bertrice Fulton and Margery Fulton Freeman enacted the contentment and the fulfillment of domesticity, of babies and marriage.

At Miss Orton's school there were the "old maids."

> They laugh at home about my "course in old maids" this winter. It really isn't a joke at all. It's quite tragically serious. There were three at school. They retold all their twenty-year-old conversations with men—conversations that of course *might* have developed into love affairs *if* they'd allowed the liberty—so that you might be led to realize that they were not old maids by necessity.[48]

Ruth distanced herself with sarcasm, then revealed her sensitivity and her empathy a few sentences later: "As we [a fellow teacher] walked the streets of lighted bungalows at night, she would drink them in one after another, and as we neared the school, she sighed once, 'There are so many homes. There ought to be enough to go around.'"[49]

Ruth recognized the pain. Striving harder to push away such delusions and finding the journal alone inadequate, Ruth turned to literature. She went back first to male writers of English literature and to the patriarchal visionaries of the Bible. Ruth looked in literature for guides to life and for a philosophy that would satisfy her own yearnings. She did not look for the kind of identification that demanded an absorption in women's lives; intense absorption in the words and the lives of other women came three years later, when Ruth had left Pasadena.

On October 25, 1912, in a "rewrite" entry, she told of reading Robert Louis Stevenson: "I cannot quote it, but it concerned aspirations. 'Aspirations are the riches of the soul,' he said. 'The man who has an abundance and a variety of them is spiritually rich.' And it might be true. Why not?"[50] The diarist sounds resigned, not optimistic or exhilarated by this lesson. In a similar spirit Ruth referred to another figure of English literary tradition, himself a deep pessimist. Carlyle, she supposed, preached gratitude: "It is nobler to be thankful, even, for the vision of what might be," she paraphrased his placing of blessedness before happiness.[51]

And then Ruth went back to her trusted guide, the Christ she had learned from since childhood. She found here the same message of gratitude—the message she needed at that moment of her life and found in the words of men not in the lives of women. "I'm sure it's what Christ meant when he said, 'The kingdom of heaven is within you.'"[52]

Yet the resignation she read in Stevenson, Carlyle, and Christ too closely resembled despair for the woman who wanted rather "one ecstasy of realization."

> And yet, why should I care? The people I love best do not. But always I know that is not the question. It is "Why do I *have* to care." If I shut my eyes to it, it pounces upon me from the dark, and my weapons are not ready.[53]

Behind the contrast between resignation and caring lay Ruth's contrast of female and male. She grappled with the old puzzle: Was acceptance a female fate, while vitality and energetic ambition belonged to males? She may have seen (others have) Stevenson and Christ as fitting the "female" half of her dichotomy. The October entry on Stevenson, Carlyle, and Christ contrasts strikingly to the next entry, made on a November day. Stevenson, Carlyle, and Christ may be the models of her mind; they were not the models of the woman's heart. In the October entry Ruth reasoned herself into acceptance. In the November entry she admitted desire, and frustration at futility:

> I have been reading Walt Whitman, and Jeffries' *Story of My Heart*. They are alike in their superb enthusiasm for life—for actual personal living. . . . Whitman is far sturdier and more healthful; but it is their common ground that impresses me: their unwavering, ringing belief that the *Me* within them is of untold worth and importance. I read in wonder and admiration—in painful humility. Does this sense of personal worth, this enthusiasm for one's own personality, belong only to the great self-expressive souls? or to a mature period of life I have not yet attained? or may I perhaps be shut from it by eternal law because I am a woman and lonely?[54]

Denied enthusiasm by eternal law, Ruth conceived a choice between dying and having a male child who would provide vicarious vitality. She dreamed too of a third alternative, a world where the "Woman-Christ" represented a dynamic unity of gentleness and energy:

> Once in my loneliness—feeling how none
> Had offered clasp to my blind groping hands—
> How for me no master had resolved
> That which I needs must ask,—I bodied forth
> Out of my woman-brain, a Woman-Christ,
> A Christ whose life should taste that bitter-sweet

The Hebrews had forgone—that passion—drop
That makes the whole cup's worth—a Christ whose words
In sheer normality of healthfulness
Should speak of love, and race, and motherhood.[55]

She wrote the poem ten years later in her thirties; she never published "The Woman-Christ." Meanwhile, in 1912–13, death exerted an enormous pull: "Oh, I *want* to stop! If there is any discomfort in the thought it's that there would be some left who would suffer."[56]

Then in May 1913 death came too close. "It was almost a month ago that the nightmare began. Suddenly when Bertrice [Margery's second baby] seemed the strongest, she was sick as few babies can be and live."[57] Although the baby recovered, Ruth felt punished for her own death wish. Contrite, she went back to lessons of endurance, of faith, and of patience. She told herself that one could wait, could hope the future would bring change, and that to chafe against the present risked tragedy. She had already practiced such thoughts, in the months before the nightmare.

> The burden of all moralizers is the praise of the present—I think I need to think far more about the future. If one cannot see any virtue in the present, at least one can firmly resolve never to put any mortgage on a future which may perhaps be more significant—never to allow any boredom to throw away a chance for friendship, nor any bitterness to wreck the carrying out of a plan one has reckoned good.[58]

The effort to embrace these conclusions strained her prose.

Through all these entries Ruth did not convince herself to look forward joyously to her own future. Her future as a woman seemed bound to compromise, calm endurance, and lacking what was given to males: a boundless, creative energy. So she built her hopes on patience, and thought about having a child. The wish gave her a different view of the future and some small faith in "fulfillment":

> Perhaps my trouble comes from thinking of the end as my *present self,* not as a possible and very different future self. . . . It is always very hard for me to feel that year after year is just added *preparation*—and for what? The great instinctive answer is for Motherhood—yes, I think I could accept that with heart and soul.[59]

But this dream offered neither an easy nor a practical solution to Ruth's difficulties. The idea remained persistent, but by the summer of 1913 Ruth discarded dreams for the "four walls that make reality."

"Ethically, if Motherhood is worthwhile, it ought to be also worthy to have a hand in the growth of a child or a woman," she wrote in the above entry. She struggled to find such worth and satisfaction in classes at Miss Orton's. Repeatedly the horror of futility filled her journal. This "lack of zest," "this loneliness, this emptiness of life"—these and similar phrases burst through reasoned entries. As the school year came to an end she wrote, "In a world that holds books and babies and canyon trails, why should one condemn oneself to live day-in, day-out with people one does not like, and sell one's life to chaperone and correct them?" What was the choice? "The only trouble is that there may not be any better way of realizing the good things of life than right here."

Ruth did not consider seriously the feminist proposal of mother-hood-without-marriage; domesticity itself seemed out for her. Not able to count on this future, she turned back to the past. Ruth returned, in daydreams and then in actuality, to the farm life of her childhood. "And yet it seems sometimes as if it would help famously to exchange chaperoning and study-hours for a garden of hollyhocks and pansies against the old apple trees and lilacs at Grandfather's. I'll do it yet!" she announced to herself one June day in 1913.[60]

A month later, after the crisis of the baby Bertrice Freeman's near death, Ruth acted on her exclamation. She decided to return to the farm permanently. She did, however, test her decision first, this time confirming her own view not through literature—and male answers— but by talking to a woman. She went to the headmistress, Miss Orton, just before the planned trip to Norwich.

Ruth told Miss Orton how she hated the "meals and the chaperon-ing" and implied enough more that Miss Orton extended perfect sym-pathy. Without probing into Ruth's private world, Miss Orton promised to rearrange Ruth's school schedule. "But it wasn't those [promises] that made the differences." Miss Orton, Ruth realized, had treated her like a mature woman with the right to make changes in her own life: "She gave me a self-respect I had not had for months—years—and I think it was because she never once implied that it is our business to live placidly through anything. Apparently it never occurred to her that I had whimpered." Even without the childish word, clearly Ruth contrasted Miss Orton to her mother: "Even mother always tells me somewhere in the conversation that life isn't all cake."[61]

Not "even mother"—especially mother. Ruth had to fight all her life against Bertrice Fulton's principles of endurance, discipline, and above all no whimpering. Miss Orton freed Ruth temporarily from her mother's principles. Another sort of woman, Miss Orton, unmarried, devoted herself to raising a new generation; not children but pupils demanded her care and absorbed her energies. Miss Orton evidently combined sensitivity and insight with a calm logic and attention to feelings. Ruth had reason to appreciate the combination. In observing this different pattern for a woman's life Ruth did not reject Bertrice Fulton. As a matter of fact, she wrote the June 15 entry describing her conversation with Miss Orton while sitting next to her mother on the train to Norwich, New York.

Ruth had promised Miss Orton she would come back to Pasadena for one year, but she carried Miss Orton's advice with her to the farm. Miss Orton separated Ruth from herself and from other teachers at the school: "We narrow our interests until we grow fossilized, as I am," she told Ruth. "And then we have to make our teaching fill our lives. We have to, to live. I want you to have many interests. You have much to expect of life."[62]

"I have attained to the zest for life"

A picture of Ruth Fulton from 1913, just before she went to spend the summer in Norwich, shows a serious young woman. Her hair is parted in the middle and waved around her ears. She smiles the half-smile that characterized virtually all the photos taken of her, and seems to be trying for a mask of placidity. Perhaps she experienced a glimmer of contentment; she anticipated the summer with pleasure.

Ruth loved Norwich and longed for a happiness she dreamed might be hers there. To maintain the dream she had somewhat to reconstruct the probable reality. Ruth felt ambivalent about the farm, or rather about what the farm stood for. She was most afraid her return signified withdrawal—"I want to *stop*"—and planned useful tasks to take her time and energy. She would accomplish something to justify the private pleasure she anticipated from being literally and figuratively "at home." She would turn the farm into a profitable business: "I'll make something off the garden and the orchard—perhaps in time it will be a prosperous business."[63]

In Norwich, family ties held far more tightly than in Pasadena. Yet Ruth expected to find an independence and freedom from others in New York that she hadn't found in California. To be on her own became part of the fantasy. But only with doubts; to be with Aunt Myra, too, must be an aspect of life on the farm: "I don't delude myself with any 'unselfish' motives, though if I could give Aunt Myra the good times she's missed, that would have its place too."[64]

Ruth and Bertrice Fulton had barely settled down when a visitor arrived. Stanley Rossiter Benedict was not a new face in Ruth's world. The brother of Agnes Benedict, a close Vassar friend, Stanley Benedict had visited Ruth in Buffalo soon after her graduation from college. He had also during the past winter made the long trip from New York to California to spend two days with Ruth in Pasadena. During the 1913 New Year's trip, and possibly even earlier, Stanley Benedict became part of Ruth's ongoing debate about woman's life and fulfillment. Being physically there, he exacerbated her privately voiced argument.

Stanley Rossiter Benedict was born in March 1884 in Cincinnati, Ohio. The Benedict family, like the Fultons and the Shattucks, extended back to New England and to Mayflower arrivals, though the Benedicts had chosen mainly educational rather than religious vocations. Stanley's sister Agnes went to Vassar with Ruth and after graduation argued in writing and in actions for progressive schooling and equally progressive family life. (Agnes Benedict may also have been one of Ruth's models for women who chose career over marriage, not a help to Stanley's courtship.) Stanley Benedict went to the University of Connecticut, received a Ph.D. from Yale in 1908, and two years later became professor of biochemistry at Cornell Medical School in New York City. He stayed at Cornell for the rest of his life.

The persistence and single-mindedness colleagues remembered about Stanley Benedict characterized his courting. He pursued Ruth with deliberation, purpose, and logical argument, though not without sensitivity to her discomforts and uncertainties. Photographs show a stern man, with a sardonic expression and jaw thrust assertively out. A letter he wrote to Ruth in 1913 reveals a warmth of feeling underlying the image of rigidity (rigidity would also be mentioned by colleagues in his obituaries): "And Ruth—what's made it worse for me was that I felt that your letters—even the one I received in Paris—were scarcely written to *me*—you've never felt that way in your life, have you? And it made my trip a little harder than you'll ever guess."[65]

The most sensitive part of Stanley Benedict's courtship involved aligning himself with Ruth's father. He knew and fully appreciated Frederick Fulton's cancer research:

> I've been reading your father's papers—and I do so wish he could have gone on. Your mother needed him, you needed him, and I think the whole world needed him. He started at the very foundation—the only real way to start—by classifying, looking for relationships. And his handling of the subject matter he had was splendid.[66]

Before World War I, Stanley Benedict, too, did cancer research, with an absolute devotion to his work that stirred Ruth's admiration. Stanley fit himself into Ruth's pattern, but simultaneously preserved distance from her father. If his own work, he wrote, was a "reason" for living, he did not have Frederick Fulton's endurance: "The problem is so terrible that I can't keep so closely to it as he did."[67]

The more Stanley Benedict brought up her father, the more Ruth leaned toward Benedict, and toward the "solution" he offered to her dilemmas. The more pulled toward a conventional solution, the more she resisted it. Stanley saw this: "But Ruth—as I intimated above—you can hardly settle everything by a letter now—your sending a man 6000 miles to Europe and 6000 miles to Pasadena doesn't give him any claim on you I'll admit—but you've had the reins a long time, and you *have* bungled things, haven't you?"[68]

Stanley Benedict represented things Ruth desired and dreaded. She wanted to be joined to a man like her father and to experience passion; she was terribly drawn to the notion of a "great love." At the same time, she feared that love would destroy her and suffocate her real self:

> All her quests
> Had sailed but for this prize, this one note blown
> To lead her captive, and white flesh and bone
> Yielded to strangeness and to sweet unrest.[69]

These lines are from Ruth's poem to her mother; Ruth saw the signs of her mother's passion and had repudiated them. At the same time, the world told her that a woman's true fulfillment lay in family and children, and Ruth struggled against such "selflessness." In the journal entry bemoaning the "terrible destiny" of being a woman, she ended with a subtly sarcastic reference to the "right man." To have family and children a woman needed a man, and Ruth revealed anxieties about her capacity for this role in sentences that mocked: we women "have not the motive to prepare ourselves for a 'life-work' of teaching, of social work—we know that we would lay it down with hallelujah in the height of our success, to make a home for the right man."[70] Eight months later, in May 1913, she crossed Stanley Benedict off: "Stanley's ruled out."[71]

Stanley did not give up. He touched directly upon another set of her concerns, about loneliness and barriers between people. "You made a good statement our first evening 'make me know you'—and I echo it to you, and I'm going to see that it's done."[72] In this January 1913 letter he painted a picture of Ruth that Ruth recognized. His insight

into her "masks" moved her, as she would always be moved toward
people who had insight into the hidden parts of herself.

> And Ruth—your mask is getting thicker and thicker—I could
> see that it is—and that's all wrong. You belong somehow
> where you never have to wear it. You're so wonderful behind
> it—I believe—I've so often and so long wanted to get behind
> it, and I've never done it. You shouldn't *have* to wear it at
> all, for it's certain to grow to be a part of you if you do—and
> then you'll be altogether alone, and it's so wrong for *you*
> Ruth. . . .[73]

Ruth had another image of herself that Stanley did not know, or
did not write. She tormented herself with an image, seeing herself as
cold, withdrawn, and nunlike.

> I see the taut preciseness of her tucked-in bed.
> And I saw—I saw my own ~~indifferent~~ [crossed-out] ~~carnal~~
>   [crossed-out] pity in her eyes.
> And now I knew I too show first gray streaks of hair,
> That I too taste white collars,
> That I too punctuate the day by going out to meals.
> I did not know before.[74]

She needed to feel her own energy and vitality. Had she had a child
to prove her passion, Ruth Fulton might not have needed Stanley Benedict. A child would have validated her emotional self, but Ruth appreciated the comforts of convention and would not undertake motherhood
without wifehood. The idea stayed, and Ruth dreamed later of a passion
separate from husband and marriage. She continued to wear black and
gray clothes until the late 1920s, as if to test her own ability to reject
the powerful poetic image she had created.

Stanley Benedict's visit to Norwich in July 1913 closed Ruth's
debate, at least for a while. His visible enjoyment of her beloved
Chenango hills inspired Ruth's affection, as had their shared enjoyment
of the canyons and arroyos of Pasadena. Ruth associated Norwich with
good, loving family relationships; her mother's character softened in the
atmosphere of an extended family, and there, too, her Grandmother
Shattuck had been able to save her soul while yet devoting her life
to others.

Ruth's journal entry for July 1913 does not mention Stanley. Rather,
she seems deliberately to reconstruct a setting of contented farm-life
into which Stanley might fit. At the farm she intended, she wrote, "to

find a way of living not utterly incongruous with certain passionate ideals: to attain to a zest for life, and enthusiasm for the adventure which will forever deliver me from my shame of cowardice, to master an attitude toward life which will somehow bind together these episodes of experience into something that may conceivably be called life."[75]

Stanley visited the farm again in August. During that time Ruth made a decision:

> How shall I say it? That I have attained to the zest for life? That I have looked in the face of God and had five days of magnificent comprehension?—It is more than these, and better. It is the greatest thing in the world—and I have it. Is it not incredible? It happened when Stanley came down last week.

She went on to narrate, in detail, the steps leading toward their decision to marry. And as if to dampen any remaining doubts and fears, she returned to the question of worth in women's lives.

> In general,—a woman has one supreme power—to love. If we are to arrive at any blythness in facing life, we must have faith to believe that it is in exercising this gift, in living it out to its fullest that she achieves herself, that she "justifies her existence."[76]

Ruth still had a promise to keep, to the woman who had in some ways allowed her to make the commitment to Stanley at all. Ruth had promised Miss Orton she would return to school for one more year. She spent 1913–14 in Pasadena, then returned to Norwich in the summer to be married. She and Stanley were married in July 1914 and moved into a house in suburban Long Island, a town called Douglaston Manor. Ruth settled into domestic "leisure," and Stanley went back to the laboratory at Cornell. A month after their marriage World War I broke out.

4

To Find Fulfillment

"A great love, a quiet home, and children"

"I HAVE BARELY WRITTEN here for a year or more," Ruth Fulton Benedict wrote four months after her marriage. "Last year I had Stanley to write to, my work to do, my small business of preparation to fill my time. This year I have Stanley to talk to, to play with, to passionately love, but no longer to write to."[1] She wrote a long entry that November 1914 day in Douglaston Manor. Stanley was at work in Cornell, she had finished her chores, and a whole day stretched ahead. She took stock, not for the first time assessing her life and her happiness.

Ruth Benedict retrieved the notebook left over from Europe and Pasadena, worn and frayed but with enough blank pages for her on-going inquiry. She may have opened the book reluctantly, remembering the pain that inspired the October 1912 entry. On the other hand, she knew she had to "measure" her life and that in words she might master the emerging agitation she tried not to see. Ruth Benedict conscientiously controlled her prose; thoroughly-revised entries suggest Ruth still wrote warily, even in private. The sheer effort of squeezing complicated ideas onto small pages may also have been a relief; her script is crowded and cramped.

She avoided the seductive rhythms of verse. In the journal, Ruth practiced an effective distancing of present agonies. She transferred her moods into "mood," a subject for debate. Ruth knew by then that prose, for her, distanced feeling as poetry did not. In the journal, the more thoroughly she revised and argued an entry, the more one suspects avoidance. She persisted in composing away her feelings, especially in the first years of marriage. Then it seemed hubris to complain, when "zest" had been—and might again be—near at hand and, from a different perspective, a hubris the greater in face of war-caused horrors. Yet Ruth picked up the old notebook, knowing she was supposed to be happy, and started an argument that for the next ten years veered back and forth between points made and confrontations begun anew.

The journal revealed a woman daring to question the "supposeds" of marriage and of love, then retreating from unexpected insight. Often she was not able to separate alternatives and she combined the notion of woman's supreme power "to love" with another notion, of "achievement" the world would recognize and value. The terms were familiar, and Ruth took up a familiar remedy for her confusion. When argument failed she turned to images, and sketched portraits as guide to her own alternatives. Ruth created versions of the woman's life she had missed: the nun in her tight, white bed; the "elderly little school-ma'am [who] hid from us her lifelong honest strivings to do her duty, striving forever unrewarded. . . ."[2] Sarcasm crept into some entries, and Ruth mocked her own efforts to clarify life's purpose.

She paraded forth another set of female figures in an attempt to come to terms. She thought about William Wordsworth's sister Mary and about being Beatrice to a Dante—about women whose fulfillment came, but came only vicariously:

> It were enough that stone should lie quiescent,
> Stone never ran quicksilver in the shade,
> Stone never gathered out of doom a singing,
> Lost now, forgotten, and its dream betrayed.[3]

Ruth did not then, or ever, decide whether her perpetual dissatisfactions resulted from her own character, from Stanley's character (not being a Dante and, perhaps, an increasingly pale shadow beside her romanticized memories of Frederick Fulton), or from an unlucky conjunction of two lives.

Perhaps another thought came to mind, hardly formulated in journal or in verse in the 1914–19 years. Ruth may have begun to speculate then about degrees of femaleness and maleness in one person. She had already established, and played with, contrasts between a female world and a male world, in verbal and in visual forms. She had refined her own ideas through the ideas of others, without yet relating her conclusions to the components of her own personality. But the more she thought about her lack of fit to the female role, the more she seemed drawn to considering the maleness in herself. She noted her craving for achievement and her resistance to the wifely virtue of loving, and wondered whether she possessed too largely the traits her society defined as male.

Much of the time such thoughts seemed too radical, especially if explicated. Ruth masked her puzzlement about sex differences in dreams of a glorious male-child, of a "true realization" of self, and of a perfect moment of passion:

> Let my slow finger trace the curve
> Above your curtained eye
> Know the lift of your lips: preserve
> The clasp of hand and cheek and thigh.
>
> Then I shall go ahead again,
> Armed now from ultimate fear,
> Always in some casual crowd of men,
> I know you near.[4]

Whatever the specific guise, Ruth's debate still circulated around ecstasy and achievement, dreams and purpose. Now she had as a living example of one kind of commitment her husband, to whom her ties were complicated and her reactions ambivalent. In earlier years she had mainly compared herself to women; Robert Freeman seems not to have triggered responses in his sister-in-law beyond the lingering criticism of Margery's marriage.

Ruth's identification with her father became problematic when she became the wife of a man whose achievements were both like and unlike Fulton's. "I can't keep so closely to it [cancer research] as he did," Stanley Benedict had written in 1913.[5] Nor could Ruth decide on a calculation of achievement: Why did Stanley Benedict's activities seem more worthwhile than her own? Ruth had expected to find contentment after July 1914; instead she experienced growing confusion: "my imagination circles round and round, as if mesmerized, above the uselessness of it all: above the long travail that brings only change, change not to be dignified as progress; above the passionate sacrifice that only damns the loved one it would save."[6]

If the marriage of Ruth and Stanley Benedict at all resembled the marriage of Bertrice and Frederick Fulton, Ruth lacked something of her mother's sources of satisfaction. She was caught still between a "male world" and a female destiny; being a wife had raised, not solved, problems.

"The ennui of life without purpose"

Ruth Fulton used the phrase "the ennui of life without purpose" in 1912, describing the "girls I know in Pasadena."[7] By the fall of 1914 the phrase came close to describing her sense of her own life. Marriage had not, at least not by itself, provided the "justification" of her life she had demanded. "What need has a happy woman to 'justify her existence'?" she asked, then strenuously built an airtight case rather than searching for a true answer.[8]

Marriage provided Ruth with a stretch of free time, and time filled up with questions and doubts. She did her chores quickly, having inherited an "efficient handiness" in spite of herself and in spite of Margery. She tried to appreciate this "abundant leisure" and the new chance to schedule hours for herself. In Buffalo she had worked steadily on "cases" and in Pasadena at her teaching. But "abundant leisure" was also hard, and not only because Ruth Benedict felt the force of Bertrice Fulton's "life is not all cake" (or any "sweet"), but because by November 1914 she was bored. Having nothing to do let in the "blue devils."

She had started the 1914 entry on a brave note: "I have so much— life seems so incomparably rich these days." By the end the diarist listed projects she determined to undertake. In between Ruth constructed an elaborate argument about a "person's happiness." "This preoccupation with happiness is almost wholly bad: the greater the possibilities in the person, perhaps, the more intensely he longs for what must grow to seem an unattainable harmony." These sentences lack the sincerity of the next few, where Ruth made plans. ". . . Then there are the 'social work' stories; I want to study Shakespeare and keep a book of notes; I'd like to read Goethe intelligently. . . ."[9] Eager to accomplish something, Ruth overwhelmed herself with possibilities. Her "plans" included intellectual "self-improvement" (reading and writing), intense physical exercise, and, by the middle of the war, volunteer work for a charity society in Westchester County. To read, to take dance lessons, to recapture an intimacy with her husband—these were goals that helped to overcome despairing thoughts.

Ruth struggled to bring the several plans together. Through purposeful activity, of whatever sort, she would prove her worth to Stanley and revive the marriage. She even tried, at one point, to involve him in one of her projects: "For amusement and for Stanley I shall try to write out the chemical detective stories for which he supplies the plots."[10] Writing together, she thought, would be a way of creating an energetic interaction and a closeness she remembered. Stanley Benedict did provide "data" for the stories, and his wife wrote them out under the name "Edgar Stanhope." Edgar may refer to Poe; Stanhope suggests her "hopes" for the partnership with Stanley.

The stories were not very good. Existing drafts are weak, uncertain, and imitative—a literary failure.[11] Ruth recorded neither her own nor Stanley Benedict's opinion of Edgar Stanhope. She hardly needed her husband's "brutal honesty," critic enough herself to recognize immediately the quality (or lack of quality) in a literary piece.

During the first years of marriage, and a world war, Ruth required a courage not part of her temperament or of her society's conventions for women. She explored her dissatisfactions in the diary: if she could not fulfill her life's purposes by loving, and if writing failed, what was left? She turned back to reading, for distraction, escape, and a guiding philosophy. The task resembled probing a wound. Ruth pushed hard to fit the lessons she read to her life, and chose as models the primary writers of her tradition. These great creative spirits of Western literary tradition were male: Marcus Aurelius, Shakespeare, Goethe. She moved swiftly from one to the other, looking for a phrase, an idea, a panacea for her difficulties.

Had she not been finally so realistic, critical, and self-aware, reading might have soothed her soul and provided answers. "The trouble with life isn't that there is no answer, it's that there are so many answers. There's the answer of Christ and of Buddha, of Thomas à Kempis and of Elbert Hubbard, of Browning, Keats and of Spinoza, of Thoreau and of Walt Whitman, of Kant and of Theodore Roosevelt."[12] She chose an array of possible models, from the crystalline medieval religiosity of Thomas à Kempis to the smiling moralism of Elbert Hubbard, from Buddha to Theodore Roosevelt; Ruth plumbed other traditions and her own. Years before, she had begun to insert philosophy where Baptist doctrine failed, suspecting religion offered a too ready-made and ultimately too abstract answer. Now philosophy, as well, seemed ready-made, impersonal, not tested in experience. Philosophy failed in face of the "stinging knowledge that for ourselves we must build up our own answer, that not even a Kant or a Christ can answer it for us."[13]

Ruth had learned her lesson by 1914–15, yet she resisted exploring where her own answer might lie. She concentrated on male writers—poets, philosophers, religious figures—almost deliberately keeping at bay the tempting urge to locate her "restless strivings" in the lives and words of "rebellious women" of other generations. She mentioned briefly the subject of "enslaved women" in her November 1914 entry and began to develop the idea a year later.

Ruth also had in mind some measure of a satisfying answer since she found nothing satisfactory in her reading of male writers during those years. The "measure" did not apply simply to content; when Ruth found her own tone of voice, she absorbed the content of numerous reading notes into her ongoing personal debates. It was then, early in her marriage, that Ruth began a serious study of the works of George Santayana, a philosopher whose attitude and whose words accompanied her until her death. The "measure" had to do with finding a resonant personal experience, with sharing the concrete events of another life, and—she let herself realize—with factors inextricably linked to being a woman: "Nature lays a compelling and very distressing hand upon women, and she struggles in vain who tries to deny it or escape it."[14]

During the winter and spring of 1915 Ruth persuaded herself that the best she could do was submit to "nature." A woman "can only hope for success by working according to Nature's preconceptions of her make-up." In fact the statement opened more questions, about her own "make-up" and the make-up of women who chose to protest and deny their fate. Ruth Benedict found herself attracted to the strong and bold women who rebelled against "enslavement." The November 1914 entry ended with a series of dots: "the 'woman problem' is a lazy man's expression of a . . ."[15] Ruth had several older issues to work through before she came back to the "woman problem" and to her identification with its heroines.

She intended first to revive her marriage, and retreated from the example of women who had challenged convention and "charted" a new way. For the sake of her life with Stanley Benedict Ruth decided, temporarily, to take refuge in the "inevitability" of woman's destiny. The decision was facilitated, perhaps, by a move from Long Island (Douglaston Manor) to Westchester County, to a new house in Bedford Hills. Stanley wanted to be farther from the city, and Ruth found her time filled with setting up household in the small, nearly rural village.

But her unhappiness surfaced again in autumn, when she looked out of the Bedford Hills house onto leaves turning gold and red before falling. (Her comparative contentment in Southern California may have had something to do with the nonexistence of autumn there.) "The Fall is always a hectic season—a time when 'things' seem to rise in the might of their manifold pettiness, when the broken days seem to accomplish nothing and I lose my head."[16] Again Ruth refused to specify, but she seemed to be afraid of losing Stanley and losing the "charter" of her own life. Her entries also suggest she feared "mussiness" and muddle quite as much as she feared ennui.

In November entries, repeatedly, Ruth despaired of setting her life to rights: "again another winter." Over ten years later, in 1939, she wrote a poem that summarized a mood; the stanzas will do for almost any year of her life:

> Let be, the bleak long winter, and the field
> Guard preciously its stubble; let no shower
> Of April mildness stir its roots to life;
> Let no stalk come to flower.[17]

Despair did not turn automatically to hopelessness. In the poem she also talked of springs to come, and her late December–early January entries often show a resurgence of hope.

The optimism came partly because Ruth and Stanley Benedict spent Christmas vacations together, at Lake Winnepesaukee in New Hampshire. There life took on a quiet contentment. Ruth may have more easily seen "worth" and happiness in her own life when Stanley Benedict did not go off to Cornell every morning. Too, January begins a new year, traditionally a time of hope and resolution, and Ruth adopted this one of her culture's customs. She resolved to sweep clear the mussiness of her incentives. The stark whiteness and severity of a snow-covered landscape set the woman to rights, and purpose seemed possible in the sharp winter light.

The peace and even ecstasy of these vacations made a less and less frequent interlude. Ruth could not make the November mood disappear with all the resolutions of January 1. When the Benedicts returned to Bedford Hills, strain, tension, and dissatisfaction once again prompted journal entries. A photograph of Ruth at this time shows her standing in front of the Bedford Hills house, looking frail, nondomestic, uncertain.

At home, she set about the series of activities she no longer pretended were anything but distractions: "Take the mere question of filling time. It's never been decided for me, and the only problem whether I could rise to the occasion. Think of Margery. I've had to set my mind to *invent occupation*, to make up something at every step of the way." Thus Ruth regarded her life, a statement written in calm reflectiveness rather than in a moment of despair and in the face of "blue devils."[18]

The worth of her miscellaneous activities lay mainly in the exhaustion they produced. Tedium, Ruth knew, drove out melancholy. Charity and day nurseries, beneficial tasks, were good but not good enough. "And surely the world has need of my vision as well as of Charity Committees; it is better to grow straight than to twist myself into a doubtfully useful footstool; it is better to make the most of that deepest cry of my heart: 'Oh God let me be awake—awake in my lifetime.' "[19] She could only express such longings in a private, dramatic language.

"The great instinctive answer is for motherhood"

Ruth Benedict brought up the subject of children in journal entries, on scraps of paper stuck into the notebooks, and in conversations with

Stanley Benedict. She had been married for less than a year when she began to doubt the "fulfillment" of wifehood. She found she could not devote herself to another without external recognition, and in spite of herself the "world's petty mathematical calculations" crept in.[20] The more she tried to dismiss a calculation of happiness, the more happiness obsessed her; she wrote in an unfinished, undated entry: ". . . Can't get food, that fact's got to be the limit of your horizon."[21] A child, she thought, would change the balance, would prove to the world the "fulfillment" of love and its "justification."

Ruth pinned more and more hope on the wished-for child, to ease her restlessness, to satisfy her longings for a "flood-tide" of love, and to rebuild her marriage. None of these expectations was unrealistic; they ballooned out of proportion when Ruth lost touch with Stanley Benedict. She hinted, too, at another aspect: A child would prove her sexuality, be evidence of the vitality of her "animal nature."[22]

She craved close communication in marriage. Stanley Benedict's initial insistence that the two tear down "masks" had conquered her gnawing uncertainties about marriage. As early as winter 1915 the valued closeness seemed to be disappearing under the indifference of their contact. Ruth remarked in her journal, and subsequently told her husband, that she could not bear his withdrawal from talk. Years later, she considered the issue again: "With the best will in the world I couldn't express *nothing*. And it was more suffering than I could bear."[23] No more could she bear his physical withdrawal. For periods of time, evidently, the Benedicts gave up both verbal and physical contact: "He rejected me—all of myself I valued—and however calmly my outward self agreed and resigned itself to a course of action, it cut the roots of my life at their source."[24]

Through the decade and a half, 1915–30, Ruth sometimes with cool retrospection and sometimes in distracted despair looked at her marriage. Once, analyzing her love, she bitterly condemned its "unhealthy growths, pity and fidelity." She needed—and by 1920 said so—a response or her faithfulness would be, in Nietzsche's phrase, a virtue of the weak.[25] But Stanley Benedict kept back responses and refused the signs she needed.

He closed himself off on many levels. He shut his wife out of his world of "worthwhile endeavor." Stanley Benedict told her little about the laboratory, perhaps reacting to her tireless plea for a world of her own: ". . . The place where he works, nor meet the men he knows best. I must have my world, too, my outlet, my chance to put forth my effort."[26] Stanley Benedict insisted upon scheduled relaxation, a need that drove him to move the household to farther Westchester suburbs and to depend upon the New Hampshire vacations. Stanley Benedict separated his wife from his work, and later she responded in kind. Few of Ruth's colleagues met her husband—once he hid in the barn when several anthropologist-friends appeared.[27] Most of Ruth's colleagues knew Stanley from her reports as stiff, rigid, and cold.[28]

A "separate world of endeavor" does not ordinarily hamper communication between husband and wife. Ruth, however, was not certain how to chart her way between a life apart and a desire for intimacy. She thought, and said, that if she could prove her seriousness at a task, Stanley would turn back to her with some of the eagerness of winter and spring 1913. But she had a hard time convincing him, especially since she had little idea of a task and of what constituted her "life apart." Her remarks on women's lives left little to compensate for love; "the one gift in our treasure house is love."[29]

Often the Benedicts' conversations ended in anger. Ruth feared and risked Stanley's dislike of issues she brought to his attention. "I know so well what he needs: . . . all he asks is to keep an even tenor. And, knowing this, for years I can keep away from subjects which disrupt the quiet—my own ambitions; my sense of futility; children—chiefly children." She could not bear his disapproval, and the pain of his criticisms remained vivid well into the 1920s—not only because he spoke them in anger but also because they struck a familiar chord.

Stanley Benedict condemned the dissatisfactions and outbursts of temper she condemned in herself. Each time she thought she had conquered uncontrollable moods, she found echoes of those early childhood tantrums. She once believed her furies had disappeared that night in Buffalo when her mother made her "swear" to control herself. Yet in marriage she again "felt kinship with the periods of violence" she disliked.[30]

Ruth saw no benefit in anger and strove to banish what she called "brawls" from her relationship with Stanley Benedict. But she could not be silent. "The greatest relief I know is to have put something in words, no matter if it's as stabbing as this is to me; and even to have him say cruel things to me is better than an utter silence."[31] She refused to have a marriage in which separation and silence ruled.

And she compared her own to other marriages: Margery and Robert Freeman, Joanna and John Shattuck, Bertrice and Frederick Fulton. All three wives had had children to absorb energies and to represent achievement. For Ruth "babies" stood as well for intimacy and for passion. Children seemed the proper outcome of her parents' love, a contrast to the mourning by which her mother later announced great love. Children became the focus of everything Ruth Benedict missed in her own life story.

Social expectations, the living models she reconstructed, and the content of her fantasies all pushed Ruth Benedict into viewing a child as a solution. But her "child" remained abstract, a focus for dreams of contentment and of an end to restlessness. The child she envisioned objectified her wishes, and like the poet picking an elaborate, often intellectualized image, Ruth created a being that contained a conglomeration of thoughts, dreams, and plans. She described more vividly, and more concretely, her nieces and nephews.

The intense dreaming she put into the child may have dampened Stanley Benedict's enthusiasm for the idea. Quite possibly he grew frightened at how much his wife depended on the child to give her life purpose and to rescue the marriage:

> I told him he should see. My past list of jobs proved nothing: until I loved him nothing had ever seemed to me worth the effort of attaining. . . . I should prove that I could do better than to drift into a meaningless routine. . . . I should prove too that whatever I could achieve in my own life was something added to our relationship with each other.[32]

Stanley presented himself as realistic and decisive, Ruth the dreamer, and she usually agreed—though not necessarily about the relative virtues. Even in sonnets, when she spoke of dreams, her opinion of their value shifted. Ruth at once feared "toy balloons" and appreciated each "perfect sphere / Of unadulterate color. . . ."[33]

She tried to convince Stanley that the dream of a child would not "burst" and that a child might cement the marriage. In the same entry in which she reported his distrust, she altered the word for their relationship from "love" to "friendship." By 1916 she thought of the marriage as a friendship, a child part of the companionship and not a proof of passion. The child no longer represented ecstasy, but could be a common interest in the shared household. For her this was still a bid against loneliness and isolation.

Ruth never became pregnant. "But with me," she wrote, comparing herself to Margery, "I've wanted three things: Stanley, and I never could build up any companionship with him; children, and I never had a chance to daydream about them, never having had even an illusion of pregnancy, and poetry. . . ."[34] But she did daydream and also found out that one reason for her failure to conceive was physiological. According to Margaret Mead, Ruth would have had to have an operation which Stanley considered too dangerous; Ruth's fallopian tubes were blocked and Stanley did not think the risk of surgery worth taking.[35] Ruth accepted his advice whether or not she wondered about the several motives for his caution. Adding to the distance between himself and his wife, Stanley increasingly removed himself from all family ties. Ruth visited his family, a duty she took on partly to see Agnes Benedict and partly to substantiate her role as wife. Stanley stripped his life bare and occasionally Ruth accepted his idea, seeing her "salvation" in total simplification.[36]

Not for long. In terror of a life without fulfillment or at least distraction, Ruth Benedict clung to motherhood against the batterings of "reality" and of her own critical insight. She desperately preserved a dream whose very enactment she regarded warily, with an intuitive and intellectual awareness of the dangers in "vicarious living" through a child. She also dreaded the emptiness in her life, and though she did not phrase the fear exactly this way, for a time the "child"—the precarious fantasy—served as guard against thoughts of suicide and the lasting desire "just to stop."[37]

The child would have served better had Ruth been better able to believe in dreaming, or had she been able to embrace the idea of being mother without being wife. Stanley accused her of dreaming no more severely than she accused herself. Accompanying the very first entries on motherhood, Ruth wrote of the "delusions" of motherhood. Finally she burst her own dreams by testing them against reality: "There is no misreading of life that avenges itself so piteously on men and women as the notion that in their children they can bring to fruition their own seedling dreams," she wrote in an undated entry. "No, it is wisdom in motherhood as in wifehood to have one's own individual world of effort and creation."[38] She wrote another, similar entry in November 1915, about the "mockery" that belongs to "our radiant faith in 'our children.'"[39] The thought here was borrowed from George Santayana, whom she read off and on.[40] Ruth realized too well that children would be at best a truce to her restlessness, never a permanent peace.

Equally, she could not relinquish the dream. Partly the dream connected to her need to prove her "animal endowment" and to demonstrate her own sexuality. Ruth's preoccupation with a child linked to her concern about her sensual side, first in terms of heterosexuality and then in terms of her own being, apart from Stanley. She never recovered fully from Stanley's physical rejection of her; she referred to it in barely disguised language in poem after poem:

> Is life no more than this? that always I should come
> Unmarked from passion, unbranded from despair?
> Shall I come always, longing for embrace
> Ultimate, irretrievable, complete,

As that you keep far out beyond that last blue bar
For those who come to claim it? . . .[41]

Even after she grew resigned to his withdrawal, she continued to explore the nature of her sexuality and her ability to give and receive passionate love. The fear of being sexually frigid and the fear of never loving sometimes joined and sometimes did not.

Ruth put off directly considering her sexuality and expressed her yearnings for a passionate intimacy in tangential, often fantastic, terms. Then in the mid-1920s she began, not always without self-dramatization, to assess her marriage and its failures.

> So, too, in those long years with S.— I was guilty because his disapproval, his dislike kept on the torture rack an even more precious thing than solitary content or willing domesticity. Love was possible; I believed it just as I believed, in childhood, that content could have lasted all day. But against his harshness I was powerless.[42]

She also started writing poetry again, using verse as a vehicle for and discovery of her feelings. There, in structure and sonnet, Ruth poured forth a sensuality whose sources and implications caused her confusion. Through complicated, combined religious-androgynous-mythic figures, who variously merged natural and spiritual traits, the poet attempted not only to describe her passions but to understand her own sexuality. She was, as well, sensitive to the conventions of her milieu, not sure how far she might safely transgress the norms for women of her generation, her class, and her temperament. A distinct puritanical streak ran through Ruth's thoughts; so did an eager appreciation of her era's encouragement of "healthy animal" impulse.[43]

She turned her journal into a series of essays about passion versus spirituality. She intended to consider sexuality, but phrased the subject in language that sometimes seems to have nothing to do with the writer. The sonnets revealed her feelings, the journal carried on a careful argument. On July 26, 1930, she argued at length about the pros and cons of animal nature and human creativity:

> Well, then, where are the good healthy functioning humans who have made momentous contributions to the spiritual treasury? . . . Christ, so far as we can tell, was blessed from the start in lacking the fundamental drive of the healthy animal, and Buddha succeeded in ridding himself of it. . . . The artists seem more often to have been forced by circumstances into impotence. . . .

The argument goes on for five full pages.[44]

These were not unfamiliar thoughts for Ruth Benedict. Stanley Benedict's rejections had prompted anxieties and sadness early on: "Touch seems such a sweet and natural human delight."[45] Nor was it new for Ruth to force herself to distinguish between a flaw—a frigidity—in herself and the responses of another person to her. In 1915 she wrote: "Anything to live! To have done with this numbness that will not let me feel."[46] Again she distanced the statement, enclosing her self-insight in a note on the eighteenth-century feminist Mary Wollstonecraft. The note anticipated forceful journal arguments and the painfully revealing sonnets of later years.

> The worst is not our anger, Hearts
> Grown icy with the bitterness
> Of calculated hurt redress
> Somehow their ruin. Love departs
>
> Thus numbly always, nor leaves behind
> One red-lipped fagot of the fire
> Of her incredible and dear desire.[47]

Ruth followed through a train of thought parallel to her concern about sexuality. She began increasingly to consider motherhood without wifehood, separating one kind of passion from another. If she had not experienced a "floodtide of love" with a man, perhaps she could find passion in the "great instinctive answer." She could have a child of her own, apart from Stanley Benedict. She also avoided such thoughts and only cautiously explored the feminist literature on motherhood. By 1917, however, she had read Ellen Key and found in the Swedish feminist a confirmation of her own early intuition that love between man and woman in twentieth-century society was doomed by social conventions. Ellen Key, wrote Ruth Benedict, believed that without "the double handcuffs of the marriage ceremony . . . men and women are capable of giving themselves to one another simply, completely, permanently."[48] Less than a year after marriage Ruth had herself written: "What are our weddings, from the religious pomp to the irrelevant presents and the confetti, but presumptuous distractions from the proud mating of urgent love?"[49] Several years later she again noted the "perpetual lock and key of marriage" which suffocated rather than inspired love.[50]

So Ruth learned to separate the idea of a child from the conditions of marriage. She could think of a child as the fulfillment of her "power of loving," a power she had not been able to exercise in marriage. At the same time, she let herself be drawn to other women who had found a "great love" apart from marriage. She read more, and more certainly identified with, women whose love expressed itself outside the fetters of social conventions.

Ruth moved in thought away from Stanley Benedict, and altered her dream of a child. She separated the child from a heterosexual relationship, motherhood from sexuality. She also created new models from the "bold and strong women" who argued that love could be "true," permanent, and dignified only when freed of social constraints. At some time, too, Ruth stopped thinking of a son and replaced the "glorious male-child" with a daughter. She "extended" her life through a female and not a male: "It's very simple: this is my daughter's life that's posing as mine. It's my daughter's love life which shall be perfect; it's my daughter's abilities which shall find scope; it's my daughter's insight that shall be true and valid; it is she who owes it to speak out her beliefs."[51]

"I long to prove myself by writing"

Ruth Benedict dreamed of a child, with acute awareness of the frailty and deceptiveness of such dreams. In the entry on "her daughter" she questioned rather than truly indulged her fantasy—the expression is less wish than wondering: "The efficacy of such spectacles I suppose no man could understand—how many women could, I wonder?" She herself doubted the efficacy and implied that "make-believe" was at once a comfort and a danger. She condemned, in other entries, her "play-acting marriage."[52]

Through critical sarcasm and in logical arguments, Ruth distanced her dreams. In one argument she concluded that a woman could not extend her life, either through a male child possessing "superb ego" or a female child who got the "big things of life."[53] There was danger in vicariousness for mother and child: "No, it is wisdom in motherhood as in wifehood to have one's own individual world of effort and creation."[54]

She also resisted a complete break from Stanley Benedict and worked to build a friendship out of mutual respect for each other's efforts. To this she added, more and more forcefully, an idea that love gained "dignity" from permanence and commitment on some terms. She strove for dignity in her marriage and in her personal life and summoned up the "endeavor" she felt would bring dignity and stability: writing. "The best seems to die in me when I give it up."[55]

At Christmas in 1916 Stanley said, "Whatever the job, it would not hold me; nothing ever had, social work or teaching. Children might for a year or two, no more. As for the question of success in such a thing having any value in our relations with each other, it was nonsense; it only meant that I'd discovered now that marriage in its turn did not hold me."[56] Stanley pointed out, once more, things about herself that she obscured in dexterous verbalization. He said bluntly and "brutally" what Ruth made elegant, and impotent, in her own writings.

> He had been seeking Ariadne always.
> Always, abandoned to the Minotaur,
> The labyrinth of his soul an empty prison
> For that great beast that ravened at its core.[57]

This was not the first, or last, time Ruth took on a male persona in her poetry. Nor was this the first or last time she feared the fate of a futile quest.

Stanley Benedict challenged his wife's seriousness and her worth, and she set out to meet the challenge. She would devote herself utterly —she used the word "slavish"—to a book. "It means that for the first time in my life, I have committed myself to the endeavor for *success*— success in writing."[58] Yet she had already recognized two years before, if not openly admitted, that marriage would not fulfill her and that Stanley would grow impatient with her perpetual discontent. Her journal entries in 1914 and 1915 read like a defense against despair.

The plans she made in November 1914 were projects to carry her into the future. She had been married for four months.

> My pet scheme is to steep myself in the lives of restless and
> highly enslaved women of past generations and write a series
> of biographical papers from the standpoint of the "new
> woman." My conclusion so far as I see it now is that there is
> nothing "new" about the whole thing. . .—that the restless-
> ness and groping are inherent in the nature of women. . . .[59]

She chose Mary Wollstonecraft (1759–97), Margaret Fuller (1810–50), and a near-contemporary, Olive Schreiner (1855–1920), but did not, in that entry, say why—or how—she made such a choice.

The biographical papers were of tremendous significance to Ruth Benedict, and her gradual awareness of this altered the content and form of the three portraits. The essays represented an opportunity to test her capacity for commitment and to explore the connections between commitment, being a woman, and social demands. She deliberately picked three bold and outspoken women who had done what she thought she could not do. "In the face of such a world Mary Wollstonecraft threw down her challenge."[60]

Her original scheme stemmed from and propelled further Ruth's sensitivity to the "woman issue." A choice of Wollstonecraft, Fuller, and Schreiner committed the biographer to a feminism not precisely her own. Ruth Benedict had advocated accommodation to conditions or, at least, to "Nature's preconceptions." She compared her conclusions to those of her models, and the complexity of her "proof" became apparent —to herself as well as to a later reader. She had announced her goal of proving to Stanley and to herself that she would not drift into meaningless routine and, synonymously, barrenness and "blue devils." She also intended, without saying so, to prove the dignity of her own personality apart from Stanley Benedict and from the world's "coarse thumb and finger." Ruth did not state this purpose; it is clear from the lives she chose to "steep herself in."

The project seems a risky one for so new a wife. Ruth admired the "rebelliousness" of her subjects and was intrigued by their willingness to flaunt social conventions:

> For Mary Wollstonecraft never spoke her part by rote. She never flinched before the hazard of shaping forth a personality not duly authorized and accepted. She was one of those persons, who, in her own words, did not "rather catch a character from the society he lived in, than spread one about him." She lived with all the alertness of her brain focused upon the abrupt experiences of her life; the knowledge she won, the price she paid, her books may hint to us, but it is her life through which we understand.[61]

Ruth did not wholly anticipate the quandary she got into by sharing, even vicariously, these "enacted principles."[62]

Ruth Benedict's engagement with three other lives shifted. Her words convey a tension between absorption in and distance from the biographical characters. And in journal entries Ruth described the pain of writing biography differently from the way she talked about the struggles of writing verse: "Just to vegetate this summer, and write in this book [journal], and, if I can, write 'Margaret Fuller'—isn't that the best, without being so wordy about my conflicting selves?"[63] For the biographies she had to find not only the right phrases and images but also a place for self.

Ruth wanted the project to be recognized, to be praised while it proved her worth to herself and to Stanley. In choosing to write about "restless women" she tried to compromise between personal pressures and attention to an audience. Over the four years of writing, shifts in her view of herself went hand in hand with shifts in her anticipated reader; the result was that Ruth left at least six versions of "Mary Wollstonecraft" and numerous unfinished sketches, notes, and references for the other two essays. The degree to which she admitted herself into the studies influenced her decisions about whether the book was "feminist," a general political statement, her "answer" to World War I. She brought up each of these possibilities in revised versions of "foreword," "preface," and "Mary Wollstonecraft."

Tugs and pushes in different directions made it difficult for Ruth to finish the book, and difficult even to begin. She had selected three women she "liked," and said so, then as writer she continually reconstructed this "liking." In journal entries she translated the resulting conflict into "mussiness" and uncertain incentives. "How far awry my plans have gone this year [1917]! I was to make good in writing—I've not touched it," she wrote one May day.[64]

When Ruth Benedict later recalled the basis of her choice and the purpose of the biographical essays, she revealed also the uncertain alternation among approaches. She had tried, through various drafts, to subdue her emotional attachment to the three women and yet to keep the energy such attachment gave her prose. She hinted at the dilemma in a letter to Houghton Mifflin Company. Ruth Benedict began by presenting her book as a study of "women leaders," part of feminist literature, and concluded by considering her "lives" "romantic human documents" for a time of crisis.[65]

She also let the editors assume that Mary Wollstonecraft was a perfectly reasonable choice. By the end of World War I, Wollstonecraft had become a model for feminists, and Ruth did not need to explain that choice of subject.[66] In fact she had found her first and primary subject four years before setting out her "pet scheme."

In 1910 Ruth Fulton stood before the Opie portrait of Mary Wollstonecraft in London's National Portrait Gallery, moved by the vision of a woman who had "saved her soul alive."[67] She never forgot the vision, and she referred to the portrait in every version of "Mary Wollstonecraft." In one passage, more journal than draft, Ruth Benedict described her "desperate longing" to "know how other women had saved their souls alive" and accorded "dignity" to the rich processes of living.[68] She read a dignity of experience in the face of Wollstonecraft.

In other drafts (none is dated), Ruth underplayed the impact of her vision. She left the incident mainly as background, the compelling personal impulse for a political and polished account; yet her description of the portrait appeared as coda to the one published version of the essay.[69] In the forewords and in her letter to Houghton Mifflin Company, Ruth went out of the way to "rationalize" her choice of the other two subjects, Margaret Fuller and Olive Schreiner, in effect rationalizing the choice of Wollstonecraft as well. She wanted, she said, the examples of three different lives in three different times and places. She also chose subjects for whom material could be easily gathered (as she told the Houghton Mifflin editors). Beyond the choice of convenient subjects, Ruth by then knew enough about the feminist movement to estimate the importance of the women and to predict an audience for her essays.

Ruth Benedict wrote a particular kind of biography. "The feminist movement needs heroines," she announced, then added that these women must be heroines through their experiences not through their writings. "We" need to know what "they attained in the adventure of living."[70] Ruth's strongest statement of feminism emerged from this argument: "feminism does not live by its logic";[71] feminism is not a system but a "passionate attitude";[72] and, in a romanticized phrasing, "the urge, the power of this woman's movement does not lie in the gift of logic; it comes from the bright stinging realms of their dearest desires."[73]

Ruth set out to write more than a "life and works" biography. She called her essays, in one note, "empirical biography" and by this meant, essentially, the evocation of a life. That is, she intended to present material so that her readers might share—reexperience—the dominant motives in a life different from their own. Her subjects well suited her intentions. Mary Wollstonecraft especially, but all three women in Ruth's interpretation, "lived life headlong," lived life with a "lavish expense of spirit." Her conclusion about Mary Wollstonecraft applied to the three: "her books may hint to us, but it is her life through which we understand."[74]

"Empirical biography" also demanded participation by the biographer. Ruth added to her notion the idea of a writer's empathy with the life she described. For Ruth, absorption had also to be controlled—a control gained from the distance of time and place. If she shared Mary Wollstonecraft's "groping restlessness," she did not share the eighteenth-century constraints on feminine behavior. She stressed the "perspective" gained from distance. Only "we" (twentieth-century women) can see the coherence and the purpose in the "swift, whirling facts" of Mary Wollstonecraft's life.[75] Only the biographer can picture the integration of experience and political rhetoric that Wollstonecraft's contemporaries dismissed as haphazard, and scandalous, rebellion.

Ruth Benedict argued the point for all three women; she viewed all three as women of bold and rebellious spirit, whose lived experiences more than their published writings made the "statement" for contemporary feminists. This point provided organization for the three essays, and Ruth found it easier to organize than to finish her book. The very idea of a "passionate determination to live life at full value and face nothing nonchalantly" upset the balance between absorption and distance she tried to achieve.

One cannot read the drafts of "Mary Wollstonecraft" without realizing the extent to which the eighteenth-century woman's life became a model and a challenge for Ruth's life. It is equally evident that Ruth would have carried themes from the Wollstonecraft section into the Fuller and Schreiner sections. She picked out of Wollstonecraft's life aspects that touched her own: the near-tragic childhood; the yearning for ecstasy which took form in close friendships with women, in religious "awe," and (for each of the three women) in a reckless love affair; motherhood; death. The biographer tied the lives of her three women together under the notion of passion and purpose—the juxtaposition of ecstasy and achievement.

The "biographical essays" completed Ruth's own life story. One could go through the Mary Wollstonecraft essay point by point to establish the terms of Ruth's ongoing autobiographical inquiry. As she wrote the essay Ruth came upon herself, and often unexpectedly. She realized, over the nearly four years of writing, that sympathy carried its own impetus and that the attraction of her subject's "lavish expense of spirit" threatened her aimed-for equilibrium.

Ruth Benedict knew the importance of reflection and of difference in biographies; a relationship between empathy and critical distance had entered into her definition of "empirical biography." Even a bare summary reveals the complex basis of her identification with Wollstonecraft, Fuller, and Schreiner—and reasons for never finishing the book. The main theme of drafts, notes, and sketches for the volume contained Ruth's familiar concern with the strength of passion (the "floodtide of love" in her journal became the "open sesame of happiness" in "Mary Wollstonecraft"), the unshakable commitment to an idea, and the dependence of idea upon passion. She read all this, by 1915–16, into the context of the "woman issue."

The biographer did not do an injustice to her subjects. She had chosen her "women" carefully, and because each demonstrated "intellect-grounded-in-passion." Nor did Ruth exaggerate the likenesses among her three subjects. She did interpret their lives in the light of her own idea —ecstasy and achievement—but always with deliberateness. She drew together particular aspects of the three lives and made these startling and significant, but no more than any practiced writer would do. She only added the caveat that the biographer deal with what resounded in her own life.

"I have loved with my whole soul," she quoted from Mary Wollstonecraft.[76] At times, Ruth seemed most absorbed by the passion in her subjects' natures. The passion, for all three women, culminated simultaneously in a "great love" and in a significant political statement—or so

Ruth portrayed the central incidents in Wollstonecraft's and Fuller's lives (and would have done for Schreiner). Through the miscellaneous collection of materials, Benedict consistently stressed the love affair and equally the conjunction of love with an articulation of feminist principles. She also devoted paragraphs, sometimes pages, to Wollstonecraft's *Vindication of the Rights of Women,* but she clearly considered the "rhetoric" less important than the "idea-as-lived."

She also wrote about Wollstonecraft's marriage and motherhood. The biographer struggled to be fair to Mary Wollstonecraft's marriage, without much success: "Her idea did not attain solidity by the congealing of icy and solitary logical processes, like those of her twelve-months' husband, the estimable and frigid William Godwin."[77] Too careful to use the word "defeat," Ruth did suggest a resigned diminishment of enthusiasm: "Truly, he was a formidable person to imagine in love. Perhaps the fascination of his dense ignorance attracted Mary Wollstonecraft, who knows? At any rate, it was the growing intimacy with William Godwin that lifted her back to genuine existence."[78]

Ultimately Ruth fit the relationship into an argument for the importance of "married standard bearers"[79] in the twentieth-century feminist movement. This was the best she could do to rescue Wollstonecraft's decision to marry Godwin; she did not here understand the motives of her heroine.

Then there were the children and, not unconnected, the deaths of her three subjects. Ruth relished the details of Wollstonecraft's motherhood and drew out the details of Wollstonecraft's tragic death in childbearing—"Why did not the desperate need of her in their childish lives force her back to life?"[80] For all three—Wollstonecraft, Fuller, and Schreiner—motherhood had linked to tragedy: Wollstonecraft died giving birth; Fuller and her young son drowned together; Schreiner's baby died in infancy. At the end of "Mary Wollstonecraft," Ruth emphasized the heroism and bravery, not the tragedy, of her subject's life: "She *had* saved her soul alive; it looked out from her steady eyes unafraid."[81] But Ruth could not move on to the next two women.

The writer had counted on publication, and Ruth claimed that Houghton Mifflin's rejection of the Wollstonecraft essay kept her from finishing the book. She needed the recognition represented by publisher approval, to bolster her sense of worth and possibly to "prove" her case to Stanley: "I told him he should see." He had doubted her ability to stick to the project and may have implied that writing for herself had limited value.

Ruth also found that the whole project drained her energies and distracted her not only from "ennui" but also from true "self-realization."

She had been ambitious; the book was to be a feminist statement, her contribution to the postwar era, a savior of her marriage and of her own soul. She discovered she had neither the passion nor the "superb ego" of her subjects to see the project through. Once again her life seemed to be a series of unconnected incidents—an "episodic" pattern—in contrast to the coherence she created for Mary Wollstonecraft.

She yearned for an overwhelming purpose, a point on which to test her powers of commitment. She jammed the drafts, notes, and sketches into a carton, acting out the "mussiness" once mainly a figure in her journal. Then Ruth Benedict sent away for the course catalog from the recently established New School for Social Research.

5
Discovering Anthropology

"I haven't strength of mind not to need a career"

HOUGHTON MIFFLIN COMPANY REJECTED the Mary Wollstonecraft essay in 1919. "And more and more I realize I want publication," Ruth Benedict had recorded three years earlier.[1] She wanted publication mainly to prove the worth of her writing. Without external recognition—the "validation" a publisher gave—the project seemed another "toy," the distraction of a bored child. Ruth had applied the words "frivolity" and "distraction" to her activities before finding in a letter of Mary Wollstonecraft's "Till I can form some idea of the whole of my existence, I must be content to weep and dance like a child—long for a toy and be tired of it as soon as I get it."[2] Ruth quoted the passage, and made the metaphor her own.

Ruth had picked up one "toy" after another: love and marriage; children; a time-consuming project. Or so she saw her life in 1916. Her self-denigration then resonated within the context of a world crisis: "And how useless to attempt anything but a steady day-by-day living with this tornado of world-horror over our heads."[3] For her three heroines—Mary Wollstonecraft, Margaret Fuller, and Olive Schreiner—war had provided purpose and their private concerns became part of a greater and a "just" cause. Each extended personal experience of the suppression of women to a battle against the suppression of any group. Mary Wollstonecraft endorsed the principles of the French Revolution, Margaret Fuller took up Italy's fight for independence, and Olive Schreiner battled racism in her homeland, South Africa.

Ruth Benedict, too, looked for wider scope for commitments. She knew she needed a valid endeavor; vague restlessness turned against her marriage and a life in Bedford Hills. She turned back to the familiar territory of academia and in the fall of 1919 enrolled in a lecture course at the New School for Social Research. Over twenty years later she explained her action in terms of World War I. She went to school to learn "what makes the U.S. a nation of Americans, France a nation of Frenchmen . . . ," she told the American Association of University Women in 1946.[4]

Ruth's retrospective account, influenced by a second world war, reflected a part of her motivation. She was not alone, in 1919, in hoping that more information about other nations would help ensure "lasting peace." The New School offered its program of courses in like spirit: "Only by an impartial and open-minded consideration of present difficulties and an effort toward reasonable readjustment can society be rescued from the forces of bitter and opposing dogmatisms, whether these spring from an excessive confidence in, or contempt for, the existing order."[5]

Ruth never said exactly why she chose the New School. Partly she may have appreciated the convenience and the flexibility: No degrees were given; students were free to come and go as they liked—"pursuing each his special study for its own sake according to his particular aims."[6] Classes began after 4 P.M. and cost twenty dollars each. Ruth could fit her classes around her domestic schedule.

Partly she may have appreciated, without saying so, the policies and the guiding theme of the school. The New School had been founded five years earlier by liberal and well-off New Yorkers (the so-called "*New Republic* group"), refugees from Europe, and various nonconforming academics. Ruth must have read about the establishment of a new school in New York City and may have read the idealistic statement of purpose before actually enrolling. The aim of improving "world conditions" resembled a goal she had heard at Vassar, though the situation, times, and personnel at the New School changed the implications of this. The students Ruth met in 1919, too, differed from the women she had known at Vassar; the concern with contemporary issues after World War I converted humanitarianism from an attitude into a specific activity.

The New School building was in downtown Manhattan on 23rd and 24th streets. For Ruth Benedict the site, among warehouses and stores, made a clear contrast to the bucolic Vassar campus—and certainly a change of view from the Bedford Hills house she left. New School founders expected students to "use" the city, its libraries, institutions, and heterogeneous population.

From the conscientiously nonprescriptive set of courses, Ruth selected from the "group of studies . . . primarily descriptive and historical in their emphasis. They will seek to give an 'unbiassed understanding of the existing order, its genesis, growth and present working.'" She avoided studies focused on "thought and ideals" and human emotions as well as those dealing "specifically with special contemporary problems."[7] She passed over courses given by the sociologist Thorstein Veblen, Charles Beard, and Harold Laski, and never took John Dewey's yearly "Method in the Social Sciences."

She wanted new perspectives, and Dewey, for one, was not new. Ruth had read his arguments on progressive education and on the importance of uniting reason and passion. She had included these ideas in her biographical essays; Dewey's notion of "intellect rooted in desire," quoted in a draft, directed the course of Mary Wollstonecraft's life and to an extent Ruth's own. But in 1919 Ruth wanted more, a sense of the social as well as the personal circumstances of "purpose" and fulfillment. She put aside philosophy and biography, temporarily, for descriptions of other "ways of life"—the old "country over the hill" idea. That first autumn at the New School, Ruth chose a class given by a sociologist-turned-ethnographer.

Ruth Benedict enrolled in "Sex in Ethnology," taught by Elsie Clews Parsons. The course consisted of "surveys of a number of societies presenting a distinctive distribution of functions between the sexes, and of topical analyses of the division of labor between men and women."[8] Parsons's material seemed to offer information on Ruth's particular concerns.

Possibly enthusiasm, possibly a little of the familiar need to "stick to it," prompted Ruth to take another ethnology course in the spring of 1920. She picked a course called "The Groundwork of Civilization," given by Alexander A. Goldenweiser. She may have heard about this "brilliant anthropologist" from other students; at any rate she quickly appreciated his attention to "neophytes" and later wrote: "The lectures were only a small part of his help; he suggested books and articles, and talked them over with me afterwards. . . ."[9] In his lectures, however, "Goldie" displayed his brilliance and his extraordinarily facile imagination. Ruth took his classes for the next year and a half. (Parsons did not teach during the next several years.)

In the fall of 1920 she took Goldenweiser's "Early Society and Politics," in spring 1921 his "Early Economics and Knowledge," and in fall 1921, "The Diffusion of Civilization." Effectively, if inadvertently, Ruth constructed the basis of a graduate program in anthropology.

Goldenweiser was a contrast to Parsons in personality and in style. He also, unlike his colleague, had been trained as an anthropologist, receiving his Ph.D. from Columbia University in 1910. He taught, or tried to teach, full-time, but the other side of Goldie's inspiring wisdom was an erratic, undependable quality that lost him job after job. Goldenweiser displayed a mixture of intellectual daring and personal melancholy that colleagues found hard to tolerate: "He indulges in the soulful vocabulary of an adolescent of the German 'Storm and Stress' period who is prepared to sing an ode to Life with the intention of putting a bullet through his brain as soon as he's finished," one described Goldie.[10]

Ruth Benedict forgave the self-indulgence for the inspiration. She also forgave Goldenweiser his flirtatiousness—a quality that led some to call him a "womanizer." She did not feel put upon by his efforts to charm, and perhaps appreciated the recognition of herself as an attractive woman. She only lost patience when his self-absorption resulted in poor teaching: "2 p.m. Goldenweiser . . . Bored!! How could he!"[11] Usually she, with others, was entranced by his sweeping accounts of diverse cultures. Goldie did not stop to cite details; instead he conveyed the whole picture of a "strange" society—a picture imprinted on his audience's mind. Ruth responded to his ethnographic portraits and to his emphasis on the "pattern" of a civilization. She continued to have lunch with Goldie after she left the New School and until he went to Oregon to teach. ". . . Went down to lunch with him [Goldenweiser]. Cut Barnard class for the purpose."[12]

Goldenweiser exuded excitement about his discipline, and Ruth flourished under his enthusiastic attempts to convert newcomers to anthropology. He influenced her as much personally as intellectually. Her other New School teacher, entirely different in manner, also influenced Ruth as much by what she was as by what she said. Goldie displayed a bold and flashy mind, Parsons a disciplined, relentless attention to facts. "Dr. Parsons writes from complete detailed knowledge of specific conditions in each Southwest pueblo—a 'labor of description,' as Dr. Parsons calls her work. . . ."[13] When Ruth wrote this review of Parson's *Pueblo Indian Religion,* both women were well into their professional careers.

Meanwhile, in the immediate postwar years Elsie Parsons exerted an influence over the younger woman through her exemplary professional devotedness. Parsons enacted, often deliberately, the role of successful career woman who had not rejected the conventional traits of womanhood. She went home to a husband and six children (only four lived to maturity), to household responsibilities and vacations with the family. She also published ten books and numerous articles.

Elsie Worthington Clews was born in 1875, in New York, her father a wealthy banker and her mother a Virginia socialite. At age sixteen she insisted on going to the recently accredited Barnard College on Madison Avenue instead of to the "proper" female colleges her parents favored.

From Barnard she went on to earn a Ph.D. in sociology from Columbia (1899). A year later she married Herbert Parsons, a New York lawyer and congressman. She had her babies and continued to lecture at Columbia and New York University while a governess cared for the children.[14] In 1915 Elsie Parsons helped found the New School for Social Research.

The Parsonses traveled frequently, to Europe and South and Central America as well as throughout the United States. A curious and energetic woman, Elsie Parsons began collecting bits of exotica: jump-rope songs; voodoo chants; details of a woman's initiation. She collected industriously and needed a system for organizing the data she gathered. In 1913 Elsie Parsons went to the anthropology department at Columbia and consulted with its chair, Franz Boas. He welcomed the potential anthropologist, and her vast quantities of data, and Parsons established a tie which lasted for the rest of her life.

Elsie Clews Parsons gave anthropology material, time, and money.[15] On principle she refused offices, honors, and full-time jobs. She claimed that others needed the professional recognition more than she did. "Honors of place should be given to men in the academic rank who would find them of practical value," she claimed,[16] but every now and then she gave in: From 1923 to 1925 she was president of the American Ethnological Society, from 1918 to 1941 associate editor of the *Journal of American Folk-Lore*, and in 1941 the first woman president of the American Anthropological Association.

A woman who believed in independence, Elsie Parsons both argued and enacted her principles. Consequently, too, she distanced many, even those who admired her work and her stamina. She represented the kind of achievement possible for a woman and, as well, the demands of that achievement. "She valued control preeminently: first in herself, next in others. Therefore, she trained her judgment to be unsparing, and sometimes seemed more coldly reasoned in her motivations than was actually the case. Toward the young and the dependent she was uniformly helpful, provided they were not parasitic," Alfred L. Kroeber described his colleague in an obituary.[17] Ruth Benedict shared Kroeber's opinion, but she felt an even more intense ambivalence than did Kroeber.

The passion Elsie Parsons controlled emerged on two subjects: the Pueblos and their glorious southwestern setting and the opportunities for individualized expression within cultural bounds. By 1919 Ruth Benedict also recognized the tensions between social convention and self-fulfillment. Five years later she understood Parsons's awe at the Southwest. Elsie Parsons linked a concern with individuality to her observations of highly regulated Pueblo life, and Ruth would have been quick to note a biographical element in her teacher's yoking of idea to data. Parsons had, in fact, pulled her anthropology out of personal experience of social constraints.[18]

Ruth perhaps read Elsie Parsons's books before 1919. A conscientious student, she in all likelihood read them after she met Dr. Parsons. Throughout *The Family* (1906) and *The Old-Fashioned Woman* (1913) a careful reader might find the concepts central to Parsons's ethnographic writings: the need for "descriptive data," precise observations, and facts before theory.[19] Both volumes criticized the conventions of American society; in 1913 Parsons took a pen name to argue against the oppression of women. The "wedding ring is a token of inadequacy as well as of 'respectability,'" wrote "John Main."[20]

To some extent a cross-cultural approach relieved Elsie Parsons of the need for disguise. Anthropology provided not so much new issues or procedures as an armory of empirical illustrations. She still focused on women, her main concern the American married woman who depended upon someone else for a "living," and she startled her readers by comparing an American engagement party to an African puberty rite.[21]

Ruth never referred to the content of her first ethnology course, but much in Elsie Parsons's lectures prompted a shudder of recognition. Underneath an unease in the classroom, Parsons conveyed a "spirit tested in experience," at least to Ruth's sensitive view. Ruth also saw her own preoccupations translated into the stuff of a discipline and, in Parsons's presentation, bolstered by "hard evidence." Ruth kept her journal and in a set of entries recorded the complexity of her responses to the New School.

The entries are undated, but judging by content were made sometime during 1919–20. She titled two of the three long sections "A Defining of the Issues" and "Goals for Women." The third, untitled, section brought home ideas developed in the first two. Ruth devoted more than her usual care to these paragraphs; they could be sketches for a paper. In one sentence, for example, she noted to herself: "(illustrate, Ibsen *Ghosts*)."[22]

Elsie Clews Parsons may well have been the actual reader or at least the projected audience. For Ruth Benedict, Parsons represented a woman who succeeded "by the world's measure" without giving up her private life and, in Parsons's case, possessing the added quality of being impressively rational. Ruth did not consistently admire the rationality, but she forced herself to judge its worth, especially in a woman. Alexander A. Goldenweiser served Ruth less well as audience for her "woman issue." His charm, his fancifulness, his flirtatious attention distracted her from clarification. "It is so easy to please Goldie," she once said.[23]

In many ways Elsie Parsons was the most complete model Ruth Benedict had yet had, with her career and her children, her commitment and her control. (Ruth's mother had always preached control, though without always showing it. And in 1912 when she gave up a career to care for Margery's children, Bertrice Fulton took back the role her older daughter had always seen her in.) In responding to Elsie Parsons, Ruth refined the dimensions of her self-inquiry. She struggled to reconcile the split between passion and achievement that seemed woman's fate, and to incorporate both into one configuration. Persistently Ruth distrusted a passion that emerged in selflessness or in melodramatic gesture. She equally feared the loss of passion, an ennui, and by 1919 the "freezing" of her "blood." "Ice when it forms upon the brooks in autumn / Stills their swift feet that ran they knew not where," she wrote in the mood of those years.[24] The poet, too, added to her "nun" the "monk of Ariège," who denied himself all beauty and his own sensual nature. Ruth's monk went mad behind his dutiful "copying."[25]

The journal entries, whether or not directly inspired by Elsie Parsons, extended the theme of Ruth Benedict's biographical essays. Ruth had filed "Mary Wollstonecraft" away, and the dilemma of zest versus duty remained. Feminism, she said in her much-drafted preface, must be told through lives. But the telling must be rational, with a clarity gained through distance, and she had, it seemed, lost her distance when writing about her "impassioned" women. In the "faithful black notebook," Ruth tried now to construct a reasoned accounting of "the woman issue."

The three entries form one piece. Ruth organized her ideas somewhat chronologically, in the order of realization. She rethreaded the strands, from Pasadena (old maids and family), her marriage (love and worth), and the events of World War I (work for self, for others). She carefully set up terms, then ended not with a logical conclusion but with a statement echoing the tone of the biographical essays: "—oh, we need so desperately to learn, syllable by syllable, this new faith in love."[26]

Ruth paved the way to this insight. She first reviewed the "economic autonomy" argument and soundly rejected it, whether formulated by Elsie Parsons, Charlotte Perkins Gilman, or any other contemporary feminist.[27] Ruth considered economic, like political, questions outmoded and boring. "The deeply-sundering issue in feminism doesn't lie any longer in paid labor vs. parasitism."[28] She did not mind, yet, being supported; a salary could not be the source of her independence. "There is no virtue even in a pay envelope to make life seem worth living," she had complained in 1912. Seven years later she put the issue in sociohistorical terms: "I think conditions are rapidly falsifying these issues: the vast majority [of women] have the right to labor now— wartimes have seen to that—in the great war-game no one is exempted. And it is a necessary emancipation; without it there would be no further step. But it is only initial."[29] Even in less sanguine moods about conditions in her country, Ruth thought economic and political changes peripheral and diversionary. "It is not political recognition, it is not economic independence: the goal could never be reached without these. . . . But the ultimate objective, the high goal remains an inward affair, a matter of attitude." And later, "The issue really and truly is fine free living in the spirit world of socialized spiritual values. . . ."[30]

She put Elsie Parsons's economic argument in perspective. Too, something in Goldenweiser's discussion of gender stuck in Ruth's mind. Ruth was drawn to Goldie's assumption, and appreciation, of innate differences in female and male.[31] This idea commanded her attention, and her prose changed. She wrote then about "the emotional part of woman's life—that part which makes her a woman," and forgot logic and distancing mechanisms. Effectively the diarist embraced a notion she had prepared for all along in words like "red-blooded" (in the first sentence of the first entry), "vitality," "dignity of robust personality." These were not new words, but familiar clues to a side of her temperament.

Ruth Benedict had not thrown over biography for anthropology. She had instead widened the range of "vicarious living" and added descriptive details about other societies to her accounts of other personalities. She also gradually widened "the issues," from women to any individual in society. But that came later.

In the 1920s Ruth remained uncertain about her answer. Next to Parsons's feminism her own seemed a little "old-fashioned," with its emphasis on falling in love and finding a perfect companion. Ruth was not a Victorian lady, but she was a somewhat Victorian liberal. Her persistent faith in "socialized spiritual values" echoed Matthew Arnold, and she recognized the echo and the nineteenth-century source of her confidence in human creativity.[32]

Behind her stronger emphasis on economic factors, Elsie Clews Parsons was as little a revolutionary as Ruth Benedict. Both women finally accepted the existing order, using "social data" to comment upon, not to challenge, current cultural arrangements. Both became anthropologists and argued for individual freedom within the social order. The two women recognized what they shared and what they disagreed about and developed a reluctant respect for one another. Respect rested on a kindred professionalism, won against odds, and turned to impatience at sharply contrasting methods for "doing" the profession. In 1919, however, Parsons fully supported the younger woman, and Ruth began to hope she might actually find a place for personal preoccupations in a discipline.

During the two and a half years Ruth came in and out of the New School, the two women became reasonably well acquainted. Elsie Parsons heard about and witnessed the intelligent eagerness of the younger woman, and Ruth welcomed the opportunity to expend her energies on a "real" piece of work. Then Parsons consulted with her colleague Alexander A. Goldenweiser, and together they decided Ruth Benedict should get a Ph.D. in anthropology. Because Parsons trusted her relationship with Franz Boas, she, not Goldie, traveled uptown with Ruth to talk to the head of Columbia's anthropology department.

"I can't tell you what a place you fill in my life"

In 1940 Ruth Benedict wrote to Franz Boas, "I can't tell you what a place you fill in my life." Twenty years earlier, when she first met Boas, she saw a fierce-looking man with a dueling scar across one cheek. He mumbled, partly because the left side of his face had been paralyzed by a cancer operation and partly—at least some thought—deliberately to challenge his listener's attention. Ruth struggled to hear, and there may be no greater proof of her devotion to the new discipline than her endurance of an initial interview with Boas.

Whatever he thought of Elsie Parsons's judgment, Franz Boas welcomed converts to the discipline he had legitimized in American universities. Behind Ruth's stutter and hesitant demeanor he heard a commitment to the study of man and society, and he had Dr. Parsons's word to substantiate his favorable impression. Franz Boas, not for the first or the last time, waived requirements and accepted Ruth Benedict as a Ph.D. candidate in the Columbia University anthropology program. Ruth did not describe her reactions to becoming a doctoral student. She may have been swept along by Boas's enthusiasm and by his assumption that she would be an anthropologist. She may also have suspected she had found a vocation and, superstitiously, not put into words her hope that this was true. She would be thirty-four years old the coming June.

In fact, Ruth did not need to write about her decision to get a degree in anthropology. She had prepared reasons, and justifications, beforehand in journal entries from 1912 through 1919. In these entries she questioned women's goals and expressed dissatisfaction with marriage and with a "make-shift time filler of a job."[33] And there was the war. Ruth saw her personal crisis in the context of world crisis, but rather than thereby achieving a sense of proportion, she chafed at her inability to contribute to ending the "raging horror." Stanley Benedict did research on poison gases, and whatever his wife thought of the exact nature of his work, she envied his participation in the "effort."

In the fall of 1919 Ruth had joined an institution with an academic program directed to "peace in the world." At the New School she met others who shared her faith in "mutual understanding" as a foundation for peace. At Columbia, Franz Boas adopted a quieter tone and walked a precarious path between political sympathies and academic policies. Bruised once by an American Anthropological Association censure,[34] he worried about university interference with his curriculum. So, his nascent anthropology program in mind, Boas subdued his political engagement—or at least he tried to: Ruth undoubtedly heard the anecdote about a soldier who appeared in Boas's office in Army uniform. The soldier was Ralph Linton, and Boas quickly made him unwelcome. Linton registered for a Ph.D. at Harvard.[35]

During World War I, Boas warned the social scientist against taking sides or, especially, blatantly announcing the side taken. He certainly thought of his science as making a contribution to international understanding and couched this in terms acceptable to a university administration. The advantage of anthropology, he said, is that it "enables us to free ourselves from the prejudices of our civilization, and to apply standards in measuring our achievements that have a greater absolute truth than those derived from a study of our civilization alone."[36] The basis on which Franz Boas taught courses matched the basis on which Ruth Benedict had, if less explicitly, turned to anthropology in 1919. The subject matter of anthropology, in the two schools she attended, gave her a way of "serving" humanity (a lesson from Vassar as well) without becoming a mere "footstool." For Ruth, the issue still had to do with women's and men's opportunities. She did not want her war effort to be restricted to ladylike charitable endeavors and Boas offered an alternative: a science, tough, useful, and gender-free. She did not either, in the flush of an unusual optimism, think that Boas waived requirements just because she was a woman. The subject of Boas's special treatment of women came up later, but Ruth never saw the problem of bias some female students did.

In 1921 Ruth still hoped to prove herself to Stanley Benedict. She intended to be a full-time student and not neglect any of her domestic tasks.

Pleased at the possibilities Columbia, and Boas himself, offered, Ruth did not acknowledge the strain of juggling two roles. When tension crept in, she argued herself out of it: "P.M. missed Dr. Boas and out on 5 P.M. train. Depression after telephoning S—. . . .—But it's just mannerisms; all right at home."[37] Her days were full, and she made them fuller with housework, visits to Stanley's aunt and uncle, lunches, dinners, and theater trips with friends. She did switch from the journal notebooks to tiny appointment books and there jotted brief references to her activities. She did not want to think about loneliness, her "abyss." "Felt very isolated today, and sent check for membership [a club]."[38]

Ruth Benedict commuted from Bedford Hills to Columbia University. Occasionally she and Stanley rode in together, and she would get off at the 125th Street station and make her way down to the anthropology offices in the journalism building on 116th Street (a less hazardous trip than it would become in the 1960s and 1970s). Boas taught required seminars and occasional classes and encouraged conversations in corridors, offices, and lunchrooms. Ruth spent the day at Columbia, and so did everyone else. The department became a "second home" for faculty and students (and many found it difficult ever to leave "home").

"Monday, January 29. In on 8 o'clock and finished typing Wintun paper in seminar [room]. . . . Met Dr. Boas for dinner at Esther's [Goldfrank]. . . . Business meeting at the Ethnological Society. . . ."[39] This was a typical entry, broken only by glimpses of depression the diarist put aside in her determination to hold on to a sense of "fit" she rarely had. "Talked of Esther and Mrs. Parsons; relationship terms. Bought jam and cards! I must remember afterwards how simple happiness is."[40] Between classes and the apparently endless informal talk about work, Ruth spent more and more time in Manhattan, less and less in Bedford Hills. She grew familiar with the neighborhood around Columbia and varied that with trips to the New School for lectures and later to the American Museum of Natural History for "tours." And somehow she found time to order coal and bring the "Chilkot blankets from storeroom."[41]

To preserve her equilibrium, Ruth drew boundaries. Students and faculty who knew "Mrs. Benedict" never met Stanley Benedict and never visited Bedford Hills. And though Stanley may have heard details of Mohave "relationship terms," he seems not to have participated wholeheartedly in his wife's newest enthusiasm. His patience could well have worn thin; few students learned from Boas without becoming preoccupied with the man, and Ruth added to verbal evidence of her absorption piles of index cards and scraps of notepaper. She was not an orderly note-taker, one suspects in contrast to Stanley, and used whatever paper happened to be available. She recorded anthropological ideas on envelopes, backs of receipts, and in the middle of shopping lists and she stored them away for future work and incidentally for posterity. Stanley Benedict valued the placidity of his nonwork surroundings and disliked his wife's mussiness. In the evenings the two played "Go Bang," a distracting Japanese checker game.

The game, not the studies absorbing her daily attention, tied Ruth to Stanley. The game was a small incident in days spent struggling with kinship terminology, with the fundamentals of physical anthropology, and in responding to Boas's urging that she find her "own topic" in the discipline. Ruth took the required courses in statistical theory and in American Indian languages. The technical matter of measurement—biometrics—probably interested her less than the argument for separation of inherited from learned characteristics, the race, language, and culture distinction of the next era. It is probably safe to say that linguistics totally tormented the student and reminded her of the unsuccessful German class at Vassar and the hopelessness of ever understanding her Polish clients in Buffalo.

Boas also taught, year by year, general ethnology courses. Official departmental lists contained the same titles year after year, but Ruth (like other students) soon realized that Boas did what he pleased, regardless of title. One semester she took "Kinship," and one page of her notes has *"boring"* scrawled across the top.[42] Judging from the appointment books, kinship represented the special challenge of her discipline: "I'll learn!" she insisted.[43] Mainly she took whatever Boas taught and took his seminars repeatedly—even after she began teaching herself.

Ruth may never have heard quite enough in classes. Boas mumbled, and his mumbles were not always English. Not only did he accidentally lapse into German, but sometimes he purposely threw out Dutch or Latin words he expected students to understand. No one found this easy, and a half-deaf student least of all. But Ruth took Boas's courses over again for other reasons. In fact, she could not count on his repeating anything from one time to the next, and the unpredictable change in content pleased rather than disturbed her.[44] Contemporaries, with different expectations for professional training, complained about the idiosyncratic teaching.

Franz Boas's course in methods caused the greatest irritation. Boas himself minimized the advantages of teaching anything firmly designated "methods" in anthropology.[45] But students expected a clear set of procedures, and he failed to provide this. Students wanted instructions, and Boas taught a point of view. Students wanted an empirical base on which to construct an approach, and Boas used Kwakiutl data to illustrate an array of ethnographic concepts. He gave the students credit for being able to read for ethnographic facts and for being able to find their "procedures" once they began fieldwork. Ruth Benedict, however, thrived on learning that demanded each student's active participation and she knew that academic issues gained substance from the teacher's personal commitment. Becoming an anthropologist at Columbia in the 1920s meant taking on an energetic interaction and, in practical terms, required a large degree of self-motivation. Ruth Benedict went from seminar room to Low Library, along with both the annoyed and the encouraged of her peers.

She read ethnographies, tested for herself the Boasian perspective on "man in society," and returned to Bedford Hills in time to make dinner for her husband. When the two did not play "Go Bang," Ruth worked and wrote to clarify her personal interpretation of this unexpectedly "personal" science she was learning. "—*Contra* Dr. Boas on culture areas. He's such a godsend. Argued with him again about the Races book."[46] She called Boas a "godsend," referring to far more than his classroom teaching (as she had when she used similar words for Goldenweiser). Franz Boas both conveyed and elicited a passionate commitment to the discipline. He taught science with what Alfred Kroeber called "icy enthusiasm."[47]

Ruth Benedict was not alone in recognizing biographical sources of her attachment to Boas and to his anthropology. She rejected the psychoanalytic phrases used by several of his students, primarily Kroeber. She also disliked the emphatically familial vocabulary of other students and adopted the "Papa Franz" nickname much later than its originators, Ruth Bunzel and Gladys Reichard. Yet these phrases and interpretations all reflected something she did enjoy: The Columbia department was a small, tightly knit community, bound by affections as much as by intellectual pursuits.

To a person like Ruth Benedict, inclined to see pattern and recurring themes, Boas appeared to possess traits she valued in Frederick Fulton. Like Fulton, Boas thought of his science in terms of the improvement of daily life. The two also shared a kind of idealism which involved testing the strengths of scientific procedures in the cauldron of actual experience. Dr. Fulton had been investigating a malaria epidemic in the field just before his death in 1888. By contrast, Stanley Benedict remained a research scientist who (according to colleagues) rarely emerged from his laboratory.[48]

Ruth Benedict might also have remembered John Samuel Shattuck in her contacts with Boas. She may have seen a likeness in the outwardly fierce demeanor, product of determination not lack of sympathy, and a similarity in their gentle treatment of her. Boas was sixty-three years old when Ruth met him in 1921, a grandfather's age, especially compared to the unchanged image of a thirty-year-old father. Boas gave the impression not of calm and stillness but of vibrant energy, of the "full-blooded vitality" Ruth always admired. As a child, she had watched Grandfather Shattuck load hay from early in the morning until evening. Throughout the 1920s and 1930s she would receive letters from Papa Franz complaining about the efforts of a fieldtrip and exulting in the total exertion.[49]

In both men, too, the energy Ruth Benedict admired went along with a stern devotion—in Shattuck's case to his church and in Boas's case to his discipline. Increasingly she interpreted Boasian anthropology to suit principles she had learned in the Norwich farmhouse. From those years on, Ruth responded to the person, poet or preacher or scientist, whose subject was—ultimately—the human desire to comprehend existence. Boas's anthropology structured the subject, discovering diverse accommodations to an "awesome universe"; in anthropology Ruth added empirical research to a question that belonged to a religious world-view. She did not do Boas an injustice; he too believed anthropology provided a basis for faith in mankind.

Ruth could have extended the resemblance between Papa Franz and her grandfather. Like John Samuel Shattuck, Boas had little patience for the doubter, for the individual who violated the principles of a discipline and, by association, distorted the terms of a life. Boas demanded a creative encounter with his ideas, not conformity, and the errors he noted came from refusal to "look" not from an individual's independence of outlook. For Ruth, these (largely unconscious) resemblances bolstered her notion of learning: an experience in which pupil took from teacher a way of developing private judgments and pursuing an individual quest. Her grandfather, her formidable anthropology professor, and many of the authors she read conveyed much the same lesson; learning meant adopting a distinct perspective on the human condition, trusting one's insights and accumulating a knowledge of significance to the world. In 1921–22 Ruth also recognized an obligation to demonstrate "good faith" to Franz Boas by somewhat unlocking her "pearls of great price," her precious thoughts.[50] Only her grandfather had been so privileged before—or so she suggested in her autobiographical fragment.[51]

Boas did not pry, leaving Ruth's "masks" intact, whatever glimpses behind or guesses he had about their cause. He came to know her particular talents and turned them into disciplinary approaches. He used his insights to establish a discipline and not to draw people into his personal orbit. Usually solicitous, Boas never demanded or liked dependency—and he brushed aside any excessive expressions of concern for him.[52] If Ruth Benedict needed one more model for her relationship with Boas, she had one in her essay on Mary Wollstonecraft. There she had written (five years before entering Columbia) about Wollstonecraft's relationship to the "prominent Fleet Street publisher" who pushed her into a writing career by giving her "hackwork."[53] Ruth called Mr. Johnson's attitude "fatherly" not to specify a generational but to eliminate a sexual relationship. In Ruth's view, Mary Wollstonecraft devoted herself to Johnson out of shared "duty" to the "world of letters," not out of passion for the man.

Ruth Benedict said none of this and wrote practically nothing about herself in 1921–23. She did not even keep the appointment books past March, perhaps dreading "revelation" beneath the determined timetabling of her life.

The tension between being a wife and a full-time student deepened when Ruth began her dissertation. Franz Boas had accepted her as just predegree, and speedily maneuvered her toward a topic. He had been directing dissertations for twenty years and adjusting specialized problems to his long-range plan for anthropological research. He also became remarkably adept at fitting student interests and backgrounds into disciplinary requirements, as he viewed these.

Going through possible topics with Ruth in the fall of 1922, Boas considered her training in literature and her obvious, if unstated, reluctance to do extensive fieldwork. He expected enthusiasm, knowing a subject was better done when done with motivation. The exact balance between Ruth's initiative and Boas's persuasiveness does not matter; sometime in the autumn the two agreed upon a library study of diverse forms of religious experience. Boas had not treated Ruth differently from other students, some of whom shared her appreciation of his attention to personal inclinations, others of whom did not.

Franz Boas expected doctoral students to do fieldwork, but not necessarily for a dissertation. Ruth had made a short trip in the summer of 1922 to visit a Southern California tribe (the Serrano, near Pasadena), but she put aside her field data in order to work on a topic that, in her words, "kindle[d] to light genuine enthusiasm."[54] During the fall she wrote "The Vision in Plains Culture" and there introduced ideas she subsequently elaborated in the dissertation, begun the following spring. In "Vision" Ruth described ecstasy and religious awe and various cultural provisions for transcending self. She structured the argument according to Boasian prescription; the theme came straight out of her own habitual preoccupations.

Under the rubric of diffusionism, Ruth Benedict traced the spread

of "vision" from culture to culture, noting the accommodation of supernatural to social patterns. She amassed data, and isolated incidents that
needed no intervening adjectives: an Indian starving himself into hallu-
cination, another cutting off his finger, a third torturing himself out of
ordinary perception. The writer might have remembered her own childhood tantrums and racking vomiting spells and taken to heart in 1922
the knowledge that one culture's extreme and punished behavior can
be another culture's expected and rewarded behavior. Her last sentences
praised the "indefinite multiplicity" of human experience.

She sent a copy to the *American Anthropologist,* and the professional journal accepted "Vision" immediately.[55] Ruth Benedict had
proven her professionalism. She had also shown she could transform
personal concern into acceptable shape, and she turned to her dissertation.

Once more the varieties of religious experience constituted her
subject, and once more Boas approved. Ruth's dissertation answered his
demand for "the detailed study of particulars,"[56] utilized the diffusion-
of-traits approach, and took anthropology a step closer to the accumulation of "empirical facts" that preceded "lawmaking." Possibly Boas
breathed a sigh of relief at not having to find field money, and Ruth
certainly went off to Low Library with more than relief at her research
site. She read voraciously, pouring through ethnographies, historical
accounts, journals, and travelogues for descriptions of the quest for a
guardian spirit. Beyond her task, Ruth welcomed the chance to find
"another country" in books, a familiar pleasure and occasional compensation for days of relentless note-taking: "Worked in Library 10–6.
Missed lunch till too late. Weary."[57]

In the introductory chapter of "The Concept of the Guardian Spirit
in North America," Ruth Benedict summarized previous literature on
religion and society.[58] The next chapters contained ethnographic data
presented in Ruth's characteristic prose style: precise wording intensified by the writer's perceptible devotion to her subject. Ruth did more
than describe; she attempted to convey to a reader the force of a
vision-experience. This was partly her old idea that fully to comprehend,
a reader must "participate vicariously" in another's experience. When
her own language failed to communicate the "thrill" of an ecstatic
moment, Ruth summoned up lines from myths and from native statements. She sprinkled quotations throughout her descriptive summaries.

There is a surprising amount of feeling in this competent dissertation. Ruth extended the thesis format to portray the power of
religious awe, to evoke the profoundly private aspects of an institutionalized moment of wonder, and to inspire a reader with recognition of

the spiritual impulse common to all mankind. She had learned her teacher's diffusionism and also his abiding concern for the play of ideas in cultural life. In the last paragraph, she extolled man's ability to create the world he lived in; until we see that, "we shall be unable to see our cultural life objectively, or to control its manifestations."[59] She incidentally, and unintentionally, in the dissertation described the poetry she had put aside for science.

Ruth Benedict finished her dissertation in March 1923 and submitted it without exhiliration. "Thursday, March 8. Finished off thesis and mailed it."[60] A similar letdown has been noted by generations of doctoral students. Boas did not ease the situation by claiming that the doctoral dissertation and the examination were "ordinary" events, the first step toward "serious" anthropological research,[61] and he even occasionally forgot to notify a student of results.[62] Ruth's successful completion was greeted by Papa Franz in this spirit, and she missed a defined, even celebrated, achievement: "To Museum for Peru with [Earle Pliny] Goddard—great help."[63]

For Ruth, receiving a doctoral degree had all sorts of ramifications; perhaps she felt a celebration could distract her from doubts and anxieties. As it was, Stanley's warning that "nothing would ever hold her" came back to trouble her. A woman who reportedly thought little about clothes, she tried a conventionally feminine release and after lunch with Goddard went downtown and "bought a suit! Weary—too weary to stay for theater."[64] At home, failure of the Ph.D. to satisfy her "longings" pressed in, and she turned to the journal. She wrote there of the pain of "awareness" and an equal dread of "indifference." She tied her thoughts to a novel, *Many Marriages* by Sherwood Anderson, a book that describes the dominance of love in a man's life: "Only that was an awareness of a life [the love] one could exist in without distaste—And then it seems to me terrible that life is passing, that my program is to fill the twenty-four hours each day with obliviousness, with work—And oh, I am lonely."[65]

Ruth did not record her husband's response to her Ph.D. Her loneliness on March 8 suggests that he either did not respond or did not respond adequately. Stanley Benedict's apparent indifference should be understood in context. His wife herself doubted the significance of this achievement. Partly, too, Stanley Benedict's dispassionate assessment of options warred with Ruth's demand for zest and fulfillment. Partly, as she recognized, her own sense of life was frail: "inconceivable that such a thing as life existed."[66] Typically she distanced her mood with melodramatic phrase.

Ruth and Stanley Benedict had drawn apart in a concrete way.

"It's as if we inhabited the opposing poles— He kept talking about a job for him at California, or for me at Wellesley," she wrote three weeks before finishing the thesis.[67] She had chosen a library topic, grateful not to have to learn an American Indian language. Ruth Benedict also chose library work in order to maintain the fabric of her marriage. She spent weekdays in Manhattan and sometime in 1922–23 rented a room near Columbia from a schoolteacher who needed the apartment only on weekends. On weekends Ruth Benedict went back to Bedford Hills, carrying notecards and drafts with her. That winter Stanley Benedict suggested the two live permanently apart, and Ruth resisted: "S— 'It isn't any laws people need [for divorce]; just the nerve'— He has a fixed idea, and he'll drive me to it—maybe."[68]

Her feelings were confused; in her diary she talked of "home" and referred indiscriminately to the New York apartment and to the house in Westchester. She dreaded being even more lonely without Stanley than she evidently was with him. Stanley Benedict had work that absorbed and pleased him and won colleague approval (if not collegiality). He also, in the mid-1920s, fell in love with another woman. "It wasn't Stanley's romanticizing about another woman that was difficult for me, but the fact that we couldn't get within a thousand miles of each other."[69] By the time she wrote this, part of an extensive self-scrutiny, Ruth and Stanley had probably decided to live apart; the decision was made in 1930, when Ruth had professional confidence, new friendships, and a self-awareness developed in poetry.

"It is only a question of the degree in which the conviction answers to the hungers of that one and only soul, and of the quality of the loyalty that it commands in that soul."[70] She had hoped anthropology would provide a "conviction," and she put a great burden on her discipline to provide the "big things of life."[71] In a poem she spoke more brutally, when she wrote of the monk of Ariège painstakingly copying documents and isolated from sensuous pleasure and "vitality."[72] Through such figures and imagery, the woman might construct her answer. Ruth Benedict revived Anne Singleton, her pseudonymous poetic side—and the sensuous side as well. "Now my best, my best 'that in all my years I tend to do,' is surely writing."[73]

"And you must send me your verses"

On June 25, 1922, Edward Sapir wrote Ruth Benedict a long letter on her "paper," read in "one breath, interrupted by supper, most necessary of distractions, only."[74] The paper was "The Guardian Spirit," her dissertation which would be published in 1923 as *American Anthro-*

pological Association Memoir 29. The letter, full of critical comment and suggestions, initiated a friendship based on the shared vocations of anthropology and poetry and on shared doubts. From 1922 until 1929 Ruth Benedict and Edward Sapir wrote about anthropology and poetry, gossiped and confided, and criticized each other's work. The correspondence was interrupted mainly when Sapir came to New York City, a trip he made frequently from Ottawa, his home from 1910 to 1925.

Edward Sapir was three years older than Ruth Benedict and had received his Ph.D. under Franz Boas in 1909. Boas trained Sapir in linguistic techniques, and Sapir turned the study of language into a precise and passionate exploration of man as a communicative being. But Sapir did not remain content with one approach and tried in various ways to grasp the meaning of human existence. Sometimes the very scope of his subject threw him into despair, a mood intensified for fifteen years by his failure to get a job in an American university. He was a brilliant creative thinker and, by report, a charismatic teacher. Obstacles to institutional affiliation may have been personal (he considered his Jewish background significant) or professional (a rigorous and demanding approach to the discipline). Edward Sapir wrote his 1922 letter to Ruth Benedict from Ottawa, where he was chief of the division of anthropology in the Geological Survey of Canada. In 1925 he was at last able to move, to the University of Chicago, with a cry of relief at being released from the provincialism of a Canadian city.[75] To Ruth he wrote, "My muse has taken a holiday. She doesn't like to have furniture moved into the house."[76] He remained at Chicago until 1931, when Yale University appointed him Sterling Professor and he founded their department of anthropology.

Ruth Benedict soon discovered that her correspondent's depressions stemmed from more than just his pursuit of awesome questions in an uninspiring environment. Sapir's personal life was disrupted by the intermittent madness of his wife Florence Delson Sapir, compounded in 1920 by the insanity of his father for whom he was responsible. The Sapirs came to New York for Florence's treatment and to check on Sapir's father; between visits, Boas seems to have helped out.[77] In the early 1920s, when Ruth Benedict first met Sapir, linguistics seemed one dependable refuge in a world of emotional upheaval: "I really think I shall end life's prelude by descending into the fastnesses of a purely technical linguistic erudition. There is great comfort in withdrawing from the marketplace of so-called human interests and resolutely following a star . . . so pale, so clear, so remote it can bring neither joy nor disappointment."[78]

Sapir, in fact, wrote that in 1925, a year after Florence had died and when he felt particularly marooned in Canada with three young children (Herbert Michael, Helen, and Philip). Five months later he moved; a year later (1926) he married Jean McClenaghan and eventually had two more children (Paul Edward and James David). Sapir wrote about his pleasure in the second marriage and asked Ruth to come visit them in Chicago. She visited once, but never knew Jean or Sapir's second family as well as she knew his first. By the late 1920s the friendship between Ruth and Edward had waned; different interests and inclinations crucially undermined the original basis for intimacy.

The basis for friendship included spoken and unspoken elements: the content of work, anthropological and poetic, but also the ever-present "abyss" of loneliness each feared. They talked of work and of poetry, and of their teacher Franz Boas and various poetry editors. Judging from Sapir's letters and from Ruth's diary notes, they also talked of anxieties and the "hauntings" of futility.

Timing played a part. When Sapir first met Ruth Benedict she had finished a dissertation and was wondering what to make of her "career." She questioned the capacity of anthropology to fill the emptiness left by marriage and, perhaps, to permit a marriage to last, though on terms different from those she set in 1914; "this ardent delight, this transforming love. . . ."[79] Part of her answer lay in turning back to poetry. In 1922 Sapir too was pulled between anthropology and poetry (he added music to the "creative" side of his life) and to all eyes was a man in grief.

"Dr. Sapir came to ask about country boarding places. He wanted me to come to see his wife today—and I went at three."[80] Ruth heard about those aspects of his grief she did not see: "I spoke of Miss R—'s paranoiac trend," she wrote the next day, "and he said, 'It's very easy for me to understand that type of person. It comes naturally.' "[81]

Ruth Benedict told Sapir a great deal by telling him she wrote poetry. For the previous seven or eight years, if she did write verse, she kept it a "precious secret." She told no one of this vocation before 1920, neither friends nor, apparently, her husband.[82] To tell Stanley Benedict constituted a threat, since the images in her verse made vivid the collapse of their relationship:

> . . . and know
> No longer any grief, who go
> Just to see love crucified.
> Down the vain ways where love has died.[83]

Ruth virtually kept the poet from herself, drawing on an array of pseudonyms to keep that part of her life separate. Once she had been "Emily" and with Stanley had been "Edgar Stanhope"; without Stanley she briefly called herself "Ruth Stanhope."[84] And there was a "Sally" who had trouble writing, "who would dictate lines only when it suited her."[85] By 1922 Ruth Benedict settled on "Anne Singleton" and kept the name for nearly ten years. She recalled her grandmother Joanna in "Anne" and conveyed a self-personification in the "single-tone" as she had in the earlier "Stanhope." In the guise of Anne Singleton, Ruth Benedict expressed a self that included "ripeness" and "ecstasy" along with high moral purpose, a self that Stanley Benedict no longer recognized and Edward Sapir would be permitted to know.

"So we grow more and more strangers to the other—united only by gusts of feelings that grow to seem more and more emptiness in our lives, not part and parcel of them."[86] Ruth expressed this pessimism in 1920, after six years of marriage. Diary entries provided one kind of relief, verse another, as she struggled with the "torture" in the relationship with Stanley.[87] She tried, first, to hold in check her "natural medium"—the penetrating poetic image—and to transfer the content into sterner prose, in her journal. Ruth Benedict kept one early poem, written to Rupert Brooke, the poet killed in 1918, until 1923 when she began to use poems to open and close her diary. She addressed the New Year: "I'll walk your desert quite / Self-possessed; / Never Nor once cry pity / At your worst any jest [her crossings-out]."[88]

Absorption in anthropology, paradoxically, led her back to poetry. Ruth Benedict entered a discipline just developing a concern for individual creativeness within cultural constraints. She met colleagues themselves variously engaged in a search for self-expression. She was encouraged at once to learn scientific procedures and to have confidence in her own voice. Edward Sapir, in friendship and in professional writings, argued for the importance of individualized expression. Ruth Benedict responded to his ideas and trusted his friendship—reassured in knowing his private vocations, among them poetry. "No, I have not written any poems lately," he responded to a nudge of hers in the letter about her dissertation.[89]

She appreciated Sapir and was attracted by his anthropological concern for personal creativity, by his poetic pleas for the "release" of "desire"—"Give the mad tonguing play"—and by his involvement with a wife and three children. Ruth Benedict knew Sapir well in his role of father. She saw him through the eyes of Helen, Michael, and Philip and modified their vision with her own. She had much opportunity. When Sapir came to New York he took his wife to doctors, and the children had to be watched. Ruth took on the task: "Helen Sapir's day—paper

dolls in my room; lunch from 'printed menu'; wardrobe of dolls; swim-
ming pool and typewriter."[90] She spent most time with Helen, or at
least wrote most often about this daughter-not-her-own. Her pleasure
in Helen existed free of the dangers inherent in "real" motherhood:
The "make-believe" that "my daughter's life is my own."[91] There would
be no "mocking of dreams" in her feelings for Helen, in Ruth's paraphrase of an idea from George Santayana.[92]

In quite another sense, Ruth Benedict experienced the reality of a
dream with Helen. Her care for a child could be construed as a favor
not as a commitment. Although Ruth became increasingly attached to
Edward Sapir, she still dreaded the "loss of self" in an overwhelming
heterosexual passion. The Mary Wollstonecraft essay provides clarification. The biographer wrote there about the "stalking mischief" of Mary's
ill-considered affair with Gilbert Imlay. She described more straight-
forwardly and appreciatively Mary's love for their daughter Fanny.[93]
Ruth Benedict understood Mary's love for a daughter but not the
circumstances, not her attraction to Imlay. Yet the "passionless" fathering
of Mary Wollstonecraft's second daughter by her husband William
Godwin received no less stern treatment from the biographer.[94]

Still passion had to have a place, though perhaps only distinct
from marriage. Intimacy, tied simultaneously to social convention and
to personal fulfillment, remained problematic for Ruth Benedict.

Helen Sapir gave Ruth pleasure while reawakening anxieties about
her capacity for "full-blooded love."[95] The presence of a child kept
Ruth Benedict from exploring the basis of her tie to Sapir; her concern
for the children justified an intimacy. Similarly, Ruth could explain the
friendship to herself when the two wrote about anthropology or when
they criticized each other's poems. Sometimes these "externals" disappeared and Ruth confronted Edward Sapir face-to-face or, in her
word, "maskless." Then Ruth oscillated between grief at his melancholy
and a snappy impatience at indulgent brooding. "Tonight message
from Dr. Sapir to me through Michael. . . . He looks dreadful. How do
we ever escape the upper and the nether millstones? Anyway he's between them," she wrote in March 1923.[96] Six months later he wrote a
stilted reply to a letter: "Dear Mrs. Benedict. . . . Thanks for your too
kind remarks about the poems."[97] Sometimes when she saw Sapir, Ruth
adopted a nearly adolescent tone: "Saw Dr. Sapir ahead of me at noon,
but suddenly I didn't care whether he looked up or not. He didn't. . . ."[98]
The tone revealed a kind of unresolved intimacy, part of the constant
seesawing characteristic of their relationship.

For Ruth Benedict, in the early 1920s the friendship filled a gap.
She appreciated the contrast between Stanley Benedict and Edward

Sapir; she habitually designed her life around contrasting images. Sapir, too, might have found relief in the change from his wife's volatility to Ruth's calm and quiet demeanor. Existing letters—all his—suggest the two avoided certain aspects of their relationship. Each most comfortably expressed affection around the children or on the subject of a poem or in professional advice. Eventually such distancing mechanisms disappeared, but for the while Sapir's friendship sustained Ruth in her efforts to build a world farther from the "chasm."

The March day Ruth Benedict avoided Edward Sapir she was on her way to Bedford Hills to celebrate Stanley's birthday. That night, like others, turned bad: "The cliff tonight. Nothing could bring life to it."[99] Ruth constructed alternatives and as firmly clung to her belief in steadiness and monogamy—preferably a monogamy of commitment not merely of contract. She envisioned voluntary devotion, and gradually accepted an ideal of loyalty primarily spiritual. This meant relinquishing sexuality, and Ruth did not relinquish easily. She speculated a good deal about her sexual nature: "Stanley finds me sexually undesirable and I've lived with him for five years on that basis. The situation has tended to fixate my interest in him as perhaps a more normal relation might not have."[100] The "fixation" must have affected her attitudes toward Sapir; the poems she sent him were full of lines like

> Beauty has blown
> Her fever through me, and every kiss that died
> On passionate flesh been flame intensified
> Upon the quick in nights I lay alone.[101]

An agreed-upon or assumed restraint deflected their discussion in letters, even when such phrases offered so much information. Edward noted only that the sonnet "is extraordinarily fine, and poignant."[102]

Ruth Benedict argued against her society's notion of monogamy, debating back and forth against the books she read, against her husband, and against herself. Her arguments focused on "loyalty" and the virtues of "faithfulness." She did not take up the subject of close friendship evolving into physical intimacy. Often when she talked of love, Ruth's language acquired an eerie bloodless quality: "To one who has glimpsed a vision of faith in love it is the first step toward any morality of any worth whatever."[103] A few pages after this she also wrote: ". . . Can't get food, that fact's got to be the limit of your horizon. It's just as bad with this other hunger."[104] As long as Ruth kept permanence as her lodestar, a casual affair would not satisfy her craving: "I can't believe that 'free love' is a way out—it seems to me that every chance love's got for dignity and distinction depends on a *belief* in its permanency."[105]

The entries are undated. Ruth Benedict did not fix her thoughts to a particular moment, in her marriage or in her friendship with Edward Sapir. Rather, she made these ideas a running thread through her self-conscious self-interpretations. Out of these musings, too, emerged a picture of Stanley Benedict as cold and rational—a Godwinlike figure. That he could be withdrawn and severe his colleagues noted; this did not blind him to his wife's restlessness. For Stanley Benedict the end of passion meant the end of marriage, and in offering divorce he offered his wife a chance to find fulfillment of her own. Possibly he encouraged her friendship with Edward Sapir, seeing a likely bond between similar natures. The only time he participated in Ruth's anthropology was on January 12, 1923: "S. went to E.S.'s lecture at Cooper Union! !" she noted, doubly exclamatory.[106]

Edward Sapir adopted his own mechanism of approach and withdrawal. Ruth Benedict attached to the last entry in her 1923 diary, describing a visit to Sapir, four poems whose titles told a tale: "At Ending," "The Worst Is Not Our Anger," "For Seed-Bearing," "Of a Great Love."[107]

> . . . Blossomtime shall flaw
> To arid seedbearing, and the hard alien pips
> Be weary consummation of the ecstacy [*sic*]
> She knew on summer mornings.[108]

When Sapir read lines like these from "Seed-Bearing" he as often as not retreated into technical criticism. He talked of her "meter" and avoided the theme.

Or Edward Sapir turned to anthropology and analyzed Ruth from her work. In his first letter to her he anticipated her wariness of psychology and perhaps suspected her dislike of individual psychoanalysis.[109] This kind of character reading, in fact, strained many of his friendships. In 1925, for example, Sapir wrote to Robert Lowie about Lowie's *Primitive Religion*: it is "conditioned by your type of personality as a garden is surrounded by a fence."[110] Ruth tolerated Sapir's insightful metaphors longer than Lowie did.

Through the years of deepening involvement with Edward Sapir, Ruth literally lost touch with her husband. He withdrew from her sensual side: "He rejected me sexually," she wrote in a journal note. And in a poem Anne Singleton played with the resonances of "benedict" and "benediction."

> For I am smitten to my knees with longing,
> Desolate utterly, scourged by your surface-touch
> Of white-lipped wave and unquiet azure hands.[111]

To uncover her sensuality in poetry was to prove she was alive, not caught in numbness.

Under the formal salutation of "Mrs. Benedict," then "Ruth," Edward Sapir understood and addressed Anne Singleton. In 1924 he wrote a poem to "A.S."

> Throw fagots on the fire!
> Give the mad tonguing play,
> Path for the flame's desire,
> Shoulder the smoke away.[112]

Two years later he wrote a poem to the anthropologist. He called it "Zuni" and took his imagery from Pueblo culture. The message was the same:

> Through the dry glitter of the desert sea
> And sharpness of the mesa
> Keep the flowing
> Of your spirit, in many branching ways.[113]

Edward Sapir and Anne Singleton used a similar symbolic idiom; his phrases resembled her own. She wrote:

> Come spring, set torch to tinder, that the flame,
> Not hooded now, not clogged with happiness,
> Lift clean its strong bright limbs. . . .[114]

When Edward took over the imagery, he penetrated behind the persona of Anne Singleton to reach Ruth Benedict. He urged her to banish the separation between selves, and to give up anthropology for poetry if necessary: "It is no secret between us that I look upon your poems as infinitely more important than anything . . . you are fated to contribute to anthropology."[115]

From 1922 through 1929 Edward Sapir and Ruth Benedict focused on the poetry each was tempted to consider more important than anthropology. But they did not ignore their discipline, and gossip about books and professional meetings filled the spaces between literary comments: "I'm sorry you found the Congress [International Congress of Americanists] so dull. Is New York more to your taste? Let me know what's up out there," Sapir wrote.[116] The two as anthropologists also shared a bond to Papa Franz, and his presence loomed over their letters, each one fearing he might scold them both for frivolous poetic pastimes. Do your verse in spite of Boas, Sapir once boldly counseled his friend. Franz Boas, however, was not unsympathetic: "Dr. Boas joined us for dessert—'He'd rather have written a good poem than all the books he'd ever written,'" Ruth noted on January 13, 1926.[117]

Ruth guided the letters to poetry and steered Edward off other matters. She readily, and occasionally eagerly, accepted his comments on poems, remaining wary of his remarks on anthropological points. This was partly the result of affectionate and loyal apprenticeship to Boas and partly because she needed the resonance she received from Edward as a fellow poet. Sapir discussed Ruth's career sometimes with too much supervision. His doubts about anthropology, combined with her "neophyte" status, elicited in him an occasional superior tone of voice: "Take your courage in your hands, mutter loving maledictions at Boas, and come across with a live project—and *you'll get* what you ask for."[118]

Sapir's influence on the content of Ruth Benedict's anthropology would be greatest in the 1930s, when she had the professional confidence to "chart her course" through advice about sources, supplementary readings, and goals. And then the influence came from his papers, not letters or conversations. Meanwhile, through the 1920s Ruth quite deliberately shifted her correspondent from serious disciplinary advice to gossip, sending him tidbits of news about Columbia, the New York group, the American Anthropological Association meetings. Edward continued to make plans for his friend. She continued to resist, and he repeated his advice, softening the pressure with humor: do, "say, a study of the declining, or increasing, mentality of Mayflower stock."[119] Sapir acted out of fondness, familiarity with the ins and outs of grant-getting, and, apparently, out of gnawing anxiety about his own academic success. "I'm constantly being surprised to see how little matters of ambition of that sort concern me."[120]

Edward Sapir respected Ruth Benedict as a professional and accepted her opinions of colleagues, rivals, and their "anthropological fathers." "I should like to meet him [Malinowski]," he told Robert Lowie. "Ruth is quite enthusiastic about him."[121] He profoundly admired Anne Singleton, and without the cynicism born of institutional travails. As poets, neither knew more than the other about the making of a poem or the publishing of a manuscript. In the realm of "creativity" they met, equally novice and similarly skilled, and read and reassured and helped one another. "I wonder if you could take off a little time and run me off four copies on your typewriter, you to keep one? My own typewriter is not in working trim yet, so I must sponge on somebody. Will you be the spongee, my dear and sweet counselor? And you *must* send me your verses," Sapir wrote in 1925.[122]

Poetry, moreover, replaced the clumsiness of talk and of epistolatory prose. Edward Sapir wrote poems to Ruth Benedict; if she responded in kind, the poems are lost. Ruth did write "occasional verses." She had dedicated lines to her mother and grandmother and in the 1920s wrote to friends. She drafted a poem to the soldiers of World War I[123] and honored Rupert Brooke in a sonnet:

> Now God be thanked who took him at that hour,
> Who let him die, flushed in an hour of dreaming.
> Nothing forever shall have any power
> To strip his bright election of its seeming.[124]

The Brooke poem could, in a way, have addressed Sapir. The subjects of achievement and futility, glory and death, were his subjects. They were also, preeminently, Ruth's subjects and finally Edward's empathetic insight frightened and distanced her. To confront by herself thoughts of ecstasy and of death, and the link of these to sexuality—echo of the John Donne she read—was one thing. The quick comprehension Sapir showed made her uneasy.

Ruth Benedict's poems had a disturbingly heightened quality manifested in an eccentric yoking of image to abstraction. Reading a typical line, Sapir turned away and talked "technically" (his apologetic word): ". . . forgive my pedantry a couple of technical animadversions."[125] He criticized her "syllabification," accuracy of detail—and asked Ruth to do the same for his verse. She apparently did: "I really shall obey your dicta—*impliciter*," he promised, after sending one batch.[126]

Toward the end of the decade, Edward increased his insistence that Ruth devote herself to poetry. By then he had stopped writing verse; he relinquished poetry: "Even the [John Crowe] Ransome is only half read, so you see to what abysmal depths I have plumeted."[127] Weary and disillusioned, he urged her to keep writing, experimenting, and submitting manuscripts. He told her to *be* Anne Singleton, even if this meant giving up anthropology: "Zuni myths are important toys, of course, but your verse, even when you're not pleased with it, is a holier toy."[128]

Both had spent time and energy submitting verse, and both were from time to time published. Ruth Benedict kept lists of her submissions: "NR [New Republic], Dial Feb. 28, Century March 7. . . .

Nation or Poetry 3/10/30, Harpers 4/10/30, Nation taken."[129] Small literary journals like *The Dial* and *Poetry,* as well as general magazines like *The Nation,* accepted Anne Singleton's verse throughout the 1920s. Sapir reported his successes in many of the same periodicals. Years earlier, on her postgraduation trip to Chicago (1909–10), Ruth Benedict had met Harriet Monroe. Now, in the 1920s, the influential editor of *Poetry,* Miss Monroe, or as Sapir called her, "Aunt Harriet," became a crucial figure in Ruth Benedict's life. "Harriet and her staff did not respond as cordially as I should have liked to your verse" was only one of Sapir's references to the editor with whom he apparently intervened.[130]

Sometime during that period, encouraging each other along, both Benedict and Sapir decided to collect their poetry into books. They each sent manuscripts out, to Harcourt Brace, A. C. Boni, and Harper's. The whole extended process occupied a great deal of space in letters, and their efforts proved futile. Disillusioned about individual publication, in the spring of 1925 Ruth and Edward talked of doing a poetry anthology and exchanged letters about possible selections. This venture, too, received no support from publishers. The repeated failure to publish turned Sapir decisively away from verse, and his departmental-institutional activities correspondingly increased.

For Edward Sapir, more than for Ruth Benedict, poetry (like music) seemed a supreme expression of man's attempt to comprehend existence—but not when unheard and not, for him, when he doubted his gift.[131] Instead he took over Anne Singleton and worked to perfect her craft. Ever the psychologist, he begged her to overcome the repressiveness that controlled and narrowed her verse. The existing letters do not refer to biographical facts; Sapir focused on Ruth's character and, especially, her self-imposed puritanism:

> Always "Thou shalt not" and "But I will!" Too much of this will bring you to a blind alley. I suspect that what you really need is something like systematic idleness. Are you not allowing yourself to be driven too much? Can't you develop an atrophied conscience? Or rather no conscience at all? Why not let things slide a little and give your fancy a chance? It seems hard to have to say, "Our *task* is laughter."[132]

Edward Sapir's remarks on Ruth's poems had always touched upon the private aspects, not only because he was irrepressibly fascinated by personality but also because her poetry cried out for such interpretation. Whether or not Ruth also talked about the private preoccupations in his verse is not evident. Edward appreciated all she did say and may have welcomed a personal comment or two—the more so when he lost confidence in his gift.[133]

The poems of Anne Singleton and Edward Sapir expressed similar sentiments while differing in form and in rhythm. Sapir, at a moment of self-denigration, noted ruefully that his poems turned to music:

> I strongly suspect that my trouble is that my richest type of expression is potentially a musical one, that my linguistic expression gets its color from rhythms, and the intellectual content of words, but that the subtler feeling value of words and phrases is deficient in me. . . . My unconscious loyalty to music is probably a bar to the subtler sorts of poetic appreciation."[134]

He minded equally the lack of music in Ruth's verse.[135] He caught her on discordant rhythms and shuddered at the "clashes of sound" in some lines.[136] Pattern to Sapir meant harmony, a felicitous "grouping of sound"; Ruth used the same word to mean design, a balance of variegated elements.[137]

Sapir reserved his special praise for Anne Singleton's "unique diction," though not without scrutinizing her specific words: "Look out for your diction, Ruth! You are beginning to use certain words too often (e.g. wisdom; comfort; comforted; comfortable; dream; mocking)."[138] He warned her about being too "precious" and literary, sometimes in gentle false modesty: "What does 'transcience' mean? I feel hopelessly stupid about this finely marching and austere poem."[139] He feared, rightly, that her complicated phrases confused a poem's argument and obscured the emotional content. From poem to poem, and within a poem, Anne Singleton juxtaposed abstract concepts against a concrete detail:

> These lips that lacking you find nothing worth,
> Are so the more deluded, that find dearth
> Where is satiety, and ropes of sand
> Where is the firm-knit earth.[140]

The reader must attend well.

The poet combined an English metaphysical tradition, biblical and Greek mythology, and her own perceptions of landscape. The settings of childhood and of dream, Lake Winnepesaukee, and, by the mid-1920s, the Southwest provided substance for an idea:

> You who have walked the misted meadowlands
> And crushed their petaled colors of bright gold
> And wine surpassing carmines, on a tongue
> Lusting for beauty. . . ."[141]

Ruth also argued and in verse displayed the relentless "morality" Sapir chided her about: "Must everybody contribute his share toward the saving of humanity? That is your faith. . . ."[142]

At the same time Edward Sapir envied Ruth her "rootedness" in an English religious, poetic tradition,[143] a comment on his own conviction of marginality couched in literary-critical comment. Ruth Benedict was not the only poet in the 1920s to take John Donne and metaphysical poetry as her model; she did work particularly hard on the intellectual content—harder than contemporaries who appeared side-by-side with her on the pages of *Poetry* and *The Dial.* Nor did she ease her reader's burden by adopting colloquial phrases, thus distinguishing herself from the women poets of her decade with whom she was often published.[144]

Sapir again caught the distinctiveness of Ruth Benedict's style when he remarked on the importance of etymological associations and connotative meanings and—a perpetual weakness—on the near-unintelligibility of a highly elaborated point. One word persistently annoyed Sapir: "And you're not to use the word 'ecstacy' except on extreme provocation and even then I implore you to spell it 'ecstasy.' 'Ecstacy' is exceedingly offensive to one's classical taste—the Greeks, who made the word, spelled it with an S. . . ."[145] He disliked the false note struck by archaic usages and deliberate obsolescence; his opinion is just.

Everything Edward Sapir said came together in his idea that Ruth Benedict's thoughtfulness, her literary resources, even her "morality," could serve and not suppress the emotional impulse behind her verse. He criticized, and she undoubtedly agreed, the "feminine self-confessional" poetry gaining popularity in the 1920s, but he likewise condemned her own tendency to become "airy" and "bodiless" in verse.

The "woman poet" of the decade, Edna St. Vincent Millay, represented much of what Ruth Fulton Benedict was not. Millay's candid and casual confessions, her easy injection of conversational gambits, her bantering rhythm—all these were foreign to Anne Singleton. Ruth Benedict resembled those of her contemporaries who were schooled in English literature and elegant composition, who believed in rhetoric and demanded seriousness. She may, too, have read George Santayana's verse along with his philosophy. His sonnets, like hers, had the diction of argument rather than of fancifulness and revealed a somber "desire to contemplate man and his destinies."[146]

Ruth also loved a quite different poetry. She had long been attracted to Walt Whitman and to an ego that embraced all humanity, transcending individual self. Edward complained to Ruth about her "careless disregard" of pronouns.[147] In fact, she may have used "he" and "she" interchangeably in order to approach an androgynous vision. Certainly the "he's" in her verse are as much the author as the "she's." She wrote in a poem:

> He could not stand against his spirit's devil;
> Better you leave him in the labyrinth.[148]

Ruth switched from masculine to feminine figures and voices, not to obscure her message but to convey to the reader an inclination, perhaps only a wish, to participate in both visions of the world.

In 1929 Ruth Benedict wrote a review of Robinson Jeffers's "Cawdor." She interpreted Jeffers's vision, like Whitman's, as embracing humanity, transcending the specific self. But she defined Jeffers's mode as tragic, not glorious as Whitman's seemed to be, and she praised Jeffers enthusiastically: "From first to last Robinson Jeffers turns up with his verse the fresh earth of experienced tragedy, the stuff of reality that *Oedipus Rex* must have had in it." And later, in a self-revealing statement, "Supreme validity is given to the passionate demand of the creative artist who fears quiet more than pain, more than degradation, who has known the terrible lapses of inspiration and would choose agony rather than quiet." And she goes on, in sentences Jeffers evidently appreciated. He wrote to her, "But you have explained my meanings more clearly than I could do, and I am most grateful to 'Miss S.' "[149]

The scope of Jeffers's verse, like Whitman's, extended beyond Ruth's classic poetic form. Edward Sapir, by chance or because he knew Ruth's fondness for these poets, told her too to try such open, expansive forms. "I should not waste too much time on the sonnet but go clean into the barer and stronger forms, which best suit your temperament and genius. Let the smoke gradually give way to flame," he wrote. He reiterated the idea, in letters and in poems.[150]

Ruth Benedict had read poetry and literature enough to assess her own talents. She very likely transferred at least some of the critical insight Jeffers and Sapir appreciated to her own verse. How she viewed Anne Singleton's poetry comes through Sapir's letters, and she certainly had mixed feelings about his insistence that she try an "ampler form" and release her expressiveness. Edward failed to convince Ruth to experiment with "blank verse," dramatic narrative, or any other extended form. She realized that her strength lay in controlled and measured verse, that a strict and limited meter allowed her to contain tumultuous emotions. "Contain" was a key notion and the origin of her dominant poetic idiom: brooks between banks, breath within a body, vessels and cups of clay.

The collection of Ruth Benedict's poetry reveals a repetitiveness in concept and in vocabulary. To the extent that she could not argue away or objectify her experiences, Ruth tended to go over the same ground, often becoming "lofty and Parnassian" before hitting upon a precise imagistic vehicle. Taken separately her poems have a forcefulness, stemming from a clear moral conviction about human frailty. It would be fair to conclude that Ruth's poetry replaced her religion, even as it expressed her sensuous side. The best poems did both. Then, in true metaphysical fashion, a tension between principle and passion unified a line of verse:

> Throw slack the reins, and keep no memory
> Of foolish dreams we dreamed of ripened corn
> In barns, and red fire on the hearth. Be free
> As unicorns, that are but fantasy. . . .[151]

At its best the poetry of Anne Singleton displayed a classical purity and disciplined cadence—the argument conveyed through sharp detail. Ruth Benedict always selected "worthy themes" and never trivialized her point or her gift with easy sentimentalism; "sweet love and my baby," Sapir described current, popular verse. At its weakest, Anne Singleton's poetry sounds distraught and self-consciously philosophic. The diction becomes an embarrassing foil for unanalyzed thoughts and emotions. An ongoing conflict between "reason" and "desire" led to half-exposure, half-closure that strained her language and discomforted her readers. Editors like Harriet Monroe and Louis Untermeyer, and Edward Sapir himself, were made uneasy by her verse partly because confession lay close to the surface and control tightened into hysteria.

Sapir hinted at the danger of "coyness" in her writings: the archaic verbal forms, the outmoded rhetorical devices, and, above all, the pseudonym. He did not dislike the name under which Ruth Benedict published poems. He disliked the whole idea: "Pen names are an abomination. You know how I feel about even toying with the idea of dissociation of personality. I hate it. Lie outright if you have to, but for God's sake don't stylize the lie into a pretty institution."[152] Sapir always objected to Ruth's need for disguise, but sometimes sympathetically. When the opportunity came to publish a poem written to her, he offered to dedicate it to "E.B." for Emily Benedict, rather than to Ruth Benedict, "to which you object."[153] But he knew the psychological implications of "dissociation" of self and suspected that masking warped her poetic gift. He urged Ruth to speak out and, primarily, to reconcile aspects of her being.

Sapir proved right, and her precious distinction collapsed. Poetry editors discovered the secret. Aunt Harriet knew in 1926 who Anne Singleton was, and a 1930 anthology attributed the poems of Anne Singleton to a "well-known anthropologist." In 1930 Ruth Benedict herself asserted, after seeing the anthology (*Modern American Poetry,* edited by Louis Untermeyer): "When he gets out another edition they'll [the poems] be under the name of Ruth Benedict; I won't be so bepseudonymed."[154] By 1930 her relationships with both Edward Sapir and Stanley Benedict had changed.

Through the decade Edward spoke without hesitation about the dangers of separating one aspect of self from another. Ruth had, in her poetry, described the agonizing split between "sensuality" and "reason." Sapir took up the point and reworded it for her in his prose, in letters, and in conversation. He shed the sharp light of analysis on matters she intentionally left obscure in the rhetoric of her verse. The two moved apart, inevitably. Ruth could not long bear Edward's pointed inquiries. Possibly, too, she minded and regretted the submergence of his pure intellect in the petty details of professional advantage. She retreated, and Sapir remarked on the distance: "When can we all get together again?" he wrote in October 1928; "I resent these distances and the hasty sketchiness of our meetings. Life should be completer. . . ."[155]

Ruth Benedict did not explain her withdrawal, and during that year an excuse came to hand virtually to break off communications. The two quarreled over an article Edward wrote on sexual frigidity in American women.[156] Ruth apparently took certain points personally; Sapir denied having her in mind:

> That you would not care for my sex article I took for granted,
> . . . but that you were outraged by a supposed quotation
> shocked as few things have shocked me. . . . You will not be-
> lieve me—yet it is the sober truth—when I say that you were
> never once in my thoughts when I wrote the paper on sex.[157]

Yet she knew how many Anne Singleton poems he had read and interpreted, poems with titles like "Winter of the Blood" (he had advised her not to use that phrase for the title of a collected volume), "Withdrawal," "Counsel for Autumn," and "Burial." He had read too many stanzas like

So at the winter of the blood we straighten
Our limbs to quiet, crying flesh to find
Oblivion as foxes, sun-forsaken
Deaf and dumb and blind.[158]

Sapir knew Ruth very well, and their communication never utterly ended. Among Ruth Benedict's papers as Vassar College is one file box, in it folders of Sapir manuscripts: his poetry.

In 1925 Ruth Fulton Benedict gave Stanley Benedict a volume of verse to read. She stuck postage stamps over the names of authors, then asked him to pick out her poems. He found every one, with perfect accuracy. She had decided to let Stanley Benedict know Anne Singleton and to unify the two selves—a goal she desired and did not need Sapir to urge on her. Ruth expressed pleasure at Stanley's recognition of her "character" behind stamps and poetic metaphors. She regained her optimism about their relationship. But he surely had been pained by the self-revelations in the poetry he read. Ruth Benedict underestimated how high she had already built the walls between "Mrs. Benedict" and the "well-known anthropologist who also writes poems."[159]

Ruth Fulton in 1887. A portrait taken in Norwich, New York. (Courtesy of the Vassar College Library)

Ruth and Margery Fulton, photographed by Heinxelman's Art Studio, Owatonna, Minnesota. Ruth is approximately ten years old, Margery eight and a half years old. (Courtesy of the Vassar College Library)

Ruth (upper right) at home in Norwich, with Grandfather Shattuck, the Fulton sisters, and younger family members; between Vassar and her marriage. (Courtesy of the Vassar College Library)

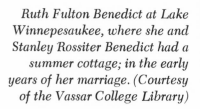

Ruth Fulton Benedict at Lake Winnepesaukee, where she and Stanley Rossiter Benedict had a summer cottage; in the early years of her marriage. (Courtesy of the Vassar College Library)

Ruth Benedict at Lake Winnepesaukee with her mother, Beatrice Fulton, and her husband, Stanley Benedict. (Courtesy of the Vassar College Library)

Stanley Rossiter Benedict, in his office at Cornell University Medical School, about 1929. (Courtesy of the Medical Archives, New York Hospital-Cornell Medical Center)

Ruth Benedict, mending socks in the Benedicts' Bedford Hills house. A picture probably taken by Stanley, an avid amateur photographer. (Courtesy of the Vassar College Library)

Edward Sapir, linguist, anthropologist, poet. (Courtesy of Philip Sapir)

A Bachrach portrait of Ruth Benedict, one of several formal sittings Ruth had as a prominent anthropologist. (Courtesy of Vassar College Library)

Ruth Benedict in her office at Columbia University. A picture taken by fellow anthropologist Helen Codere. (Courtesy of the Vassar College Library)

Ruth on her 1939 fieldtrip, with two members of the Blackfoot tribe. (Courtesy of the Vassar College Library)

6
The Anthropologist

"It was Dr. Benedict who communicated to me a sense of urgency . . ."

SOON AFTER SHE ARRIVED at Columbia, Ruth Benedict found herself caught up in a time-consuming, encompassing "endeavor." Not only did she take classes, she also ended up teaching seminars and guiding graduate students who were not much behind her in their careers. Ruth became, inevitably and increasingly, an essential part of the Columbia program and moved further from the Bedford Hills routine of cleaning house, cooking, and maintaining ties with Stanley Benedict's family. (Agnes Benedict did remain one of Ruth's close friends.) Playing "Go Bang" in the evenings alternated with, then gave way to, disciplinary tasks: editing papers, translating Spanish words from myths collected among Southwest Indian tribes, working on vision quest material for her dissertation and first publication.

Franz Boas took advantage of Ruth's eagerness and asked her to teach his classes when other obligations pressed upon him, as they often did. Ruth did not record her responses to teaching anthropology or to working with graduate students. Her previous classroom experience had been in private schools, all girls and adolescents whose determined conventionalism kept them from embracing the literature she taught. Columbia in the 1920s had a different sort of student—older, more confident, less completely committed to American conventions. One of these, Margaret Mead, came to Columbia at approximately the same time Ruth did, though as an undergraduate and fourteen years younger than Ruth. Not at first in the anthropology program, Margaret was also not as discontented with American society as were some of Ruth's colleagues and students.

In 1920 Margaret Mead transferred to Barnard from DePauw

143

College (Indiana) to be near Luther Cressman, the man she planned to marry. During her senior year Margaret enrolled in an anthropology course taught by Franz Boas and his teaching assistant Ruth Benedict. Mead immediately took to the subject—"the development of men from their earliest beginnings"—but the professor frightened her as much as he had other new Columbia students.[1]

Ruth Benedict was Boas's teaching assistant. "She was tentative and shy and always wore the same dress."[2] Margaret set herself the task of "drawing out" Mrs. Benedict. She also propagandized anthropology courses, giving Ruth the mixed blessing of doubled enrollment and busier office hours. Ruth eventually acted on Margaret's abundant, and voiced, enthusiasm for anthropology. In the spring of 1923 she urged Mead, then a graduate student in psychology, to switch to anthropology for her Ph.D. degree. Behind Ruth's hesitant manner lay the clear conviction that anthropology had superlative potential for serving mankind. "Professor Boas and I have nothing to offer but an opportunity to do work that matters," she told Mead, and won the younger woman's devotion.[3]

The teacher herself had only begun to suspect the significance of anthropology in her life. Margaret Mead started a step ahead; anthropology courses, she wrote, fit a family interest in cross-cultural studies.[4] Beyond the specific impulse toward social science, Mead had been generally encouraged to pursue her intellectual interests wherever these led.

Margaret Mead has described her childhood, pampered, loved, and admired from her birth in 1901.[5] Her father, Edward Mead, pushed the firstborn "original punk" into successive achievements, and several generations of professional women in the family left no doubt about a woman's capacities. Margaret expected to combine vocational achievements with love, marriage, and children, and she had reason for optimism. The year she began graduate work in anthropology she married Luther Cressman, a high school classmate. (Cressman, studying for the ministry, eventually shifted to sociology and then anthropology. In 1929 he went to the University of Oregon to teach first in the department of sociology, then in anthropology.) Margaret Mead wanted to have children—at least six—after she finished her degree.[6]

Ruth saw in Margaret Mead a woman starting out on "the adventure" and apparently determined to "chart her own course." Margaret also, gratifyingly, asked to be taught, advised, and socialized into the discipline. Her unabashed enthusiasm bolstered Ruth's confidence: She could teach students anthropology and she could communicate the virtues of comparison as a way of understanding one's own society.

By 1923 Ruth had finished her dissertation and she turned her attention to student work. Diary entries reveal the extent to which she concentrated on the anthropology students at Columbia, but Margaret Mead was an exception. Margaret quickly passed from one of many lunch appointments to a special category, vying mainly with Edward Sapir for space in Ruth's daily schedule. "Margaret lunch" and "After seminar talk with Margaret Mead about her future" are only the written-down references to their meetings. Departmental activities buoyed Ruth's spirits, and Mead added emotional intensity to a contentment Ruth greeted cautiously: "Heaven send it lasts!"[7] The combination gave Ruth the temerity to interfere in another person's plan. "Lunch with Margaret Mead—discussed her going into anthropology. I hope she does it."[8]

The merging of professional and personal in their relationship had qualities at once unique to the two women and typical of the Columbia department in those years. When Ruth first met Margaret she focused on the academic contact and on the student who asked persistent questions. Mead seemed an ideal student. "She was intrigued by anthropology and read omnivorously," Ruth recalled. "I used to meet her on the campus with dictionary-sized monographs under her arm that were almost as big as she was."[9] Margaret played the part of perfect student apparently without embarrassment, asking questions in class, doing extra reading, and following Ruth Benedict from seminar room to office. "Another section 3:30; Margaret Mead waited afterward."[10]

Margaret Mead proved the effectiveness of Ruth's style of teaching, one that depended upon recognition by each student of the emotional component in a reasoned inquiry. For Ruth teaching was a mutual exchange, resulting in new point of view and behavior for teacher and pupil. Her impatience at the apathy she saw in students at Miss Orton's contrasted to her pleasure at the active enthusiasm of students like Margaret. With Margaret, too, an exchange of anthropological insight turned into a permanent personal intimacy.

Ruth's pedagogy, grounded in her experiences as a child, a student, and a teacher, also had backing in contemporary theories of education. Once, in 1923, she gave a seminar on John Dewey's *Human Nature and Conduct*. Not a specific pedagogical treatise, the book does contain phrases that resonate to and probably validated Ruth's understanding of education. Margaret Mead, and others, heard phrases like "intellect-grounded-in-passion" and recognized a partial source of Ruth Benedict's approach.[11] From Dewey, Ruth borrowed the idea of passion-yoked-to-reason and, another significant element in her teaching, the notion of "inner conviction" for the "true" comprehension of "fact."

Margaret Mead was perceptive and carefully watched her teacher-turned-friend. At the same time, Ruth began to reveal more of herself to others. When the two women first met, common circumstances outweighed differences in personality and in status, drawing them together. In Edward Sapir, Ruth had found a kindred spirit and a disconcerting psychological acuteness; in Margaret she found a person different in temperament but sharing with her a debate over the "woman issue." The two women had each fully embraced anthropology, but each still debated the ways of reconciling devotion to a career with devotion to marriage and (future) motherhood. Margaret intended to have six children; she would not forego the experience of being a mother.

For a while too, Margaret, like Edward Sapir and Ruth Benedict, wrote and published poetry. Not as serious in this as the others, Margaret yet practiced the craft with determination and, typically, with a group of fellow poets. Margaret Mead talked about her poetry before Ruth mentioned hers.[12]

Sometime in 1923–24 Margaret Mead introduced Ruth Benedict to her "poetry group," which included Leonie Adams, Louise Bogan, and Eda Lou Walton. Around that same time, a favor returned, Ruth introduced Margaret to her poet friend, Edward Sapir. "It's such a satisfactory friendship," Margaret later wrote to Ruth, "defaced by no tiresome preliminaries (that's thanks to you) and founded on such sure ground of likemindedness."[13] Ruth, perhaps with the self-mocking smile of some of her photographs, joined Margaret's group and exchanged her verse with women who became prominent poets of the twentieth century. The exchange of criticism, comment, and comfort sustained Anne Singleton, though also producing an unfortunate derivativeness in some lines.[14]

Another exchange developed simultaneously among Edward Sapir, Margaret Mead, and Ruth Benedict, involving every aspect of Ruth's life and not just the "be-pseudonymed" half. For almost four years the three poet-anthropologists moved through an intricate choreography of intimacies. They expressed emotions in published and unpublished verse, and through rhetorical devices each considered and reinterpreted terms of friendship even as these terms changed in everyday interaction.

In 1925 Edward Sapir dedicated a poem to Margaret Mead:

> Of the heedless sun are you an Ariel,
> Rising through cloud to a discovered blue,
> The windy, rocking landmarks travel through
> And clamber up a crazy pinnacle.[15]

Ruth Benedict wrote to Mead the next year:

> He smiled, knowing the gray
> And dusty journey for the same
> Man saw unwinding through the stars;
> Himself no less infinity
> Than they.[16]

The closeness of theme and of imagery demonstrated how thoroughly the three had become intertwined and how well they knew each other by mid-decade. The poetic statements presupposed hours of conversation, letters, and comments on professional and private writings. Sapir's poem, "Ariel," was published in *Voices* (1925) and Ruth's "This Gabriel" was published in *Palms* (1926). Mead published several poems to Ruth:

> Curve those tense hands so tightened in disdain,
> To eager chalices for falling rain.
> Break and elaborate that frozen line
> With golden tendril and swift sinuous vine.[17]

The same few, small poetry journals accepted verse from Edward Sapir, Margaret Mead, and Anne Singleton. Sapir stopped sending manuscripts when his sense of futility overwhelmed any residual optimism about his talents. Mead claimed she stopped submitting poetry when she learned she was being published as an anthropologist not a poet. Ruth persisted, using metaphor and meter to express her preoccupations after her friends had stopped. Too, she worked on her craft more conscientiously, almost more desperately, than the other two.

All three had used poetry to communicate matters otherwise left unsaid, about fear and love, dread and yearning. All three expressed in images and poetic figures a sense of the human dilemma, Edward Sapir and Ruth Benedict with somewhat more fatefulness and horror. Death struck a clearer chord in their poetry than in Margaret Mead's verse. By the end of the decade, however, poetic conversation shifted. Edward Sapir, absorbed in a new family and new job, grew distant, while Margaret and Ruth struggled together over collapsing marriages and uncertain vocational status.

A death, in fact, had cemented the intimacy between Ruth and Margaret. On February 7, 1923, soon after they met, Marie Bloomfield, a graduate student at Columbia (and sister of the linguist Leonard Bloomfield) committed suicide after a severe illness. The event upset Ruth not only by its immediate horror but because suicide recalled her own speculations about the "gift" and the "torment" of life. "Marie Bloomfield's suicide in papers. It's unbearable that life should be so hard for them [students or women; unclear]. I know it's all wrapped up with my wish for children—and dread that they might not want the gift."[18] Margaret Mead came to comfort Ruth. "She came to my room before bedtime."[19] Mead added, nearly half a century later, that Ruth "was the one person who understood that suicide might be noble and a conscious choice."[20] Margaret may not have known in 1923 the attraction suicide held for her friend, not unless she had already seen Anne Singleton's verse and detected the woman behind the screen of metaphor:

> We weary of the earth, its madrigal
> Of still-renewing autumns, and the sky
> Spread as an azure curtain on the heavens,
> Marking our sight its confines.[21]

The friendship between Ruth Benedict and Margaret Mead flourished along with a growing professionalism and was expressed in verse, letters, nonstop conversations. The years of writing poetry coincided with learning to be anthropologists for both teacher and student, and no one at Columbia particularly noticed the deepening bond between the two women. Boas appreciated and encouraged a personal basis for intellectual collaboration, and Ruth and Margaret each deferred to his strictures for practicing the discipline. All in all the friendship made few ripples in Columbia's corridors. Close ties had become part of the curriculum: students shared books and offices, meals and rooms, lent beds for the night and apartments for the week. A constant interaction characterized the Columbia experience throughout the 1920s and 1930s.[22]

Ruth and Margaret eventually so intertwined their anthropological ideas that they were—or claimed they were—unable to distinguish the source of a significant argument. Moreover, conversations about anthropology went on in the midst of other conversations, about marriage and children, money and autonomy, the problems of finding enough hours in a day to talk, read, write, and enjoy oneself. In many ways Ruth was the more deliberate and cautious thinker, and whether or not she liked it, she did assess an idea slowly, circling around an insight and exploring the boundaries and implications of an intellectual discovery. Margaret Mead swooped more quickly and confidently upon an idea, often taking an issue the two had mulled over and rewording it for wide, popular appeal. But that too—the ability to express anthropology effectively—Margaret had learned with Ruth. Because so much was shared, with such compatibility, Ruth did not feel the envy and irritated dislike evident in some of her relationships. As much as Margaret needed Ruth, Ruth needed the admiring, enthusiastic student. Ruth helped Margaret sift through her enthusiasms; Margaret buoyed and bolstered Ruth's all too frail contentment, turning melancholy away with a sharp question about work.

In 1925 Margaret decided she must take a fieldtrip, but she did not want to work with a North American Indian tribe—Boas's usual prescription for students and especially for the women at Columbia. Margaret wanted to go to the South Pacific and live with people she had so far only read about. (Mead, like Ruth, eventually did a dissertation that drew heavily on library materials. She finished her thesis, "An Inquiry into the Question of Cultural Stability in Polynesia," in 1928.) Boas did not approve of the Pacific plan. Margaret was too young, too frail, too vulnerable to travel across the world by herself, he wrote to Edward Sapir and to Ruth Benedict.[23] There ensued a four-way discussion, by mail and in person, though Sapir withdrew after his initial insistence that "Margaret was too nervous to go."[24] Mead argued the value of her project (culture change), Ruth Benedict the "stamina" of her student, and Boas the "risks" of the whole project. To argue Mead's case required that Ruth not only announce her commitment to the younger woman but also uphold her ideal of the professional woman.

Boas did not make a rash, ill-considered, or sexist judgment when he advised against the trip. In 1924–25 Margaret Mead did seem vulnerable; she was tiny and thin and had been sick sporadically during graduate school. She continued to have what Ruth called "spells" after she came back from the field; if Ruth's 1928 diary is any guide to earlier years, Boas in fact showed the better part of wisdom. "Margaret Mead sick," "Margaret here. Sick." These and similar entries dominated several months of Ruth's diary from 1928 to 1930.[25]

As her teacher, however, Ruth Benedict insisted that the fieldtrip in 1925 would do Margaret Mead more good than harm and that to keep her home might damage her health. "Sapir has written me his anxiety about Margaret's going, and I am trying to reassure him," Ruth wrote Boas. "It would certainly seem to me disastrous to stop her. She was most enthusiastic.—But it is her lack of physical resistance I am really troubled about, and fortunately that is something about which she can be quite frankly warned."[26] Ruth persuaded Papa Franz and herself at the same time that Margaret possessed boundless will and "common sense."[27] Mead contributed to Boas's change of mind by agreeing to do the study Boas suggested, of adolescent girls in Samoa. Edward

Mead made the decision practicable by offering to pay expenses (he had reneged on a promised "world tour" when Margaret married Luther Cressman).

Ruth supported Mead's trip for several reasons. She hardly needed to stress the importance of fieldwork, since Mead couldn't wait for a "tribe of her own."[28] To do fieldwork, both recognized, meant to become a "real" anthropologist. More than that, traveling to the other side of the world, alone, established Mead's professionalism and announced her willingness to stand on principle whatever the emotional costs. This spirit appealed to Ruth Benedict and had from the days she called Mary Wollstonecraft's "the story of a life that achieved an idea."[29]

When Ruth encouraged Margaret to make the trip, her encouragement extended the influence she had already had on the young woman's life. Ruth influenced Margaret without fear of suppressing her own desires and without fear of too thoroughly molding Margaret to an idealized image. The first fear related to Ruth's thoughts about having a child; she might give up her own wishes and demands if a daughter could satisfy those wishes. The second fear came from a less explicitly stated concern about molding other people's personalities, in love and in well-meant instruction. But Margaret was strong-minded, purposeful, in command of her direction and goals. She knew when and how to ask for advice from mentor and friend. Margaret's character offset Ruth's fears and her reluctance to involve herself in another's decisions. So did the fact that the two in many ways faced exactly the same situation, a need to balance professional and personal pressures.

There was always something of a mother-daughter bond in Ruth's feelings for Margaret. Partly, both saw in that bond a perfect expression for the inspiration, instruction, and nurturing within a friendship between women. Partly, by assimilating theirs to a mother-daughter bond Ruth and Margaret distinguished it from other commitments, according the friendship unique traits and a "natural" permanency. To this they added reciprocity and a complementarity of temperament. The notion of mother and daughter came to represent not a fixed pattern or specific roles but an accurate and useful description of intimacy. "Mother-daughter" offered a vocabulary for their love, without threatening either one's self-image as a woman in American society and without violating the standards for friendship set by a probably judgmental culture.

Margaret wrote, retrospectively, about her own vision of the "perfect pupil," a student obviously and utterly *hers*.[30] An eagerness to instruct, to inform, and to mold character merged pedagogy and parenthood for Margaret Mead. Ruth saw the parallel between teacher and mother a bit more uneasily, but she too eventually merged a desire for children into an attitude about instructing and advising a "next generation." As it became less likely and finally certain that she would not have a child, Ruth converted her dream of the "perfect daughter" into a vision of ideal friendship—mutual, intellectual, and passionate. "Daughter" stood for the child she never had and for the kind of woman she most admired; described in her journal, this woman—younger and a new generation—possessed "abilities which shall find scope" and an "insight that shall be true and valid; it is she who owes it to speak out her beliefs."[31] Ruth described here both a future possibility and an immediate source of personal pleasure. Abstractly, "daughter" stood for woman's potential, for the likelihood of combining career, love, and a quiet domesticity. "Daughter" became equivalent to a faith in the future, a weapon against despair. Ruth advised Margaret, alone in Samoa, to try "playing you're your own daughter" when fieldwork turned tiresome, hopeless, and dreadful.[32]

Ruth's letters to Margaret Mead demonstrate the extent to which circumstances modified the contours of a projected mother-daughter relationship. The friendship shifted and changed, depending upon each woman's professional efforts and academic positions. A shared discipline profoundly affected their private feelings.

In the spring of 1925, when Margaret prepared to leave for the South Pacific, Ruth gave her a book of poetry. Ruth had put the collection together herself, a specially bound volume of Anne Singleton verse. "I am glad you know how much of me is shut into your book of verses," Ruth wrote on August 25. "I shall delight in having you feel me speaking them to you. Will you do one thing?—jot down the verses you wish you had or the ones that haunt you brokenly, and I'll send them to you."[33] Ruth communicated through verse a love that ran a strong undercurrent to sensible professional advice. Margaret received doses of advice from Papa Franz, but less reassurance than she craved on the first fieldtrip; five- and six-page letters back and forth from Samoa to Manhattan were not unusual.[34] Ruth advised, and she actively reassured: "But I know there is no clear-sightedness nor course of reasoning that will help—you have that already. God bless you . . . and make life easier for you."[35]

Ruth also sent packages of books, journals, and poems to the South Pacific, as good a field guide as any for a fieldworker instructed to feel "comfortable." She underlined the writings she sent, a certain way of making her presence felt in Samoa. She also wrote faithfully—not a habit of hers—to be sure Margaret did not lack contact for long.[36] (Boas had chosen Samoa for Mead because a steamer went there every three weeks.[37])

Ruth Benedict recorded on January 1, 1926, "2 A.M. 2 hour letter to Mead."[38] She had spent the evening before, New Year's Eve, with Edward Sapir. The one intimacy reminded her of another, and almost in rebound from Sapir's problematic affections, Ruth turned to a predictable, nonstressful friendship. She portrayed Margaret thus, restful, comforting, soothing: "She rests me like a padded chair and a fire place."[39] The "padding" suggested less Mead's physical bearing than her psychological state, her reassuring confidence, youthfulness, and admiration of Ruth Benedict: "I say it's the zest of youth I believe in when I see it in her. Or is it that I respond understandably to admiration?"[40]

Ruth harbored uncertainties about her capacity for love and friendship, evident even in remarks about Margaret. For Ruth, love and commitment entailed risk, and in moments of gloom she grew anxious about the permanency of any relationship. Her greatest need, she said, was to express herself, yet this involved exposure, and she chose to voice love through concern about practical matters. Five days after the New Year's night letter to Margaret, a tornado struck the South Pacific. Seven anxious days passed before news came from Margaret. "Letter at 10 A.M. from Mrs. Mead referring to tornado in Samoa. Telephoned everywhere and could find no news. . . . Sent cable for Dr. Boas to Margaret—asking for reply."[41] Anthropological activities distracted Ruth until her palpable relief on January 12 when Boas telephoned. "A telephone from Dr. Boas when I got home at 10:30— Margaret cables 'Well.' I sent telegrams to the Meads and to Marie [Eichelberger], and took hot bath like a ritual."[42] Ten days later Ruth herself got a simple telegram. "Home, and a cable from Margaret 'Love.' "[43]

Ruth Benedict and Franz Boas would have worried about any student in danger on a fieldtrip, and parents had been involved before and after Mrs. Mead. Ruth's restrained responses in her diary reveal little more than expectable concern, only the "hot bath" gives her away. How much she said directly to Margaret, then or afterward, cannot be known. Ruth never dared relinquish all privacy, and she kept parts of her life even from the woman she trusted and loved.

Margaret Mead spent time with Stanley Benedict once, tellingly on a visit to New Hampshire. (Another time when Mead arrived unexpectedly, Stanley Benedict hid in the barn—or so Margaret reported[44]). Mead rarely encountered either Bertrice Fulton or Margery Fulton Freeman. There were problems of geographical distance; beyond this, Ruth wanted Margaret mainly to see the childhood and young womanhood she had created over the years. Ruth asked Margaret to respect her points of view and self-interpretations and not to probe too closely. Mead accepted the picture Ruth presented, in anthropology, in poetry, and in 1935 in a brief autobiographical statement. Like Ruth, Margaret detected changes in a person by observing variations in gesture and demeanor; she read Ruth's moods from her face and physical appearance. In the summer of 1926 the two women met in Rome. Ruth had spent the summer with Stanley Benedict (in Europe for meetings), and Margaret was on her way to meet Luther Cressman after a year apart. Margaret described Ruth then as dejected; she had cut her hair short and a "helmet" of gray surrounded a pale and drawn face. Mead saw beauty in the image, the beauty of a tragic heroine not an energetic, contented woman.[45]

Ruth herself tried to ignore appearance and to convey her moods in sharp, verbal details. A metaphor, a striking figure, conveyed the spirit and the contained "animal vitality" of the woman. Ruth drew a self-portrait in verse, and the poems Margaret saw she read carefully and sensitively. In verse, too, Ruth conveyed her view of this friendship and its difference from other relationships. Poetic intensity was punctuated by stark notations in Ruth's diary: "Margaret Mead here," "Margaret Mead overnight"—by the end of the 1920s the two spent a good deal of time together.

Poetry, appointments, intellectual exchanges—these served to obscure and to protect intimacy from the pressure of social conventions, a pressure Ruth considered threatening to the "dignity and beauty" of any love.[46] She had drawn an ideal friendship in the Mary Wollstonecraft essay and possibly projected the interpretation onto her feelings for Margaret Mead five years later. In the World War I essay, Ruth compared a friendship between two women to the passion between a woman and a man and to a "reasonable" marriage. "The most vivid experience of her girlhood was her friendship for Fanny Blood," Ruth wrote about Mary Wollstonecraft. "Until she was past thirty it was her only adventure in romance. Mary was sixteen, Fanny but two years older, when they met; and from that time until long after Fanny's death ten years later, this friendship was, in Godwin's words, 'so fervent as to be the ruling passion of her mind.' It had a momentous influence upon her."[47] Mary Wollstonecraft named her daughter after her best friend.

The biographer did not speculate about sexual passion between Mary Wollstonecraft and Fanny Blood. Ruth applied the word "romance" to the friendship not to imply sexuality but to convey an absolute and permanent devotion. In her view, the bonds between Mary Wollstonecraft and Fanny Blood transcended physical passion;

loyalty had other sources. She argued the point in her journal, wanting sensuality to be the "natural" (animal) counterpart of "spiritual" affinity.[48]

In the biographical essay, Ruth Benedict revealed a greater comprehension of the tie between Mary Wollstonecraft and Fanny Blood than she did of the undertow of eroticism in Mary Wollstonecraft's love for Gilbert Imlay. Ruth often used water imagery; she described Mary Wollstonecraft's love for Imlay as a "floodtide"—the essence of heterosexual passion was to be out of control, violent, destructive. (By contrast, Ruth Benedict wrote in verse of "still pools" and reflecting ponds, for a different love affair.[49]) Sexuality eroded the fidelity pledged by Imlay and Wollstonecraft.

The idea that sexuality, specifically heterosexuality, undid the "whole self" persisted in Ruth Benedict's writings. She showed vividly how Mary Wollstonecraft's cogently argued and desperately lived feminist principles collapsed immediately when she met the "charming" Imlay. Ruth implied an analogous giving-in when she wrote about her mother and sister. She did not wholeheartedly approve of either marriage and seemed sometimes discomforted by the evidence of sexuality in a "trail of children"[50] and in excessive touching. The idea that her mother and her sister had abandoned self dominated Ruth's judgments, despite the fact that both women maintained a career more or less alongside family.

Ruth Benedict did not argue against passion or against sexuality. She wrote about her mother and her sister in order to understand her own passions. Much that she said about the marriages—her parents', her sister's, and her own—explained her relationship to Margaret Mead. Ruth linked the several intimacies together under a notion of choice.

Marriage, the customary permanent union between two individuals in her society, constrained and compelled sexual expression. For Ruth marriage represented an imposed bond and a restricted sensuality. Her own marriage testified to the impossible meshing of conventional contract and an eager sensuality. That marriage affected a woman particularly prompted Ruth into an uncharacteristic directness. Marriage forced a woman into dependence upon a man, and Ruth meant "spiritual" not economic dependence. She did not ever consider economics the crucial point. Altogether the conclusion was inescapable: Marriage denied a woman expression of her sensual nature and of her spiritual goals. And what good was one without the other, Ruth cried in her journal, not knowing the difference a child would have made.[51]

An alternative lay in perfect friendship, and, to be free of the "force of custom," a friendship between women. Ruth developed a theme implicit in much of her writing; constraints on expression destroyed the bonds between individuals. In debating the "woman issue" and a woman's chance for "fulfillment," Ruth never dismissed love. On the contrary, passion remained a powerful current next to her intellectual ambitions. By the time Ruth met Margaret Mead, she had somewhat turned from the purple prose of journal to the cool metaphysics of a sonnet in order to delineate her "lavish expense of spirit."[52] She had begun expanding the expression of her own sensuality when Mead came, a confident, enthusiastic, open-minded woman. The resulting intimacy was not legislated and therefore not limited. Spared notice, the friendship escaped the "world's thumb and finger." No one judged its enactment.

Ruth simultaneously recognized the difficulties and the constraints on women's options. She daydreamed of nonconventional love, but she never tore down the "four walls of reality." Poetry became both the necessary and the liberating mode of communication. In verse she tried to achieve the multifaceted passion she admired in Walt Whitman and Robinson Jeffers. Poetry challenged Ruth's capacity to embrace experience, to open her eyes to her surroundings, and to expose herself to diverse sensations. Her poems do not describe love for one woman, but talk of love itself.

> I lie so in quiet at your breast,
> And, mailed in certitude, entreat our loves
> Climb tangled flamewise past the utmost star;
> I am so safe with you, so blindly blest,
> Trust me immutable as brooding doves
> Who know safe hiding where their treasures are.[53]

Edward Sapir commented uneasily on Anne Singleton's disregard of pronouns. In doing so he misperceived and narrowed the poet's intentions, whether addressing her writer to writer or friend to friend. Most likely the writer who talked pedantically of grammar hid the friend who wondered at a haphazard exchange of "he's" and "she's" and male and female personae. Sapir's unease had a firmer biographical basis than critical justification; generally, Anne Singleton chose the gender of her figures with care, to substantiate a tightly made argument. For her, poetry did away with categories, a freedom not possible in real life. The personae in Anne Singleton's verse carried multiple and usually abstract messages about life and death, love and religion. A male as often as a female figure represented the poet, a beloved individual, a deity, or a spiritual principle:

> Now you are gone
> And if another lover for a space
> Reads his moons in your eyes on some far lawn,
> What's that to me? Over this stricken place
> The moon rides righ, watching with me till dawn.[54]

Ruth Benedict published a number of her poems and submitted more than were accepted. She had rewritten the emotional themes and did not anticipate a mistaken or cruel reading of her play with gender. She also steered away from specifics, even—often—specifics of context. Ruth considered the poet an impersonal voice, a spokesman for human dilemmas in all times and places, and she drew on biographical matters primarily to transmit a universal understanding.

At the same time, Ruth expected those who knew her to read her poems differently from the audience of *Dial* or *The Nation*. Her private audience consisted of Edward Sapir, Stanley Benedict, and, for the most intense years of Anne Singleton's life, Margaret Mead. Ruth expressed her feelings not in spite but because she had a wide audience; she simultaneously enclosed and explored her feelings in the framework provided by a critical public. As long as she spoke with "strange" readers in mind, along with the familiar, she had to "design" her desires and her dreams.

Ruth did not publish everything she wrote to Margaret. Some verse was simply too outspoken and revealing; some verse was simply bad—and often the qualities coincided. She wrote to Mead in the late 1920s:

> How in icy winter's time
> Shall roses glow, lilies chime
> Can you guess
> When in winter's icy land
> Valentine may yet command
> Heart's happiness.[55]

Ruth was critic enough to recognize the weakness of such unformed verse.

Through the early 1920s Ruth Benedict and Margaret Mead established a lasting mutual dependence. Passion characterized not one but several strands of their relationship—the anthropological conversations no less than the despairing confidences had an aura of intensity. And because the friendship did not, in Ruth's view, carry with it the "shoulds" of marriage, she did not feel compelled to sift out and analyze various components of her attachment to Margaret. Ruth Fulton had somewhat forced passion into her relationship with Stanley Benedict; her entry on his proposal of marriage contrasted in tone to everything she wrote about Margaret.[56] Ruth applied melodramatic phrases and shrill poetic metaphors to her relationship with her husband, not to her relationship with Margaret Mead and other women friends. The absence of words like "ecstasy" testified to Ruth's comfortable acceptance of the intimacy within her daily domestic life. For no matter how lofty their exchanges, how intense their contacts, the friendship still rested in ordinary and often trivial interactions. The two women's loyalty lodged itself in a persistent and acknowledged familiarity with the details of each other's lives.

Ruth Benedict appreciated the continuity into which zest and contentment fit. She did not extract and overemphasize any component of the friendship. She had achieved her valued "permanency" with Margaret Mead. The permanency rested on all manner of exchange, from caresses to gossip, from recipes to psychological theories, and included confidences about teaching, about addressing fellow professionals, about the problems of bringing up children, and of—at last—buying a new dress. The two women lived together only once, for a month one summer, and eventually circumstances prevented frequent "overnight" stays. But the dominant traits of the pattern had been set, indelibly.

> *"There are a lot of new students, and how good they will prove to be is still on the lap of the gods"*

Margaret Mead became a prime commentator on Ruth Benedict, as a teacher, an anthropologist, a wife, and a friend. "She was tentative and shy and always wore the same dress," Mead remembered about the teacher.[57] She also remarked upon Ruth's deafness and the effect of this on the class discussions. Mead did not mention a hearing aid and may not have known until later that Ruth tried such a device. "Monday, Jan. 11 Shopping for earphones!" Ruth noted in 1926.[58] She had been teaching anthropology for nearly three years. But she found the idea difficult to accept and the mechanism awkward and embarrassing. "Got earphone from Western Electric for trial and didn't have nerve to take it out in class!" she wrote the next day.[59]

Ruth revealed here a degree of vanity somewhat counter to her "same dress." The unchanging, monochromatic wardrobe nearly everyone remembered may have indicated a withdrawal from the complications so far produced by her physical attractiveness. Her pleasure in her own beauty had been bruised by Stanley Benedict's rejection. Students who met Ruth Benedict in the 1920s were not as struck by her beauty as would be those who met her first in the 1930s; much had changed for Ruth by then.

Meanwhile the hearing device also interfered with a style Ruth had developed for presenting herself in a classroom. The benefits of hearing seemed outweighed by the comforts of familiar gestures. Ruth returned the earphones on Wednesday, January 13, her flurry with such props over. From Western Electric, the supplier, she "ran off" to an art show; among pictures she felt at home and revitalized: ". . . and beyond everything Picasso's 'Sad Mother'—a study in blues with a mother shut-eyed in an ecstacy of foreboding (?) [hers] holding an old-faced, indifferent child."[60]

Students reacted variously to Dr. Benedict's deafness. Some, like Mead, appreciated the accompanying behaviors. Ruth listened attentively and watched each facial expression, so as not to miss a single word. Like Margaret Mead, those who appreciated their teacher's intent look often appreciated, too, the repetition and careful rewording of a question. Ruth Benedict, people said, could wonderfully transform the groping remarks of a student into the cogent hypothesis or argument of an anthropologist.[61]

Some students disliked the repetitiveness, the back-and-forth discussions, and waited impatiently for "point" and "purpose" in her ethnographic descriptions. More than Ruth's meandering, students minded the awkward stammer, an occasional consequence of her deafness. In the small department students went from Boas to Benedict, not an easy transition. Boas mumbled because of his facial paralysis and compounded the difficulty with multilingualism. Ruth Benedict mumbled because of shyness and discomfort at not catching everything that was said.[62]

Ruth also provided little relief from Boas's general academic limitations. Students who complained about his failure to teach anthropological methods, fieldwork procedure, and cross-cultural comparison did not find a very different approach in Benedict's seminars. She reluctantly and uneasily taught "Methods," considered "Kinship" a burden and a trial, and did best in "Mythology and Folklore," a specialty only some graduate students appreciated. A polarization emerged; Ruth's teaching inspired both harsh critics and loyal converts. "Mythology was a marvelous course," remembered one student nearly fifty years later. The converts benefited enormously, taking on Ruth's discipline and the commitment that determined her approach. These students learned to "do work that matters."[63]

Franz Boas taught a point of view on man and his cultures. Ruth even more than her teacher communicated a perspective rather than a set of procedures. She increasingly took over seminar teaching from Boas, and learning anthropology at Columbia became a matter of adopting a particular outlook. Ruth's teaching suited the state of the art in anthropology and ideas on education she had applied for nearly ten years. In her view the discipline depended upon individual motivation for the shaping of inquiry; background and current convictions provided the strategy and the goal of research. Ruth Benedict, following Franz Boas, considered scientific method a matter of fitting questions to data in an ongoing process of readjustment. From such a perspective anthropology had to be a highly empirical and inductive science.

This scientific method bore a striking resemblance to the concept of "empirical biography" which Ruth had outlined six years before arriving at Columbia. In literature she had developed an approach perfect for her new endeavor. As Ruth listened to Boas tell of daily activities in another society, she extracted from his accounts a principle of fieldwork that echoed her biographical techniques. Absorption in unfamiliar customs, self living through other in order to "know" the other—Ruth heard echoes to the theoretical paragraphs in her preface to "Adventures in Womanhood."

A method that relied upon willingness to immerse oneself in available materials and trust one's responses was in accord with a contemporary philosophy of education. Ruth knew John Dewey, from his statements and from Vassar friends (including her sister-in-law Agnes Benedict) who publicized the progressive-education movement. Further in the background lay Ruth Benedict's childhood religion and an acknowledgment of individual spiritual autonomy. The Baptist church stressed a personal appropriation of religious principles, a doctrine not incompatible with either progressivism or Boasian anthropology.

Ruth gathered these strands together when she began training graduate students. (She did not often teach undergraduates. Boas liked undergraduate classes and took over most Barnard and Columbia college courses himself.) If slightly idiosyncratic, what Ruth did suited well the needs of her discipline in the 1920s. Then fieldworkers, and anthropologists, required less a firm set of instructions than an absolute conviction that their work mattered, that their data meant something to themselves, to societies, to the world. Ruth underplayed method in order to stress faith, or at least inspiration. Students complained of the vague "romanticism" in her lectures, but she had a plan.[64]

Backed by Boas, Dewey, and the techniques she developed for biographical studies, Ruth Benedict provided an effective field guide for the study of "diverse designs for living." (The phrase she applied to her cross-cultural research came close to her concept of biography.) According to Ruth, the student eager to explore other modes of life had to be open to eventual "illumination"; fieldwork for Ruth had the revelatory quality of her literary experiences. One saw a life whole and all of a sudden, she wrote, after finishing Walter Pater.[65] Moreover, with Dewey she believed that learning based on sudden insight, the result of individual grappling with the stuff of experience, was learning that stuck.

And like Dewey, Ruth placed great importance on recognizing and utilizing personal "desire" in the formation of a reasoned inquiry. The anthropologist, like any student, organized his impulses in the process of learning. Dewey's notion of the "organization of impulse" attracted Ruth for many reasons, one of which was its perfect fit to her own view of education as the progressive ordering of dreams and experiences. Ruth put a premium, always, on arrangement; arranging one's dreams and convictions became a way of arranging one's perceptions. The arrangement of personal impulses did not precede but became part of the arrangement of so-called "objective" data.

By emphasizing the experiential and the "personal design" in learning, Ruth Benedict minimized the actual classroom encounter. Her expectation that a student would grasp her vision did not include methodology and did depend on chance conversations as much as on formal lectures. This was the way she had learned anthropology, supplemented by exposure to Boas's stern advocacy of collecting facts from diverse societies. In her classes, and frequently in her conversations, Ruth combined a trust in sudden insight with an ability to summon up and effectively arrange facts—that is, data interpreted. The combination constituted her anthropology, an argument for the significance of "exotic" customs to illuminate the familiar.

She liked anthropologists whose style resembled her own and in the 1920s grew close to Paul Radin, an imaginative and charming Boasian anthropologist. (Radin received a Ph.D. from Columbia in 1911 with a thesis titled "The Ritual and Significance of the Winnebago Medicine Dance." Like Goldenweiser, he had a hard time holding a permanent job, and like Sapir he worked for years for the Canadian Geological Survey.) Ruth's attraction to Radin was reciprocated. On visits to New York, Radin took Ruth to dinner (once at the "Russian Bear," she noted, and on January 11, 1926, he gave her his "RBAE [Reports of the Bureau of American Ethnology] set out of storage!"[66] Ruth admired Radin's work, and she went to lectures he gave at Cooper Union: "All about Winnebago things he knows and loves."[67] Both anthropologists were fascinated by the issue of individual creativity and the "unique" personality in a small-scale, homogeneous society. Ruth found her lunches with Radin usually amusing: "Lunch with Radin—much anthropological divergence."[68]

Through the 1920s, then, Ruth Benedict both learned and taught anthropology, in a single process involving classes and seminars, conversations and informal encounters, reading, writing, and friendships. It was an intense time, and her eagerness to be a professional anthropologist dominated a great part of her activities and her emotions. Columbia events, anthropology meetings, colleagues, and students took attention and effort, as she moved toward developing a definite disciplinary approach of her own. Students realized the importance, and the value, of catching her at unexpected moments to confront her on an anthropological matter. Ruth left a kind of pied piper impression in the memory of many: students trailing after her, through the corridors of the Journalism Building into no. 705, her office.[69]

And she began to achieve a modicum of contentment. Ruth was busy, engaged, doing work that mattered. She had energetic conversations in her office, over ice cream near Columbia; she dashed from a seminar to an appointment—and increasingly found Franz Boas an anchor, a source of comfort and affection as well as of anthropological wisdom. When Boas left New York, Ruth kept him posted on the state of her work, the department, individuals, and their families. She filled her letters with talk of classes, people in the field, money:

> I have sent the draft for two hundred dollars to the bank in Vancouver. . . . Miss Bryan [Ruth] sent on the Comox mss too. Mid-terms was passed this week; you wont [*sic*] like to contemplate that so well as I do. The classes are all quite pleasant, though, and, granted the time has to go that way, I've enjoyed them more than I ever have before.[70]

In others she talked more about herself. "I'm doing nothing—i.e. extraneous—and seeing nobody, and working long hours in Gladys' [Reichard] office" and of how much she missed him: "I'm so glad you are coming back before the trip to Vancouver. . . . I hate to think how I shall miss you this winter, and a fortnight will break the sentence."[71]

Details changed little over the decade as Ruth kept Boas involved even when he was not in New York—or the United States.

> I enclose a letter just received from Jules. The extra $500 is available and no better use could be made of it. . . . Amelia

> Susman has also written me about staying on in California.
> . . . If there is any objection you have on this score to her pro-
> posal, will you write me what you have told her? . . . Is Mel
> Herskovits still at your house? He will tell you that he recom-
> mended Bunny for Reed College. . . . I wish you could take
> occasion to mollify Mel about Ruth Landes' going to make
> the negro study in Bahia. . . ."

And so it went. It was no wonder outsiders called the group a "family."[72]

Her favors for students ranged widely, from the exceedingly personal to the most thoroughly bureaucratic problems. Ruth Benedict
intervened with Boas, edited papers, waived requirements, and provided
comforting cups of tea—as long as she trusted the students' intentions.
When she doubted the "good faith" of a student, she displayed a caustic
impatience startling in the ordinarily subdued woman.[73]

If the cause seemed just, Ruth handled the trouble. She reassured
a student about an absolutely "terrible paper" written for Boas: "My
mental processes seemed to stop that afternoon"; and when one unfortunate woman lost her seminar paper and all the notes, Ruth fixed that
"crisis" up too.[74] And she lent numbers of books, sending packages to
students unable to come to campus. In 1930 a woman wrote from
Connecticut, mentioned her children, then thanked Ruth for some books:
"You've been so jolly good to me ever since I met you, I thoroughly appreciate it."[75] On at least one occasion, Ruth administered a complete
"mock oral" exam.[76]

The most effusively grateful letters among Ruth Benedict's papers
were from women. Ruth won the devotion of both male and female
students, but over the years her interactions with women acquired special
intensity. (By 1930 women made up nearly half the number of graduate
students in anthropology at Columbia.[77]) On the one hand, women
appreciated working with a woman professor; role-model apart, there
was comfort in shared experiences (as Ruth implied when she wished
Mead would "join me in harness"). On the other hand, Ruth teasingly
distanced at least some male students. She called male students "the
boys," a clearly asexual and somewhat condescending reference. On
fieldtrips Ruth treated those boys like rowdy and good-spirited adolescents—writing into her Mescalero budget money for "tennis," magazines, and a great deal of food. "Canned sausages," she remembered,
are "most useful with cornmeal dodgers."[78] She occasionally called
women "the girls," but generally in a serious and respectful context;
"girls" had a less childish connotation in that era.

Women students often were older than men, having come to

graduate school from a job, perhaps a husband, sometimes children. Mature women, by age or by experience, gravitated toward Ruth, and she appreciated the individual who had puzzled over problems of career and marriage, woman's "nature," and public standards of success. But Ruth Benedict did not make exceptions for female students. She recognized their difficulties and demanded the amount of work and commitment she demanded from male students. Hearing about their backgrounds, listening to their dilemmas, Ruth urged women students to utilize these materials in anthropological inquiries.

And she consistently advised fieldwork. Like Boas, Ruth considered the exposure to strange customs crucial and illuminating. She also, as she showed in Margaret Mead's case, thought women especially had to make the commitment announced by a trip away from home and husband. The decision to go away provided professional validation as certainly as the Ph.D. Moreover, Ruth believed in endurance and struggle, in fighting through to a won fulfillment. This too might be signaled by fieldwork and again especially for women born in the late nineteenth century, coming to adulthood with World War I.

A number of women who came to Columbia in the 1920s and 1930s had previously done volunteer work, social work, or elementary school teaching.[79] With Ruth's encouragement, women carried the skills learned in those occupations into the field; rejecting unpaid, undervalued work did not mean discarding the associated talents. Other women without similar backgrounds started fieldwork afresh, perhaps with an articulated political position, rebellion against their circumstances, a yearning to get away and have an adventure. Ruth Benedict encouraged each woman to convert her "natural talents" into a framework for field-study.

She tried to persuade women that personal experiences fit professional training. The subjects they knew best at home and the talents they had because they were women, she said, might constitute one major route to professionalization. And Ruth constructed field guides, not to circumscribe a topic but to reassure women of the validity of their perspective. She urged women to study family and marriage; to facilitate this, in 1936 she drew up a set of questions: "I have been making up fieldwork questions about family life—lots of them—and I'll send them to you as soon as a copy is typed," she wrote to one doubtful woman.[80] She made up questions less to systematize participant-observation fieldwork than to distance the familiar, and to convert accepted patterns into points of comparison. Her goal, once again, was increased alertness to one's own situation.

Ruth paid attention to women in a context where individuality—

background, skills, training—became part of the master research plan. Paying attention to women, she encouraged them to explore their life stories and dominant motives, but she never encouraged indulgent, confessional stories. Reportedly Ruth could heap biting scorn on "true confessions" and on the romantic woes detailed by "lonely-heart types."[81] A carefully considered and arranged life story remained essential to anthropological inquiry. Ruth had equally little patience for spilling out and for suppressing self. Awareness of one's "organized impulses" also made anthropological inquiry valuable for a wide public.

Ruth Benedict did not admire unqualifiedly either the radical feminist or the docile wife and mother. She was pulled toward both alternatives. Some of her habits could be read as feminist: her mannish wardrobe and her early cigarette smoking, for instance. (In 1931 she told Boas that she had given up smoking and had no matchbook covers to send him. She did not sustain this "abjuration."[82]) Clothing and gestures, however, were offset by her general demeanor; to many Ruth appeared almost stereotypically feminine: soft-spoken, delicate, and graceful.[83]

Ruth's dislike of doctrine and of absolutes made it hard for her to resolve the "woman issue" and impossible for her to be a truly radical feminist or a truly contented wife. (In this, Stanley Benedict's judgment matched her own; children would not have guaranteed contentment in marriage.) Just as she judged her own life situationally, so she considered each woman's story individually—a "tale" to be treated on its own terms. Ruth attended to women in the department, and quite noticeably so. Among the letters in her files are virtual love letters from women students. But Ruth also attended to the unusual story wherever and however it came to her attention.

In many ways she paid more attention to any demonstrated eccentricity than to traits of gender. Without being explicit, Ruth gave the impression of favoring uncongenial temperaments, anyone who—on purpose or unintentionally—failed to fit the mold of his setting. She liked the nonconformist, attracted by individuals seemingly out of place in the familiar milieu and oppressed by American customs. A number of such people arrived at Columbia in the years she taught there.

Ruth Benedict felt at home with the "not at home." She could claim a mainstream ancestry; she also believed gender denied her mainstream prerogatives. Consequently women fell fairly automatically into the "left-out" category she informally applied. (Elsie Clews Parsons shared Ruth's view of convention and gender; Margaret Mead did not and, refreshingly, built her feminism from a position of inclusion not exclusion.) By and large, however, the women at Columbia in the 1920s and 1930s were resourceful not revolutionary; even Parsons expressed critical surprise at Esther Goldfrank's "personal arrangements," her alliance with a man with children.[84]

Ruth Benedict also fit male students into her categories. Gossip in the department claimed she encouraged students who rejected customary patterns of behavior, of personality, and of success for American men in the twentieth century. Ruth certainly responded to erratic personalities. But students complained about favoritism, saying she neglected anyone with a plain, middle-class background and a workmanlike interest in anthropology. If she did pay less attention to the more placid student, Ruth was not entirely to blame. She taught an apprenticeship discipline, and like-mindedness was not a negligible consideration.

On the practical side, when a student asked for attention Ruth Benedict responded quickly and efficiently. One midwestern, relatively untormented anthropologist has recalled, gratefully, her support of his innovative interdisciplinary dissertation.[85] Maybe asking for help marked off a student in her eyes; at any rate, colleagues praised Ruth's efforts to legitimize interdisciplinary programs, and these tended to be, before World War II, individual programs. "Her courtesy and imagination with students—those from other departments as well as from her own—have for years been one of the things that gave human vitality to our campus."[86]

Each year Ruth looked forward to what fate might bring. "How good they [students] will prove to be is still on the lap of the gods," she wrote to Franz Boas more than once, anticipating the incoming class.[87] Like Boas, Ruth waived requirements for special cases. This was because, again like Boas, Ruth welcomed the unusual personality, the less conventional student, not only for personal reasons but also for anthropological reasons. She believed her discipline depended on a critical distance often the result of "uncongeniality."

There were many special cases. In 1933 Ruth received a letter from the psychiatrist Harry Stack Sullivan.

> I am presuming on my slight personal and fair scientific acquaintance with you to refer the bearer, Mr. Leon Cohen, in a rather unusual connection. . . . A superficial routine contact with the admitting office at Columbia was, however, flatly unfavorable. Something tells me that this arose from his being included in some social grouping marked "undesirable." I do not think that this young man has communistic or other anti-institutional leanings.[88]

Gossip about Ruth's favoritism did have a certain basis and sometimes bordered on more insidious accusations. Robert Lowie expressed in print what discreet colleagues said in private: "And the American super-intelligentsia—Goldenweiser, Radin, Benedict, Sapir—had already decreed years before that I was devoid of imagination."[89] Lowie's remark suggested a kind of cult, as did Leslie White's references to "immigrants." Lowie here clumped Ruth Benedict with three Jews, and he knew that Boas had a Jewish background. Some Columbia students did think Ruth herself was Jewish.[90]

As with many such rumors, there were some supporting facts in statements and in behaviors. Ruth made no secret of her likes and dislikes, and the students she chose to help were often Jewish, partly because—as in Mr. Cohen's case—they did face difficulties. But her demonstration of concern for students like Jules Blumensohn (Henry) annoyed fellow students, and she may have caused him (and others) as much harm as good. "Jules Blumensohn has got along well with the Indians," she wrote to Boas from the Mescalero Reservation in 1931. "If anyone's results were to be estimated singly, his would outrank the others'. . . . The other boys have snubbed him pretty badly; they're all hearty extrovert boys and they tend to resent him."[91] The following summer, when Jules Blumensohn planned a Brazilian trip, Ruth sent several S.O.S. letters to Boas, asking whether Jules "should go" to "bad malarial country."[92] On the subject of (certain) white, Protestant, male students she could be very nasty.[93]

Once Edward Sapir had teased her about her love of "psychic irregularities." He spoke truly. Ruth distinguished not on the basis of Jewish and non-Jewish, or male and female, or any inherited trait, but on the basis of imaginativeness, daring, and willingness to transgress the patterns set by American society. Admittedly her implicit, somewhat romanticized, distinction between the dull and those with flair often corresponded with gender and with minority status. Ruth was only partially responsible for a situation temporally and disciplinarily created. Anthropology provided a haven for the individual who did not fit, and Ruth only took full advantage of a given circumstance. Her lectures conveyed less rules and methods than a particular stance she knew would attract her audience. "I learned tremendously from her, even though I never got a neat formulation of her methods.[94]

Whatever the extent and the pros and cons of personalized teaching, students left Columbia with a belief that anthropology mattered. Graduates acquired less a body of step-by-step procedures than an attitude of mind, and Ruth wanted nothing more.

Ruth Benedict's departmental duties were imprecise and extensive, performed out of fondness for Papa Franz and commitment to the discipline. Her style of teaching demanded complete absorption in the program; practically, her tasks lacked definition because she had no regular appointment. For almost a decade Ruth was appointed year by year, and her official career might be read as a parable for women in academia—though she resisted such a reading. From 1923 until 1930 Ruth was given temporary jobs, waiting each spring to hear about the next fall. She might teach at Barnard or at Columbia, and once (1923–24) she taught fine arts to a university extension class. In 1931, finally, she became an assistant professor and in 1937 an associate professor; in 1948 Columbia granted her a full professorship in the department of anthropology.

Franz Boas planned Ruth's teaching schedule and effectively determined her professional advancement. Though he maintained an official equality between men and women students, in actuality he advanced those who needed jobs, usually men facing familial and social pressures. Men, and women on their own, received the "plums" of anthropological advancement.

In 1923 Barnard College had a job in anthropology. Franz Boas decided to give this "real" job not to Ruth Benedict but to Gladys Reichard. (Reichard graduated from Swarthmore College in 1919 and, preceded by an impulsive letter to Boas, came to Columbia for a Ph.D. in anthropology. She wrote a dissertation on Wiyot grammar [1925] and did fieldwork with Navaho Indians.) The incident troubled Ruth, although (maybe because) she recognized the logic in Boas's decision. According to Boas, as long as Ruth was married she did not need support. Gladys Reichard was young, unmarried, and apparently on her own. When Pliny Earle Goddard teasingly congratulated Ruth on Gladys' job, Ruth reacted with sharp annoyance.[95]

The rivalry between the two women continued. Ruth habitually sent "love" from the field and included Gladys. But she also referred to Reichard in belittling phrases, revealing discomfort, dislike, jealousy, and a combination of all three. Remarks about Gladys's "pep" and boundless energy and comments on her cheerfulness and chatter, were not flattering; they reflected Ruth's opinion of Gladys's work.[96] Edward Sapir agreed with Ruth, and when Gladys Reichard went to Chicago to study linguistics with him he told Boas "she wasn't serious enough."[97] For her part, Gladys Reichard was not as entranced with Ruth Benedict as some students were. When she heard, in 1927, that Ruth Bunzel had a fellowship to study Zuñi she told Boas she was glad Zuñi would at last be "so well and completely done."[98] The two women granted each other a reluctant professional respect while competitiveness characterized their personal relationship.

In the beginning Ruth Benedict did not want a permanent job

and official promotions. She appreciated the flexibility and the chance to try her talents in a loosely structured setting. She was also reluctant to test the strength of her marriage against the demands and the symbolic significance of a full-time job. Stanley Benedict wanted her to take summers off and spend time at Lake Winnepesaukee. Too, during the 1920s Ruth paid as much attention to Anne Singleton as to "Dr. Benedict" and to, another persona, Mrs. Stanley Benedict. By 1930, however, the poet and wife became less important and Ruth reassessed her career. The mark of success was no longer contentment, but a job, honors, fellowships, and grants.

Ruth was not an especially successful grant applicant. She found the writing difficult and irritating, though she stalwartly persisted. Boas helped, writing enthusiastic letters of recommendation: "I wish to add that for the purpose of our knowledge of the anthropology of the southwest, the study [of family] she is proposing is indispensable and that we cannot find a better equipped investigator than she is."[99] Ruth Benedict lost one fellowship because of her age: "The Board has been quite inflexible with reference to the rule not to consider applications from candidates over thirty-five years of age,"[100] and another because her project did not have "wide implications."[101] Edward Sapir intervened in the process, also noting that her projects seemed narrow. Ruth did not appreciate his remarks.[102] Nor did she do the proposed study of family in the Southwest.

She did receive honors and a few job offers. In 1927 Ruth Benedict was elected president of the American Ethnological Society, a New York City association and virtually a club; still, election signaled her professional achievement. Presiding, she arranged meetings and acquired letterhead stationery. That same year Leslie White wrote to Ruth about a job at Smith College.[103] This, like any job outside New York, posed threats, to her marriage and to her pleasure in the congenial environment of Columbia University.

Through the 1930s Ruth devoted herself more concentratedly to student projects and departmental business. She struggled to find money for students and colleagues, writing to foundations, corporations, and sympathetic individuals. Every now and then, too, someone might find a check in the mail, sent from Ruth's personal bank account.[104] This *was* a family. Ruth did not treat lightly the importance of feeling at home, nor did she disregard her affections for Franz Boas, an element in professional decisions. Letters conveyed their mutual attachment, and the relationship kept Ruth in New York as much as anything else. Boas reciprocated both the affection and the respect; neither wrote effusively, but each depended on the fondness and the steadiness of communication.

Franz Boas shaped a good part of Ruth's career, directly and indirectly, by regulating promotions and by setting an example of devotion to the discipline. He knew what anthropology was about, how the work should be done, and the strain his science put on people's usual expectations about degrees, research, and final publication. Like her teacher, Ruth acquired and transmitted an attitude, with the associated demand for expenditure of energy and of emotion.

Like Boas, too, Ruth argued strenuously and consistently for fieldwork. Through the 1920s and into the difficult Depression years Ruth advised students to go to the field, whenever and however they could, and to take the risk of upheaval and financial setback. Her own fieldwork constituted an interesting and problematic aspect of her professionalization, a mirror of changing commitment to the discipline, to Papa Franz, and to social science as a political as well as an academic endeavor.

"When I'm God I'm going to build my city there"

In 1923 Ruth Fulton Benedict had a Ph.D. in anthropology but had not yet fully experienced her discipline's "rite of passage," extended fieldwork. The Serrano study had been limited, and a month before she finished the thesis Ruth began thinking about a longer trip. "Dr. Boas talked to me about a fellowship in SW [Southwest] folklore," she wrote on Monday, February 12, 1923, knowing the fellowship required spending time with an Indian tribe.[105] She also knew Boas expected students to learn anthropological method in day-to-day exposure to an unfamiliar culture. Much later Ruth herself wrote that Boas's "insistence on inclusive and systematic field investigation" defined a methodology for his science.[106]

She suffered over the fellowship decision. "Worst sick headache I've had in years," she noted on Tuesday, February 13.[107] Two days passed, and on Friday, February 16, she wrote, still indecisive: "~~Couldn't / Wrote Mrs. Parsons I'd take the job~~. Wrote Mrs. Parsons I was interested."[108] The sick headaches symptomized several problems. Ruth recognized the problems, and not just psychosomatically. Problems included learning a Native American language well enough to record tales, working for Elsie Clews Parsons (who apparently *was* the fellowship[109]), and threatening her relationship with Stanley Benedict by a summer apart.

The 1922 Serrano trip presented fewer difficulties. This study of a "dying culture" fit Boas's plan to "salvage" data on disappearing American Indian tribes and certainly suited Ruth; she combined work with a visit to the Freemans in Pasadena. But the trip did not accomplish her "initiation," and in August 1924 Ruth Benedict went to New Mexico to live in a Pueblo community for two months. A year later she went back to the Southwest. In 1926 she and Stanley Benedict spent the summer in Europe, and in 1927 she once more made a fieldtrip. The 1927 trip to a Pima reservation was the last Ruth made on her own. After that she directed student research in the field, in 1931 on a Mescalero Apache reservation and in 1939 on a Blackfoot reservation. She intended to do her own field study again in 1943–44, in Europe and Asia, but wartime conditions prevented her.

Ruth Benedict softened her first field experience by visiting her sister and mother at the same time. The remnant Serrano tribe lived near Los Angeles, and Ruth stayed in the Freeman house rather than on Indian land. A seventy-year-old Serrano woman, Rita Morongo, came regularly to talk to the anthropologist. Under careful prodding, Rita Morongo remembered details of food growing and preparation, of marriage and family customs, and—a vivid section in Ruth's account—a puberty rite for females.[110] Ruth especially appreciated the "informant approach" of Boasian anthropology. The use of one individual to tell about his or her culture became a standard technique for the Columbia fieldworker in the early twentieth century, its origins in Boas's own experiences. (In 1896 Boas met George Hunt, who became an indefatigably prolific informant on Kwakiutl culture for nearly forty years.)

Whatever awkwardness Ruth felt from her half-deafness eased when she could isolate her informant, and in 1922 she established a lasting pattern of encouraging informants to meet her away from their group in a quiet and undistracting environment. On the Serrano trip, she missed not informants to put together a picture of tribal life but a view of the landscape and the physical background of traditional behaviors. On later fieldtrips scenery crucially affected Ruth Benedict's understanding of a culture, and she always responded first to her surroundings.

In 1924 Ruth published "A Brief Sketch of Serrano Culture," a competent account of a "broken culture."[111] She had had trouble writing—"Struck snag in Serrano paper and put it aside"[112]—partly because data were scant and partly because she did not see a design in the disparate remaining elements of Serrano culture. The Serrano did give her a quotation: " 'They all dipped in the water,' he [a chief] continued, 'but their cups were different. Our cup is broken now. It has passed away.' "[113] In 1934 Ruth used the quotation as an epigraph for *Patterns of Culture*.

"Our cup is broken." The cup of clay given to all people had shattered for the Serrano. Ruth became intrigued by a notion of social life in fragments and drafted an article to develop the theme. In the "Cups of Clay" sketch, she applied to culture her ideas about an individual life story and recalled her despairing remarks on the "episodic" quality of her own life in 1912–13. Ruth contrasted episode and fragment to "coherence" and wholeness, a sense of perfect fit. In the early formulations, she shifted her vocabulary, uncertain about the process by which "fit" or design emerged from an apparently haphazard collection of traits. The Serrano material did not provide the substance she needed in order to transfer her insight from biography to ethnography. Before culture wholeness became her disciplinary idea, Ruth Benedict had to see a culture with a vivid and complete design.

On February 16, 1923, Ruth decided to accept the Southwest fellowship; she did not actually go to the Southwest until over a year later. Before the trip, she tabulated, cross-indexed, and summarized themes from Pueblo myths much like the ones she would be collecting. She found the work dull and tedious, reminiscent of the "painstaking copying" she projected onto the monk of Ariège. But she endured and worked on mythologies throughout the summer of 1923, at Lake Winnepesaukee with Stanley Benedict. She told Boas: "All summer I've worked on the mythology and I don't suppose a day has passed that I haven't wished fervently I could ask you some question, or wondered what you thought of some difficult coincidence in the stories."[114] And she proudly reported her progress in learning Spanish, the *lingua franca* of the Southwest and not so inaccessible as Zuñi and other Pueblo languages. Speaking Spanish, Ruth could contact individuals in the area who were responsible for introductions into Pueblo society. For relief from language and mythology she exercised her memory on recapitulations of complex kinship systems, bane of the student and teacher of anthropology. But that was her "enduring" side; Ruth also went canoeing and hiked over the New Hampshire hills with her husband. "And it's much more enjoyable to work out in a canoe than in the Columbia library."[115]

Ruth Benedict spent the school year 1923–24 teaching for the Columbia University Extension Program. She spent half the summer with Stanley Benedict, and in August 1924 left for the adobe dwellings of New Mexico. Her assignment was to collect material for Elsie Clews Parsons's compendia of Pueblo myths and folktales. Another Columbia anthropologist shared the Zuñi Pueblo with Ruth. Somewhat by chance, Ruth Bunzel also spent August 1924 observing the Zuñi Indians. When Boas heard that Bunny planned to travel to the Southwest for a vacation, he told her she "may as well" do a field study while she was there; so the departmental secretary became a Ph.D. candidate overnight.[116]

Although for a time they lived in the same house, the novice ethnographers did not interfere in each other's work. Ruth Benedict sat for hours collecting tales, ad infinitum she sometimes thought. Bunzel, in turn, spent her days observing Pueblo potters at work. "Ruth seems to be getting along very well with her tales," Bunny wrote to Boas in August 1924.[117] Benedict, judging by her field notebook, certainly was getting along. She saved a worn notebook from the first trip, filled with the scrawled lines of a story (in longhand and in English), Zuñi words to be translated, notes to herself for future reference.[118] She crossed out, drew arrows and lines, rewrote—all in the interests of an accurate rendition. Ruth knew the work required to capture the spirit of an "original" and to transmit it to others; her field notes are as revised as her "Mary Wollstonecraft."

Occasionally Ruth Benedict identified her informant: "José Maria" and "Merced" appeared frequently. She must have had clues for identifying others; narrators are identified in the published volumes.[119] She did not characterize her informants, and idiosyncrasies emerge only in narrative style. Nor did Ruth describe in the field diary her responses to the place, the people, or the project itself. She apparently worked relentlessly, throwing herself into strenuous mental activity, then taking a break with physical exertion. The first fieldtrip stretched her intellectual energies, and she ended days of note-taking—sometimes eleven hours at a time[120]—in utter exhaustion.

No full account remains of Ruth Benedict's private reactions to the 1924 Zuñi fieldtrip. But she stored up sensations and her impressions of the Southwest landscape. She used the details in her poetry. The summer before, the poet had looked out on a New England countryside for her images: stark green pines and red berries; bright blue sky and white birches: "arbutus bed, / And the dark pines, thick-carpeted."[121] New Hampshire's defined colors contrasted to the tawny reds, browns, and golds of a desert:

> Serpents lengthening themselves over the rock,
> Indolently desirous, feel the sun
> Cover their flanks with sweetness. . . .[122]

Her poetry hinted at the extent to which Ruth had succumbed to the Southwest, as had others before her—ethnographers, travelers, poets, and artists. In poems inspired by the Southwest, Ruth at last "loosened" the "psychic machinery,"[123] a change she acknowledged in prose on her second fieldtrip.

In August 1925 Ruth Benedict boarded a train from New York to Santa Fe. That August Margaret Mead rode with her, leaving Ruth at the Grand Canyon while she went on to San Francisco and a boat to

Samoa. Both women were eager to do fieldwork, and Margaret's bold adventurousness counterpointed Ruth's hard-won, practical acceptance of the rigors of a trip away. The two, brought closer together by the shared *rite de passage*, comforted each other through months that were often difficult and sometimes fiercely depressing. Just before the two left, Edward Sapir wrote to Ruth:

> I am very glad that Margaret has obtained her desire. She will enjoy the year in the South Seas hugely and will profit greatly by it, I feel certain. . . . Are you not glad to be going to the Southwest? Will it be Zuñi again? If so, I presume it will not be mythology only this time, though ritualism has its *longuers*, too, no doubt.[124]

It was not mythology "only," and it became a study broader than either Sapir or Ruth anticipated. The 1925 Pueblo study expanded, less from added topics than because Ruth opened her eyes.

In 1925 Ruth Benedict gave the impression of being at home with fieldwork. The change affected her letters to Margaret, across the Pacific, and altered her day-to-day participation in Zuñi life. She never achieved Bunny's amused involvement in the bustle and gossip and disputes of a Pueblo community, but during her second year Ruth learned the details of daily life and the fine points of personal relationships.

Bunny arrived in Zuñi two or three weeks after Ruth. The two women saw different aspects of the Zuñi Pueblo, even when they lived in the same house, shared the same primary informants, and deferred, in letters, to the same professor of anthropology.[125] Ruth Benedict perceived a kind of composition, a scene in which physical features formed backdrop to a sedate and regulated society. She conveyed the ceremonial pace of Zuñi life, while Bunny reported on sudden, "pick-up" rabbit-hunts.[126] The Pueblo setting filled Ruth Benedict with close to a religious feeling, and she wrote in exhilaration: "I've discovered in myself a great fondness for this place—it came over me with a rush—We [a Vassar friend] drove in with the rain pouring down in great white separate drops and sunlit clouds, and soft veils of rain shifting and forming against the far off mesas."[127]

On her last morning, waiting for Bunny to arrive before she went regretfully to the Cochiti Pueblo, Ruth emphasized the spiritual quality: "Yesterday we went up under the sacred mesa along stunning trails where the great wall towers above you always in new magnificence. . . . When I'm God I'm going to build my city there."[128] Ruth drew on the language of religious awe to express and to embody an overwhelming sensation. Perhaps too she detected the resemblance to an erotic emotion and in reaction stressed the "sacred" component of her responses. Ruth Benedict had not experienced a total "thrill of ecstasy" since childhood, and she returned to a mode of expression in which intense passion took color from religious doctrine—the habit of her years in Norwich.

She was pleased with herself. Ruth outlined to Mead and to Boas her various triumphs, ranging from managing the necessities of everyday life through winning the affection of Zuñi informants to learning to deal with the "terror" of loneliness. And so, contented, Ruth used the results of her own experience to sustain Mead on her 1925 venture to Samoa. Experience prompted advice like the following.

> I know I can't make all the beauty you'll be surrounded by,
> anything but aching pains. . . . And other times you must just
> love it because you are you and indomitable in the long run.
> After all this is the only safety in life . . . and we always fight
> through to it in agony of soul. . . . There is only one comfort
> that comes out of it—unbelievably—the sense that there is
> that sure something within us, no matter how often it is laid
> in ruins, that cannot be taken away from us.[129]

Beneath the abstract phrases, Ruth Benedict conveyed a hard-won lesson. On a less exalted note, a month later, teacher told student that brushing your teeth did wonders for warding off depression.[130]

Ruth realized a source of strength for the fieldworker in small self-indulgences: "Be very good to yourself. Eat all that is stupid and wholesome, sleep when it seems impossible, experiment with the light touch when it seems treachery."[131] Being able to transform discomfort into livable conditions marked a victory. Ruth described one such achievement (a letter from Cochiti, not Zuñi). "There are drawbacks in this abode. The menu is somewhat difficult since neither bread nor milk are known here. . . . Presently the Indians will begin to provide, and I'll be eating field corn with the rest of them." Food was one thing, bedbugs another: "Therefore as soon as he'd [an "old Indian"] left I managed to scramble up an amputated ladder to the roof with my bedding on my back. It was much better, but even daytime gives no surcease as yet."[132]

Living alone could be a pleasure, and Ruth happily borrowed an empty house for her two-week stay in the Peña Blanca Pueblo. She also liked managing domestic details, and these demanded a fair amount of attention.

My diet is expanding. The chief difficulty was that I was wholly unprepared to find flour unknown in these stores. But the keeper of one of these little rows of shelves they call "stores"—there are two—unearthed three little cartons of Aunt Jemima pancake flour, and I am saved. My muffins are excellent, and as for butter, even Peña Blanca butter was inedible, so I'm already at ease about that omission.[133]

Even more a source of pride, Ruth learned to get along with people. "My old man is ninety and a great old character," she reported, right after her account of muffins and butter.[134] This particular informant (a Cochiti not a Zuñi Indian) made her sorry she needed an interpreter. Ruth Benedict never knew a Pueblo Indian language well enough to use it—"It's lucky you never have been on a field trip with me, you'd be outraged at my slowness in language"—but in spite of that, "Nick and Flora both eat out of my hand this summer."[135] The Zuñi Nick, more than his wife Flora, turned out to be Ruth's best informant. Not only did he talk and talk and talk, but he also had a literary flair Ruth could not resist:

He told me the emergence story with fire in his eye yesterday through twenty-two repetitions of the same episode in twenty-two "sacred" songs. He'd try to skip but habit was too strong. He would only interrupt, "Zame zing, zame, zing"—and go on with the same endless phrases to the end. There's something impressive in the man's fire.[136]

"Nick is an old rascal who wants to see which way the cat jumps," Ruth Bunzel reported to Boas, probably the more realistic interpretation of the ever-cooperative informant.[137] Ruth Benedict controlled her usual sharp insight into character, relieved at finding a "reliable informant." Everyone knew Nick, the Zuñi informant—even Margaret Mead, who never went to a Pueblo.[138] His involvement with whites ultimately caused trouble for the man "with fire in his eye," along with his unusual (for Pueblo culture) outspokenness. In 1939 Nick was branded a witch and briefly hung by his "arms behind his back over a church beam."[139]

Ruth Benedict usually got along better with male informants than female informants. She "grew fond" of Nick and admired an old Cochiti Indian: "He hobbles along on his cane, bent nearly double, and is still easily the most vivid personage in the landscape."[140] Her portraits of the men have a vitality her references to women lack. "I am tired of working with old women," she once confessed to Boas.[141]

Her alertness to males had an unforeseen consequence. "As soon as I
go out for water the men begin to come in. One amorous male I think
I have got rid of, dear soul! He's stunning, with melting eyes and the
perfect confidence which I can't help believing has come from a successful amour with a white woman."[142] Her lighthearted, asexual tone
reflected aloofness from even gentle flirtatiousness. The "amorous"
Cochiti echoed strangely back to her past. "He hopes I'll be another
Mabel Dodge; he's all ready to take Tony's part and I will say he's a
better catch than Tony."[143] Years before, in Buffalo, Ruth had admired
the self-assured Mabel Dodge; now she knew her married to Tony
Luhan, a Taos Indian.

Primarily in 1925 Ruth worked, and worked not as a distraction
from melancholy but in order to complete a valid task. She was grati-
fied when people gathered to tell her stories, even if most were men
and even if, it sometimes seemed, they gathered for money and for
prestige within the pueblo. "Meanwhile the whole village vies to sit
with me for a seance. Joe disperses appointments as he would a poor
fund and I'm in luck that my old shaman is poor—otherwise he'd be
frowned on. One of those who rob the poor working girl, you know!"[144]
Her self-mockery more than anything suggests her unexpected satisfaction.

The Pueblo Indians ultimately provided an overwhelming supply
of tales and myths—a "bulk," Ruth said, and did "nine hours of dictation
a day." Her informants chose the content. Nick proved to be more forth-
coming than Cochiti informants. "But the tales I'm really curious about
I don't get—the katcina stories," she complained more than once. In
general the Cochiti Pueblo seemed less open than the Zuñi. Ruth
needed the help of missionaries and the Santa Fe Museum to get in
at all.[145] Boas had predicted obstacles to doing research there.

Cochiti "secretiveness" accompanied widespread attention to the
anthropologist at work. "Everybody in Cochiti seems to know my
occupation.[146] People crowded around, until the cacophony of sound
troubled Ruth, as it had twenty-five years before in the Norwich farmhouse when fourteen people sat down for supper. The Cochiti were
curious and guarded and like the Zuñi kept their secrets well, watching
the ethnographer while she observed them. Nick did talk with unusual
candor, but Ruth Benedict had other reasons for thinking she knew the
Zuñi better than the Cochiti Indians. In Zuñi she saw a culture that fit
together, where the single element revealed the whole design. She never
had a similar insight into Cochiti integrity, either because, as she concluded, Cochiti was in fact more "fragmented" or because (the probable
explanation) her pleasure in Zuñi set the context for an intuitive perception of culture coherence.

Ruth encountered in the three Pueblos (Zuñi, Cochiti, Peña Blanca) a people who controlled their "public face" and presentation of self. Informants edited information; masked gods protected the secrets of a religious system; deep inside an underground chamber lay objects of high veneration. Ruth respected the secrecy, and privacy became one dominant theme in her Pueblo portrait. Ruth Bunzel told another story, of open conflict, malicious rumor-mongering, and political machinations.[147] For Ruth Benedict, hidden turmoil and conflict did not disturb the reigning impulse of pueblo life. And from her perspective, the placid surface constituted an accurate portrait of Zuñi culture precisely because this was the way the Indians chose to present themselves. She retold their story.

Ruth Benedict tread a fine line between information and secrets and was startled to receive a letter in the spring of 1925 condemning her willingness to "expose" the Zuñi. Just before she went to Zuñi she got a letter from a half-Zuñi, sometime anthropology student Jaime de Angulo.

> Don't you understand the psychological value of secrecy at a certain level of culture? Surely you must, but you have probably never connected it with this [Zuñi]. You know enough of analytic psychology to know that there are things that must not be brought to the light of day, otherwise they wither and die like uprooted plants. . . . Why do you want to know these things? . . . It is all right to talk about it in a general way, with certain reservations, the necessary care that must be always used in handling all esoteric knowledge. It is as powerful and dangerous as the lightning.[148]

He went on for several dramatic paragraphs reiterating his "horror." Ruth liked de Angulo and persuaded him of her good intentions "over whiskey and soda till after midnight," five years later.[149]

Ruth Benedict had been, and would continue to be, scrupulous in her field inquiries, partly out of respect and partly out of empathy for Pueblo traits. She appreciated the significance of masking sacred subjects, and perhaps her quick understanding allowed her to gain access where others had failed. "I never do seem to find the spiked fence Elsie talks about—and Papa Franz for Cochiti, too," she wrote on September 1, 1925. Two days later, marveling at her success, she repeated the words: "I never do get this sense of the spiked dangerous fence that Elsie, and Dr. Boas in this case, make so much of."[150] She was rightly proud of her success in the reportedly difficult Pueblos. A reserved people, the Pueblo Indians had been subjected to persistent observation over the past half-century and they had reason to be wary.

She also somewhat lost her terror of loneliness. "I like this place. . . . By mid-morning the clouds have formed over the range [Jemez range], still as mountains, and more varied, and with the constant beauty of their shadows heightening the beauty of their range." And, after a few more descriptive phrases: "In the isolation of this month . . . three years ago it would have been enough to fill me with terror. I was always afraid of depressions getting too much for me. . . . But that's ancient history now.[151]

In 1927 Ruth went back to the Southwest, again with Ruth Bunzel. She left Bunny at Zuñi and went on to the Pima tribe in Arizona. Benedict wrote little specifically about the Pima—a paragraph here and there in 1930s articles. But the Pima gave her a significant anthropological concept. In Ruth Benedict's eyes, the Pima represented the Dionysian, exuberant and ecstatic, unlike the moderate and proportioned Zuñi. Though she did not elaborate the contrast for three years, she immediately reported to Boas, "The contrast with the latter [Pueblo] is *unbelievable.*"[152]

The Pima trip turned out to be the last Ruth Benedict did on her own. By 1927 she had time-consuming responsibilities in the department, and her two subsequent fieldtrips involved training students. She made the shift for personal, professional, and financial reasons—the third no minor consideration. Ruth had received money, for her 1924 and 1925 trips, from the Southwest Fund and Elsie Clews Parsons. She reluctantly borrowed money from Stanley Benedict for the Pima trip: "It wasn't half bad about the money," she wrote to Boas on August 17, 1927. "Stanley advanced it to me and will cash the check I gave him when I hear the money is deposited to my account."[153]

Throughout the 1930s, Ruth scrambled for funds so that Columbia students could do their fieldwork. Some students did go out independently. Ruth Underhill recalled Boas's delight when he learned she had a car and could drive to the Papago reservation in Arizona.[154] According to Frederica de Laguna, Boas instructed her to "hop a train west and ride until the money ran out."[155] Many students did not share this at least retrospective good humor, and they depended upon Ruth Benedict's resourcefulness in applying for money from various agencies, foundations, and "anthropology angels."

By the 1930s Ruth Benedict realized the practical and the personal advantages of team fieldwork. Not only did the likelihood of financial support increase, she also gained the chance to prove her theory that the more "views" the fuller the picture of another culture. One person saw one aspect; clues and pieces put together ultimately gave the whole picture. One started with "steps," not a "capital letter" project, she told a student.[156] Ruth did her first teamwork when she took students to New Mexico under the auspices of the Southwest Laboratory of Field Research (Santa Fe). The group lived with Mescalero Apache families on the reservation. Eight years later Ruth led another student team, with the cooperation of the University of Montana. The second group lived on a Blackfoot reservation. These were not Ruth's trips but, as she called them, "the boys' trips." (If not "boys," she occasionally called students the "kindergarten" with a gentle contempt colleagues commented upon.[157]) In 1931 the "boys" who studied Apache culture included Paul Frank, Morris Opler, Sol Tax, Harry Hoijer, and Jules Blumensohn (Henry). The "boys" lived with families; one "girl," Regina Flannery, lived with Ruth in the Indian agent's house.

By choice and by chance, Ruth Benedict acted more the teacher and less the ethnographer in 1931. Weary of her Pueblo field research for the moment, she looked forward to directing students in a new area. "I feel much more like this summer's work than I did when I came across the continent with you [Boas, earlier that month]. All I wanted to do then was to crawl into a hole and stay there. But that's passed. I'm even looking forward to the party," she wrote on June 28, 1931.[158] A few days later she reported on living arrangements, on language-training, and on work: "The girls' adolescence ceremony began at sunrise this morning, and we have all been following that today."[159]

At the end of her stay Ruth reported her satisfaction with student progress: "The results would be creditable to any group of ethnologists, and I'm satisfied that the boys have really learned something in the process."[160] She was less happy with her own progress. Ruth Benedict found little to catch her interest in Mescalero Apache culture. "The Apache culture is unbelievably thin, and I don't think it's a real case of the loss of traits under white influence. . . . My biggest disappointment of the summer has been that I haven't done a problem on my own."[161]

Ruth was stymied by the "thin and patchy" quality of the culture, not by the presence of other people in "her" field. She never equated being alone in the field with "good fieldwork," and from the first of her trips she had welcomed the company of people she knew, either for part of the journey or to live in the same house or to share an informant. What bothered her about Apache culture only gradually came clear. She had to think back to her frustration over the Serrano material, and the stubborn refusal of her data to produce a "whole" picture. And she had to put next to that experience her pleasure and ease of mind in Pueblo culture, and remember the soothing and inspiring effect when a culture "made sense." The Apache situation puzzled Ruth; here was not a depopulated or a scattered society, yet something seemed to be missing—

something was lacking in the picture she tried to create for this particular culture.

Eight years later when she took a second group of students into the field, she had a vocabulary and the concepts of culture-coherence, integrity, and pattern. Ruth Benedict expressed eagerness to trace the design of Blackfoot culture and to discover what held together a culture quite different from any she had yet studied. A new place, a new tribe, new students—Ruth would have been enthusiastic without ambivalence except that the world seemed to be collapsing around her in 1939. She managed nevertheless to find some gratification in working with the students. Her letters to Boas, few and distracted, reflected her assurance as a teacher and a fieldworker. "So far we have been attending funerals. There was one last night, one today and the big Indian one tomorrow. We are invited and welcomed at all of them, and our 'families' [with whom they lived] are eloquent in their courtesy to us."[162]

The Blackfoot trip proved Ruth's ability to transmit Boasian principles and an anthropological perspective. In 1939, however, she—and the students—faced a new era and a new regime at Columbia.

"Dying like him; like him with faith unshaken"

In 1931 Boasian field methods received a stern trial. During the winter of 1930–31 a young graduate student, Henrietta Schmerler, persuaded Ruth Benedict and Franz Boas to let her spend the summer on an Apache reservation. She was killed there in July 1931. Both her insistence and their ultimate agreement fit Columbia traditions. Students were expected to demonstrate a commitment to fieldwork; students also knew they would leave without exact field instructions.

Ruth, like Boas, recognized the risks of sending a student into the field in sink-or-swim manner. Generally they trusted that the dictum to treat each culture on its own terms would carry students through. "Cultural relativism" was the conceptual side of a field method built on respect for unfamiliar customs and behaviors. Henrietta Schmerler had seemed somewhat naive in her certainty that she could recognize strange customs and feel at home with them, Ruth remembered.[163] But Schmerler wanted very much to study the White Mountain Apache in eastern Arizona, and, a not-insignificant factor, she funded her own research. Too, Ruth made a point of encouraging women to pursue their interests, and without introducing a sharp feminist note, she did stand behind any woman who stated her eagerness to do a particular piece of fieldwork. Boas retained a kind of chivalrous attitude toward women in the field, concerned about their health, safety, and vulnerability. But he could be, and usually was, persuaded by Ruth Benedict to trust each new student.

Schmerler was one such instance. In supporting women students, Ruth did not counteract Boas's plans. Rather she pushed to a logical end policies he had established at the beginning of his tenure at Columbia. He early accepted women students: in 1914 Laura Benedict completed a dissertation titled "Bagobo Ceremonial, Magic and Myth," and four years later Martha Beckwith got her Ph.D. with a study of Hawaiian mythology.[164] Boas accepted women for "selfish" reasons only to the extent that he defined the discipline himself until World War I. He assumed women had access to areas of social life men did not have; he considered women more "intuitive" and skilled in interpersonal relationships and urged them to collect data on the "emotional," expressive sides of life. He did not scorn the subjects he assigned women, and he made similar collections of myths, ritual expressions, and blueberry pie recipes from the Northwest Coast Indians.[165]

Ruth Benedict supported, advised, and intervened for women students. Henrietta Schmerler, however, stretched the terms of Ruth's advocacy. Reviewing the Schmerler case later, Ruth recalled the student's romanticism and an enthusiasm that stood in lieu of a specific topic for research. Schmerler insisted upon going to a reputedly fierce tribe and without a well-defined project. "I know it is one of those unprecedented things that cannot be foreseen or guarded against," Ruth wrote Boas right after Schmerler's death, "and yet I think of endless points at which I might so easily have made different arrangements. I think especially of your saying as we came down 119th Street, 'Isn't it a rather untamed tribe?' "[166]

With some anxiety, then, Ruth had seen Henrietta Schmerler off to Arizona in the summer of 1931. At the same time, Ruth left for her summer trips, to Pasadena and then to meet the Southwest Laboratory group in Albuquerque. She would be spending most of her summer on the Mescalero Apache reservation, in contact with Boas mainly by letter. On July 25 she heard: "News of Schmerler's death. In bed."[167] Across the state from the tragedy, Ruth tried to find out exactly what had happened. From letters she learned the story and told Boas. Evidently Schmerler, in her determination to know all aspects of Apache life, had ridden out into the desert with two Apache "braves." The men interpreted her ride as a sexual invitation, and when she failed to cooperate, they killed her.[168]

Besides having to deal with officials, like the Indian agent for the White Mountain Apache, Ruth Benedict also had to deal with Henrietta Schmerler's father. Mr. Schmerler planned to bring suit against the Columbia department. Ruth's letters back to Mr. Schmerler sound a bit cold and indifferent. Partly she took refuge in a professional tone and tried to ease the father's grief by outlining the inevitable hazards of anthropological fieldwork. Partly she tried to deflect him from legal action by absolving the department of blame. She hoped he too would want, finally, to avoid the publicity of a court case.

Ruth Benedict dreaded the impact of a lawsuit on the anthropology program for several reasons. Not least among these was the importance of preserving amicable relationships with the Bureau of Indian Affairs and not irritating anyone by allotting blame for the Schmerler death. American anthropologists did their major fieldwork among American Indian tribes; Ruth had to ensure that fieldwork would go on relatively untroubled by pressures from the outside. She eventually succeeded in convincing Mr. Schmerler to settle out of court.

In her letters to Mr. Schmerler, Ruth adopted a characteristic calm in the face of crisis. She did not see virtue in intensifying the drama by displaying sentiment. Whatever she felt—and she had worked with Henrietta Schmerler before the trip—she subdued her emotions in order to handle the situation. Wisdom lay in minimizing the aftereffects and settling the dispute quietly. By the spring of 1932 everyone involved relievedly saw the "Schmerler incident" into official files. Ruth regretfully missed her Christmas trip away from Manhattan.

Henrietta Schmerler's death was the second student death in Ruth's ten years at Columbia. The first, Marie Bloomfield's, had clearly been a suicide; eight years after Schmerler, another student died on a fieldtrip. In 1939 Buell Quain died under initially mysterious circumstances on a trip to Brazil. Again Ruth Benedict had to deal with the event, uncertain about the details. She had supervised Quain's work and seems to have been particularly fond of him.[169] She wrote feelingly about Quain's death in letters, a contrast to the distance in her Schmerler letters.[170] Ruth expressed her sympathy for the bereaved Mrs. Quain; Buell Quain's mother, for her part, appreciated her son's fieldwork and wanted Ruth to put together a memorial volume of his papers. Mrs. Quain also decided that her son's inheritance should be used for anthropological research.

Yet the Quain matter caused Ruth Benedict more problems, pain, and confusion than the Schmerler death had. By the late 1930s Ruth had a recognized place in the department and in the profession. Colleagues in and out of New York knew about her supervision of student projects and about her personal enthusiasm for the Brazilian work. The other side of her disciplinary recognition surfaced after Quain died. Ruth and her friends heard that people blamed her for his death. She reported to

Boas rumors that she had deliberately sent Quain to a dangerous area, suspecting he would be killed, in order to get his legacy for the department. Ruth had little way of determining the source of the malicious gossip, whether in envy, rivalry, thwarted ambitions, or pure dislike.

For months, Ruth wrote letters about the Quain legacy and about the rumors attached to the money. She also became convinced, in spite of Mrs. Quain's protests, that Quain had killed himself. In August 1939 she told another student (William Lipkind) of Buell's death. "It will be a great shock, for there is no doubt that it was suicide. We still do not know very much, but he wrote letters to the police official exonerating his Indians and saying he was a victim of a contagious disease." Suicide complicated both her personal responses and the practical matter of the legacy. Eventually Ruth managed to give the Quain money to several student fieldworkers. She expected fieldwork in the Amazon to be carried on. Quain's legacy, more than a matter of money, constituted an ongoing contribution to his science through the work of his colleagues. To die young, in the "hour of dreaming" and "with faith unshaken," was a resonating theme in Ruth's life story. Suicide struck a special note.

Ruth had written about suicide in her journal and would again. She also brought the subject into her poetry and into her anthropology. Once she wrote: "Months and years were just a routine to keep suicide from becoming too strong for me in an unguarded moment. There were years and years when the only motive that drove me was dread, and all my hope was to be able to circumvent some moment of unbearable reckoning."[171] Mixed with such moments of dread and misery, however, had been—and would increasingly be—moments of glory, exhilaration, satisfaction in her work, and some certainty (at last) about her ability to exercise the "supreme power" of woman, "to love."

7
Patterns of Culture

"He said nice things about the SW paper too"

ONE DAY IN JANUARY 1929, with her usual trepidation, Ruth Benedict gave Franz Boas three papers to read. Almost immediately she reported to Margaret Mead in New Guinea, ". . . And I trembled when he said he wanted to see me about a point. I'd told him that I thought he'd hate the *Century* article. But no, 'he thought an article like that would do more good than his book.' "[1] In addition to the *Century* article, "The Science of Custom," she had shown him "Psychological Types in the Cultures of the Southwest" and "Animism." From these, plus "Configurations of Culture in North America" and notes on the abnormal in cross-cultural perspective, Ruth Benedict constructed her first book, *Patterns of Culture*.

The book was a central event in Ruth's life, a statement of her professionalism and her commitment to anthropology as well as a demonstration of her understanding of the discipline and its implications for American society. The book also marked a turning point in Ruth's personal life. In the early 1930s she considered her role in the profession and, more specifically, her place in an anthropological community dominated by Papa Franz. An intensified demand for rewards from her career accompanied an agreed-upon separation from Stanley Benedict in 1930, a meeting with Natalie Raymond sometime in the late 1920s, and her decision to stop writing poetry for publication (though she continued to write for herself and close friends).

She did not voice all her expectations, but it becomes clear that she asked a great deal from the publication of a book. A book might provide —at last—that sense of fulfillment she wrote of in journal entries through World War I and the 1920s. A book might also prove to her that anthropology was not a futile endeavor, another time-filling distraction: "I should prove that I was no rolling stone," she had pledged years before.[2] Ruth wanted publication, and recognition from colleagues and a general audience. Such stated and implicit motives lay behind the diary and letters she wrote in preparation for *Patterns of Culture*. Such motives also influenced her progress through drafts and sketches and "papers" to a completed book.

Ruth spent the summer of 1926 with Stanley Benedict. They divided their time between the house in New Hampshire, on Lake Winnepe-saukee, and Europe, where Stanley attended meetings. Ruth also went to a professional meeting in Europe, attending the Congress of Americanists in Rome: "My chance to put forth my effort."[3] She wanted to be a full-time anthropologist, but not to relinquish her private "precious moments." She wanted intellectual achievements, but not at the risk of emotional satisfactions. At first Ruth rather severely adjusted her career to her marriage, then she set her anthropology more generally against her need for "love," in friendship, a perfect companion, some kind of passionate attachment.

A year later, in 1927, Ruth decided she ought to have another field-trip. She traveled west, risking Stanley Benedict's annoyance and displeasure. He had jealously guarded their secluded New Hampshire vacations: "He loved the isolation and leisure of a New Hampshire summer; for many years he spent the entire vacation on the shore of Lake Winnepesaukee . . . leading a regular life with as few intrusions as possible," Ruth wrote in December 1936.[4]

Possibly she went to the Pima reservation to please Papa Franz, who generally urged regular, revitalizing fieldwork. She may also have been more ready than she said to prove to herself and to Stanley that career now came before Stanley Benedict's treasured summer vacations. Ruth had spoken often enough about a woman's need for independent interests, an "individual world of effort and creation."[5] But if Boas urged her to do another field study, with the Pima, he did not help her finance the trip. Somewhat reluctantly, she borrowed money from her husband. "It was alright about the money," she wrote to Papa Franz in August.[6] Undoubtedly Ruth was more relieved than her teacher; he expected husbands to support wives in the field and, a more usual occurrence, wives to support fieldworking husbands. Ruth Benedict was reaching for an independence beyond Stanley Benedict's personal demands and Boas's professional expectations. She wanted not money or approval but her own definition of worth. "I mean something so strenuous that the quests of the Grail are but faint shadows of a reality."[7]

That summer she gained a fair confidence, expressed in letters, in her professional involvement and in her relationships. Anne Singleton's name was known; readers of *The Dial* and *Poetry* praised the delicate thoughtfulness of her sonnets. The problematic friendship with Edward Sapir had been replaced by a closeness to Margaret Mead. Furthermore, Ruth had successfully done fieldwork behind the Pueblo "spiked fence." Two years before, she had tested Stanley's insight and was victorious: he unerringly recognized her poetic voice. "This inaugurated the best years of their marriage," Mead concluded.[8]

The "best" was only temporary and more precarious than Margaret realized. Deeply involved with her New Guinea data and absorbed in her divorce from Luther Cressman (to marry Reo Fortune), Margaret did not fully perceive all the strains in the Benedict marriage. "All our fires go out in nothingness," Ruth had written in a sonnet. Passion had disappeared. She said this explicitly in 1926: "Passion is a turncoat, but death will endure."[9] Sometime in the 1920s—Ruth wrote about it only retrospectively—Stanley Benedict fell in love with another woman.[10] Adding to the pain, Ruth read in the rejection the end of any chance to have a child. Motherhood seemingly impossible, and that source of "zest" gone, she turned back to her discipline. Ruth immersed herself in anthropology once again through her discipline's rite of passage, a field-trip. The stimulation of a "new country" and an alternative pattern invigorated her and bolstered her hope that work could conquer depression and "ennui."

In 1930 Stanley Benedict moved into his own apartment. According to friends, Ruth Benedict helped find and furnish his new home. Theirs was, eventually, an amicable separation and never a divorce. Ruth had her apartment on Central Park West, a manageable walk to the Columbia neighborhood, especially for an energetic woman. And if Central Park did not exactly resemble the hills around Shattuck Farm, at least Ruth looked out on green spaces and the park reservoir to relieve the "gray pavements" of Manhattan:

> . . . the gray pavements.
> These are lord and master over me.
> They have murdered my dreams.[11]

During the years following her separation from Stanley, Ruth spent her summers in Norwich, sometimes with her mother. "Mother is wonderfully peaceable. The two days we spent driving up from the Catskills and visiting college friends of hers were a perfect way of passing time together," she wrote from Norwich in July 1932.[12] Perhaps she had begun to free herself from her mother's precepts, if not yet to be certain of the conditions of her own "peaceableness." That summer, too, Ruth Benedict worked on the chapters of *Patterns of Culture*, adding the Pima notes to those she had saved from several Pueblo trips.

The year before, in January 1931, Ruth received an appointment as assistant professor of anthropology. She had been teaching full-time for nearly ten years without a regular appointment; her permanent departmental position coincided with the separation from Stanley Benedict, and not entirely by chance. Boas "validated" her professional independence and her growing absorption in departmental activities, as well as providing her with the income she now needed. With the appointment came even more responsibilities, including service on committees and panels outside the department and, over the years, outside the university. Papa Franz came to depend more and more on his "left hand" for emotional sustenance and administrative support.

Just before Christmas, December 1930, Marie Boas had been run over and killed. Boas, by then seventy-two years old, felt overwhelmed by her death and was himself weak and depressed through most of the following year.[13] He began considering giving up the chair of Columbia's department and perhaps retiring from the university altogether. He needed a successor and wanted one of his special choosing. During the winter of 1931 he wrote to California, urging Alfred Kroeber to leave the department at Berkeley and come and chair Columbia's department. After prolonged correspondence, Kroeber refused. Ruth may not have seen the letters and may not have realized the urgency of Boas's request —or the quality of his disappointment: "I do not think I need to tell you that I am very much disappointed," Boas told Kroeber in March. He had also been negotiating with Sapir, for a visiting position: "I had hoped that you and Sapir coming here would create a center that would be of real importance and further the development of anthropology in this country."[14] Ruth might have been somewhat tempted to welcome Sapir—looking forward to a renewal of old and strong ties; the two had shared "values of existence" for almost ten years, a temperamental and attitudinal similarity she found with few others. She knew Sapir's professional commitments and his emotional frame of mind "on her pulses," as well as from his statements. But Sapir did not leave New Haven.

Ruth Benedict admired Kroeber, and for three decades the two kept up an intense intellectual debate. Theodora Kroeber remembered their concentrated conversations at dinner parties and told how Ruth once simply ignored the accidental fall off her plate of a Rock Cornish hen.[15] Ruth may also have envied the man Boas apparently favored and regarded as heir. Kroeber himself chafed at the pull Boas exerted and, schooled in psychoanalysis, mulled over the father-son aspects of their relationship. Ruth coveted the respect Boas accorded his first, brilliant and remarkably prolific, student. She trusted Boas's affection; she worried about his approval. Boas expressed fondness in letters, conversations, and comments on her work, but a note of gentle concern crept into the collegial exchange. Ruth received these expressions of wary concern with ambivalence. Such expressions did not accord with her image of the "professional" woman, seriously committed to her "endeavor."

By 1931, when Boas asked him to come to New York, Kroeber had published three books and eleven major articles, had participated in archaeological digs, had practiced lay analysis, and had raised a family.[16] He had started and sustained a significant department of anthropology and established basic disciplinary approaches. By 1931 Ruth Benedict had published five articles but no full-length book. She had published her dissertation—all Columbia dissertations were published in the pre-World War II years—and a collection of myths: *Tales of the Cochiti Indians,* with brief introductory notes.[17] A desire to prove herself to Boas and to write something substantial and encompassing were among the motives that led her to take on a book, wondering at her own bravado.

"Perfect summer weather," she wrote to Margaret Mead in July 1932. "And I've got the library work done that I planned, and written a fair amount for me. I have to keep your rate of production out of my head, for I can't do anything like it even at my best."[18] At Shattuck Farm, Ruth found the most congenial setting for a major endeavor. She relaxed there and let her mind wander; in the familiar landscape, she discovered the stamina for writing a book. The impulse to complete a manuscript came as much from contentment as from her bothersome envy of Alfred Kroeber.

"Taking such delight in her I have the happiest conditions for living"

Ruth Benedict never expressed complete satisfaction in her work or felt herself completely fulfilled by her anthropology, ". . . for I don't identify myself with anthropology."[19] During the late 1920s her personal life changed greatly. She and Stanley Benedict made their separation official; Margaret Mead was away, involved in a second marriage and collaboration with Reo Fortune, and Ruth herself discovered a new "perfect companion."[20] Around 1930 she offered to share the Central Park West apartment with a woman named Natalie Raymond.

Margaret Mead does not mention Nat—her name is not in the index of *Anthropologist at Work.* Apparently Nat and Margaret were in "separate rooms"[21] and in rooms without adjoining doors. This may have been one of the relationships Mead only learned about after Ruth's death.[22]

Whatever Margaret Mead knew or guessed about the friendship between Ruth and Natalie Raymond, she did not include anything in her memoirs.

But Ruth did not keep her friend a total secret. Judging from references in letters, she neither minimized nor disguised her attachment to the younger woman. Regards to Nat, love to Nat, and similar phrases appeared at the close of letters written to Ruth through the early 1930s. Those who knew Nat best were the students Ruth Benedict took to the field in 1931. Natalie Raymond traveled to the Mescalero Apache reservation with Ruth in August, and she stayed long enough to meet members of the Mescalero team.[23]

Ruth typically went to the field with company, sometimes a Vassar friend, once Boas, and on several occasions Ruth Bunzel. Nat would have had to take a break from her own schedule for a summer trip. Like Stanley Benedict and like Frederick Fulton, Natalie Raymond was a research chemist. Her laboratory was at the then Rockefeller Institute (now Rockefeller University) on York Avenue in New York City. A block away from Cornell, Nat may have known or worked with Stanley Benedict; Stanley may even have introduced her to his wife. Perhaps he wanted to counteract Ruth's self-denigration and doubt, feelings she expressed in diary entries: "There's one obvious fact about my personal life: it's always been built around refusals."[24] If so, Nat would have been virtually the only colleague Stanley Benedict did introduce to his wife. His "rooms" were more separate than hers, and Ruth knew as little about her husband's workplace as he learned about hers.

Yet over the years and despite the failings recorded by Ruth, Stanley Benedict demonstrated considerable insight into his wife's character and demands, her restlessness and "yearnings." Whether or not he was responsible for the meeting, Nat certainly filled an important place in Ruth's life.

In 1916 Ruth had quoted Godwin's opinion of his wife's attachment to Fanny Blood: the "ruling passion of her mind."[25] In writing about Mary Wollstonecraft, Ruth Benedict accepted Godwin's account of the intimacy between the two women, though she otherwise disliked his portrayals. Like Godwin she recognized how thorough and "momentous" an influence a friendship could be.[26] Ruth's association with Nat fit into an ongoing puzzlement over the role of passion and sexuality in her own life as a woman, a preoccupation prompted by Stanley Benedict's dismissal of her as "passionless."[27] One learns from the biographer's description of the Mary Wollstonecraft–Fanny Blood friendship not the facts of Ruth's friendship with another woman but the quality of Ruth's expectations. Poems carried revelation further:

> We look on her—and Lo! as any woman
> She folds us to her hair, her breasts, her kisses
> And we are impotent, and dream we are content.[28]

Ruth did not analyze individuals or friendships; her writings, from "Mary Wollstonecraft" through sonnets and diaries, conveyed the intensity of perfect companionship.

For Ruth Benedict the very intimacy she valued brought anxieties. She worried often about whether she trapped Nat, tied her down: "She has so much more of life ahead of her than I have, and so many choices still to make."[29] She referred to their age difference with concern and, made self-conscious by her assessment of Mary Wollstonecraft, struggled against mothering her younger friend. "The passionate protectiveness of a mother for her frailest child," she said in "Mary Wollstonecraft."[30] The little that is said about Natalie Raymond reveals the woman's firm purposefulness and no special frailty. Nat seems to have been a conscientious researcher; regards sent to her through Ruth asked about her work and wished her well on "findings."[31] In the end, Nat appeared to have been a solid and reliable woman, not a "timid, clinging" Fanny Blood.

The friendship remained a powerful force in Ruth Benedict's life at least through the 1930s. In August 1936 Franz Boas asked Ruth about Natalie, her feelings and health and work.[32] That month a crisis had occurred which Ruth greeted with melodramatic phrases characteristic of moments of concern: "Nat's gallstone attack. Drove down from Norwich by night." A week and a half later she recorded "Nat's improvement."[33] On July 16, 1937, Ruth Benedict wrote a will; she left Shattuck Farm to Natalie Raymond.[34]

"40,000 words already together for a book"

The satisfactory domestic arrangement of her shared apartment buoyed Ruth's spirits. Personal contentment underlay her determination to finish a book, even at her reported slow pace.[35] Ruth habitually mocked her own ambitions, stylistically undercutting her fonder dreams. Style evinced the wariness she felt about the unfolding pattern of her life. Before starting *Patterns of Culture*, Ruth had not only stopped being a wife and become an assistant professor, not only stopped living with Stanley Benedict and met Natalie Raymond, but she had virtually stopped writing poetry and spent long hours editing the *Journal of American Folk-Lore*. All these experiences influenced her book; some of the influences she recognized, others remained unconscious. Ruth Benedict composed a self-conscious "life story" and remarked in her poetry upon the need for passionate vision and creative endeavor; her studies of folklore, a different version of this idea, also became an important part of her ethnographic approach. The degree to which personal changes impelled not only the decision to write but also the style of writing may not have been a constantly present factor—Ruth also recognized that too much awareness led to her ever-lurking sense of futility.

When Ruth Benedict began writing she thought back over gathered evidence and former arguments. She drew her arguments, to an extent, from the articles Boas read in 1929. Evidence came primarily from her fieldwork in the Southwest Pueblos. She remembered the "cliff-dwellings dug into the sheer face of the precipice, or built on a ledge hundreds of feet from the valley floor."[36] She remembered even more sharply the rhythmic regularity of Zuñi life, a rhythm that affected her poetry and her prose: "We are so wise. And out across these sands / They plant their feathered prayersticks in the moon / Tonight, praying the gods of ancient pueblo sires," she wrote in a stately cadence.[37]

The writer, and anthropologist, needed to construct an order in her personal, professional, and poetic responses. She needed to arrange her impressions for a credible and scientific account, and she started with three organizing concepts: the expressed theme of Pueblo life; the contrast between Pueblo and Pima Indians; the Apollonian-Dionysian characterization in Nietzsche's *Birth of Tragedy*. Behind these choices lay the emotional and intellectual experiences of her past forty years.

The contrast Ruth noted during her 1927 fieldtrip inspired her approach. She wrote to Boas in August, comparing the Pima to Pueblo Indians: "The contrast with the latter is *unbelievable!*"[38] Next to the moderate and peaceful Zuñi with whom she had spent two summers (four months), the Pima seemed fierce, warlike, immoderate. Fascinated by the differences, Ruth Benedict elaborated each group's dominant characteristics. Her Pueblos *are* more self-contained and placid than the Pueblos described by other anthropologists and, though little has been published on the Pima, one suspects that Ruth—calculatingly—exaggerated their outbursts and frenzy. But she had a purpose, a motive for her literary liberties: "It is not possible to understand Pueblo attitudes toward life without some knowledge of the culture from which they have detached themselves: that of the rest of North America. It is by the force of the contrast that we can calculate the strength of their opposite drive."[39]

To portray the Pueblos distinctly, the anthropologist set them against their neighbors. Nearly fifteen years before, in her biographical essays, she had similarly planned to delineate one woman's personality by comparison to two other women. In 1930 Ruth had larger ambitions and anticipated a wider audience, yet for manner of presentation she turned back to the biographies, along with poems, slight sketches, and abundant "reading notes." Developing a style for her book, Ruth gained confidence in her point of view and learned to trust the "worth" of her endeavor—even measured by the world's "coarse thumb and finger."[40] She spoke out loud her passionate principles, a task left undone when she put aside "Mary Wollstonecraft."

At the same time, she searched for something beyond her observation of "striking" differences between the Pueblos and the Pima. "When you read it in Nietzsche it's more clearly the right—poetical way of seeing," she wrote to Margaret Mead in an uncharacteristically clumsy set of sentences.[41] She took "Apollonian" and "Dionysian" from Nietzsche, admiring his exuberant and arrogant assumptions about whole societies and whole personalities. A similar admiration for "sweep" led her to mention Wilhelm Dilthey and Oswald Spengler and in 1919–20 to be attracted by Alexander Goldenweiser's presumptuous summaries of "primitive cultures."

While Ruth Benedict was writing drafts of *Patterns of Culture*, she read a recently published book, Virginia Woolf's *The Waves* (1931). Her pleasure in the experimental and difficult novel relates to her use of Nietzsche's "names" and to her attempt to convey a culture in a single phrase. In *The Waves*, Ruth responded to the idea of evoking essential spirit rather than detailing elements of character, displaying inconsistencies and rough spots. "Did you like *The Waves*? And did you keep thinking how you'd set down everybody you knew in a similar fashion? I did," she wrote in January 1932.[42] Virginia Woolf conveyed the complexity of human character through the juxtaposition of distinct individualities and "moments of being." But Ruth also found something lacking: "I suppose I'm disappointed that she didn't include any violent temperaments, and I want my group of persons more varied."[43] She thought about *The Waves* while writing her own book, in which the complexity of human society is conveyed through the juxtaposition of distinct, particular types. "What you can spin is all you have to work with, and the result is altogether dependent on that. Don't you think, given the limited types she allows herself, she's done it beautifully?"[44]

Like the novelist, the anthropologist needed more than one pair of contrasting types to illustrate the variety in "designs for living." Her descriptive evocations of Pueblo, Dobu, and Kwakiutl cultures have to be read as part of a calculated plan. Ruth Benedict wrote nothing carelessly, and her first book was no exception. *Patterns of Culture* drew on previously outlined arguments, but as the writer gathered her thoughts and her data other modes of interpretation stretched and altered the text.

Ruth chose the Zuñi as her first example, a perfect illustration of the Apollonian type. She needed other, equally distinctive examples of an accommodation to the natural environment and to the "wonderful power" of the supernatural.[45] She also wanted to move away from the "essentially mild" she objected to in Woolf.[46] Three years earlier she had read Reo Fortune's description of the Dobu Islanders. "I enjoyed the Dobuan material immensely. After I'd read a couple of hours I'd feel they'd all been sold to the devil," she had written to Reo Fortune in January 1929.[47] A few sentences later she revealed another source of her interest: "For thorough-going difference from our own ways of behavior, you could hardly have hit on a better example."[48] Sometime after this she decided the Dobuans made a perfect foil for the mild Southwest Indians. She had finished the Pueblo chapter and drafted one on Dobu. "If you think it would be awful of me to take the words out of your mouth this way, cable me collect, just 'Don't,' and I'll understand."[49]

She had already picked a third culture, repeating, whether intentionally or not, the structure of "Adventures in Womanhood." Ruth knew Boas's Kwakiutl almost as well as he did—or as well as she knew the Zuñi. The self-aggrandizing, greedy Northwest Coast Indians had been present in Boas's seminars and classes from the time she arrived at Columbia in 1921. Ruth learned Kwakiutl culture, then taught the material when she took over seminars for Papa Franz. She undoubtedly added field notes to the published sources cited in *Patterns of Culture* and probably borrowed bits of information from Boas's conversations and references to the Kwakiutl at dinner parties in his New Jersey home.

Franz Boas had an enormous store of information on the Kwakiutl. His eager accumulation of fact included kinship terminologies, myths, observations on marriages and child-rearing, details of vocabulary and of cooking—the list goes on. And he kept collecting, for in spite of homesickness, occasional depressions and ill health, irritation at smoky fires and yapping dogs, Boas traveled to the Northwest Coast until he was nearly eighty.[50] He made more than thirteen trips, and when he could not be in the field (or chose instead to vacation with his wife, Marie, and after her death with his family), he depended on a stream of letters from his informant George Hunt. Hunt's faithful reporting both helped and hindered Boas; along with the material, Boas had to face accusations that the *Kwakiutl Reports,* if his at all, were at best collaborative.[51]

At any rate, Ruth Benedict realized her good luck. She had abundant data on the Kwakiutl and a vivid secondhand impression of the landscape and of individuals to match her memories of the Pueblos.[52]

Boas never completed a Kwakiutl ethnography, and in this respect his data, as she said, resembled straight anthropological field notes. "Tons of raw material entirely reliable, and a minimum of interpretation or explanation," Ruth noted.[53] Reo Fortune's material came in a different form, carefully arranged and argued. "But I hadn't really thought I'd need to take one of yours [to Margaret Mead] or Reo's cultures—because you do them so well I can only parrot your points. And with the pueblos and the NWC that isn't so."[54] Ruth clearly considered Boas's material "raw" and Fortune's "finished." But her own purposes dominated altogether, and she did not ever really "sponge" from the *Sorcerers of Dobu* as she anticipatd she might: "You have said it so well in your book that I can only sponge."[55] Ruth had chosen two cultures to go with her Pueblos because she could consult with the fieldworkers, and she wanted to consult as she carried out her intention of thoroughly reworking the data. Fortune pointed out how she rearranged even his material: "It [*Patterns of Culture*] looks fine—and you really are kind the way you take it [*Dobu*] and you say it all so well—it makes me think of the place and the people and not of my book at all . . . and is such an improvement in its ready quick but adequate passage . . . ," he went on in his "lumpy bumpy" style.[56]

Ruth Benedict neutralized her various sources (including hundreds of published pages on the Zuñi Indians). She molded the information to her particular "idea," and (as Fortune realized) maintained an absolutely consistent and evocative style throughout chapters 4, 5, and 6.

"I discuss my reasons for choosing just these three cultures"

Ruth Benedict had hinted at her reasons for choosing the three cultures in the January 1929 letter to Reo Fortune. "For thorough-going differences . . . you could hardly have hit on a better example."[57] In the ethnographic chapters, she displayed distinct "designs for living," the integrity of each, and the impact of custom upon individual members of a society. She also had in mind, the statement to Fortune revealed, a review of American customs, the cultural dictates her readers knew too well to recognize. "It is the inevitability of each familiar motivation that we defend, attempting always to identify our own local ways of behaving with Behaviour, or our own socialized habits with Human Nature."[58]

Looking at primitive societies did not simply satisfy curiosity—though there was undoubtedly that; it also provided the material for instructing her readers, colleagues and citizens alike. The aim, educating, brought together her personal, political, and anthropological concerns.

Ruth Benedict had undertaken a difficult task, and she proceeded care-fully. *Patterns of Culture* shows a writer at work and an orderly process built on "rehearsals" and sketches already approved by Franz Boas. "I hadn't realized till I came to plan this work how all the points I've worked on all fall into the same outline," she commented in the summer of 1932.[59]

Two articles especially established the logical framework for *Patterns of Culture*: "Psychological Types in the Cultures of the Southwest," first delivered in 1928, then published in the *Proceedings of the Twenty-Third International Congress of Americanists,* and "Configurations of Culture in North America," published in 1932.[60] (For her concluding chapters, Ruth used notes and data on self and society and, primarily, on the diversity of "normal/abnormal" from culture to culture.) To lighten the tone of the introductory chapters, Ruth included phrases and images from "The Science of Custom" (1929),[61] a piece admired by Papa Franz for its conversational style. From the titles and locations of her articles, it appears that she rehearsed not only the substance but also the style of her book and that she intended from early on to appeal to more than an anthropological or even a solely professional audience. When Ruth began to compose the book, she added vibrant examples to carry home her thesis—to embed "dry logic" in details of living, breath-ing cultures.

The theme of *Patterns of Culture* is, as Ruth put it, "cultural con-figurations again."[62] Her remark was modest; her theme extended be-yond "configurations again" to include advocacy of culture-over-nature and of personal creativeness within social constraints. She pointed to the *range* of configurations and to the *integrated* quality of any one arrange-ment. Deliberately, her word "integrity" echoed descriptions of person-ality, and through her vocabulary Ruth implied the conditions of indi-vidual development in a society: "the fundamental and distinctive cul-tural configurations that pattern existence and condition the thoughts and emotions of the individuals who participate in those cultures."[63] Ruth Benedict saved the issue of "adjustment of the individual to his cultural type"[64] for her last chapters.

The anthropologist also took on the responsibility of justifying the study of others, anticipating a "why bother" question at the least and a suggestion of "exploitation" at the most. She had formulated her justi-fication in "Science of Custom" and brought the point into her book. "The whole problem of the formation of the individual's habit-patterns under the influence of traditional customs can best be understood at the present time through the study of simpler peoples."[65] In fact she sprinkled the point liberally through *Patterns of Culture*; phrased vari-

ously, the "transparency" of the "simpler material"[66] became her persistent theme. One important version appeared immediately, an adap-
tion from "Science of Custom" and repeated in drafts of publicity
blurbs.[67] This was her "laboratory" analogy.

Primitive cultures "are a laboratory in which we may study the
diversity of human institutions. . . . It is the only laboratory of social
forms that we have or shall have."[68] In these sentences, Ruth expressed
her belief that the "simple" illuminated the "complex," showing in outline the content and the development of elaborated forms. Primitive cultures are simple in the sense of being clearly phrased: a comprehensible
articulation of social arrangements and their impact. Ruth referred, on
the one hand, to experimental sciences and, on the other, to aesthetic
concepts to further her argument. (She would not "bore" her readers
with explication.[69])

For Ruth, above all the study of others was justified by reference to
"self"—to individual and social self. She said this not in so many words
but between the lines of all eight chapters. The primitive is a laboratory
because interrelationships characteristic of *any* culture emerge sharply
in uncontacted, uncomplicated groups. Ruth Benedict added to the thesis
of "Science of Custom" a corollary: the array of diverse customs in an
anthropologist's laboratory proved that no one culture was natural or
best or permanent. Comparison led to change. Ruth did not, evidently,
conceive of a hierarchy when she compared "primitive" to "civilized"
societies; rather, she offered evidence for the vast flexibility in human
arrangements. Further, she stressed the distinct quality of each of her
samples—each was a unique type, she said, extending the thesis of
"Psychological Types."[70]

Distinction related to integrity, to the special coherence of traits
Ruth called a "configuration."[71] A configuration resulted from the judicious, ongoing recombination of traits. The argument in summary sounds
intricate, but Ruth wrote it out in a persuasively easygoing style. Ethnographic details and consistent analogies enlivened the prose, and—
when successful—implanted her concepts in her readers' minds. *Patterns
of Culture* exudes greater forcefulness than any previous formulation of
the same idea.

Ruth Benedict had followed Boas's suggestions. Throughout the
early years of the twentieth century he had encouraged anthropologists
to study individual cultures and culture processes before positing general laws of human behavior. Students, Ruth among them, took the
prescription to heart, exploring distinct cultures and showing the unmistakably "particular" historical factors in culture coherence. Ruth wrote
culture biographies.

> *"A culture, like an individual, is a more or less consistent*
> *pattern of thought and action"*

How integration came about and the probable implications for individuals in a society emerged in the book, subsumed under the notion of "pattern." Before Ruth Benedict chose that word, she experimented with biographical and historical approaches, and tried the usefulness of notions from the physical sciences and from aesthetics. In each case she revealed her reluctance to analyze, her prejudice in favor of swift, vivid characterizations.[72] Her goal was to evoke a "whole-greater-than-parts," an accurate rendering of her idea of culture. In pursuit of the goal, she adopted the phrases now firmly associated with her name, like the comparison of a culture composite to "gun-powder."[73]

Another figure, the "arc" of behaviors, represented Ruth's more important idea of selectivity and arrangement.

> In culture too we must imagine a great arc on which are ranged the possible interests provided either by the human age-cycle or by the environment or by man's various activities. A culture that capitalized even a considerable proportion of these would be . . . unintelligible. . . . Its identity as a culture depends upon the selection of some segments of this arc.[74]

Selectivity was essential to her theme, though Ruth did not precisely explain what she meant. Figures of speech made her argument, and her central rhetorical figure involved the analogy of culture to personality. "A culture, like an individual, is a more or less consistent pattern of thought and action."[75] She supplemented this with aesthetic concepts, references to the development of an art style.

Ruth Benedict knew what she was doing when she composed. Little in *Patterns of Culture* was random or gratuitous; her references to art, like those to personality, indicated both a process and a product. An unconscious process resulted in an artful, often wondrous product.[76] The pattern emerged over time, in a cathedral, a culture, a person. Sometimes Ruth seemed frankly in awe at the mysterious component that remained, an element in patterning unknown both to the creator and the observer. Her life story, too, indicated a view of pattern as precious and not fully comprehensible. She had experienced the precariousness of patterns, and she assumed a similar truth about cultures.

She tried yet another analogy, of culture and language, to clarify her notion of pattern. This analogy emphasized the impact of particularized changes on underlying "order" and simultaneously the constraints of order upon particularized changes. But for Ruth Benedict, language, or the linguistic analogy, slighted the aesthetic connotations of pattern. Her interpretation of culture included the drive toward satisfaction and pleasure in an elegant design; she saw this aesthetic motive compelling cultures—and people—to design and redesign the terms of their existence. Though phrases like "unconscious canons of choice" suggested passivity, Ruth always meant an active and a creative process when she talked about culture patterns.

Her most powerful trope in *Patterns of Culture* yoked culture to person. To convey her point she used "integrity" and "configuration" along with "pattern." The words are straightforward borrowings from Gestalt psychology and reflect that view of a person. "Have you read Koffka?" Sapir asked in 1925.[77] On his advice, perhaps supplemented by Margaret Mead's enthusiasm, Ruth read Kurt Koffka's *The Growth of the Mind* (1924)[78] and added the book to other, selected readings in social psychology. The concept there of "wholeness" of personality suited her intuitions, as did an emphasis on selectivity, a continual arranging of traits taken from surroundings by self. The link between any self and a setting was dynamic and distinctive, changing over time according to biographical determinants. As the lines of pattern emerged, arranging became a conscious process; pattern could become plan and the ordering deliberate, for an individual and a society. Ruth Benedict certainly had "self-conscious" in mind when she coined the term "culture-conscious" in *Patterns of Culture*.

Edward Sapir influenced Ruth's book, not so much through his linguistic discoveries as through his psychological insights. She did not cite his essays on language (one appeared in the *Encyclopedia of Social Sciences* with her essay on "Animism"), nor did she cite his "Culture Genuine and Spurious," though she must have known this fine essay in its several versions.[79] She did cite "Cultural Anthropology and Psychiatry,"[80] a piece close to the aim of *Patterns of Culture*. In general, Sapir like Ruth talked about the integrity of a culture on the way to talking about individual distinctiveness within a culture unity. "There is no sound and vigorous individual incorporation of a cultured ideal without the soil of a genuine communal culture; and no genuine communal culture without the transforming energies of personalities at once robust and saturated with the cultural values of their time and place."[81] Ruth elaborated the intricate links between "incorporation" and "transforming energies," in her words, the person molded by and molding his culture.

With help from the philosopher George Santayana, her Zuñi informants, and her biographical studies, Ruth took on the issue of how an individual can absorb, even epitomize, cultural values without being submerged. The problem of "fitting" without "giving in" had long bothered the woman; in *Patterns of Culture* the anthropologist added a further formulation.

Ruth Benedict enjoyed Santayana, and sentences from his writings crept into her journals and essays. Santayana described the individual who represented his culture by articulating its dominant themes.[82] Articulation did not have to be verbal. Ruth herself put above words the articulation of cultural values through gesture, fantasy, and individual experiences. The anthropologist, however, qualified the philosopher-poet's finest praise for the individual whose life and art embodied his society's highest ideals. Her essay "Mary Wollstonecraft" had praised the individual whose expressions embodied, artfully, alternative ideals, the possibility of a new society. Recognition of the importance of the divergent individual became a major point and a critical note in Ruth's anthropology. She had described Mary Wollstonecraft as a woman who refused to accept the "dominant themes" of her culture until the last years of her life, when she found fulfillment in marriage and mother-hood. Ruth did not solve the problem she there introduced, the conflict between self-fulfillment and limiting, necessary conventions, between articulating a critical idea and attaining a measurable contentment. She did not judge or evaluate the matter of a feminist submitting to social conventions and to "woman's nature" while proclaiming, in the *Vindication of Women's Rights,* a message of rebellion against any constraints on the individual person.

"The ideal man"

In *Patterns of Culture* Ruth Benedict focused on a topic with personal ramifications and a professional legitimacy; self and society was not a new topic for her or her discipline.[83] She went beyond the self-is-nothing-without-society theorem and, though readers did not always notice, beyond a mere equivalence of personality and culture. Ruth claimed that individuals needed society for their very individuality and that societies needed individualities in order to survive, adjust to crisis, and change.

Ruth also had a particular idea about how to present these points. In proper anthropological fashion, her fieldwork experiences gave her a clue. She applied a Zuñi concept of "the ideal man" to her discussion of self and society and in the process substantiated her notion of "pattern."

Through their "ideal," Zuñi Indians perpetuated a standard of individual behavior. The standard reflected cultural values and became a vehicle for transmitting pattern from society to individuals. Ruth Benedict borrowed the idea to express connections between individual and culture without attributing cause or direction. She avoided Reo Fortune's occasional emphasis on institutional causes (overall, the two anthropologists agreed remarkably, perhaps with Margaret Mead's help). She also avoided an implication that individual (or personality) simply reflected culture, the person being only a blotter for cultural expectations.

"The ideal man in Zuñi is a person of dignity and affability who has never tried to lead, and who has never called forth comment from his neighbours."[84] The Zuñi ideal man reiterated the culture pattern. The Dobuans, too, told of their ideal man, and Fortune wrote: "In other words the desirable man is he who has sought and gained the dangerous values unhurt by the black art of his rivals."[85] And the Kwakiutl, never to be outdone, recreated an ideal man for future ethnographers: "You knew my father, and you know what he did with his property. He was reckless and did not care what he did. . . . He was a true chief among the Koskimo."[86]

These are the protagonists of *Patterns of Culture.* The three figures are not biographical subjects; rather, they represent personality types, embodying the "type" of the culture.[87] Much as she relished her "heroes," Ruth in fact kept biography out of ethnography, in regard to persons if not to approach. She was not interested in particular personalities when she drafted *Patterns of Culture* and, with notable restraint, did not describe any of the people she met in the Pueblos. She wrote about the ideal person Nick and Flora recognized and, presumably, valued. Or maybe not Nick. According to Elsie Clews Parsons and other Southwest ethnographers, Nick embodied antithetical traits and was by no means the typical mild and unambitious Zuñi. Nick succeeded, thanks to visiting anthropologists and a last-minute rescue from the punishment due a witch, anyone who, like him, contradicted Zuñi prized virtues.[88] Nick was exceptional. According to Ruth Benedict, usually the individual who most closely approximated the "ideal" succeeded in his or her setting. This congenial individual expressed in behavior and beliefs the dominant values of his culture. The congenial individual also won prestige and material rewards. Ruth added an important point: the accommodating and successful individual could effectively modify existing patterns. Here, however, she raised a problem and postponed discussion until her last two, nonethnographic chapters.

For Ruth Benedict individuality was a matter of expression, and the "ideal man" set boundaries for the expression of self in a society. Every culture provided channels for expression, in action and in gesture, channels that were both limiting and releasing. Ruth also included in her account the possibility of individuals for whom provided channels were not adequate or satisfactory or possible at all.[89] The conventional forms of expression had to allow for the emotional as well as the intellectual impulses of human beings. Thus, Ruth returned to an old preoccupation, a fascination with the forces of irrationality in every society. That was her theme in "Animism" and in coincidental reviews of Lévy-Bruhl.[90]

"The death of a near relative is the closest thrust that existence deals."[91] Death tests the ability of a culture to handle profound individual emotions and to restore to a group its order. Ruth Benedict had picked a subject whose resonance to her life would not be noticed under the traditional attention given death customs in anthropology.

Death and mourning rituals dramatized the emotional content of an individual-culture link. Rituals, especially, highlighted the significance of conventionalized, formulaic expressions for individual grief. "Prayer in Zuñi is never an outpouring of the human heart. . . . And the prayers are never remarkable for their intensity. They are always mild and ceremonious in form."[92] Ruth knew the value of structured expression for relieving agony; she also knew that individuals might be variously attuned to conventional patterns. Death, the supreme crisis for individual and society, was faced and handled uniquely by every person and every culture.

The Dobuan reacted to death with malice and vengeance. "Dobu in Dr. Fortune's words, 'cower under a death as under a whipping,' and look about immediately for a victim . . . the person to charge with one's fatal illness."[93] On the Northwest Coast the Kwakiutl pitches his will against death: "Death was the paramount affront they recognized."[94] The Zuñi individual hardly mourned and minimally acknowledged grief.[95] The typical Zuñi accepted death calmly, expressed sadness only with others, resigned to that as to everything in life.

Ruth's conviction that individual "terrors" can be brought to bay within formal conventions and available traditions colored her middle three chapters. A reader remembers the Zuñi rhythmically scattering black cornmeal, the Dobuan locating and punishing the inevitable killer, and the Kwakiutl burning his house in arrogant protest against death. Through such vignettes the anthropologist reiterated but did not dissect the links between an individual and his culture. The artist in *Patterns of Culture* exploited the stylistic potential: Death comes near the end of each chapter.

Death provided a further lesson in the book. During her fieldwork Ruth Benedict asked the Zuñi about suicide and to her amazement found that no one recognized the idea. Even more startling, the Zuñi did not seem to require an idea of self-destruction: "They have no idea what it could be."[96] (This point, among others, elicited severe criticism; anthropologists who objected to Ruth's approach stressed the violence in Zuñi life, toward oneself and others.[97]) The Dobuan killed himself and the Kwakiutl did, each in characteristic fashion. In suicide, each carried out the themes of living.[98] Absorbed by these contrasts, Ruth made a crucial suggestion: a culture pattern may entirely exclude certain attitudes and behaviors so that, not on the "segment," these do not even negatively affect individuals. Told of suicide, the Zuñi listened politely, then laughed.[99]

There would always be in all cultures individuals unable to take the available channels: the suicide in Norwich (an act condemned by Ruth Fulton's grandparents and praised in books she read), the bitterly weeping Zuñi, the gently grieving Dobuan. And such individuals "have all the problems of the aberrant everywhere."[100] There were always people who did not fit.

"Cultures in which these abnormals function at ease and with honor"

"Just as those are favoured whose congenial responses are closest to that behaviour which characterizes their society, so those are disoriented whose congenial responses fall in that arc of behaviour which is not capitalized by their culture. These abnormals are those who are not supported by the institutions of their civilizations."[101] Ruth Benedict's phrases in the last chapter of *Patterns of Culture* have an intensity and poignancy revealing a more than disciplinary interest in her subject. Her protagonist in chapter 8 is the "disoriented" person whose "characteristic reactions are denied validity" and who faces a "chasm between them and the cultural pattern."[102] She had long mulled over the problem of normal and abnormal, and she published an article nearly simultaneously with *Patterns of Culture*, "Anthropology and the Abnormal."[103]

The last two chapters of *Patterns of Culture* focus on the individual in society. In her conclusions, Ruth not only completed the logic of the previous six chapters but introduced ideas and approaches central to her subsequent work and to the work of anthropologists from 1934 to the present. In these chapters, too, she revealed the grounds of her commitment to ethnographic inquiry. She asked how far an individual might depart from expected standards of behavior and of temperament without being ostracized, tortured, driven insane. In answering the question, Ruth Benedict embarked on a comparative evaluation of cultures in terms of permitted variations.

She phrased the dilemma as one of creativity versus congeniality. Her book illustrated the dynamic quality of individual encounters with culture, the constant "creating" necessary to cultural survival. The self, Ruth knew, strained against conventions while depending on these for making sense of experience. The challenge was to accept convention yet fully realize self-integrity. "But no anthropologist with a background of experience of other cultures has ever believed that individuals were automatons, mechanically carrying out the decrees of their civilization."[104] Being congenial, she said, did not mean conforming into self-obliterating passivity. Individuals do not drown in "an overpowering ocean" of custom,[105] although every action, every decision, every intimate mood is colored by custom. A culture, she said, can be intricately patterned without submerging the component individualities. In a more venturesome vein, Ruth Benedict hinted that the intricately patterned culture might show the greatest tolerance for diversity.

The "passionately thought," not very disguised message of the book was that in other places, in other times, being congenial had other meanings. This was the hinge of a multiple-stranded argument. Ruth wrote her book and the article to controvert assumptions of "natural" human behavior, universal "personality types," and permanency of customs. In the process she showed how branding a "type" unnatural could lead to madness, neurosis, irreconcilable conflict.

Sexual and religious experiences were her prime examples for the varying definitions of normal and abnormal from society to society. One can speculate on the private impulses behind these publicly expedient choices. Sex and sexual behavior were popular topics in the 1920s, and Ruth never denied her desire for a wide audience.

> When the homosexual response is regarded as a perversion, however, the invert is immediately exposed to all the conflicts to which aberrants are always exposed. His guilt, his sense of inadequacy, his failures, are consequences of the disrepute which social tradition visits upon him, and few people can achieve a satisfactory life unsupported by the standards of their society. The adjustments that society demands of them would strain any man's vitality.[106]

Society, not biology, produces the "aberrant" individual, frail and "useless to society."[107] Ruth's version of culture-over-nature went with another point: culture can be changed.

Religious trance was her other example. "Trance is a similar [to homosexuality] abnormality in our society."[108] Like the homosexual, according to Ruth Benedict the religious mystic had been branded "abnormal" and *therefore* became "neurotic and psychotic."[109] With religion, she had chosen another biographically weighted subject to bolster her case for an enlightened, sensitive, and respectful social psychiatry.

For the moment, however (and this shifted over the next ten years), Ruth concerned herself less with cross-cultural psychiatry than with the intolerance of "abnormal" and marginal individuals which she detected in American society.

"He is an arid and suspicious fellow"

The force of custom (i.e., culture) had a positive side. Throughout *Patterns of Culture*, Ruth Benedict attempted to persuade readers of the possibilities and the mechanisms for changing the conditions under which they lived. Customs, she argued, are historical, arbitrary, and controllable. Her efforts had a personal motivation: "I can't swallow the solution in Plato's Republic," she had written more than ten years earlier.[110] And the translation of mysticism into the approved channel of poetry no longer satisfied her. Anne Singleton expressed "visions" for a while; by 1930 the woman and writer reached for a wider audience, a more public statement. Ruth Benedict spoke about diverse societies to her own complex, and she thought constricted, society.

Exactly because of the personal motive and because Ruth was a persistently private person, she couched her pleas for change under the general rubric of "social engineering." The concept, if controversial, also struck a familiar chord for professional and lay readers of the time.

Ruth Benedict accommodated her "social engineering" to the ideas of John Dewey, to progressivism, and to a liberal-humanism that recalled Matthew Arnold and the nineteenth century. Social engineering, in her view, operated through the individual and through the individual's enlightened attitudes toward himself and—inseparably—toward his society. A teacher all her life, Ruth knew how attitudes should be changed. Offered the "right kind" of information, an individual would naturally take it upon himself or herself to alter a perspective, to expand horizons and rearrange circumstances. In *Patterns of Culture* Ruth presented the "right" information in ethnographic portraits that were unmistakable reflections of her own society. Experience convinced her that knowing self was a result of continuing contrast and comparison.

Ruth Benedict chose the Dobuan and Kwakiutl cultures because, she told Mead, she could talk to their ethnographers. She also chose the two cultures because each echoed American society in a particular way. That echo constituted another aspect of her comparative approach; differences cannot be so great as to make unrecognizable the alternative ways of meeting basic human needs.

Virginia Woolf composed a central persona from the reflections of six other characters; their voices created the "arid and suspicious fellow," Percival.[111] Ruth similarly drew American culture from the images and reflections of three other cultures. She described the Dobuans so they sounded like American Puritans: stingy, prudish, suspicious—in a word, paranoiac.[112] The Kwakiutl, in many ways the most vivid figure in *Patterns of Culture*, resembled a side of American character that Ruth Benedict inclined toward while acknowledging her own stronger puritanical streak. The ebullient Kwakiutl stood for a spirit of greed, accumulation, confidence, encompassing ego—the megalomaniac trend in American society and the foundation of American "free enterprise." Like Walt Whitman, whose ebullient and greedy poetry Ruth admired, the Kwakiutl risked his pride to embrace experience, and Ruth envied the "ecstasy." She wrote of Whitman's "unwavering, ringing belief that the ME . . . is of untold worth and importance."[113]

The Zuñi represented a potential, a goal for the culture built on the schizophrenic traits of puritanism and expansiveness. Ruth perceived in Pueblo life an ideal, a reference for America's future. She did not envision Utopia in the Pueblos; she emphasized traits out of which her contemporaries might create a better way at home. Nor did she recreate a portrait of herself in "The Pueblos of New Mexico" (really "The Zuñis of New Mexico"). Ruth admired the Pueblo design and did not hesitate to convey her admiration. But she did not read into the Pueblos her own "ideal virtues"; rather, she stressed in Pueblo life examples for careful melioration in American society.

The portraits resulting from the author's determination to open her readers' eyes onto themselves might be (often are) called one-dimensional. The portraits are not "flat."[114] Ruth Benedict vividly and emphatically presented each unique type and, as vividly, an unmistakable contrast. She summarized her intentions for Houghton Mifflin:

> She has chosen three strongly contrasting primitive cultures, and described them in all their customs, from the way they plant their yams, or divorce their husbands, or go headhunt-

ing at death, as well-knit and internally consistent attitudes toward life. The details of their behavior have great intrinsic interest because of their striking character.[115]

She expected, too, that her readers ordinarily saw the world in such sharp characterizations. Ruth was not far off; through a parade of epic figures from Puritan divines and witch-burners, through Paul Bunyan and Jesse James, to the Babbits of her own century, Americans realized their culture values in personality types. Ruth brought to her discipline a common-sense perception, and articulation, of culture pattern through individual type.[116]

She chose the Dobu, Kwakiutl, and Zuñi cultures carefully, and equally carefully a vocabulary that would be immediately evocative— as recognizable as Paul Bunyan and Lewis Babbitt. Nietzsche's words bordered on the esoteric, but Ruth found his phrasings overwhelmingly persuasive. "The basic contrast between the Pueblos and the other cultures of North America is the contrast that is named and described by Nietzsche in his studies of Greek tragedy," she wrote, and happily included several quotations.[117] She knew his contrast "on her pulses" as well as intellectually.

One December 3, probably 1930 (a diarist remembers the year), Ruth Benedict wrote:

> By the time I was eight I knew what Dionysian experience was, I had had to take account of fury, an experience that swept over me from somewhere outside my control—as I figured [?]—, lifted me like a tornado and dropped me limp at the end. But I'd also got also [sic] by that time my great response to this violence, and it was disgust. After a periodic scene I was likely to vomit . . . .

And she went on, in an extraordinarily Dionysian vein.[118]

Disgust at excessive gestures and uncontrolled responses turned Ruth toward the Apollonian—the remembered calm of her dead father's face. She herself rarely achieved a "true" Apollonian attitude; she insisted upon the "moderation and measure" in Zuñi society almost in compensation. Zuñi culture did "objectify" a version of Ruth's dream, an order of life she admired. But she did not make up the Zuñi or imagine the relentless regularity and controlled ceremonialism. Before and since, visitors to the Pueblo have described these qualities, and if Ruth focused on ritualized expressions because of resonance to her private perceptions she also did so out of professional ambitiousness. Competing with colleagues, she wanted her book to achieve a unique standing.

The material available on Pueblo Indians when Ruth wrote seemed either so full of detail or so narrowly analytic as to obscure any sense of what these people were truly like.[119] Ruth recreated the personality of Pueblo culture, an identifiable and integral entity that was perfectly distinct from her own culture and objectively distinct from her private values.[120]

In many ways, in fact, the Dionysian more than the Apollonian "mirrored" the author. Dionysian objectified Ruth's wishes and suggested a strongly compelling motive of her life and her career. The Dionysian appeared mainly in poetry and in journals, and then insistently. "There is only one problem in life: that fire upon our flesh shall burn as a knife that cuts to the bone, and joy strip us like a naked blade."[121]

The non-Nietzschean terms, paranoiac and megalomaniac, are farther from Ruth's private mode of interpretation. She expected her readers to recognize the popularized Freudian terms and from these form a lasting impression of Dobuan and Kwakiutl cultures. Ruth Benedict presented her protagonists so they would stick in her readers' minds. "People need to be told in words of two syllables what contrasting cultures mean," she told Reo Fortune.[122] By "need" she referred to her ameliorative aim; with eyes opened to diverse constructs of life, people would engineer, reconstruct, the design of their own lives.

If Ruth thought her readers needed two-syllable words and graphic descriptions, she also had faith that these readers would become "the culture-conscious," the aware and self-critical individuals she trusted to change American society and (perhaps) the world.

"Men are never inventive enough to make more than minute changes"

Ruth Benedict wrote for an America over the "zesty" optimism of the 1920s and ready for the suspicious, stingy, tight-belted atmosphere of a depressed economy. Given the impending economic crisis, her Zuñi example takes on special meaning, an alternative to Dobuan malicious possessiveness and to Kwakiutl "conspicuous consumption." Zuñi culture also offered an alternative to the Marxism embraced by several friends and colleagues.

In the chapter titled "The Pueblos of New Mexico" the anthropologist made a statement about social policy, grounded in a liberal-progressive humanism. Ruth counted on individuals to move from envisioning to engineering alternatives. In her book the Zuñi are a persuasive alternative, a lesson in cooperativeness and harmony of interests that is hard to resist. But Ruth did not impose her lesson. From teaching she knew that a chosen lesson was a lasting one; she only tried to make the choice inevitable. With the Zuñi she described a culture of proportion and fairness where no one starved and no one was judged by property or power.[123] She also described a culture sure of itself and well-enough integrated to avoid being destroyed by a dominant white culture.

"The Pueblos of New Mexico" bore a substantial burden. The chapter demonstrated the rightness of aspects of Zuñi culture and presented a set of images that would make agreement with the author powerfully "logical." But chapter 4 was one version of a many-sided argument, directed to a range of readers. Ruth Benedict did write a pedagogical anthropology; she thought of her discipline in terms of an audience to be instructed—the individuals "in the street" who, startled into awareness, worked toward an improved society. "Where else could any trait come from except from the behaviour of a man or a woman or a child?"[124]

This belief in the power of every human being to recreate, repeatedly, the terms of existence underlay Ruth's humanism and her anthropological approach. Her faith in individualized and revisionary change prompted her support of New Deal policies and a hope that Franklin Roosevelt would prove congenial to American culture, spokesman for "dominant motives," and therefore an effective innovator. But she postponed discussion of these and other political issues until after her book was safely published and out, in bookstores all over the country. "Even Macy in this city does not have the book in stock, as every person I know who ordered one has waited ten days to have the order filled."[125]

Ruth Benedict had constructed, implicitly, another heroic personage: the informed, creative individual who, understanding patterns, successfully altered surroundings. In the face of leaders like Hitler and Mussolini—men who seemed "congenial" to their cultures and times —Ruth even more strenuously counted on "common people" and "sanely directed change." Books like hers *had* to sell, and she made no effort to hide from friends and editors her intense desire that *Patterns of Culture* sell and sell widely. Her concern led to discussions of title, jacket color, and price, as well as to several revisions of publicity blurbs. At Houghton Mifflin, Ferris Greenslet patiently answered urgent and irritable letters.[126]

The title took considerable time and thought, Ruth not knowing that the phrase she settled on would be ineradicably associated with her name. She did not pick "patterns" right away. "I've turned over titles and titles. I want the title of the book to clearly indicate that my competence is in anthropology, nothing else. That is, I don't want any psychologizing title. I shall suggest 'Primitive Peoples: An Introduction to Cultural Types.'"[127] This August 1932 version nearly implied an equivalence: the isomorphism of "peoples" and "cultural types" Ruth tried to avoid in the text of the book. The links between "peoples" and "types" are part of the book and are implied finally by "patterns."

The early version may well have sounded pompous and pedantic. Ruth insisted upon the accessibility of her material, a priority as strong as that she be thought competent in anthropology; she had to keep both professional and popular audiences in mind.

> I have turned over in my mind some fifty titles for the book, and I find I have the strongest possible preference for a title as exact as possible under the circumstances. . . . Would you consider "Patterns of Culture"? "Patterns" has been used in the sense I have in mind and it is besides a pleasant English word.[128]

Years earlier the "crowd" at Columbia had talked about "patterns."[129] A small group of Boas students discussed patterns of behavior, of personality, of everyday interactions—an array of arrangements and habits both inter- and intrapersonal that reflected and confirmed the dominant values of culture. The word "pattern" stood for the ordering of a culture and the patterning in individual lives. Ruth and her friends added the "patterning" of words, in poetry and (with less enthusiasm by Ruth) in language itself: the creating of a coherent and comprehensible statement. They added process to stasis, and Ruth's word referred not just to "shape" but to "shaping."

Ruth considered several words more or less synonymous with pattern, especially "integrity" and "configuration"—or if not synonymous at least filling out the connotations of "pattern." For her book, it seems clear from letters, pattern had the special attraction of being a common-sense word with a strong link to poetry and art. Unlike the "configuration" of her 1932 article, pattern evoked responses that, she hoped, would carry without laboring a complex argument. Common-sense understandings of the word do clarify the anthropological meaning and to some extent relieved Ruth from having precisely to define her word. (Others later took up and all-too-thoroughly disputed the definitional issue.)

She meant by "pattern" what most people mean, a formal arrangement based on a theme or tendency. Theme can be considered interchangeable with propensity and motive; the Apollonian motive is a theme of Pueblo culture. Around a theme, pieces fall into place over time. The existing pattern determines the quality and structure of internal elements and, as well, the incorporation of new traits. Grammar and vocabulary come to mind, but Ruth Benedict preferred to relate her word to psychology and poetry. "A culture, like an individual, is a more or less consistent pattern of thought and action. Within each culture there come into being characteristic purposes not necessarily shared by other types of society."[130] These frequently quoted sentences might be rephrased: the integrity of a culture and of an individual lies in the "unfolding" of pattern according to dominant tendencies, over time and uniquely—Ruth did not slight the biographical and historical past tense of a present constellation.

Patterning referred to culture and to personality at once. This way Ruth suggested a mutually creative connection and a similarity in type between culture and person. She did not explain the connection in *Patterns of Culture*, except to say that individual character and actions followed culture patterns, and that the individual with more awareness of patterning could change himself and his surroundings. Ruth Benedict dealt in implications and assumptions; personal patterns reiterated culture patterns in content (what they were) and in form (how they came about and worked). Pattern also recalled Ruth's claim that individual personalities fit cultural types while retaining an idiosyncratic response, the distinctiveness of component pieces without which there could be no pattern. Again common sense illuminates the anthropological point.

Most broadly, Ruth Benedict talked about an aesthetic dimension in human life. She talked about the yearnings for order and the satisfactions in a coherent and selective presentation. She had appreciated the comprehensibility and strengths of a well-constructed statement. She applied similar standards to a person (who did not chafe against cultural expectations yet maintained self-integrity), to a poem (which used traditional forms to express innovative perceptions), and to a culture. Underlying all these judgments was Ruth's belief in the importance of making sense of existence and arranging—often wonderfully—the natural and supernatural forces that impinged upon any "living."

Poetic references were not accidental. In 1934 Reo Fortune, prompted by Margaret Mead, asked Ruth whether she had borrowed "patterns" from Amy Lowell's poem of that name.[131] "I walk down the patterned garden path / In my stiff brocaded gown. / With my powdered hair and jewelled fan, / I too am a rare pattern. . . ." In her lines, Lowell conveyed a message about boundaries and taming and the end of desire that Ruth must have understood personally, whatever she thought critically. Edward Sapir disliked the poem: "'Patterns' is piffle, like much of Amy's work," he told Robert Lowie in 1917.[132] Ruth undoubtedly knew Amy Lowell's poetry. Whether she considered "Patterns" to be "piffle" is not known, nor is her answer to Fortune's question. One can only guess at her memories when she chose "pattern" for the book. Aesthetic connotations did influence her decision, whatever their source.

The aesthetic introduced an ethical dimension. Ruth consistently and self-consciously used the word "integrity"; she implied in pattern a kind of "truthfulness" of being, honesty in a sound arrangement. For Ruth the scattered and haphazard culture seemed not "neurotic" (as critics said) but literally of less integrity (one remembers Sapir's "genuine and spurious"). She drew this insight from her experiences— her dislike of the "random"—and in subsequent years refined notions of "soundness" in person, in culture, and in relationships between the two. She retained, as well, the cross-cultural perspective of chapter 8, making untenable any absolute definition of the "well-integrated" personality and any fixed definition of the ideal environment for personal development. (The consequences of varying cultural tolerances for diversity became a major focus of her later writings.)

"Pattern," then, had not been lightly chosen. The word contained a wealth of meanings, some outlined and some merely hinted at in the 1934 book. Ruth apparently liked the encompassing and connotative quality of the word. Supplementing the common-sense and the poetic references, the word also referred to her ongoing self-interpretations. "It is curious to see how the basic patterns of our life hold from babyhood to decrepitude."[133] Ruth eventually settled on "pattern" with a feeling of satisfaction; she kept the word for her 1946 book on Japanese culture.

The title stood out nicely on the turquoise-blue jacket, a color achieved after some negotiation. "The color of the back-strip paster I should much prefer in some more saturated color," she wrote to "My dear Mr. Greenslet" in June 1934; "this seems too light a turquoise, and difficult to read the printing on it in the bookcase. I am clipping onto this letter a slip of paper that seems to be more nearly the right tone."[134] She wanted a bright Southwestern turquoise. She had other demands. The spelling should be British, not American (using "——ours" instead of "——ors," for example); the price should be as low as possible. She bargained Ferris Greenslet down from $3.75 to $3.00 to

$2.50. And she asked about distribution. "I have received another letter from California saying that my books are not available there. This letter is from a person very used to purchasing books in Southern California. . . ."[135] The publicity should be precise: she was an anthropologist, a present, "not *former*" (her emphasis), editor of the *Journal of American Folk-Lore*, "Mrs." not "Miss" Benedict.[136] When asked, however, to write a brief biographical sketch, she withdrew. "Be a darling and do this for me," she scrawled across a letter from Greenslet and sent it to Margaret Mead.

Mead may have done the favor. She did publicize the book, in conversations, reviews, and comments. Her reviews acknowledged the dual audience Ruth projected. Mead praised *Patterns of Culture* for contributing to anthropological theory and method as well as for determining the contours of everyday thought. Acutely, Margaret Mead recognized that readers of *Patterns of Culture* would make "culture a household word," and use the concept in their daily conversations.[137] These were the "Macy shoppers," the ordinary men and women who, according to Ruth Benedict, created a culture. Other anthropologists wrote favorable reviews—and Boas a guardedly pleased, short introduction. Some colleagues dismissed the book entirely, as poetry not social science. Few, even those most positive about the book, tried to do what Mead did and merge the "poetic," imaginative content with the anthropological argument of the book. Kroeber came the closest, since he like Mead understood the "impressions" not as fluff but as essential to the logic of *Patterns of Culture*. He praised the book, in a remarkably apt if awkward phrase, for its "quality of distinctive, almost passionately felt, balanced thinking precisely expressed."[138]

Lively debate about the book lasted for well over ten years. Ruth's colleagues seemed unable to let go of *Patterns of Culture*, picking at its thesis, doubting the accuracy of ethnographic accounts, questioning the woman's method and her role in anthropological thought, and probably above all envying the style and success of the book. One of the most popular anthropology books of the twentieth century, Ruth's *Patterns of Culture* inspired more than small twinges of envy and rivalry. Readers throughout the world remember the Zuñi, the Dobu Islander, the Kwakiutl Indian, if not the revision of the "functional approach"[139] or the argument about cross-cultural psychiatry. Readers remember the distinct contrasts and the vivid possibilities for arranging human life, if not a "comparative method" or the meaning of "typology" in Ruth Benedict's book. Finally, too, readers of *Patterns of Culture* must recognize that an existing state of affairs is neither permanent nor perfect nor inevitable.

Patterns of Culture established an intellectual attitude and conveyed an optimism about the ability of individuals to change their lives—a lesson from the author's life and badly needed in the 1930s. Ruth Benedict transmitted a powerful principle through the concrete data of her cross-cultural examples. The book, perhaps, conveyed more optimism than the author felt.

> *"Like eating and drinking it [anthropology]*
> *has a necessary place in my life"*

The message of *Patterns of Culture* is essentially a hopeful one. The anthropologist displayed her "laboratory samples" with the conviction that her audience would realize the force of custom, the arbitrariness of custom, and the opportunities available when culture was put over nature as regulator of human lives. Ruth Benedict displayed as strongly her belief that any reader could become "culture conscious" and, aware of patterns, be the precipitator of a "sane and scientific direction of society."[140]

Patterns of Culture seemed to represent the fulfillment, personal and professional, that Ruth had craved for so long. Houghton Mifflin attended to her many requests and packaged, publicized, and priced the book as she wanted. Her colleagues responded, if not always with praise, at least not with indifference. And readers from hundreds of different places read the book. *Patterns of Culture* would become a standard statement on cultures and a lasting guide to culture change. In December 1934—in time for Christmas shoppers—the *New York Herald Tribune* described Ruth's book as one of the ten most "worthwhile and 'solid' books of the year," she proudly told Mr. Manley Jones, sales manager at Houghton Mifflin.[141]

Six months before, on June 9, Ruth had written a lengthy journal entry.

> What is this need I have so strongly and which comes over
> me only the more overwhelmingly after I've been faithful for
> a while to my jobs and duties? . . . Work even when I'm satis-
> fied with it is never my child I love nor my servant I've
> brought to heel. It's always busy work I do with my left hand,
> and part of me watches grudging the waste of lifetime. It is
> always distraction—and from what? It's hard to say.[142]

Natalie Raymond, sharing the apartment, filled Ruth with love and with doubts about her love. The doubts focused on age differences and on incompatible demands for intimacy. In another long entry, six days later, Ruth wrote:

> I ought to have enough self-knowledge to know what would make life meaningful to me. Not my work in anthropology, much as I owe to it. Like eating and drinking it has a necessary place in my life and adds to it, but the role it plays in Margaret's life or Boas' is impossible for me. Companionship comes close to the core of the matter, and loving Nat and taking such delight in her I have the happiest conditions for living that I've ever known. If I have to cultivate a background role and school myself to the precariousness of my happiness —since she has so much of life before her and so many choices still to make—after all, that is something I can very well do in terms of my own temperament.[143]

The old fear of futility, rejection, and despair had not disappeared.

Through the early 1930s Ruth struggled to maintain her faith in an individual's ability to accommodate to and at the same time change surroundings, alter the significant, pressuring customs. She struggled to believe in the power of daydream, expressed in poem or myth or "another country." She would not minimize the importance of an envisioned alternative for the judicious revising of existing reality. Emotional and political commitments, running through her professional and personal life, were in those years severely challenged by events. Placidity—the peaceableness Ruth saw in her mother—was hard to come by. As the decade passed, external circumstances impinged dreadfully on the modicum of contentment she had attained with Nat and on the satisfaction she gained from being a "world famous anthropologist." In 1933 Ruth Benedict became one of the first women included in the *Biographical Directory of American Men of Science*—a gratifying if somewhat mistitled honor. *Time* magazine reported the news, and that "Dr. Benedict was 'shocked' at the small number of women named."[144] The two women named with Ruth Benedict were zoologists, laboratory scientists.

Her professional scientific standing was undoubted, her attachment to Nat deepened in happiness and in concern, and her distance from Stanley Benedict grew nearly unbridgeable.

Ruth and Stanley had talked about the need to live apart. On their New Hampshire vacations—interspersed with canoeing, reading, and relaxing—they talked, with a frankness not characteristic of their wintertime conversations. They talked of their differences and their inability to be in touch and tried not to blame or to feel guilty.

During the summer of 1930, at Lake Winnepesaukee, Ruth wrote long entries in her diary, puzzling over the relationship and her part in it. On July 26 she spent five pages trying to convince herself she could "suppress" her animal spirits and knowing she could not.[145] This was not the first, or last, time she wrote about rejection of her "healthy nature." By 1930 she debated the issue with the calm of familiarity; between the lines pain was evident, but also, finally, an admission that marriage had failed. Ruth and Stanley had first established a relationship on walks through the Pasadena arroyos and Norwich hills. Appropriately the marriage came to an end on walks bordering the New Hampshire mountains.

"Stanley died," Ruth Benedict noted on December 22, 1936, with an arrow drawn up to the December 21 space in her appointment book. "AM to S's grave," she added on December 30. She wrote nothing more about his death except thank-you letters for condolences and obituary notices. On December 26, Ruth went off to Washington, D.C., for the Anthropology Association meetings. Her brief diary entries on Stanley Benedict's death, and her immediate attention to professional activities, represented not coldness but one characteristic response to death. Ruth had many reasons, not all unconscious, to moderate her grief and control her mourning; she managed the shock of her husband's death (unexpectedly, of a heart attack) by immersing herself in the dominant concerns of work.

That year, too, Franz Boas insisted on her promotion to associate professor of anthropology. Ruth's job was full-time, more than full-time by 1936, and had completely replaced her marriage. But anthropology did not fill all her needs. "I ought to have enough self-knowledge to know what would make life meaningful to me. Not my work in anthropology, much as I owe it, and committed as I am to it. . . . Companionship comes closer to the core of the matter."[146] In those mid-1930s years Ruth demanded much of her discipline and, a parallel, demanded a great deal from her domestic arrangement with Natalie. Increasingly, too, world events required, and disturbed, her commitment to a science, forcing a reconsideration of contentment and responsibility.

But even had external crises not impinged, Ruth would still have seen the edge of chasm. Happiness was always "precarious" and achievement ephemeral in face of the "blue devils." To accept precariousness, Ruth said the year *Patterns of Culture* was published, "implies a strength and collectedness in myself that is the strongest need I have."[147]

8
Folklore and Mythology

"My years-long effort to get another editor"

A YEAR AFTER *Patterns of Culture* appeared, Ruth Benedict published a second book utilizing Southwest materials collected a decade before. *Zuñi Mythology* offered another view of the Pueblo Indians and a turn in the prism of Ruth Benedict's concept of culture. In *Zuñi Mythology*, Ruth presented a theory of myth that tied together past notions and anticipated her future course in anthropology. Her idea of myth as "compensation" and "wish-fulfillment"[1] reflected private speculations as well as current preoccupations in the discipline. The theory, to be validated cross-culturally, showed the effect of personal and professional changes over the previous ten years. The mythology volumes appeared in the midst of Ruth's term as editor of the *Journal of American Folk-Lore* and perhaps reminded her of past pleasures in the characters and plots of "primitive" stories.

On her first Southwest trip, in 1924, Ruth collected tales from the Cochiti Indians. Seven years later the Smithsonian Institution printed *Tales of the Cochiti Indians* at the reasonable price of 40 cents.[2] *Tales* was a competent piece of work, acknowledging the influence of Elsie Clews Parsons and Franz Boas; the booklet only suggested what became a distinct approach to the study of myth. Ruth added a brief introduction and an appendix arranged to show: "(1) the mythological concepts of Cochiti . . . , (2) its hero tales . . . , (3) the fictionalized versions of Pueblo life. . . ."[3] These statements, and a sentence in the introduction, hint at her theory: "The fundamental material in these tales, and the fundamental factor in their formation, is the daily life of the people."[4] She advised comparing "fictional" elements to the content of daily life, recalling a point made in her "A Matter for the Field

Worker in Folklore," published eight years earlier. "This lack of corre-spondence between the statements of folklore and the customs and beliefs of the people is often of great importance."[5]

On the 1925 Pueblo trip, Ruth Benedict continued to collect tales, though that was not her main purpose. She had begun to think about culture configurations, and myth-collecting became a means for under-standing Pueblo "personality." But she also listened to Boas, and he typically expected fieldworkers to gather legends, stories, anecdotes, and myths. Beyond his constant pressure for data, he emphasized the unique insight into a culture "genius" provided by verbal materials. Folklore told of the culture's world-view, through the native's own words, and without distorting either his categories or his imaginativeness.[6]

Such a viewpoint suited Ruth, who knew the value of verbal testi-mony for revealing "character." In line with her emphasis on the verbal, she treated tales as a kind of literary document, only occasionally as a song or chant and rarely as part of a group interaction. She could not hear tales when people gathered around. For Ruth the context of a tale was the whole culture, not the moment of its telling and hearing.

She did not differ from fellow Boasians; most fieldworkers in the 1920s and 1930s tended to ignore the performance of a story. After her 1927 Pima trip, however, Ruth Benedict expressed some dissatisfaction with listening to and recording one person's version. "I wish that I could give with these mere words . . . the powerful recitative chant" and demonstrate the "heightened handling of the stuff of life itself," she jotted in a note.[7] Tone and gestures filled in the content of narra-tives, she began to see, and she considered the use of "recording instruments" in the field—though she confessed to hardly knowing how these "machines" worked.[8]

There were several implications of a Boasian single-informant approach, especially for Ruth. For one, she did not have to interpret audience response in a crowded setting or delve into turns of speech in a language she never learned. For another, Boas's approach involved considering *all* narrative forms and treating as equally valid various modes of expression. Ruth found the Boasian approach to myth an ideal starting point for her own work. "It is impossible to draw a sharp line between myths and folk tales," Boas wrote in several different pieces, over twenty years.[9] These verbal materials gave evidence of the cul-ture's past and present, specifically of its "way of thought." If, in Boas's view, folklore did not explain, it did "make sense" of life.

Ruth modified this perspective to suit her insights, her field data, and her anthropological purposes. She studied tales in context in order to delineate a culture "personality"; the unifying thread was literary and poetic rather than solely diffusionist and historical. From 1923 until the completion of *Zuñi Mythology*, Ruth Benedict sought to understand expressions of self and fantastic versions of a life, in essence, to accord an imagined world "real" significance. She worked toward her understanding in personal writings (poems, journals, and letters), in anthropological pieces, and in editing the *Journal of American Folk-Lore*.

In 1924 Franz Boas decided to give up editorship of the *Journal*. (He had been editor since 1908, and influential before that.) He did not relinquish his strong voice in editorial policies when he withdrew from the official position. He picked his successor, and few folklorists could have been much surprised at the choice of Ruth Benedict. In fact, Ruth had not been Boas's first choice. The name "Gladys Reichard" appeared on a list, crossed over and replaced by "Ruth Benedict."

Why did Ruth accept a job likely to be time-consuming, irritating, and full of personal conflict? She had worked on folklore ever since her arrival at Columbia, usually doing the monotonous indexing—so tedious she took refuge in kinship terminologies. "When laboriously and meticulously setting down the occurrence of incidents or themes . . . became unbearably tedious, she turned to working out half-recorded kinship systems."[10] Yet tedium also drove away her "blue devils," and for that she welcomed mindless tasks: "After all perhaps I'm something of a masochist—I can get a kind of thoroughgoing convincing relief from the devils out of a terrible chore that I don't get out of any holiday . . . and I was in rotten shape when I began collating [tales]—sick headaches and a toss up swing [possibly her vomiting]. . . ."[11] The (sometimes) "mindless" tasks of editing a journal at least brought recognition and influence, to a degree. Ruth had a share of ambitiousness and, equally, appreciated the validation of a defined professional role. In 1924, the Ph.D. a year and a half behind her, she welcomed an institutionalized location, a world of her own. Perhaps, too, she welcomed a chance to perpetuate and to expand Boasian approaches to folklore, on her own and through editorial decisions. Finally, she enjoyed (and said so) having contact with colleagues and overseeing personal and professional projects.[12] She had shown herself to be a good editor, on her compositions, her own and Sapir's poems, and on colleague papers.

With the small amount of prestige, the incoming editor acquired a number of problems. Ruth may have anticipated some of these problems; she certainly complained about many.[13] Immediate difficulties arose over transfer of control: Would Ruth Benedict be a mouthpiece for Franz Boas, a docile advocate of Boasian policies? At first, cautious and tactful, Ruth did not rush into changes. Then, little by little over the years as editor she made decisions that considerably altered *Journal* policies. The content of the *Journal of American Folk-Lore* did change under Ruth's direction, gradually and sometimes awkwardly. She proceeded slowly, partly out of deference to her teacher, partly because major shifts disrupted a still family-sized group, and partly because as editor she had no money.

Ruth Benedict edited the *Journal* through the years of America's Depression. Her correspondence revealed a constant, gnawing preoccupation with sources of support—for the next issue, for a Folk-Lore Society memoir, for the badly needed services of a secretary: "Naturally the woman wants to know whether she could count on the job October 1st, and I shall certainly try hard to garner the salary together. Have you any suggestions," she as much as stated to Boas in 1929.[14] Without Elsie Clews Parsons's reliable support the *Journal of American Folk-Lore* would several times have folded. "Thanks to Elsie Clews Parsons" became a standard addition to Folk-Lore Society minutes. From 1925 until she left the position in 1940, Ruth spent her editorial letter-writing energy on budgets and printers; articles piled up alarmingly on her desk and papers for the Folk-Lore Society remained uncompleted.

It is hard to judge exactly how aware Ruth Benedict was of the growing antagonism toward her editorship. She did not admit, if she knew, the extent to which she conscientiously observed Boasian dicta, not looking for new articles or fresh contributors. Ruth had reasons for letting matters slide at the *Journal.* Manuscripts came unfailingly— Boasians seemed tireless, collecting, interpreting, and submitting material. By the early 1930s, too, she had acquired substantial unofficial responsibilities at Columbia and was in the midst of her own writing; it helped to depend on the "New York group."[15]

The developing controversy about content and purpose of the *Journal* could not remain totally secret. Ruth either withdrew—to work—or tried to control the dispute. Though she could be sharp-tongued in conversations, many report, she generally avoided disciplinary and organizational battles, especially in the early years. The disagreement that surfaced had originated before she became editor and involved "ethnographic" versus "literary" approaches to folklore and myth. Lines were drawn between "white" or "regional" folklorists and "anthropological" folklorists. Ruth's position resembled Boas's. Like Boas she regarded folklore mainly as ethnographic data, adding to the information on a culture; her expansion to include "emotional constellation" and, increasingly, the individual-social relationship did not really bring her closer to the "white" folklorists. This self-designated opposition voiced two main complaints against Ruth Benedict and "anthropological folklore": the concentration on materials from "primitive societies" (few from "home") and the (apparent) failure to look at the literary and artistic significance of mythologies wherever collected. Ruth *did* look at literary aspects, but in order to improve the data; she ignored folklore in complex societies almost entirely, whether in the form of regional folklore or in the guise of "myth in literature."

Three years after she became editor of the *Journal*, she witnessed one version of the dispute. In 1928 Stith Thompson ended the affiliation of the Modern Language Association and the Folk-Lore Society because, he said, bookkeeping had become "too complicated."[16] Evidently Thompson suspected that the anthropological folklorists had slighted the literary and linguistic folklorists for too long—and he was right.

The *Journal* did reflect the dominance of anthropologists, fieldworkers, and a Columbia Ph.D. program. For two decades the table of contents read like a Boasian roster; most articles were by Boas students and associates. An "in-group" policy had positive effects: the *Journal* showed consistency and published otherwise unwieldy pieces (too long, too specialized, and so forth). By 1930 the *Journal* gave the impression of being an archive for ethnographic data, emphasizing the North American tribes where Boasians did research.

The "white" folklorists protested vociferously, and gradually, with a combination of inertia and relief, Ruth acceded to their demands. In a manner of speaking she let the "literary people" in the back door, and they stayed to take over. From the book review section, literary approaches spread into the front pages. Around the same time, Ruth herself described folklore as a "humanistic science."[17] By "humanistic" she meant attention to human creativity and to modes of expression in any cultural setting.

In 1931 Martha Beckwith submitted a review essay of Constance Rourke's *American Humor* (1931), calling the book a "classic" in "literary circles."[18] In deciding to publish the review, Ruth Benedict acknowledged the judgment of a woman who was her colleague, friend, and fellow Boasian. She also this way encouraged white folklorists. Four years later, in 1935, Ann Gayton became book review editor and strengthened the move away from ethnographic folklore. (Anna Gayton Spier received her Ph.D. from Berkeley in 1928, writing on the narcotic *datura* in aboriginal American culture.[19]) With the support of George Herzog, Gayton expanded *Journal of American Folk-Lore* coverage through a book review section that eventually took up fully half the *Journal*. (Herzog, a student of Ruth's, showed her influence on his work in his 1937 dissertation, a comparison of Pueblo and Pima music.[20]) The white folklorists at last had equal time. Simultaneously Ruth began to withdraw from *Journal* matters and Society decisions. If a rug was being pulled out from under her, she had already stepped partway off.

George Herzog, with Ann Gayton and others, set matters going faster. As the 1930s came to a close, he held informal, more-or-less secret meetings to plan renovation of the *Journal* and the Folk-Lore Society. The year of Herzog's most concerted efforts, 1939–40, Ruth was in Pasadena. She had taken a sabbatical and left Columbia, folk-lore, and New York City behind to be with her sister's family and to write a book (*Race*). Herzog kept in touch and tactfully, discreetly, let Ruth know of probable changes. Herzog was more outspoken in letters to others, where he complained that the "Journal and the Society were directed for too long by people in NY City" and that the nonanthropological folklorists who "represent a majority of our members . . . have had little to say in the direction of affairs—partly because the society usually meets together with the AAA whereas the white foklore [*sic*] group tends to go to meetings of the MLA."[21]

In January 1940 Herzog wrote to Ann Gayton about the editorship: "I am wishing against hope that you would accept." One week later Gayton declined: "I have a quantity of work laid out for the next year or more."[22] Perhaps she did not want to do what would largely be a "clean-up" job;[23] perhaps she did not want to hurt Ruth's feelings. The second choice for editor, Gladys Reichard, accepted.

Whatever their complaints, the white folklorists remained tied to Boas, Columbia, and New York City. The group, under Herzog, appreciated Gladys Reichard for her connection with New York anthropology and also for her administrative skills, her energy, and her good nature: "I understand Gladys is swinging into action with the journal with zest," Herzog wrote in March 1940.[24]

Ruth expressed relief at being out of the job: "In view of my years-long effort to get another editor no letter of resignation from me is necessary. No, I had had no word of the action of the Council in Chicago," she added with less equanimity, "but I wish Anne [*sic*] Gyaton [*sic*] might have been prevailed upon to accept. . . . I gather from your letter that the chage [*sic*] was suggested in the form of strong criticism of me? . . . But even the criticism is secondary to your good news," she concluded.[25] Whether she found equally "good news" in the person who succeeded her is not clear. Since the mid-1920s Ruth and Gladys had been rivals for anthropology jobs and, maybe, for Boas's affections. This was a different sort of succession from Ruth's own.

"Peoples' folk tales are in this sense their autobiography"

Ruth Benedict *was* relieved, if she was simultaneously distressed at hearing the long-standing criticisms of her regime (the letter to Herzog has an unusual number of typographical errors). Editing the *Journal* had not been entirely a matter of worrying over finances, answering dissatisfied folklorists, negotiating with printers and distributors. During those fifteen years, Ruth developed themes and approaches that had an important effect on her professional writings of the next decade.

As editor, Ruth refined Boas's views on the significance of narrative by adding her characteristic insights, stressing the style and the purpose of story-telling for individuals and for societies. She introduced techniques for interpreting verbal statements which recognized information in contradictions as well as in correspondences to "recorded" fact. Along the way she expanded her concern with human creativity into a concept of culture.

Ruth further clarified her ideas in the classroom, and that, for her, included office hours and personal conversations. She taught "Folklore and Mythology" one year or another from 1925 until the late 1930s, her "very best classes," according to students. Her syllabi are remarkably consistent and show the construction of a theory through the gradual replacement of diffusionist with her own "intensive," particularist approach. Columbia students compromised between "extensive" and "intensive" studies and began to explore the literary elements in narrative for information on the values and beliefs of a culture. Columbia folklorists added the psychological to the historical function of myth, under the tutelage of Ruth Benedict.

Folklore remained primarily a tool of ethnographic research, in Ruth Benedict's eyes as in Franz Boas's. She agreed with her teacher that folklore provided the best insight into the character of a people. From casual tales to accounts of the origin of the world, narratives carried and, carefully read, yielded the "dominant motive" of a culture. In 1923, when Ruth wrote "A Matter for the Field Worker in Folklore,"[26] she took her first step beyond Boas. He regarded folklore as document on a culture's past and on its present configuration; he read the material, chronicle and "art," at "face value." Ruth, too, regarded verbal as special evidence. But she did not read the material at face value, "the definite recording of tribal custom."[27] She treated folklore instead like an autobiographical account, with the complexities and manipulations peculiar to modes of self-presentation. Though she did not say it in so many words, the idea of autobiographical expression informed her writings on myth and folklore.

Ruth hinted at her point of view in a crucial sentence in the 1923 article. "This lack of correspondence between the statements of folklore and the customs and beliefs of the people is often of great importance in the correct understanding of the material."[28] To judge the "information" in a statement, autobiography or folklore, an interpreter must investigate the setting and discover, by matching text to context, the "meaning of the story to the people who tell it."[29] In lack of correspondence between the "said" and "done" lay clues to the "true" personality.

An autobiographical notion fit Ruth Benedict's general organizing analogy: culture is like personality. Specifically, she brought to the study of folklore a belief that people often did not know, and surely did not blatantly expose, the pattern of their lives. Realization, for a culture and for a person, came in disguise; a parade of masked figures through vivid scenes illuminated the elements of pattern. According to Ruth Benedict, then, a society like an individual protected its sources of integrity in symbolism, masks, and mythic plots. The folklorist's job was to sift through distortions and gauge the truth in fantasies. Ruth attributed to group, and to person, a guardedness combined with an urge to comprehend the terms of existence, and this summarized the function of folklore—close to the function of poem and story in her own life.

The anthropologist drew on her familiarity with autobiography and poetry to expand ethnographic interpretation of conventionalized expressions in myth, tale, ritual, and gesture. Boas had taught that such expressions revealed the "mind of primitive man."[30] Rejecting the "explanation" theories of his predecessors, he yet left the impression that in their statements natives made *sense* of the world, communicated and preserved a "world-view." Ruth added an emotional component; she recognized the press of unfulfilled desires, frustrations, and yearning for beauty behind any statement. Sacred myths and occasional tales testified to an ongoing compromise between "thinking about" (conceptualizing) and "experiencing" (responding to) a given situation. For Ruth, stories revealed an emotional accommodation to as well as an intellectual formulation of otherwise "unmotivated" forces.[31]

In 1924 she wrote a grant application, proposing a study of the "emotional bases of primitive folk-lore." She also planned to analyze the "elements of culture incorporated into their literature" by a people.[32] The proposal did not indicate the links between these aims. Ruth did not get funded, and in 1924 she went to the Pueblos supported mainly by the Santa Fe Laboratory and Elsie Clews Parsons. The work of collecting and collating myths meant postponing her "lack of correspondence" idea, though in doing extensive collecting Ruth acquired a valuable familiarity with Pueblo tales.

The following summer at Zuñi Ruth pursued the text-context theme. Zuñi myths were an active part of daily life, not a repository of tradition or the remains of a collapsing culture. The fieldworker had her chance to investigate the "emotional bases" by noting the correspondence (or lack) of described to practiced customs. With Zuñi materials, Ruth Benedict could study not only *choice* of cultural elements but also the *manner* of presenting these: realistic and unadorned versus exaggerated and supremely distorted details. The "meaning" of stories lay in these rhetorical reflections upon events and observed circumstances. "Meaning to the people themselves," she had said; why a story was told, elaborated, and revised became her subject. Consequently Ruth turned her focus inward, unlike Boas who focused (at least primarily) on the diffusion of "external" mythic elements from group to group. She knew the importance of private stories and assumed (daring a personal premise) that folklore could be better understood by thinking about story-telling in individual psychology.

When Ruth Benedict applied autobiographical notions to the study of folklore, she made several assumptions. Sensitive to the contradictions between statement and context, and aware of the remarkably diverse rhetorical manipulations that served to establish and to guard integrity, she ended up claiming the absolute necessity of fantasies, daydreams, and wishes for cultural, and personal, survival.

The change of term, from Boas's "genius" to her "personality," had not been random. Ruth accorded "personality" (and, to some extent, psychology) meanings that reflected a literary as well as a current psychoanalytic milieu. In keeping with the literary bias she looked for formal, composed expressions rather than free associations, and valued the deliberate construct rather than the accidental confession. Similarly, Ruth showed little desire to unveil unconscious impulses and concentrated instead on motives made visible and therefore (according to her) effective. Over all, Ruth Benedict recognized that a society, like an individual, accommodated to the known and unknown forces of circumstance by devising a rhetoric and building a symbolism; "a cathedral of concepts," she read later on in Nietzsche.

Her ideas were long-standing. At Vassar in 1909 Ruth Fulton had written, "Man is always reaching out beyond the world he sees and hears."[33] Moreover, men created diverse ways of "reaching out," redoing ordinary circumstances, injecting the extraordinary into the day-to-day, imagining anew the natural and supernatural universe. In these pages, too, the college senior anticipated another principle of her later anthropology: "The most fascinating study of the ideas of different nations is through the revelations of their peculiar sense of symbolism."[34] She implied, there and elsewhere, that symbolic sense and rhetorical gestures must be unique, varying from culture to culture, from person to person, from nation to nation. Individuality expressed itself in symbolism and style; this would be a key thread in Ruth Benedict's folklore and in her anthropology. Cultures reworked and transcended the stuff of everyday, each uniquely.

In 1928 Ruth gave a paper titled "The Complexity of Literary Forms Among the Indians of the Southwest" and in 1929 one on "Figures of Speech in Pima Poetry"—each to the American Folk-Lore Society. Despite the titles neither was strictly literary analysis. Rather, the ethnographer showed how a close study of "figures of speech" provided clues to culture character. Ruth Benedict had brought her 1924 grant proposal to a satisfactory conclusion; she linked "elements of culture" to the "emotional bases" through a discussion of style and the revelation of desires and despairs in rhetoric. Choice and presentation of cultural elements in a narrative revealed personality, its dynamic as well as existential features. Ruth did discuss literary aspects of folklore, for ethnographic purposes. In doing so, she somewhat modified the usual meaning of "literary forms" and included rhythms, phrasings, and more explicit content than did standard "literary" interpretations. Nothing, for Ruth Benedict, shed so clear a light on Zuñi character as the reversals and ludicrous backwardnesses in Zuñi origin myths. The picture of "sacred" beginnings in a world full of accident and misbehaviors gave special insight into Zuñi personality. The beginning of a life story had a special place in her own imagination; she knew the importance of an initial unwinding of pattern.

Ruth was literary in yet another way, in a sheer and evident pleasure in Zuñi imagery and dramatic sensibility. She quoted narrative in *Patterns of Culture* to add information, but also with pure pleasure in the sound of a prayer or a sentence. Occasional Pueblo figures and cadences crept into her sonnets written after 1925. "Asking for their breath," she quoted from Zuñi, "Into our warm bodies taking their breath, / We shall add to your breath."[35] And she wrote, as Anne Singleton:

> This breath, blown out upon the casual air,
> Lost as it passes, formless as the light,
> We have for blocks to build with. . . .[36]

Ruth Benedict developed a view of primitive folklore that reflected her own practices of self-interpretation. Once she wrote an autobiographical fragment; usually she presented herself in the "masked" short stories, sonnets, and statements of professional commitment. Autobiographies, she recognized, were necessary, and necessarily disguised—frequently passing beyond the verbal into motion and gestures. The private bursts of daydream and yearning, however expressed, shaped the public presentations in sketch, poem, and anthropology.

"The great opportunity for wish fulfillment"

In 1923 Ruth Benedict stressed the importance of collecting folklore from a living culture. The idea remained central to her writings on folklore throughout the 1930s. Her juxtaposition of stories and observed behaviors contributed to the final formulation of a theory of myth, published twelve years later in *Zuñi Mythology's* introduction. In 1923 she mentioned "lack of correspondence"; by the early 1930s she had arrived at an estimation of the meaning of distortions. "The role of daydreams, of wish fulfillment, is not limited to these [fantastic] cases of distortion. It is equally clear in the tales that most minutely reflect the contemporary scene."[37]

With the idea of wish and daydream, Ruth extended Boas's thesis that narratives especially revealed the "genius" of a culture. She added to insights based on Pueblo field data her familiarity with forms of autobiography—telling a life—and developed a theory about the content and function of wishing in all societies. So, too, Ruth Benedict combined ethnography and literature, though not exactly the way the white folklorists did or expected.

"The presumption that is indicated by a study of the distribution of this folkloristic pattern [marriage with eight wives] in North America is that in the Pueblos polygamy is a grandiose folkloristic convention partaking on the one hand of usual mythological exaggeration and on the other of a compensatory daydream."[38] In her introductory section, Ruth pointed out that people tell stories about themselves, full of exaggeration, improbabilities, and nonhistorical and totally incredible incidents. Exaggeration and daydream are known by comparison to reality, or in context; she drew here on simple common sense.

People's stories, like any imaginative construct, are necessary fictions, the material for an ongoing identity just as surely as historical events and adaptations to the surrounding, natural environment. Ruth Benedict recognized the importance of expression ("my greatest need," she said[39]) and went on to assume that expression of self constituted a creation of self, the exaggerations and wishes along with the reporting and chronology.

Autobiographical sketches and versions of a life in prose, poem, myth, and tale illuminated the pattern, highlighting threads for future rearrangement. Behind the measured beat and intricate imagery of her verse, Ruth outlined her perceived boundaries and "dreamed" the means of transcending these.

I shall have gladness of you. Now at last
I am not blinded any more by those

Sweet promisings of flesh that we hold fast
Only so long as one cry comes and goes.
In my two hands I have held starry things. . . .[40]

The other side of melancholy, in her stanzas, might sometimes be hope.

Ruth Benedict brought to folklore these insights into the truth of wish and exaggeration. And, one suspects, she had more interest in the distortions, in the odd incompatibilities and eccentric representations, than in the match of tale to "historical or contemporary occurrences."[41] According to Ruth Benedict, folklore, while certainly providing information on the past development and current constellation of a culture, also satisfied a psychological need. Societies, like individual human beings, needed to "make up for" the missing and legitimize the secretly desired: "recast the universe."[42]

The wishes of a group, like those of a person, ranged widely, from the utterly fantastic to the familiar redoing of an awkward moment. To accompany her somewhat expedient distinction between tale and myth,[43] Ruth distinguished between wishes referring to the customary and wishes referring to the "supernatural." In tales people adjusted the givens of every day and compensated for failings; in myths people confronted the wondrous and the mysterious. In his tale, a Zuñi man wished for another wife, to be pregnant, to kill an enemy violently. In her tale, the Zuñi woman wished to escape marriage, to participate in a rabbit hunt, to abandon her children. In their myths, Zuñis wished for a universe that "man can entreat and make propitious."[44] Myths expressed a wish for design, for a perceptible and alterable arrangement of the universe.

Wish in myth, compensation in tale: ultimately content and function were much the same. The stuff of experience provided material and inspiration for mythmaker and storyteller. So, too, "for the purposes of study, myth can never be divorced from folklore."[45] Ruth did not use psychoanalytic definitions of wish and of compensation, though she may have appreciated a recognition of such meanings on the part of readers. She distrusted all universalistic explanations and saved special sarcasm for psychoanalysis.[46] She objected to psychoanalytic interpretations because she disliked grand assumptions about human character and destiny, because she (like Boas) distrusted "laws" of human behavior and because, finally, she believed expressions of wish and fantasy were unique to the individual, consciously created and worthy of respect.

Wishes *were* unique—a reference to her autobiographical notion—and addressed the immediate concerns of a person and a society. Wishes expressed specific not general human tragedies: "the meaning of the story to the people who tell it."[47] Along with this emphasis on individualness, Ruth rejected any assumption of panhuman symbolic meanings.⁴⁸ Dreaming might be a universal impulse; content and form varied from place to place, time to time, individual to individual. Again, if dreaming served one purpose all over, it was by incorporating precisely designated dissatisfactions and ambitions.

For Ruth Benedict the human need to express wishes, tell stories, and make up fantasies constituted a culture's primary justification and supreme challenge. She remained fascinated by the devices any culture established for preserving integrity and charting a new course—its path-breaking imaginative exercises on available material. Visions and day-dreams were a first step into the future—a glance over the "four walls" of reality.

In 1923 Edward Sapir wrote Ruth that he expected from her a "really fruitful treatment of myth."⁴⁹ Sapir's remarks continued their previous conversations about anthropology, poetry, and psychology. He suggested that his friend show, "unless you balk at psychology under all circumstances, how the crystallization [into pattern] could form a suitable frame for adequate individual expression."⁵⁰ Sapir ended the letter by yoking "anthropologizing" to "poeticizing," equal passions for both (the first not the second, his word). In the 1920s each faced a choice between, as Sapir put it, the two desirable "toys" of anthropology and poetry.⁵¹

Ruth Benedict and Edward Sapir also shared a pessimistic streak, and, to an extent, pessimism inspired their fascination with the ways people coped with the unpredictable and the relentlessly predictable in life. With a characteristic mixture of personal relief and professional calculation, the two focused on creativity as the escape from fatalism and "cultural determinism." Notions of creativity dominated their writings on self and society, personality and culture links. But, inevitably, Ruth moved away from Sapir, partly through her studies of myth and folklore.

She had incorporated mythology into her earliest experiences. Ruth Fulton's first readings had been the myths of her culture, sacred and secular. The Bible, Shakespeare, and Victorian fiction formed her perceptions, and she adapted inherited themes and symbols to intensely personal statements. An awareness of working within literary conventions marked Ruth's writings in prose and in poetry; the "pattern" that framed *her* individual expression was evident in vocabulary and in technique. When she came around to studying primitive narratives, Ruth added to her own experience of composing within a tradition further perspectives on art in society—characteristically testing hers against the answers of others.⁵²

In 1926 Edward Sapir wrote to Robert Lowie, "I would like to meet

Malinowski; Ruth is quite enthusiastic."[53] (Sapir and Malinowski would be colleagues at Yale in the 1930s.) Ruth met Malinowski in 1926 and liked him: "You'd like him a lot," she wrote to Mead. "He has the quick imagination and the by-play of mind that makes him a seven-days' joy."[54] He had recently published *Myth in Primitive Psychology*, and the short account of Trobriand myth influenced her interpretations of folklore.

In Malinowski Ruth Benedict recognized a view kindred to her own, of man struggling to understand himself, his actions and attitudes, in an unpredictable universe. Feelings of helplessness propelled men into constructing systems of order and of intervention. For Malinowski, myths like other elements of culture satisfied a particular psychological need, in this case for guidance and security. He considered myth a set of precedents, instructive but also reassuring—a traditional plan of action that left men with few questions and some grasp on existence. Myths are a "statement of a primeval, greater, and more relevant reality, by which the present life, fates, and activities of mankind are determined, the knowledge of which supplies man with the motive for ritual and moral actions, as well as with indications as to how to perform them."[55] Frivolous stories, casual tales, did not accomplish this purpose, and Malinowski dismissed legends, anecdotes, and such—distractions at least and at best confirmation of social ties.

Malinowski emphasized the instructive, and moral, aspect of myth almost to a fault: prescriptions clothed in fantasies. But he revealed a sensitivity to the fearfulness marking the human condition. Myths bridged the gap between the terrifying and the trivial, normalizing the one and exalting the other. In myths men accorded the mundane a higher reality and simultaneously brought the spiritual down to earth. Malinowski wrote, in myth "elements of human error, of guilt, and of mischance assume great proportions. Elements of fate, of destiny, and of the inevitable are, on the other hand, brought down to the dimension of human mistakes."[56]

Ruth borrowed from Malinowski's study of Trobriand myths the idea that narratives can counteract the sense of futility and helplessness in human lives. She agreed: myths introduced a superior truth into daily activities and provided justification for customary behaviors. Ruth may have, as well, found Malinowski's account too pragmatic; instruction and even comfort excluded the awe and pure fantasizing she valued. Though his word "charter" appeared throughout her own writings, in ethnographic studies of myth Ruth Benedict emphasized less guidance than revelation and realization. Malinowski wrote of an imagination tailored to the requirements of the everyday. Ruth accepted that, but she also believed fantasy provided relief from tedium and cast an entirely new light on the ordinary. Myths contained a "vision"—embodied "spirituality"—and Ruth considered mystery as important as mastery in conducting a life. "Contiguous to our lives on one side there exists a life of the spirit—a world wherein we are as babes, and yet have to learn to stand upright."[57]

For Malinowski myths had to do with rules, and vaguely with ethics and religion, but little to do with dreams and wishes. Trobriand myths allowed Trobriand Islanders to live in the world they knew. For Ruth Benedict a culture's myths allowed people to envision, then to create, a "world new minted."[58]

Ruth continued to read, along with her anthropology, Nietzsche and Santayana, philosophers who represented to her the "right—poetical way of seeing."[59] In those two unlike thinkers she found confirmation for her idea that myths, tales, poetry—any art—not only reassured men about existing circumstances but also provided a glimpse into fundamental truths. Man's dreams, however expressed, illuminated his reality: "Only his illusions have ever given him a sense of reality," Santayana wrote.[60] Art displayed truth, in proper guise. Myths and poems were a mode of perception, different from a vision quest, but with ultimately similar sources and significances.

Ruth Benedict read Nietzsche while writing *Patterns of Culture* and could not have forgotten his passionate panegyric to art in *Birth of Tragedy* and in *Zarathustra,* a book she read in the 1920s.[61] As a reader she had before been swept along by an egomaniacal confrontation with ideas, and the assertiveness of abundant self always attracted her.[62] In *Birth of Tragedy,* Nietzsche proclaimed the role of art in civilization and of the artist in society, and he argued for the necessity of "transforming" reality. "Art alone is able to transform these nauseating reflections on the awfulness or absurdity of existence into representations where with it is possible to live."[63] Insights must be masked; there is danger in a sheer exposure to reality. The Plains Indian after his vision had to return from the mountaintop, Ruth had written. Prolonged, an exposure to truth served mankind no better than dry and abstract argument; art made principles tolerable and effective.

Ruth responded to Nietzsche because he resonated to a side of her temperament and because his statements echoed back to her past. She too connected moments of realization and nausea; during childhood sudden insight brought on vomiting or temper tantrums. Once, Ruth had learned to take refuge from too much "daylight" in the haymow's secret, imaginary world. Then, years later, she responded self-consciously to a similar intuition in Nietzsche: "The symbol-image of the myth delivers us from the immediate perception of the highest cosmic idea."[64] She, too, would come to believe that myth, all imaginative creations, protected man from his truths; a screen of "symbol-image" made perception of reality bearable, and perhaps alterable—from time to time, society to society.

Nietzsche's often violently expressed ideas resonated to Ruth's own, quieter "Light the more given is the more denied."[65] She explored the meanings of "illumination" in her poems, exploring in metaphor the dangers of exposure to truth.

> Lest, at arm's length, pebble to pebble lying,
> Life's farthest depths show clear as whitened bone.[66]

"Whitened bones" dotted the Pueblo landscape;[67] once more Ruth found form for an abrupt comprehension in her ethnographic experiences. But particularly the figure on his lonely vision quest gripped her imagination, and so did his certain return to society.

In folklore, the anthropologist began to assess the cultural significances of metaphor and mask. She argued there that modes of symbolizing, of creating "pictures" to embody values, constituted a unique design for survival in every society. Art, it followed, affected "every man, woman, and child" in a society. Ruth Benedict could not avoid discussing the intervention of vision in life; the Plains Indian, enlightened, re-immersed himself in everyday duties. And she found herself compelled to deal with religion, ethics, and morals, as long as she wrote on myth and folklore. Vision intervened in life; Ruth implied a "should" and recalled George Santayana.

Turning from Nietzsche to Santayana is like turning from Dionysian to Apollonian, and Ruth may have appreciated the change. The Dionysian/Apollonian distinction came from within Nietzsche's pages, but his philosophy and prose itself represented, often enough, the Dionysian spirit. By contrast, Santayana's prose is stately and serene, a voice of proportion and of the "civil." (Santayana's influence crept so thoroughly into Ruth Benedict's writings that she occasionally omitted the quotation marks.) Ruth admitted her appreciation of the shift between Dionysian and Apollonian mainly in her diaries and letters, where "red-blooded vitality" contrasted with puritanical restraint, zest with moderation, in a continual dialectic.

In tone and in point of view, Santayana added another dimension to Ruth's approach to myth. His statements on poetry, religion, aesthetics, and morality occupied essays and whole books and provided background for nearly everything he wrote. Ruth brought the religious-ethical and the aesthetic into her interpretations of myth and folktale, but she debated the equivalences of art (aesthetics), ethics (proper conduct), and religion Santayana posited.

"Our bewilderment about the essential bases of religion"

While thinking about the introduction to *Zuñi Mythology*, Ruth Benedict prepared five articles for the *Encyclopedia of the Social Sciences*. In "Mythology" and "Folklore" she established her distinction between "supernatural" and "secular" narratives. In the other three, "Magic," "Ritual," and "Animism," she worked out a notion of the supernatural to accompany the myth-tale distinction. At the same time, Ruth began to draft a chapter on religion for Boas's textbook, *General Anthropology*. The chapter took a long time; Boas's book did not appear until 1938— though apparently Ruth was not the only tardy contributor.

"I sent Ruth Bryan [typist] my chapter for the BOOK last week," she wrote to Boas in 1932. "She wrote that she hasn't received yours yet, and was free to copy mine. As soon as she returns it I'll send it on."[68] Revisions and delays followed. Ruth Benedict was always a careful writer, but this chapter seemed to take longer than the assignment warranted or the result justified. The chapter vacillated between a general discussion of "attitudes to the supernatural" and an eager display of cultural diversity—the range of religious customs.[69]

The anthropologist, it would appear, had not reached an understanding of religion she found satisfying. Boas had considered Ruth's intellectual and her personal inclinations when he asked her to do the chapter on religion (Ruth Bunzel wrote the Zuñi chapters). He also, if unsuspectingly, put pressure on Ruth Benedict to discuss professionally a subject she might rather have left unformulated.

In the *Encyclopedia* articles she had distinguished between sacred (i.e., supernatural) and secular with somewhat less than full conviction—her prose does not persuade. Furthermore, in the "Ritual" article she identified ritual with daily habitual behaviors, treading perilously close to the psychoanalyst's idea of "neurotic" symptom.[70] Finally, in the "Magic" piece, Ruth portrayed magic as a substitute for technology.[71] She could not, however, readily dismiss the compulsions behind such expressions; man's confrontation with the "wondrous," his "awe" in face of the "supernatural," a "spiritual voltage" in the universe—aspects of her vocabulary suggested anything but indifference to "spiritual" matters. "Animism," referring to the "illogical" in all cultures, revealed a further problem implicit in the other four pieces. Ruth had yet to deal with her own society and its varieties of spiritual experience. She called the primitive her "laboratory" and considered primitive mythology a useful "sample," but she approached religion in complex societies indirectly, in statements embedded in discussions of Pueblo customs and in her poetry.

There was much to intrigue a woman of Ruth's temperament in her sources on myth, in data from her fieldtrips, and in her quick responses to Zuñi ways of handling "natural" and "supernatural," man and god, good and evil. She *was* intrigued, and doubly so because the nexus of myth and religion touched her past.

Ruth Benedict called her volumes *Zuñi Mythology*, but she had not collected only sacred stories. The distinction between sacred and secular was not the important point, and "mythology" sounded dignified for the title of a two-volume publication. Throughout, the editor demonstrated how fully Zuñi religion interpenetrated the pettiest, most "natural" aspects of Zuñi life. The Pueblo Indians seemed remarkably comfortable with a hodgepodge of sacred and profane and with their sensible concepts of good and bad. Theirs was not a sharply divided universe: "They do not picture the universe, as we do, as a conflict of good and evil. . . . [Witchcraft] derives among them from no Satanic majesty pitted against a good God."[72] Evil was impish, mischievous, recognizably clumsy, not absolute or permanent. Ruth was also fascinated by the absolute "scandalousness" in Reo Fortune's interpretation of the Mundugumor universe, another distinctive display of human accommodation.[73] Malice and evil attracted her as they had Reo.

Ruth Benedict had come upon a version of the classic anthropological dilemma: Was religion a universal phenomenon or simply an idiosyncratic cultural decision, another "selection from the arc"? She made the dilemma even more pronounced in personal statements than in professional writings and alternated between considering religion "everything," the fantasies and daydreams that sustained individuals and societies, and considering it "nothing," a destructive delusion or a coldly logical doctrine.

"Isn't it unbearable that that is all about nothing," Ruth commented to Margaret Mead one summer day in 1926 as the two sat in front of Notre Dame Cathedral.[74] Mead concluded that her friend had given up religion; Ruth had given up a religion she thought inaccessible, schematized, impersonal, and distanced from the everyday—the "insubstantial fables" of her verse.[75]

Ruth Benedict rejected the equation of religion and church (institution), religion and mythology (dogma), religion and ethics (code of conduct.)[76] She did not give up her private quest for "spirituality," and she continued to grapple professionally with the meaning of "religious complex." Her always provisional formulation related to wishes, day-dreams, imagination, and thus inevitably to myth—as in poem not doctrine.

"We are rare in identifying a religion with a mythology," she said in the *Encyclopedia* entry on myth.[77] Yet she did not dissociate myth from religion. Myth like poetry, she claimed, is an "accessory after the fact."[78] Myth and poem were not equivalent to but embodied and com-municated religious feelings. Ruth continued to believe that the experi-ence of awe was an essential part of human existence and that societies, like individuals, required moments of "visionary ecstasy." In her jour-nals Ruth yearned for the "knife that cuts to the bone,"[79] for "zest" to relieve monotony, and for "illumination" to balance accumulated fact. Somewhat the signs of her restlessness, these phrases also represented a considered principle. Without moments of revelation, daydream, and quest (she tried various synonyms) the pattern stayed hidden, the lines indistinct and unalterable. Ruth did not mean anything mystical; she was talking about the not uncommon experience of a sudden compre-hension.

She was also talking about an illumination that influenced day-to-day events. Ruth Benedict never minimized the impact of vision on the commonplace. Poetry is called religion when it intervenes in life, San-tayana had said. Ruth brought up a similar idea when she discussed the appearances of gods on earth.

It was not new for Ruth to think about appearance in both senses: how gods looked and how gods arrived on earth. She had not forgotten being reprimanded for "seeing" her father in a picture of Jesus Christ—an identification of man and god she later observed in the Pueblos. Like most Southwest fieldworkers, Ruth marveled at the pervasiveness of re-ligion in Pueblo life. Zuñis regulated their business by ceremony and obeyed a governing priesthood.[80] Ruth Bunzel complained about "danc-ing gods" constantly "interfering" in her work;[81] Ruth Benedict was en-tranced. In their feathered headdresses, symmetrically colored masks, and regularized performance, Pueblo gods dominated Pueblo life. These gods were domesticated, familiar, and approachable. A neighbor was likely to "be" a god, without straining either "humanity" or "divinity"; human traits corresponded to divine traits. "When they pray they say to their gods, 'We shall be one person.' They exchange intimate relation-ship terms with them. . . . They speak of exchanging breath with their gods."[82]

Myth and ceremony expressed and confirmed the closeness of man and god. The Zuñi did not know a distance from his theology, a distance Ruth Benedict portrayed as vast in her own religious tradition: "The gold stars / Stood fixed in austere heaven," she wrote in the theological poem, "And his eyes were opened."[83]

Ruth had toyed with Catholicism, mainly in her poetry. She found attractive the lush imagery of "purple grape" and "honeyed wine,"[84] but in an undated, unpublished poem when she imagined "god" a "lily-rod," she transmuted the sensuality into severity. "And the god / A moment lets descend his glory thinned / To the forked slightness of a lily rod [ ]," she wrote in a poem called "Too Great Has Been the Tension of My Cloud."[85] The Catholic cast of her poetry revealed the sensual side of her nature, a contrast to the puritanical streak. Ruth's poetry also suggested her efforts, in the late 1920s, to chart a course through the "religious complex" in her own society. The Roman Catholic church was not like the Baptist church of her upbringing. An intricate Mass replaced the instructive sermon of a minister, Communion replaced the lonely bedtime prayer,[86] and a solemn ritual pageantry outshone the quiet domestic religion she remembered.

The appeal of Catholicism did not last. Ruth criticized in metaphor the cold distance of God from man and the long, arduous road to spiritual comprehension demanded by this religion.

> Only those
> Storm-driven down the dark, see light arise,
> Her body broken for their rainbow bread
> At late and shipwrecked close.[87]

Everything seemed intellectualized and ultimately unsatisfying. The Catholic mass, with wafer and wine, no longer served:

> They come like quiet waters
> Again from sacrament, their hands
> Clasped on dear volumes, their demands
> Divinely satisfied: O daughters
> Of an antique beauty lost
> From our tormented fingers, then
> Are you comforted again?[88]

Ritual failed. A catechism and man's essential loneliness summed up Catholic and Christian doctrine for Ruth Benedict. Contact with the gods in Western religion was through words or disembodied.

> "Unceasingly," God said, remote in heaven,
> "This man child beats his head upon the stone
> Desiring knowledge; has he not computed

> The stride of the wind, the little crumbling ash
> Left, at the last, of bone?[89]

Ruth pictured an inevitable separation; even during worship, man remained alone and his God a fatefully isolated figure, "the labyrinth of his soul an empty prison."[90]

The contrast with Pueblo religion was "unbelievable." Pueblo gods danced on earth; individuals personified their gods, sharing identity and bodily participating in divinity. The Zuñi, too, never danced alone but always shared a communal "thrill." This was *not* Dionysian: the Zuñi never succumbed to a wild and isolated frenzy. In his dance he joined others, every step meticulously controlled. Zuñi ceremonies excluded the self-absorption and unboundedness that resulted in ecstatic loss of self. But what the Zuñi lost in ecstasy and brilliant individual vision he gained in contact, closeness, links to the whole universe. This was, again, a side of Ruth's character and often deeply valued by her. The Zuñi ritual was elegantly and perfectly Apollonian; the dancer "retained his civic name."[91] In Ruth's pages even the pounding, visceral drumbeat became a regular, ordered sound.[92] And the priest who went alone to pray was questioned about this aberration.[93] Ruth Benedict portrayed an ideally congregational religion and a strikingly down-to-earth one.

The myths of Pueblo and of Western traditions articulated the differences in religious complex. Zuñi myths no more than Zuñi gods existed at a cold distance from ordinary men. The Zuñi did not contact his god timidly, on special occasion, through an intellectualized dogma. He learned divine principles "on his pulses," dancing, memorizing, repeating the themes in a powerful pattern. Zuñi was an absorbing not an analytic religion, fostering a bodily not a "chaste" encounter with gods.[94] Zuñis did not listen to tales of a god, dead and reappearing in a shroud:

> Cruelly you returned, a ghost the food
> Of darkness, laying by
> The perfumed garments of the burial.[95]

Zuñis heard about gods who were tricky and tricked, lustful and generous and sometimes ugly.[96] A god might escape punishment for a mischievous deed; so might a man.

These were gods born of passion and often a painful pregnancy. In 1928 Ruth wrote "Annunciation," paraphrasing the birth story of her tradition.

> . . . This god shall disarray
> No fold of your slight garments.[97]

She had tried another version. In "The Woman-Christ" she described a mother who bore a god and a female deity and implied an identity, thus merging fully natural with purely supernatural traits.[98] In the myths she collected, Zuñi gods shared human birth, the joys and the risks, and Zuñi gods lived always close to mankind. Common origin and common emotions allowed gods to help men out of predicaments (and sometimes vice versa)—not free men of sin. Christianity's sacrificial death, and atonement, had no counterpart in Pueblo myths. Errors, misjudgment, greed, and ill will were privileges of men and of gods; punishments fit the deed and the individual. Ruth Benedict noted the contrast to the Christian doing penance for a sin or for sinfulness, and she conveyed the differences between two traditions in her sonnets, in *Patterns of Culture* and, the "spoken proof," in *Zuñi Mythology.*

Divine intervention in the lives of men, as narrated by Zuñis, was not sternly moralistic. Neither god nor man stood for absolute good or absolute evil; both struggled through temptations, part of everyday existence. Caught in recognizable difficulties, mythic figures guided Zuñi individuals by example not precept. Sinless, the Christian god forgave man's sinful behavior. In more than one poem, Ruth expressed the conviction that such guidance, from an abstract and pure being, could be "terrifying."

In 1928 Ruth wrote a series of poems, an effort still to understand the "appearances" of god on earth. The previous summer she had visited the Pima tribe and added an "intoxicating" religious complex to the Apollonian, and compared both to her own. These 1928 poems *are* remarkable, as Edward Sapir said; in them, the poet's metaphysical strain issued in a strikingly personal imagery. " 'This is my Body' is a profound poem," he added.[99] Several stanzas have been quoted: the God, remote in heaven, while man futilely beat his head on stone; the quest that ended in ash, man with "hands bleeding and his brain sick on its leash."[100] The last stanza brought together the whole:

> "And all the while, a child curled in the brain,
> Quiet lies smiling in a swaddling sheet."
> A wise man spoke this riddle to the deaf
> Once in Judea, handling the bread and wine:
> "This is my body. Eat."[101]

One can read the poet's emotional constellation in these phrases, the sense of being bound between silence and wisdom, symbolism and satiation.

That same year Ruth Benedict wrote the poem "Myth," a gentler version of her speculations. The stanzas combined memories of Norwich and of Pueblo rituals:

> A god with tall crow feathers in his hair,
> Long-limbed and bronzed from going down of sun. . . .
> He gathers where we dropped them, filling full
> His arms' wide circuit, briars and sterile shrub.
> And all alone he dances, hour on hour,
> Till all our dreams have blooming, and our sleep
> Is odorous of gardens,—passing sweet
> Beyond all, wearily, we till and reap.[102]

And yet the poem showed more ambivalence than resolution, a continuing uncertainty about the relationship between god and sorrowful, weary, unwise human beings.

By inclination, and with encouragement from anthropological and philosophical writings, Ruth linked myth, poetry, and art to man's state of grace and conduct in the world. Her 1933, 1935, and 1938 pieces all in one way or another discussed men's approaches to forces seemingly beyond control and often beyond comprehension. Under the several distinct titles, Ruth Benedict reflected on the human conditions and "spiritual attitudes."

"Christianity is the moral autobiography of mankind," Santayana had written.[103] He meant a *type* of autobiography, to go with the kind of poetry he had in mind. Both were "epical," displaying the triumph of Good over Evil. An epic, a "high" poem, became religion because it embodied, persuasively, notions of Right and of Wrong. Ruth would have amended the philosopher: "high" poetry became, specifically, a Christian religion. Distinctions between good and evil did not dominate either Zuñi myths or Zuñi religion; in fact, Ruth Benedict did not accept a Platonic view of good and evil or any absolutes at all.

She had, however, used a phrase resembling Santayana's. Folklore is a peoples' autobiography, she said, not an epic, but narratives of small annoyances and compensatory wishes, of frustrations and liberating fantasies. She stressed the importance of expressing self and confirming fundamental values. The necessary fictions varied; the ways people constructed an autobiography took diverse and wonderfully elaborate forms. Ruth had combined Malinowski's pragmatism, Nietzsche's "nauseating," unmasked reality, and Santayana's "poetry and religion are two sides of a coin."[104]

By 1935 Ruth formulated a view of myth and folk tale that left religion somewhat in abeyance and somewhat the implied point of all her writings. People, she wrote, are stirred by their wishes and daydreams, expressed in poems, myths, anecdotes, and visions of the "country over the hill."[105]

Ruth Benedict did not preach the value of vision, of seeing and fore-seeing. She did occasionally adopt a moralizing tone—especially on the importance of "spiritual attitudes" which, for her, had to do with the readjustment of a society. People's dreams commented on their reality, embodying at once a criticism of the existing arrangement and a passionate hope for the future: "I mean something so strenuous that the quests of the Grail are but faint shadows of a reality, something so costly that there are few indeed who dare reckon on paying that price. . . . The growth of the world in that direction alone is able to excuse its existence."[106]

"The world new-minted"

"Poetry as certainly has something to do with morals, and with religion, and even with politics perhaps, though we cannot say what."[107] Ruth Benedict shared T. S. Eliot's vagueness and his optimistic conjunction of the significant aspects of human existence. She also shared his belief that men made wishes in a moral universe, that wishes were moral—a serious endeavor, not a frivolous distraction. Wishes, for Ruth, were serious to the extent that they were specific, and tied to earth.

In myths and poems men envisioned an alternative design, based on while modifying the one they knew. Dreams were fanciful and were intimately linked to the failings and the tribulations experienced every day. The quest to attain "paradise" depended upon an acute perception of the actual—so Ruth implied in much of what she wrote in private and in her discipline. This idea marked for her the nexus of myth, morals, religion, and politics.

> Being despoiled, not heir of Paradise,
> His senses raw and hungered after long,
> He dreamed it worth the consummate song.[108]

The poet did not discuss how paradise might be gained or lost; the poem did redo arguments hidden between the lines of her anthropology. Those who consider their lives a paradise make no wishes and no changes.

> He reckoned closer, Adam, who had lived
> With Eve in Paradise; it was not worth
> The taking.[109]

Those who are prompted into dissatisfaction by introspection, imagination, or comparison will wish and perhaps aim for paradise:

> . . . he was strong
> To brook unbroken, spent for Paradise.[110]

Ruth Benedict reminded her readers that "paradises" must be grounded, their content the material of "real life." The conviction underlay her progressive-liberalism, her support of Franklin Roosevelt's ameliorative New Deal programs, and her cautious entry into late 1930s national and international politics. All wishes, she said in another poem, had strings attached, a globe of "unadulterate color" fastened to earth by a sturdy thread.[111] The phrase comes from "Toy Balloons," a poem Edward Sapir called "splendid."[112] The poem is a resounding reminder of the principle behind Ruth's politics, her spiritual attitudes, and—certainly—behind her commitment to anthropology. "Toy Balloons" also showed her persistent doubts:

> Vendor, of your pity,
> Do not sell these to children.[113]

She saw both risk and necessity in vision. "All things fail save only dreams," she wrote, also in 1924. This poem contains images of isolation and of fragility: "A lonely / Pool no cloud can shadow" and "No other thing / At crest of being, with unbroken wing."[114]

Six years later, in 1930, Ruth wrote again of dream and fantasy.

> Throw slack the reins, and keep no memory
> Of foolish dreams we dreamed of ripened corn
> In barns, and red fire on the hearth. Be free
> As unicorns, that are but fantasy
> Unpledged to any truth, a single horn
> Against reality.[115]

Freedom, the poem implied, came from testing conventional precepts and probing common delusions—"riding" the fantasy as far as possible, with feet on earth:

> Pawing the leafy-hidden track
> With forefeet that are slim and velvet-black.[116]

Fantasy and creativity became crucial concepts in Ruth Benedict's anthropology. She wrote about a culture's dreams and a culture's wishes.

Beneath the anthropomorphic vocabulary Ruth meant shared dreams, transmitted through and, importantly, recreated by individual members of a society. Ruth Benedict ignored the artist except as worker and re-worker of common dreams; a few paragraphs in *Zuñi Mythology* describing personalized and gender-linked narrative techniques did not tip the balance.

Again and again, Ruth claimed that dreams and visions bolstered the structure of a society. She knew that a coherent and vital culture depended upon the quests and visions experienced by individuals; she knew, too, that fantasies, contained preeminently but not exclusively in myths, provided the means by which a culture perceived and projected values into the future: "the world new-minted." The individual might unravel the threads of an existing pattern, only to rewind them into a better-pleasing and "precious" shape.

> And jewelled
> Loveliness his holy grail.[117]

"The precariousness of those rationalistic attitudes"

Ruth Benedict was an anthropologist, and her writings on folklore con-stituted strong advocacy of an anthropological perspective. Reading folk-lore in context meant more than looking for history on the one hand and clues to unconscious impulse and "illegitimate" desire on the other. The folklorist-as-ethnographer did not expose an underside of Zuñi person-ality but a distinct mode of perception and of self-presentation—an aspect of Zuñi character. Ruth maintained her culture-personality anal-ogy, and she no more tore down a peoples' disguises than a person's masks. The "cathedral of concepts" did not hide character, but repre-sented it.

Readers of *Zuñi Mythology*, of *Cochiti Tales*, and her shorter pieces on folklore, myth, and ritual occasionally missed Ruth's point. She was concerned with the significance of cultural self-interpretations and their diverse expressions across societies. She was not (as some assumed) especially concerned with transcultural types: the frustrated culture find-ing relief in violent tales, the rigid culture exhibiting wildly uncontrolled fantasies. Ruth Benedict's "accuracy" lay in pinpointing, with Zuñi data, a psychological mechanism by which societies adjusted to and altered existing conditions; whether or not the Zuñi showed themselves to be "really" gossipy and greedy was not her point. Critics, however, often focused on the accuracy of an ethnographic portrait, and the publication of *Zuñi Mythology* exacerbated an already acrimonious debate about true Pueblo character—a debate Ruth in large part ignored.

In her review of *Zuñi Mythology*, Elsie Clews Parsons commented that there was no need for "retaliatory compensation" in myth because, she said, "Zuñi children are not neglected; as Dr. Benedict indicates, they are cherished." And she added, emphatically, "Psychological interpretation without accompanying analysis of distribution is ever precarious."[118] The review perpetuated the rhythm of dispute between Elsie Parsons and Ruth Benedict—the one drily factual, the other applying insights from psychology, personal "myths," and life stories to get at the meaning to a people of "facts" in their lives. The two women never totally agreed about the Pueblos and probably not about how to read folklore. Like her first anthropology teacher, Ruth treated folklore as an ethnographic source, but for modes of perception not details of behavior. For Ruth, folklore revealed the "emotional constellation" of a culture and its dynamic renewal. In folklore she uncovered the complexities of how a culture managed, not just the consequences of its managing.

Franz Boas, too, misunderstood the general thesis of *Zuñi Mythology*, reading for a kind of information rather than for indication of human creativity in the face of doubts and of inherited certainties. Ruth sent him a draft of her introduction in the spring of 1934; in August he wrote from Connecticut:

> I am a little doubtful whether it is justifiable to explain the tales of devoted children and the like entirely on the basis of the play of imagination with possible and real situations. . . .
> I cannot help thinking that this style of narration may have exerted its influence regardless of cultural patterns.[119]

He made the diffusionist point, but added a comment closer to Ruth's intention: "The final reconciliation is, of course, typical of the Pueblos."[120] The "typical" Pueblo pattern, expressed variously and retold continuously, inspired her thesis.

Zuñi Mythology does offer information about the Zuñi Indians along with a theory of myth. The mythic portrait accompanied the bird's-eye view in chapter 4 of *Patterns of Culture*. In *Patterns*, Ruth gathered significant details to evoke a particular personality; she substantiated an elegantly abstract conceptualization with carefully chosen impressions— the mode of her sonnets. In *Zuñi Mythology* the Zuñi spoke for themselves, bluntly and (Southwest folklorists complained) repetitiously, fulsomely, endlessly. Speaking for themselves, the Zuñi revealed distinctive strategies for coping with a perceived and less-than-perfect world. The pages of *Zuñi Mythology* offered colleagues and critics not a Zuñi different from the one in *Patterns of Culture* but the Zuñi in a different mood. The monsters and stubborn wives, the pregnant men and runaway children, the deceitful stepchild and nasty god—all rang changes on a dominant theme. In their stories, the Zuñi confirmed and commented upon the traditional Zuñi "road." The stories preserved a dominant attitude, Apollonian in content, moral, and rhythm. The pattern held; only the emphases shifted from myth to tale, from ceremony to individual experience. In her book the ethnographer quoted myths to color in a clearly outlined Zuñi character.

So it would be wrong to set *Zuñi Mythology* against *Patterns of Culture,* to test Ruth Benedict's accuracy as a fieldworker. She collected myths, tales, and observations in order to convey a coherent culture entity, in effect, a "re-presentation" of the Zuñis' own presentations. It would also be wrong to consider *Zuñi Mythology* a set of permanent data, still-life versions of Zuñi wishes and fantasies (though it is partly that); *Zuñi Mythology* illustrated a process. People go on telling tales and remaking myths because changing circumstances require a renewed psychologically and aesthetically satisfying sense of things. Each culture maintains a characteristic rhetoric for recasting the universe, background for and responsive to the skills of an individual innovator and a single storyteller.

In the end Ruth's most important achievement, in *Zuñi Mythology* and other folklore pieces, was to incorporate a notion of imaginativeness into the study of cultures. Her notion reflected her understanding of psychology, of patterning, and of self-consciousness and revision in a life. She did not limit imaginativeness to one area of life or to one segment of a population, but assumed imagination was crucial to any person-culture relationship. (Cultures, she made clear in other writings, varied along exactly this dimension of permitted "imagining.") The person who was subject to conventions also revised and revitalized the accepted rules, acting out and challenging the primary values of his society. In effect, every individual participated in a moral universe—a "religious complex"—because, according to Ruth Benedict, every individual claimed a guiding vision and pursued a "quest" that altered daily living.

Vision and quest, an individual experience, stemmed from and sustained the culture pattern. As Ruth saw it, the imagination of an artist, a poet, a narrator, an ordinary man, existed within tradition—and had to. She outlined some of her point of view further in a series of letters she exchanged with Richard Chase.

In 1945–46 Ruth Benedict was living in Washington, D.C., with-drawn from the Columbia department but still advising graduate students. Sometime that fall she agreed to read Chase's dissertation on myth, written for a Ph.D. in English. The correspondence began respectfully enough, then quickly fell into irritated bickering. Chase expressed growing annoyance, possibly reflecting the anxieties of a degree candidate but mainly defending his case—with notable self-possession. Ruth, for her part, revealed the seriousness of her commitment to students and the importance to her anthropological thought of literature and folklore. But her persistent if flattering misunderstanding of Chase's topic did not ease their conflict. His "book," Chase told his reader more than once, dealt with the "opinions of folklorists, not folklore itself." The book is a "short study of opinions on myth," he reminded Ruth.[121] Told, she expressed little sympathy and much doubt, deciding that the subject did not utilize his literary skills. "Did you compromise for the degree?" she asked over his repeated denials.[122]

Ruth Benedict encouraged Chase (albeit late in the game) to concentrate on a particular folklore, to exercise his talents on a single body of material. The advice led straight back to her 1920s argument for "intensive" folklore study: the psychological (autobiographical) approach she added to Boas's historical-diffusionism. Writing to Chase, she again urged that text be put into context; expressive elements were evidence, requiring thoughtful and concentrated analysis.

The disagreements between Ruth Benedict and Richard Chase did not amount to a difference between anthropological and literary interpretations, though both phrased it that way. Ruth's "culture" was always in a sense literary, her "humanistic" referred to human creativity and man's imaginative constructs.[123] The difference lay between a focus on the art and a focus on the artist. But the edges of the debate remained fuzzier than either admitted. Chase once described myth in words whose style if not whose purpose in argument Ruth appreciated: "a fusion of calm potency, grandeur, and mysteriousness."[124] Each—student and teacher—stood in awe before the stunning evidences of human imagination, Chase because of the displayed power of "a man's mind"[125] and Ruth because of the remarkable power of words to contain pervasive, existential terror.

"You see myth as a cultural phenomenon. I see it as the aesthetic activity of a man's mind," Chase wrote, further to distinguish his view from Ruth's. For her, to be myth the art had to transcend the individual and become "common coin of a whole tribe or civilization."[126] She did not push Chase out of anthropology, though he accused her of building "barriers" between her discipline and his. Rather, she urged him to analyze the aesthetic, effective components of myth, a step toward accounting for the impact of art upon a society. She told him to do what he did best: "stay ~~being~~ [hers] a literary critic."[127] She said he could best contribute to the study of mythology by studying myths, not individual mythmakers and (certainly) not critical opinions on myth.

Ruth Benedict did not dismiss the poet or the mythmaker or the artist; she even had sympathy for the literary critic.[128] In writing to Chase, she had returned to her view of creativity as a cultural phenomenon carried by the individual. She never implied that a "creation" springs full-blown: "There is no conceivable source of any cultural trait than the behavior of some man, woman, or child."[129]

To become property of a "whole tribe or civilization" the "trait"— if art—must embody shared wishes and fundamental beliefs otherwise unadmitted or unperceived. The true creator in any culture, Ruth Benedict implied, rose above the specifics of "personality" to represent common themes and, on rarer occasions, to speak for the human condition "under the form of eternity."[130] The "great" poet like the primitive narrator translated his personal experiences into an aspect of shared humanity. The anonymity of the artist, for Ruth, linked the Zuñi storyteller to the Bible and to Shakespeare (who, especially in the pre–World War II years, lacked a "biography")—the central myth and tales of her own civilization. She admired J. W. N. Sullivan's biography of Beethoven: "Beethoven is not describing to us a spiritual history [i.e., his personal history]; he is presenting to us a vision of life."[131] Through a precise image, a dramatized incident, a sounding crescendo, the artist in any society confirmed and expanded the premises of human existence. "The highest endowments do not create—they only discover," Ruth Benedict had written during World War I.

> All transcendent genius has the power to make us know this as utter truth. Shakespeare, Beethoven—it is inconceivable that they have *fashioned* the works of their lives; they only saw and heard the universe that is opaque and dumb to us. When we are most profoundly moved by them, we say, not "O superb creator"—but "O how did you *know*! Yes it is so."[132]

Ruth Benedict's correspondence with Richard Chase in 1945–46 also reflected the studies of complex societies that for the past ten years had occupied her time and thoughts. Between 1935 (*Zuñi Mythology*) and 1945, when she agreed to be on Chase's committee, Ruth had shifted her attention away from the "laboratory" to the "marketplace." She used literature and art as ethnographic sources for modern nations, insights into a complex personality, and thus further developed concepts and approaches that threaded back to Norwich, to Anne Singleton, to the years at Columbia and on the *Journal of American Folk-Lore*. Ruth did not become a white folklorist; she instead made imagination and expressiveness the core of her studies of culture-as-a-whole.

Over those ten years, too, "humanistic" became an increasingly important word in Ruth's anthropological writings and speeches. At the center of her anthropological inquiries lay the problem of individualized expression within cultural conventions and a recognition of the integrating function of wish-fulfilling fantasy and daydreams. The anthropologist had a responsibility to uncover the hopes and the despairs a people themselves did not always recognize and, all too often, released in conflict, oppression, and war.

The end of Ruth Benedict's folklore studies, typically, marked a beginning, an awareness of the need for "imagined alternatives" in all societies and in a war-torn world. She posed against the "precariousness of rationalistic attitudes" the solidity of a well-considered dream and hoped the dream would survive.

> . . . what profit then?
> Losing that song, what chatter being men.

9
Anthropology: Science and Politics

"We need only to obtain a little perspective"

IN 1939–40 RUTH BENEDICT took her sabbatical and went to California to write a book. In her sister's household in Pasadena, then a few blocks away in a house she shared with Ruth Valentine (a psychologist and California friend), Ruth worked on the manuscript of *Race: Science and Politics*.[1] She had exchanged the "gray pavements" of New York City for the sunny warmth of Pasadena, but 1939–40 was not a year of contentment or ease of mind. *Race* addressed the crisis around her and revealed a shift in her interpretations of herself as a woman and as an anthropologist.

At first glance the book seemed to be a break from her previous writings. *Race* issued a warning to her society in more urgent tones than Ruth had used before. *Race* also confronted subjects she had slighted in earlier writings: conflict and competitiveness, accumulation and privilege, power and oppression. The book has an unmistakable political message; the author's stand on events in her home society could not be clearer—there are no parables here, only a sharp reminder to her society to "open its eyes."

Six years before, in 1934, Ruth had complained to Margaret Mead, "He has given up science for good works. Such a waste!"[2] She referred to Franz Boas's increasing political activity, and her concern covered more than regret at Boas's distraction from science. Ruth also feared the consequences of giving up the "neutrality" of the academy, such as it was. In those years the president of Columbia, Nicholas Murray Butler, was not above overseeing class discussions.[3] Too, World War I events and the American Anthropological Association censure of Boas were not far behind, and Ruth Benedict thought back to the First

247

World War as conditions in Europe visibly worsened. The problem of the scientist's duty had by no means been laid to rest.

Ruth also worried about Boas's health and stamina. Close to eighty years old, Papa Franz had not been wholly well since 1930 when his wife died. Through the decade he added to his university tasks and tiring fieldtrips, lecture tours, letters of protest, and involvement with refugees—finding them housing, money, and security. In October 1938 Gladys Reichard wrote to Boas: "Why don't you limit your refugees to one day or something? I don't think it is age which tires you out so much, it is the everlasting hopelessness of all these people"—but he wouldn't stop.[4] A year later, in the winter of 1939, Boas confided to Ruth Benedict his concern about his health, asking her not to repeat the matter: "And I get tired without cause, I mean without having done any work. I am really concerned about putting all my materials in hands that can use it, but I do not know how to do it. Please, do not mention all this to anyone."[5]

Ruth, not alone of Boas's students, accepted the obligation of carrying on his efforts. She, especially, shared his notion of the scientist's duty, and when he asked her to provide the public—the common man —with anthropology's perspective on racism, persecution, and human potential, she took the assignment without question. The result, *Race: Science and Politics*, is short, simple, and angry, but consistent in motive and content with Ruth's whole anthropology.

Race at once validated her work and fit the history of her discipline. Ethnographic comparisons of "primitive tribes" to "civilized nations" had continually raised the question of fixed differences in peoples' capacities to advance. Franz Boas, out of a political liberalism, and Ruth Benedict, out of a personal debate over the "natural" versus the "conventional," each concluded that all human beings learned equally and were equally able to change. At moments Ruth openly marveled at the "plasticity" of human nature, and she urged greater recognition of man's infinite potential upon her contemporaries—scientists and politicians.

Her book was a plea, a tract whose every sentence alerted people to the assumed "inevitabilities" and challenged a placid submission to pattern. Ruth's book also translated Boas's ideas, rewording them for a popular audience. People who did not read his *Race, Language, and Culture* did read her *Race*.

As she wrote, Ruth battled despair and apathy. Luther Cressman (Margaret Mead's first husband) visited Ruth in the fall of 1939 and later recalled how "bitter" and "frail" she looked.[6] During those months Ruth was tormented by events and uncertain about the effectiveness of her participation. Moments of painful anxiety alternated with weary boredom. Being in Pasadena with her sister's family did provide relief and comfort; writing *Race* at least allowed her to put to use her tumultuous emotions.

"To my tribe alone he gave the ceremonies which preserve the world"

Race: Science and Politics contains a relentless array of detail, designed to shock readers out of complacency and deflect the world from its precipitous course into disaster. Along with politics, Ruth tackled a central issue in her science, what is now called culture versus nature and what she put in terms of "learning" versus the "innate." In *Race* she would argue for learning, with phrases that conveyed both her meaning and a process of thought. This was precisely what she had advocated in twenty years of teaching and of reviewing books.

Ruth Benedict made her argument along two fronts in *Race*. Sometimes she stressed learning and the capacity of human beings to alter their attitudes and interactions; then the book praised human "plasticity." Other times she focused on the innate, specifically on race. Then Ruth returned to Boas's distinction between biological race, the *science*, and race as a category, an excuse for persecution, the *politics* of her title. Race was a biological fact; the use made of "race" was social.

"As the author says in his foreword, 'intellectual protests can perhaps never be efficacious in a world of action,' but the attempt nevertheless must constantly be made," Ruth quoted from Paul Radin's *Racial Myth*.[7] She had been preparing her "intellectual protest" for a decade. *Race* was polemic based on reliable scientific data gathered from diverse tribes and nations; her sample ranged over history and included a variety of culture patterns.

Nor did Ruth omit Western societies, least of all the United States. Her Americanism came to the fore in *Race*, and she criticized her nation from the perspective of a particular brand of patriotism absorbed in the schools of central New York State and the Midwest. One has only to add the Baptist upbringing she never quite rejected, and the emotional underpinning for Ruth's trust in individual motivation becomes clear. She returned in *Race*, too, to her oldest question about fitting in without conforming, about being different without being denied access to the valued "goods," the rewards of society. Her political statements of the 1930s reached back, to Norwich, to her self-conscious "written" feminism of World War I, and to a general intellectual liberalism. By 1939, when she began *Race*, Ruth had substantiated these long-term, often vague principles through her discipline. Anthropological data and method bolstered her convictions and sharpened her insights into American society. Comparison to other societies, even those not seen, prompted in Ruth a coolly distanced view of her own landscape.

An example of this came up before *Race*. During the 1930s Ruth paid increasing attention to Latin America, specifically its "cultural pluralism." In her interest she responded to students who, finding it ethically and financially difficult to work with North American "minorities," chose to work in Latin America instead. Neither financial nor ethical difficulty plagued Latin American research, and Ruth gratefully accepted corporation funds that allowed fieldwork to go on in the Depression years. Columbia students discovered, among other things, a superior form of race relations: Brazil emerged heroic.

Ruth was intrigued by the discovery, but the closest she came to seeing the situation firsthand was a summer visit to Guatemala. In 1938 she and Natalie Raymond went with Ruth Bunzel on a trip that combined work with vacation. "Nat has driven me all over the country," she wrote to Boas on July 3, 1938, hoping the letter would arrive in time for his birthday. "Happy Birthday! I shall be thinking about you on the day and hoping that all your family are with you and that the sun shines and the breezes are cool."[8] She and Nat stayed in "Bunny's village," Chichicastenango, in "a first class hotel." But, the anthropologist added to her teacher, the hotel had badly disrupted Indian life. "I wish they'd put it somewhere else and left these earnest, hard-pressed Chichicastenangans in peace."[9] At the end Ruth submitted an optimistic report on a working cultural pluralism.[10]

By the following summer her optimism, and to some extent her interest in Latin America, had severely lapsed. That summer, on a Blackfoot reservation in Montana with students, Ruth expressed nervous pessimism about the United States and the world. "I feel very far out of the world, but at least I know no world conflagration has flared up yet," she wrote to Boas.[11]

In September she went to Pasadena, not feeling better. That fall Ruth was dispirited, lethargic, absentminded: she several times forgot to send her rent check to New York.[12] It was Boas's turn to worry about her health. "I was shocked to hear that you are sick. I trust this will find you well recovered. Please, let me know!"[13] After a debilitating bout with pneumonia, Ruth summoned up the energy, or at least the well-learned endurance, to work steadily on the manuscript of *Race*. Boas urged her to write, knowing that work kept her "blue devils" at bay.

The first chapters of *Race* closely followed Boas's precepts. Of utmost importance was the matter of distinguishing inherited traits from learned traits, the "given" from the "customary" in human behavior. The scientist's obligation to demonstrate these distinctions increased as societies failed to do so. With this in mind Ruth effectively described the enormous individual variations within one racial group and the great changes in behavior and temperament of a "race" over time and in different environments. She wrote confidently on the subjects of learning and change but less confidently about physiological facts, the other half of her thesis. Scrupulous about data, she did not hesitate to ask Boas for advice on the *science* of race.

With chapter 6, "Who Is Superior," Ruth Benedict prepared her strongest thrust. And in part two, chapters 7 and 8, she carried out the attack, turning her rhetoric on the *politics* of race. She wrote about name-calling, assumptions of "better" and "worse," and about the taunting of one group by another—behavior as old as human society and part of nearly every individual's biography. Taunting and persecution were a constant feature of human societies, varying only in motive and in content. Social conditions prepared the way for such behavior, setting context for the attack of one group upon another. This had been true forever, but the phenomenon reached an excruciating and unforgivable extreme in 1930s Germany. As Ruth implied in her book, the appearance of Hitler and his triumphant Nazism was at once too understandable and too horrifying to accept as part of an inevitable pattern of human behavior. "It was not so difficult as it might seem to change the German racist theories from the boast of all-conquerors to the use of a humiliated and despairing people."[14]

In chapter 7, "A Natural History of Racism," Ruth wrote about Germany, and condemnation blistered through her account. In chapter 8 she talked about the United States. Nazism, she suggested, was not a unique aberration; persecution and racism ran through American history as well. Racism was "merely another instance of the persecution of minorities for the advantage of those in power," she said with ironic understatement.[15]

Elsewhere she was blunt. Americans had never faced the nature and the extensiveness of their own racism. "The racist literature [i.e., *on* race] of the United States deals hardly at all with our great national racial problem, the Negro," she claimed.[16] Actually Ruth herself dealt hardly at all with the "negro problem"; the Negro formed one case in her argument. She had good reason for not emphasizing Negro-white relationships at that moment. On the brink of war, Americans needed to recognize unity—not be reminded of disunity. Rather than condemning, Ruth sternly instructed her country in how to eliminate the conditions that led to racism and persecution.

In *Race* Ruth presented data and examples so vividly that the course of change would be self-evident.

> If civilized men expect to end prejudice—whether religious or racial—they will have to remedy major social abuses, in no way connected with religion or race, to the common advantage. Whatever reduces conflict, curtails irresponsible power, and allows people to obtain a decent livelihood will reduce race conflict. Nothing less will accomplish the task.[17]

This was one of her strongest statements, followed by recommendations that ranged from "providing full citizenship rights" to "improving material conditions."

> Until housing and conditions of labor are raised above the needlessly low standards which prevail in many sections of the country, scapegoats of some sort will be sacrificed to poverty. Until the regulation of industry has enforced the practice of social responsibility, there will be exploitation of the most helpless racial groups, and this will be justified by racist denunciations.[18]

Not a revolutionary tract, *Race* did contain firm advocacy of state intervention and government "social engineering."[19] Behind this ran another argument. Giving individuals material security, Ruth wrote, increased their sense of worth and with it their willingness to cooperate in the running of society.

Race's arguments, though stronger, were not entirely new ones for Ruth Benedict. Although she had not before focused so explicitly on material conditions, she had discussed the bases for individual autonomy and full participation in a society. She had talked about the benefits to a whole society when every individual contributed and won acknowledgment for that contribution. She had persistently argued that a society must provide everyone with a source of livelihood; she had not, however, argued that a society must provide everyone with a job or a salary. There were other ways of defining livelihood.

The possibility of various connections between work, wealth, position, and individual autonomy appeared throughout her writings. Ruth compared societies, noting the diverse bases for freedom to act, and considered the child and the woman as persons whose contribution came from non-wage-earning activities and whose independence was therefore often, though not invariably, at risk.[20] In 1937 she temporarily left aside ethnographic parable to write programmatically about her own society. "No society we know has consistently demanded, as ours has, the toll of human frustration that results when human beings find no place in the social framework and share no common goals."[21]

For Ruth Benedict the solution involved not redistributing income but spreading responsibility. In recognizing the different contributions of different individuals, societies might eliminate conflict, intolerance, and depression. If a naive solution to racism, persecution, and hatred, this also represented Ruth's best hope at the end of the 1930s. Her hope was rooted in an ambivalent Americanism, a faith in human nature, and sturdy confidence in a people's impulse to envision a better world and to adjust behaviors to the vision. "Our Founding Fathers believed that a nation could be administered without creating victims. It is for us to prove that they were not mistaken," she ended *Race*.[22]

"All things fail save only dreams"

Race was an accomplishment of a certain sort. In her book, Ruth Benedict had done what Boas wanted; she had publicized the science they shared, and in a cause to which both lent full allegiance. She had taken her stand and made the "intellectual protest" that still, in 1939, carried weight. But the year had been a difficult one for Ruth. Her fieldtrip with students, something she usually enjoyed, paled before her concern about events in Europe. In 1939, too, she heard from George Herzog of dissatisfaction with her work on the *Journal of American Folk-Lore*. She herself had been ill, dispirited, in despair through much of the fall. Then in December that year Edward Sapir died. He was fifty-five years old.

The two had grown apart over the past ten years; nevertheless, his death resonated through her life. The timing accentuated the severity of the loss. December was a month when Ruth typically reviewed her life, experienced doubts, and felt the need to rearrange and reorder her significant themes. *Race* itself provided mixed satisfaction; she fulfilled her citizenship obligations and she paid tribute to Boas, but her heart had not been fully in the subject. Ruth never said much about the reception of her books, and the positive responses to *Race* prompted no more recorded comment from her than had other reviews. When she heard the news about Sapir, in the midst of her "intellectual protest," she might have wondered how far she had come from the viewpoint the two shared in the 1920s. Then both had had the sense that life presented extraordinarily complex problems, demanding a response in poetry, music, and friendship as well as in science.

"A tract for our times," reviews said, praising the simple and un-ambiguous polemic of *Race*.[23] And Ruth would go on to simplify even more. *Race* turned into *Races of Mankind*, written with Gene Weltfish in 1943.[24] *Races of Mankind*, in turn, spread through public schools, churches, and labor unions in the form of comic strips, films, and dra-matic representations. The sections on intelligence testing disturbed the Army, and in 1944 the House Military Affairs Subcommittee forbade dis-tribution of the pamphlet, calling it "communist propaganda."

By 1939–40 Ruth had already become a political figure and had taken her anthropology a great distance since the time Edward Sapir had written to her in a poem called "Zuñi": "Through the dry glitter of the desert sea / And sharpness of the mesa keep the flowing / Of your spirit, in many branching ways."[25] Their personal intimacy had dis-appeared during the 1930s, but the undercurrent of a shared under-standing of anthropology remained. Ruth's late-1930s activities nearly obscured this kindred interpretation of a discipline.

In the 1920s Ruth Benedict and Edward Sapir had both struggled with the significance of doing anthropology. "I somehow feel in much of my work," Sapir wrote in 1916, "that I am not true to my inner self, that I have let myself be put off with useful but relatively unimportant trifles at the expense of a development of finer needs and impulses, whatever they are."[26] Sapir, like Ruth, questioned anthropology from the point of view of his ability to contribute to a science and pursue his search for an endeavor that would truly express the "human spirit." Each tried to satisfy "inner self" and science by fitting humanity in, adding to an-thropology man in his agony and his creativeness.

Ruth wrote an obituary for Edward Sapir. Her piece, published in the *American Anthropologist*, revealed virtually nothing of the tension and the intricacy making their relationship and giving it staying power.[27] She conveyed little of the man in her short formal piece, either because she was self-conscious about her audience or because she feared the display of her emotions. "Give the mad tonguing play," Sapir once wrote to Ruth,[28] advice she found hard to take—in poetry, in person, and in public statements. Control provided a refuge from emotion.

Reasonably she left much of the assessment of Sapir's work to more qualified commentators. Ruth could not do justice to his linguistic work. But Ruth also, surprisingly, barely suggested the impact Sapir had on culture-and-personality and, especially, on her own contributions to the field. The strong continuity between her ideas and his does not appear in Ruth Benedict's memorial for Edward Sapir.

Uneasy with the form, unhappy with the reminder of so much changed in her world since the first years of their friendship—it is hard to say exactly why Ruth so restrained her comments on Sapir. Perhaps she felt she had adequately acknowledged Sapir's extraordinary impact on her life in her professional writings; the course of her anthropology had as much to do with Sapir's influence as with anyone's—except Boas's and possibly Mead's. Too, the strongest influence on her work came from Sapir's nonwork, from his poetry, from his personal acuteness about character and conflict, from an insight into her spirit that startled her by its clarity. Ruth could not easily put those aspects of a friendship into the obituary.

No doubt Ruth was immeasurably saddened by Sapir's death—the more, not the less because it occurred in December 1939, when the world seemed dark, winter thoughts plagued her, her book was nearly done, and the future loomed. Edward Sapir would have understood her fear of futility: "To amass data, to write them up, to discuss 'problems' —how easy, but *cui bono?*"[29] His words, in poems and in prose, had often brought Ruth's thoughts to the surface readily and powerfully.

Through it all, Ruth Benedict and Edward Sapir shared a commitment to and a questioning of their science, as well as a humility in face of the effort to understand man beset by conflict and blessed with imaginative vision. As long as Ruth did anthropology, as long as she considered hers a science of the human dilemma and a bid against meaninglessness, she maintained the bonds formed with Edward Sapir in the 1920s. She too might have wished to claim as he did:

> I cannot bend my soul to the twist
> That will make it fit with the brutal fate,
> That will make it yield to the tyrant world.
> My soul stands firm.[30]

In Ruth's version, "All things fail save only dreams."[31]

10
The Duties of a Discipline

"We may train ourselves to pass judgment upon the dominant traits of our own civilization"

IN 1937 FRANZ BOAS retired from chairmanship of Columbia's department of anthropology. His presence no longer held Ruth Benedict to departmental duties, duties that had involved her in more or less running the department. She had little hope of being appointed his successor.

> My own position is that I'm all in favor of getting the best man possible, and if a better man will come over me than under me, I should be enthusiastic about it. But if the powers that be decide against Lloyd [Warner] and [Ralph] Linton they will have to consider younger men, and there's no reason why I should passively agree to a beginner's being made head of the department because I'm disqualified by being a woman.[1]

Neither the Columbia administration nor the Faculty of Political Science (where anthropology was located) would risk appointing a woman to head a department. "As Dean McBain said, the universities will have to come to it, and he didn't believe it was bad policy to take the bull by the horns and accept the necessity."[2] But they did not take the bull by the horns, and instead considered several men. Ralph Linton emerged as the favored candidate. He came to Columbia as a visitor in the fall of 1937, along with an archaeologist, William Duncan Strong, and George Herzog, Ruth's associate from the Folk-Lore Society. In November of that year, speeding up usual procedures to avoid controversy, Columbia appointed Linton head of the department of anthropology.[3]

With Franz Boas out and Ralph Linton in, the department changed enormously for Ruth Benedict. The style of anthropology shifted, from Boasian emphasis on wholeness, culture as a unique entity, and man's "subjective" view of his environment, to Linton's more sociological, systematic approach. Not only had Ruth lost a man to whom she was attached emotionally as well as intellectually, she now had to work with a man she thoroughly disliked. (Boas, too, had disliked Linton.)

The personalities of Ruth Benedict and Ralph Linton were utterly antithetical, and Linton's arrival at Columbia precipitated open antagonism. Each accused the other of determined persecution and evil intent, virtually of sorcery. Ruth worried, then became convinced, that Linton was trying to take the department away from her. "All that I know— except for Bunny's [Ruth Bunzel] wild forebodings—is that Linton and Strong and George [Herzog] had a meeting in which they named certain required courses for all PhD candidates," omitting hers, she wrote in an "S.O.S." "I knew when I asked for a sabbatical that it was on the books that they'd try it." The whole letter reveals a conviction that Linton, and his allies, were eager to get rid of her. "All I can see is that I am in a minority and students might not be advised to take my courses" was a mild version of what she dreaded.[4]

Ralph Linton was not the sort of person Ruth liked. His third wife described him as a "vigorous and imposing figure. He was over six feet tall and weighed well over two hundred pounds. He was fond of food, being both a gourmet and a gourmand at table. Music, dancing, cards, and alcohol had not been permitted in his home and he never developed any interest in the first three. But he overcame the last taboo."[5] Adelin Linton sketched in the figure; others elaborated: Linton apparently overcame the "taboo" with a vengeance and added a few indulgences.[6] Ruth Benedict, tall for a woman, also struck people as being wispy and vague; Linton found her unbearable, aloof, cold, and finicky.

Ruth accused Linton of trying to "eliminate" her. Linton believed that Ruth intentionally turned students against him. People still wonder whether Ruth actually circulated the petition against him Linton claimed she had.[7] Whether or not such a petition existed, Ruth certainly conveyed to students her lack of enthusiasm about their new chairman. She had her supporters and Linton had his—and he continued to marshal allies in his battle against Ruth even after he left Columbia for Yale in 1944.[8]

On the subject of Ralph Linton, Ruth Benedict lost her usual restraint. She wrote letters, their tone shrill with irritation and the growing suspicion that Linton planned to destroy her. "There is also Bunny's [Ruth Bunzel] foreboding that I am to be liquidated."[9] Such

outraged letters, sent broadcast across the country by a woman who
was not a habitual letter-writer, caused concern. Her friends worried
that Linton would, purposefully or not, drive Ruth to distraction, into
a debilitating depression, or worse.

Though a note of hysteria crept in when Ruth talked about Ralph
Linton, she was neither alone nor inaccurate in her judgments. Linton
precipitated waves of discontent among undergraduates, graduates, and
other faculty members. "I don't make Linton out at all. For some
reason I can't get acquainted with him," the sociable Gladys Reichard
complained. "From my girls' [Barnard] letters it seems to me that he
is not able to hold his class in leash. There must be some student
hecklers or something."[10] Others remembered Linton as being a "bit
off his head," unable to control his reactions. For people used to a
"family" under Papa Franz, Linton introduced a dreadfully discordant
note.

Why had Linton been chosen, at risk of competitiveness and hostility in the close-knit department? At the time, Linton's interest in
anthropology resembled Ruth's own. Both focused on culture-and-
personality, from different enough perspectives to create a strong
departmental specialization. Linton's sociological approach comple-
mented Ruth's notion of a personality common to individual and to
culture.[11] Both were moving toward a "psychiatric anthropology," as
Ruth said in a letter inviting A. I. Hallowell to join them for lunch
at the Maison de Winter.[12] In addition, Ruth like Ralph Linton became
intrigued by the seminars Dr. Abram Kardiner held at the New York
Psychoanalytic Institute (1936–39).

Ruth went to these seminars with Bunny, and the two women
presented Zuñi data for Kardiner's secondary psychoanalysis. Linton
brought data from Pacific Island societies, and these ultimately formed
the basis for Kardiner's theory of "basic personality."[13] The seminars
suited Linton very well, Ruth not so well. She withdrew, turning to
social psychologists and neo-Freudians like Karen Horney and Harry
Stack Sullivan. Ruth's ability to respect Linton's work and to accept
him as chairman at Columbia survived mainly because she went to
Pasadena for her sabbatical in 1939–40, spent her New York time on
committees and at interdisciplinary conferences, and generally kept her
distance from Schermerhorn Hall.

During those years as well, Ruth Benedict moved out of the
academy. Horrified at contemporary events, she looked at American
society, its character and the sources of that character. "No society
has yet attempted a self-conscious direction of the process by which
its new normalities are created in the next generation," she had written

in 1934.[14] The end of the decade seemed the time to start; societies had to create the conditions for "new normalities" or disintegrate. The time had also come, Ruth realized, for the anthropologist to pass judgment on her own society and to offer it alternatives.

"We need data on the consequences for human
life of different human social inventions"

Teaching greatly influenced Ruth Benedict's anthropology. She taught through decades distinctly marked in mood: the contentment of pre–World War I years, ebullient optimism after the war, the demoralizing Depression of the 1930s. In addition, Ruth's thoughts about teaching and molding the next generation paralleled her thoughts about motherhood. Margaret Mead remembered her dream of "being stolen away to educate a child; when she was grown, my friends recognized that she must have been my pupil, for only I could have brought her up."[15] Ruth, sensitive to the temptation of living one's life through a child, tried to keep the role of mother separate from that of teacher. Her fears about the risk of living "vicariously" through a daughter did not accord with her growing confidence as a teacher. Nevertheless, when she wrote about the relationship of one generation to the next, her absorbed interpretations of motherhood gave energy to conventional progressive-education ideas. Ultimately Ruth made respect for individuality and separateness of pupil and teacher the cornerstone of child-rearing wherever it occurred.

From the beginning of their friendship Ruth and Margaret talked about motherhood and, very likely, about teaching as well. Each woman wanted a child, but from different perceptions of their own "independent purposes." They did agree on the flaws in child-rearing practiced by their friends and sisters and by American society as a whole. As anthropologists, too, Ruth and Margaret discussed children, comparing America to primitive cultures. Margaret Mead collected data in her Pacific Island societies; Ruth remembered Pueblo children and incidents in Zuñi myths. When she reviewed Mead's *Growing Up in New Guinea* in 1930, Ruth praised the book for instructing Americans about their inept child-rearing practices.[16] Eight years later Ruth published her views of child-rearing.

"Continuities and Discontinuities in Cultural Conditioning" first appeared in *Psychiatry* in 1938[17] and has subsequently been widely reprinted. The article outlined an argument that dominated Ruth Benedict's work for the next ten years.

The argument of "Continuities and Discontinuities" sounds slight; the ideas are by now thoroughly a part of our thinking. In her article Ruth utilized a characteristic device: common-sense references and a conversational tone make her points sound familiar, the lesson seems easy. Children should be taught traits appropriate to the adult world. "Appropriate to"—a key phrase—meant that a child learned nothing he would have abruptly to unlearn in growing up. The child learned no habits that would be scorned or useless in an adult world.

Ruth Benedict chose three dimensions for her discussion: "responsible-nonresponsible," "dominance-submission," and "contrasted sexual role." Responsibility, dominance, and sex, she claimed, were sternly denied to American children and equally sternly demanded of American adults. The result was a sharp disjunction that threatened individual personalities and social structure. Ruth condemned discontinuity, not a particular set of habits or characteristics. And, on the other side, she advocated continuity, not a particular method of child-rearing. But a value did emerge.

"Continuities and Discontinuities" repeatedly stressed "responsibility." Ruth stressed the benefits of teaching children to take responsibility for themselves and for their actions. When and how was relative, to culture and to individual; again she avoided absolutes. "They sat gravely waiting till the child succeeded and her grandfather gravely thanked her," she described the Papago elders waiting for a small girl to close a heavy door. The gentle fondness behind this example shaded an unambivalent message: "The essential point of such child training is that the child is from infancy continuously conditioned to responsible social participation, while at the same time the tasks that are expected of it are adapted to its capacity. The contrast with our society is very great."[18] Responsibility implied self-confidence and resiliency, the ability to chart one's own course. "The young child is taught that it has only itself to rely upon in life."[19]

Although short, "Continuities and Discontinuities" had a great impact. For readers then (and since), Ruth's argument powerfully explained the character flaws in American people and American society. She certainly intended to bring her readers up short, to alter their customary attitudes: "Our culture goes to great extremes in emphasizing contrasts between the child and the adult." Ruth wrote with insistence and with vigor, aware of the urgency of the anthropological lesson in a time of economic and moral collapse: "These doctorings [of "natural" growth] should not be read off in any one culture as nature itself."[20]

"Continuities and Discontinuities" tied together themes in Ruth's personal and intellectual pattern. In it "custom" emerged victorious; that culture invariably intervened in the "facts of life" gave men freedom. "Childhood situations provide an excellent field in which to illustrate the range of cultural adjustments which are possible within a universally given, but not so drastic, set of physiological facts."[21] Ruth rephrased her anthropology then, stressing the importance of deliberate adjustment and conscious direction of the life course. "Insofar as we invoke a physiological scheme to account for these neurotic adjustments, we are led to overlook the possibility of developing social institutions which would lessen the social cost we now pay; instead, we elaborate a set of dogmas which prove inapplicable under other social conditions."[22] American culture had so far failed, its child-rearing creating a selfish and weak character, unable to handle crisis.

By the winter of 1939–40 Ruth had completed two major statements on American character, "Continuities and Discontinuities" and *Race*. She did not look forward to returning to Columbia the next fall. Winter months, even in Pasadena, prompted thoughts of endings and gloomy statements like those in her diaries of the World War I years.[23] In January 1940 she received a letter from Frederica de Laguna, an anthropologist at Bryn Mawr College. (De Laguna had received her Ph.D. in anthropology from Columbia in 1932.) Freddy asked her former teacher to give a series of lectures at Bryn Mawr, beginning in February 1941. Ruth wrote back, agreeing to the proposal.[24]

The Bryn Mawr lectures are interesting both in their ambitiousness and their incompleteness. Ruth attempted to formulate a theory of society—for her, a theory of culture-and-personality. Then, uneasy about premature generalization, she destroyed most of her notes. The salvaged material, published in the *American Anthropologist* in 1970 as "Synergy: Notes of Ruth Benedict,"[25] together with her letters to de Laguna, contain the rudiments of a theory linking social structure and personality-type across societies. Her aim was grand: a theory that incorporated ideas on individual dignity, social participation (responsibility), and the conditions for efficiency and freedom in cultures.

After an initial misunderstanding, Ruth realized she had taken on several duties at Bryn Mawr. Besides the evening lectures, she was expected to participate in a seminar with de Laguna and a social-psychologist Donald MacKinnon, and to cooperate with de Laguna on a student research project. Although Freddy patiently repeated the details, Ruth continued to mix up the seminar and the research project. In the process of responding to tactfully posed, firm instructions, Ruth explicated her current interests.

On January 29 she told Freddy, "Your letter was full of problems."

Mainly Ruth objected to organizing a research project around the "stability of cultures." Such research, she said, required comparison across many groups. She suggested instead concentrating on significant topics in a few societies and specified: frustration-aggression; dominance-submission; leadership—obviously taking note of world events. These topics, Ruth thought, would also be good for the seminar, "The Individual and Society" (a title that echoed, perhaps deliberately, Abram Kardiner's seminars). In her reply on February 13 ("I have been laid up with flu"), Freddy ignored the "aggression" idea and picked Ruth's "simpler project," a study of religion.

That took care of one detail. For the seminar, de Laguna more or less reiterated her original list, though in the February letter she added "reactions to frustration" and "dominance-submission." The two women did agree on the importance of data to substantiate and validate theory. Freddy, with less-than-perfect faith, promised to give students a "full dose" of ethnographic readings before Ruth arrived: "But you can not expect much from them when you come, so our attack on problems will have to be as simple and direct as possible."[26]

Whatever her accomplishments in the seminar, Ruth effectively outlined in her evening lectures the beginning of a theory of self and society. "Now more than ever," she told the Bryn Mawr audience, "we need data on the consequences for human life of different social inventions. . . . We need a broader base for our social thinking. We need firsthand observations to study the consequences of these varied [cultural] solutions." Once more Ruth Benedict used the laboratory analogy, this time thinking about persecution and war. We need, she said, to ask "whether or not these social restraints are such that they add or take away from the individual's ability to conduct his life as he desires." She compared primitive to complex societies explicitly on the basis of personal dignity, civil liberties, and human freedom.[27]

On those February evenings in 1941, Ruth described the conditions producing dominance, aggressiveness, hostility, and cruelty in individuals. She also constructed the alternative, conditions that fostered self-reliance, responsibility, mutual tolerance, and "toughminded respect."[28] Typically, Ruth offered an encompassing concept to "measure" culture integrity and individual autonomy. "Synergy," like pattern, incorporated ideas about personality and society, distinctiveness and shared attitudes, self-realization and sociological success. And, like pattern, synergy came out of Ruth's background. She borrowed synergy from medicine and theology, where the word meant "combined action." "I shall speak of cultures with low synergy, where the social structure provides for acts that are mutually opposed and counteractive, and of cultures with high synergy, where it provides for acts that are mutually reinforcing."[29]

The speaker clearly admired "high-synergy" societies: cooperation at a maximum, conformity at a minimum; specialized contributions essential but the criteria for "contribution" flexible. High-synergy societies, she told her Philadelphia audience, resembled corporations and joint stock companies. And, she added, these societies, simple or complex, demonstrated good will and fine morale.

At the end Ruth added a coda to her theory, a discussion of religious systems. In religion a people projected ("imaged") the primary elements of their character and the proper relationships between people. "For in their religion, societies have transcribed and apotheosized the cooperativeness or the aggressions their cultural life arouses."[30] Not fully developed in the undestroyed notes, the argument did connect to Ruth's folklore studies and to her poetry. "In any integrated primitive society, religion is a work of the imagination in which people have stated their thoughts and emotions, whatever they are, that their life in society has allowed them to have."[31]

Imagination, rephrasing thoughts and emotions in symbolic form, envisioning alternative patterns—the "Synergy" lectures drew on Ruth Benedict's usual themes. How receptive to individual autonomy and impulse could a society be and still remain whole? How far could an individual push natural inclinations before society intervened? Questions like these absorbed energy from Ruth's personal debate, as her "woman issue" expanded into consideration of necessary versus distorting cultural conventions. Overall Ruth asked simply, urgently, at what point did natural traits lead to pain and frustration? Under what conditions did natural traits become the basis for names that branded, distinguishing normal from abnormal and the fit from the unfit? These concerns threaded through "Continuities and Discontinuities," *Race*, and "Synergy."

Ruth Benedict had written about deviance in *Patterns of Culture*, her examples being religious trance and sexual "perversions." She continued to use sexuality as a way of exploring the pressure of culture on nature and the risks in customary definitions of "human nature." Sexuality was a good example, for many reasons and for many points. Speculation about sexuality had been part of Ruth's autobiographical inquiries, phrased variously in her diaries, in the androgynous imagery of her poetry, and finally in her anthropological research. Sexuality was also her culture's issue, prompting the gathering of data, new theories, and much propaganda. Ethnography became a main source of data, introducing problems of evidence, intention, and rhetoric. In 1935 Ruth praised Margaret Mead's *Sex and Temperament* for demonstrating the power of culture without pleading a special cause.[32]

Both Margaret Mead and Ruth Benedict shared their era's inclination to search outside the United States for better arrangements of sexuality and sex-roles. Sex was viewed as the prime symptom of a "neurotic" American character, and a change in sexuality the route to improved character. The result of looking out was at worst an ethnographic free-for-all and at best a needed reminder of how thoroughly cultures modified a presumably "natural" impulse. In 1929 Edward Sapir wrote: "The present sex unrest has been nibbling at more or less reliable information reported by anthropologists from primitive communities. Any primitive community that indulges, or is said to indulge, in unrestricted sex behavior is considered an interesting community to hear from."[33]

Ruth approached the topic of sexuality with similar concern about glorifying "primitive freedom." She feared the effects of programmatic rhetoric, but like Sapir (and others) recognized the importance of sexuality in the formation, and the flaws, of American character. And though she generally agreed with Sapir, she was also suspicious of his insights in the 1929 article on female frigidity. By the early 1930s Ruth had turned from Sapir to other guides. In the spring of 1935 she wrote to Karen Horney, the neo-Freudian analyst, asking for her paper "The Problem of Feminine Masochism." Horney sent the paper, along with an invitation to dinner, and that winter Ruth enrolled in a course given by Horney. Two years later, reviewing *The Neurotic Personality of Our Time*,[34] the anthropologist explained her attraction to Horney's approach. She fully agreed with the emphasis on social causes of individual abnormality and on the central role of sexuality in precipitating and signaling tension between individual inclination and cultural conventions.

Through the 1930s and 1940s Ruth Benedict continued to consider sexuality a clue to cultural determinants of normal and abnormal, as well as to individual responses to imposed designations. In 1939 she described to the New York Academy of Medicine the range of known sexual behaviors and warned against branding any one behavior "unnatural."[35] Nine years later Ruth reviewed favorably Kinsey's detailed demonstration of the diverse sexual practices considered "normal" by Americans.[36]

In talks and writings on sexuality, Ruth still posed the problem of cultural patterning and individual expression. When in 1940, "at long last" and two years after publication, she read Henry Murray's *Explorations in Psychology*, she found a resonant formulation: "I should have been told the day the book was off the press that it was my meat." Murray's notion of social "press" and individual "need" in a constant, creative interaction suited her anthropology.[37]

Or at least partly—she also wanted a theory geared to change. Sometime during the 1930s Ruth read Harry Stack Sullivan, thus indirectly admitting Sapir back into her approach (Sapir and Sullivan had collaborated at Yale). Friends report that Ruth did not like Sullivan personally, but she came to appreciate his formulation of a social—in fact, a political—psychiatry. Sullivan's insistence that social conditions had to be changed in order for individuals to thrive and find satisfactory self-expression appealed to Ruth, the more strongly as the world seemed dominated by aggressive, hostile, and neurotic characters.

To "fuse" psychiatry and social science, Sullivan (with Sapir and Harold Lasswell) established the William Alanson White Foundation, and in 1944–45 Ruth gave a series of lectures at the foundation's Washington branch. She also served as editor on the foundation's journal, *Psychiatry.* "The Journal is addressed . . . to all serious students of human living in any of its aspects, and to those who must meet pressing social needs with current remedial attempts"—the journal's statement echoed her views.[38]

Like her service on the editorial board of *Character and Personality* (1937–45), a journal similarly oriented to context and character, Ruth Benedict willingly lent her name and less willingly her time. She shared with the founders of *Character and Personality* and *Psychiatry* the certainty that conditions must be changed for new, and better, generations to be created. But she had already decided on her course of action: she would teach her society about alternatives and thus direct the creation of "new normalities."

"Our chance lies in loading the dice"

Ruth Benedict became increasingly active in various reform groups during the Depression and in face of an anticipated world war. To an extent she followed Boas's lead, joining committees he was on and often chaired. She also followed her own inclinations; Ruth's activism was a form of teaching. Generally, too, the committees she joined proclaimed as their central purpose educating the American public, whatever the disparity of manner and ideology behind the "educating." Ruth, like Franz Boas, shut her eyes to potentially disruptive political factions within committees organized to spread information.

The neighborhood she lived in itself encouraged activism. By the

1930s a confirmed New Yorker, Ruth participated in the distinct culture of Manhattan's upper west side. On Central Park West she lived amid changing ethnic populations, as well as Columbia colleagues. The combination of a miniature melting pot and liberal professors gave rise to community associations, local newspapers, evening meetings. Ruth belonged to several groups, but less actively as she moved into national and professional organizations.

By the late 1930s Ruth Benedict represented anthropology, at least for some. She was in demand, her name to be on letterheads, her presence requested at a conference, her opinion solicited on cross-cultural matters. Usually she was contacted by committees whose programs emphasized teaching: exchanging information to establish the foundation for thoughtful tolerance. Her activism accorded with the "shoulds" in her writings. Ruth had always practiced her discipline as a pedagogy, instructing the public in available options. Essentially a version of progressive education, Ruth's program for change was also hugely ambitious. She aimed for nothing less than an alteration in peoples' outlooks that would alter the world.

For Ruth, teaching anthropology meant teaching the experiencing of another way of life. When asked to introduce the discipline to schools and communities, she developed plans for facilitating such experiencing at home. New Brunswick, New Jersey, was not a trip to the Pacific, but in its neighborhoods individuals could experience "strange customs."

In 1938 Ruth joined the Bureau for Intercultural Education, established to promote " 'cultural diversity' through the schools of America." She applied her methods: in schools throughout Manhattan children tasted new foods, learned folk dances, and met the foreign-born parents of their friends. She also tried to find out about anthropology in high schools for a manual on intercultural education. No, David Mandelbaum wrote from Minnesota, there was no anthropology in Midwest high schools. His report was typical.[39] The manuals, Ruth knew, had to be carefully prepared. She remained wary of abstract presentations of exotic customs that ultimately kept people in their places. "In a situation where aliens regard the majority's culture as attainable and desirable, they [an elite] plan that aliens shall demonstrate their differences; in a situation where the alien hopes that he may show that he can function *as an American,* they organize material for 'tolerance' courses."[40]

Her arguments, presented at meetings and for committee action, attached cultural diversity to choice. To choose to conform or not to conform should be the privilege of every human being. "To improve intercultural relations in America it is necessary to capitalize on the aliens' will-to-function as an American," she wrote, reminding her readers that "pride in one's own traditional background is not contradicted by desire to be an American."[41] As Ruth participated in discussions on "Defending America's Future," she revealed her loyalty to aspects of American society. She also changed her vocabulary; "cultural diversity" gave way to "cultural democracy" in an emphasis on choice and election of differences.

Education provided the means by which ethnic groups could acquire American customs without relinquishing their traditional values. The possibility of maintaining ethnic identity while enjoying equal opportunity applied to the American Negro as well.[42] Schools could train all individuals in self-reliance and awareness, the wherewithal for choosing one's own direction. Ruth also saw dangers, in the power of education to coerce and the state to control the classroom. In 1941 she objected to the Hatch Act, culmination of a series of onslaughts against academic freedom. The classroom, Ruth said, must be an open forum where everyone could take a stand.[43]

On December 7, 1941, Ruth's beliefs were put to a test. She had been actively if indirectly involved in her country's policies for over five years. With war she was asked to contribute directly by working for the Office of War Information (OWI) in the Bureau of Overseas Intelligence.

"Efficiency rating: excellent"—Office of War Information

"I'm so glad you are in Washington doing exactly what you alone can do," Dorothy Lee wrote to Ruth Benedict in January 1944.[44] Another former Columbia student put the matter differently: "Was Ruth deceiving herself when she went to Washington?" she asked in the mid-1970s.[45] Ruth's wartime work for the federal government raises questions about neutrality and duty, science and patriotism, which remain problematic today in a changed anthropological and political context.

Ruth did not go to Washington right away but stayed in New York working on the numerous committees and councils she belonged to at the time. "Being an anthropologist in wartime seems to have made me a jack-of-all-trades. Anyway I'm working on national committees on anything from food habits to race, from the legal status of women to postwar worlds."[46]

She had not immediately favored American entry into the war, and on September 1, 1941, she told *The New Republic:* "Declaration of war should be a last resort, kept in reserve with full knowledge that war itself never decides crucial interests."[47] Two years earlier, in 1939, bored with *Race,* she had drafted a piece called "The Natural History of War." Ruth used "natural history" in the scientific sense; her article classified *types* of war, distinguishing between nonlethal war—did not destroy the groups involved—and lethal war that destroyed whole civilizations. "We wage the lethal variety of the genus War and the poisonousness of it comes not from what man is but from what society is. . . . Then war becomes a sociological tragedy."[48] She had also made a point significant in view of her subsequent activities. War of any type, she said, is *learned;* war is a social behavior not a "natural instinct." Furthermore, war—a man-made havoc—can be eliminated by men.

Not published (but approved by Papa Franz),[49] the piece established a rationale for Ruth's OWI activities. The tone is urgent and the message repeated. If men learn to wage war, men can learn to avoid war by contemplating the consequences and by establishing alternative modes of interaction. She called for a thorough revision of "the rules of the game."[50]

Revision of rules involved knowing the rules by which "others" played and, equally, the rules by which "self" played. Ruth Benedict went to the OWI knowing its wartime purposes but looking ahead to its peacetime possibilities. "Psychological warfare" certainly meant the use of information to influence an enemy, but from another vantage point had the benefit of requiring investigation into national characters. For Ruth information about national character was crucial for establishing a lasting peace.

Ruth Benedict joined the OWI in 1942 with the conviction that knowledge prepared the way for a reasonable postwar reconstruction. She acted on her faith in man's ability to utilize positively an increased awareness. Her actual OWI position, like everyone else's, came about by chance and by contact. She followed Geoffrey Gorer into the Office of War Information as "Head, Basic Analysis Section." (Gorer, a British social anthropologist and her colleague in groups like the Council for Intercultural Relations, left the OWI to work for the British Embassy.) Ruth was not spared a civil service investigation and security test. In June 1943, six months after she took the job, she received her P-5 rating, a title, and an office: "Head, Basic Analysis, Overseas Intelligence, Office of War Information, Social Security Building 1646-B." Her salary was $4,600, her immediate supervisor Leonard Doob, a social-psychologist from Yale. Nearly a year later, in April 1944, she heard that "as a result of investigation the person named below has been rated eligible on suitability." According to Doob, Ruth Benedict never received "high security" clearance and did not work on projects of "utmost confidentiality."

At some point Ruth prepared her own description of the OWI job. In an undated typescript[51] she summarized goals and procedures, and revealed the completeness of her affiliation. "1. When detailed cultural study of some nation is requested by an Operational Division or by B.O.I. [Bureau of Overseas Intelligence], I familiarize myself first with the literature and statistical studies available on these countries." She planned to collect material from government agencies, "to interview first and second generation immigrants and refugees now in America" and "to follow current cables, press news intercepts and intelligence from these countries." Finally, "a basic manuscript is prepared describing the institutions and aspects of adult life in the nation. It analyzes the patterns of behavior that are prevalent, the way in which these patterns are rewarded and sanctioned, attitudes toward authority, toward violence, toward destiny and the like," to which will be attached "suggestions for psychological warfare." She had her "design" well in mind; did she deceive herself about "psychological warfare"?

Ruth Benedict had constructed her science around the importance of providing information to those who could make changes. Her blindness, or naiveté, during World War II lay in not questioning the precise uses to which others put the information she provided. Ruth offered guidance as an anthropologist and a citizen; she recognized her obligations. Moreover, the notion of "psychological warfare" only extended her view that learning about others substituted wise social engineering for random dice-throwing. In her OWI work Ruth Benedict was moved to an extreme application of her knowledge by the strength of her belief in its importance for designing interpersonal contacts and social conditions. The crisis was extreme.

In winter 1942 Ruth moved from New York to Washington, D.C., and took an apartment in the Northwest section of the city. She had a few months to settle in, before becoming fully engaged in wartime work. On July 2, she received her first assignment, from George Taylor, head of the Asian division, to do research "for building up plans for psychological warfare" in Southeast Asia. Ruth Benedict was to complete a study of Thailand by August 7.[52]

Subsequent assignments came in quick succession. Ruth finished the Thailand project on time, on August 7, 1943; a month later (September 13) she turned in a report, "Background for a Basic Plan for Burma." Four months later she finished "Rumania" (December 1943), then on January 10, 1944, received a memo "in connection with the Netherlands." The memo requested a "brief list of 'dos' and 'don'ts' which can guide the writers of booklets designed for the inhabitants in order to mitigate somewhat the friction."[53] She must have ignored much bureaucratic language in those three years.

For the full-scale reports, Ruth closely followed her outline of methods and goals. First she summarized the nation's background, establishing historical, religious, political, economic, and day-to-day context. She then presented an account of personality and the formation of personality in childhood training. At the end, she offered her suggestions for psychological warfare, for defeat of the enemy and adjustment of American attitudes. "This paper is an attempt to collect and present information about Burma and its people which is relevant to psychological warfare. It is not intended as a directive but as a convenient arrangement of material from which a basic Burmese plan can be prepared," she stated in the introduction. The ethnographic sections contain surprising simplifications: the Burmese "psychologically show a quasi-spontaneous criminality."[54]

"The Propaganda Problem" reveals a woman committed to her job. Half her suggestions dealt with separating the Burmese from the Japanese: "producing acts of violence against the Japanese" in well-timed, well-planned fashion. The other half dealt with bringing Burma to the side of a United Nations: "by emphasizing that these [salt packets] are 'profits' from United Nations victories, it may be possible to make them [Burmese] feel that our victories are their victories."[55]

"Thai Culture and Behavior" (1944) was a more rounded report, with a suggestion of Ruth's usual awe at a distinctive, unfamiliar culture—especially one that showed such remarkable consistency. She modified the propaganda section and emphasized the character of the people; the result resembled her best anthropological writings. Moreover, aside from a few facile assumptions—the "Siamese by nature a quiet people," orderly, cheerful, convivial[56]—the Thai report substantially advanced national-character study. "Only by treating the whole culture—its sociological as well as its psychological aspects—its child-rearing as well as its international relations—is it possible to see what consistency emerged and how far certain patterns of Thai behavior can be stated."[57]

Ruth was charmed by the Siamese much as she had been by the Zuñis. The Siamese possess "self-reliance" and autonomy, she wrote, and find life "so enjoyable that they rarely indeed seek oblivion from it"—an echo of the Zuñi characterization.[58] Ruth missed being able to take a fieldtrip to Asia, not only because she respected her discipline's method but also because she suspected she might find sources of a congenial character and culture in the daily landscape of Thai life.[59]

Ruth completed her Rumanian assignment efficiently, conscientiously, and rather tediously. Rumanian switch of sides in 1944, she noted, could be explained by a child-rearing filled with inconsistencies.[60] Ruth did not know the fate of this report; nor in fact could she predict the use of her Thai, Burmese, and even Dutch materials. Apparently no one really knew what happened to reports that circulated through the OWI offices. A report might land on someone's desk and, depending on timing and tidiness, might or might not be passed along. Whether or not information ever reached an "operator," military personnel, or an administrator remained a mystery. From all accounts the OWI had a somewhat left-hand-ignorant-of-the-right atmosphere, plus the jealousies that accompany a "personalized" workplace.[61]

Yet Ruth thrived, carrying on her research with reported energy and imagination. Unlike those who regarded their service in the government with mixed feelings, Ruth apparently ignored the confusion and the rivalries between scientist and policymaker. She did not worry about the use of her information—she might have done so twenty-five years later, along with colleagues who lived to reconsider wartime participation. For the while, a sense of obligation dampened doubts; more, Ruth Benedict *was* doing exactly what she could do: using disparate materials to get at the "spirit" of a culture. She pursued national-character study for her country, examining official documents, radio broadcasts, literature, films, and interview data from refugees and immigrants in the United States. Throughout Ruth applied to complex societies principles from her studies of primitive societies; in the process and with the help of colleagues, she clarified her use of psychoanalytic, sociological, and biographical methods for learning a "culture personality."

"America loses one of its greatest scientists"

Ruth Benedict recognized the importance of the war to her work, just as she recognized the importance of her anthropology to the war. At the OWI she justified anthropology even by her severe standards, turning disciplinary techniques to the problem of war and the likelihood of peace. Ruth's long effort to connect the "force of custom" to the "creativity of every individual" became part of plans for postwar reconstruction.

During the World War II years Ruth Benedict came into her own as an anthropologist. The OWI work, its purpose, the required collaborations, the setting, suited and stimulated her. A note of confidence came into her letters, evidence of a satisfactory reconciliation between scientific endeavor and humanistic ideal. Ruth had envied Stanley Benedict that reconciliation in World War I; a combination of science and humanism in research also dominated her memories of her father. But for Ruth, above all Franz Boas represented the scientist motivated by a lasting faith in human capacity to create a better world.

Shortly after Ruth arrived in Washington, Franz Boas died. On December 21, 1942, at a Columbia dinner, Boas collapsed in mid-sentence. Wine glass in hand, he was about to proclaim a "new theory of race."[62] He was eighty-four years old when he died. Margaret Mead may have telephoned Ruth, to comfort while imparting the news. Ruth must have been stunned; she did not record her responses in journal or in letters. Once before she had been in Washington to hear news of a death in New York—in 1936 when Stanley Benedict died. The death of Boas demanded an even more strenuous review of her life. Ruth's commitment to anthropology stemmed back twenty years to a first meeting with Franz Boas; her heightened awareness of anthropology's significance in 1942 must also have recalled her first, post–World War I years in the discipline. Boas's death removed one of the guideposts by which Ruth had charted her own course.

That she had grown used to Boas's reported illness and despair did not mean she had accustomed herself to his death. Throughout the 1930s, when one or the other wasn't in New York they kept touch by letters, and Boas wrote increasingly of weakness, an "inability to walk far," his melancholy. "Walking, even a short distance, makes me short of breath. Attacks of shortness of breath will even come on without any apparent physical activity, and I get tired without cause, I mean without having done any work," he reported sadly to Ruth in 1939.[63] He made these remarks, but he also continued to take fieldtrips, conduct classes, give speeches, and serve on committees. Ruth heard about his failing health and mood, and as much about his constant activities and apparently endless endurance. Boas's death seemed far in the future. Too, death played a large part in her self-conceptualizations, and that may have deflected her thoughts from the deaths of others.

Ruth Benedict wrote four obituary pieces for Franz Boas, three in 1943 and one in 1947. The four, together with a brief statement in 1931, present a public side of her debt to Papa Franz. The articles barely hint at a personal relationship crucial to the history of anthropology in America. But beneath the restrained prose lay unqualified admiration. Ruth assumed Boas's greatness as a thinker and creator of a discipline. "It is seldom that one man has been so largely responsible for the history of a scientific discipline," she wrote in 1931.[64]

The formal remarks in fact contained Ruth's personal responses to Boasian anthropology. While she did concentrate on Franz Boas as a scientist, she also revealed her attachment to a particular view of human nature and human creativity. Ruth's description of Boas's achievement carried her own commitment: "He saw the necessity of gathering new first-hand material on conditions as they actually exist in human experience," she wrote.[65] In her emphasis on "actual human experience" and on his inclusion of the human being in his anthropology, Ruth characterized the man. She considered Boas's awareness of man's struggle to create meaning and to improve his world the heart of Boasian anthropology and, by implication, the dominating theme in Boas's life.

In *Science* Ruth quoted, without citation, Boas's definition of the dynamics of culture, "by which I mean the life of the individual as controlled by culture and the effect of the individual upon culture."[66] The impact of culture and the "effect of the individual"—these phrases appeared throughout her pieces on Boas, the watchwords as well of her anthropology. She noted how Boas "gradually" came to stress the individual's view of culture and individual articulations of natural and supernatural forces.[67] She dealt at length with "subjective worlds" and "manmade conventions," two phrases that indicated man's ability to see and to revise the conditions of his life. For Ruth, Boas's science was a counsel of hope: A man-made world can be changed by men. His anthropology spoke of human potential, and his accumulation of empirical data represented an effort to preserve that potential.

Apart from these official testimonies, Ruth Benedict published nothing directly about Franz Boas, his writings, the anthropology program, or his discipline. So, with the exception of the 1931 piece, Ruth commented on Boas primarily at moments of grief and loss. In fact, she commented on his work and its sources in his character throughout her professional life. The anthropology the two shared rested on mutual respect—by the mid-1930s Ruth could say "love." She had met Boas at a time of intense personal upheaval in her life; she had gone to Columbia, in 1922, searching for something that would totally absorb her energies. Her demands then were great, and only Boas could come close to satisfying them since he, too, as Ruth realized, looked in anthropology for fulfillment of a quest. Over the years Ruth learned the passionate depths of Boas's commitment to science, and the knowledge wove through her obituary pieces.

She wrote of Boas's humanitarianism during a world war, her readers' minds on mass killings and a "tornado of horror." Under these circumstances Ruth especially stressed Boas's faith in mankind and especially forcefully reminded her readers of the value in an undying respect for human dignities.

The *Nation* article of January 1943 said it definitively. There Ruth portrayed Franz Boas as a tireless champion of human liberties. She spoke with insistent admiration of Boas's engagement in world affairs. For her, his conviction that the scientist must intervene needed no defense and no further explanation. "It was as a scientist, too, that he took up heavy responsibilities in the world outside of the classroom. He never understood how it was possible to keep one's scientific knowledge from influencing one's attitudes and actions in the world of affairs."[68] Ruth expressed through her tributes to Boas her own desire to make "a world safe for differences" by teaching the worth of uniqueness and the limitlessness of man's potential.

Behind her formality, intensified by the circumstances of writing, Ruth showed how thoroughly Boas had created the conditions for her anthropology and for anthropology in America. He had encouraged by precept and example the importance of "taking a stand." Ruth claimed that Boas had trained her in scientific procedures; he had also trained her to "keep faith with ideals."[69] Guided by the man and by her responses to his principles, Ruth related her own science to world affairs. Three years after Franz Boas died, Ruth Benedict began the only book Boas did not read before publication, *The Chrysanthemum and the Sword*. Here, in her last book, Ruth revealed her "passionate principles" and, simultaneously, her profound attachment to the founder of her discipline. The book demonstrated an anthropology she had learned from Boas and helped shape an international encounter.

11

The Anthropologist as Citizen

"We must have a plan which is equally radical"

WORK FOR THE OFFICE OF WAR INFORMATION was war work directed to peace—so Ruth Benedict considered her participation, and so did a number of her colleagues. Such concern about peaceful cooperation and planned reconstruction had begun before the United States entered World War II.

The concern took two forms: a look at one's "own household" (Ruth's phrase in *Race*) and a look at other nations. Preserving peace and maintaining cooperation demanded changes on a domestic level and on an international level. Change to be "wise" had to be informed, a recognition of diverse "cultural versions of human life."[1] Knowledge, information, awareness, and self-consciousness provided routes to a permanent peace and an accompanying tolerance. "To realize that goal [of peace and freedom], we shall have need of the kind of knowledge which results in understanding."[2]

Ruth Benedict was not alone in believing that peace had to be based on knowledge and that ideas gave substance to world politics. "The Conference on Science, Philosophy and Religion is an effort to face the crisis in our culture by an experiment in corporate thinking."[3] Ruth attended the 1941 meeting (at the Columbia University Men's Faculty Club) and commented on Margaret Mead's outline of the "Purposive Cultivation of Democratic Values." In her comments Ruth repeated the true meaning of cultural relativism, by then a much maligned phrase. Cultural relativism meant the "inescapable interdependence of cultural traits one with another, and of the individual and his society."[4] Cultural relativism referred, on the one hand, to the uniqueness of every culture and, on the other, to the place of each individual in a culture. For Ruth recognition of the uniqueness and the force of culture resulted not in suspension of judgment but in judgment of the whole.

Another issue in Mead's paper took Ruth's attention—Mead's substitution of the word "direction" for the word "end" in talking of change. End prescribed, Ruth noted, while direction only indicated, on the basis of existing conditions. "The 'directional' attitude bases any current decision upon strong cultural habits and the absence of alternatives; it takes its cue from the present situation and can adapt itself to changing conditions without tragedy," she wrote.[5]

In one version or another, that was essentially the message Ruth preached throughout the war years. Change must be accommodated to existing conditions. There were several implications. Change was to be imposed not randomly or broad-scale but with consideration for dilemmas faced and decisions made in the past. Too, no system could be taken as absolutely "good"; Ruth warned her countrymen and fellow liberals of the dangers in assuming a democratic system was best for everyone. "The absolute is a fire which burns men's fingers," she told those who were too certain.[6] She condemned any sign of ethnocentrism, even couched in an ideology of "liberty for all."

"Existing conditions" included by-now-familiar components: the interconnection of traits (traits in context); the significance of individuals within a culture; the distinct character running through social institution and personal temperament. In fact, Ruth was restating her concept of pattern, and she argued strenuously for the necessity of perceiving pattern and obeying its dictates—a lesson for politicians taken from her discipline and from her life. "This does not mean that change is impossible, but that changes have to be adapted to the existing building."[7]

Maintaining her emphasis on integrity and cultural diversity, Ruth's wartime statements also acknowledged the impact of recent events. A peace that considered existing patterns had to consider upheaval and rapid change, a part of pattern for every contemporary society. Ruth argued that international negotiations could no longer depend on traditional balance-of-power arrangements; power differential itself bred conflict and war. She suggested instead balance of responsibility and an exchange of obligations among united nations.

In 1942, when Ruth wrote about nations cooperatively united, she in effect extended to the world her previous, local solutions. Different individual units cooperated while preserving distinct characteristics and traditional beliefs. "If we are to prevent the consummation of Hitler's plans we must have a plan which is equally radical and equally tailored to the world as it has become as a result of modern invention. [There are] two alternatives which could keep the world in order: Hitler's or a United Nations'."[8]

The United Nations organization was then mainly an idea about co-operation; at hand was the matter of future, guaranteed disarmament, and Ruth wrote on this subject too: "Parking the deadly weapons ["as in some South American tribes"] is not the only simple rule preventing war among savages, of course, but it is elementary. Under modern conditions it means disarmament."[9] She added that disarmament had to be coerced, legislated, enforced. Her tone became less than neutral, less than tolerant, and she preached her own absolute. "My own feeling is that disarmament will have to be legalized and we will have to trust to its fruits to justify it. I doubt if we can trust to showing Indian princes and African kings the fatal kickback in war under modern conditions."[10]

The near condescension stemmed from dread at the alternative to disarming. Ruth knew the frailty of rules, law, even coercion, unbacked by a thorough change in attitude. People, and nations, must be convinced of the horror of modern warfare, its potential for destroying all civilization. To change attitudes once more involved vividly displaying the alternatives so there could be no question about the proper course. Ruth applied her domestic solution to the world, showing the material and the moral benefits of preserving differences. "In exactly this fashion we must admit human differences, admit them to the hilt and not deny them. Differences are the most precious thing in life," she wrote.[11] She envisioned a world society of "high synergy," and the political vision gained strength from its personal significance.

To appreciate, respect, and ultimately use differences, one must know them and their origins.

> With every occupied country the United States assists in freeing from Axis domination, with every Asiatic country where we operate in cooperation with the existing culture, the need for intelligent understanding of that country and its ways of life will be crucial. . . . The danger—and it would be fatal to world peace—is that in our ignorance of their cultural values we shall meet in head-on collision and incontinently fall back on the old pattern of imposing our own values by force.[12]

This was the justification, and justification enough, for national-character study.

"The stamp each nation and tribe puts upon its men and women and children"

"During the war years, however, the problem of national character became a matter of grave political importance. There were crucial questions as to 'the nature of the enemy,' the receptivity of satellite nations to certain kinds of appeals and not to others, and the opposition of certain of the allied nations to measures easily accepted by others."[13] National character was what Ruth Benedict had spent her time and energy on for nearly three years during World War II. "In 1943, I was asked to join the Office of War Information, and to work on national character in enemy and occupied countries." She recognized the difficulties and responded to the criticisms of national-character study; "civilized nations are too difficult to study," said critics.[14]

Criticisms of content and method in national-character study were not unjustified. Pressed by time and deprived of usual anthropological access to a community, students of national character frequently adopted simplified explanations, psychoanalytic and other (links between toilet training and adult personality became a cliché). Ruth had never depended entirely on the fieldtrip, nor did she have complete sympathy for psychoanalytic theory. "To the anthropologist, the study of national character is a study of learned cultural behavior."[15] Learning was her key, and she used the word to cover all individual learning. Ruth thought of national character as the acquisition of a particular personality over time. Like her 1930s work, her national-character studies focused on the way individuals learned to be members of a group. In national-character study, however, she added to the importance of knowing what *was* learned the importance of knowing what could *be* learned.

Another source of difficulty in national-character study was the "unit" being studied. As Ruth Benedict wrote, wartime anthropologists studied "complex nations" not "compact primitive communities,"[16] and nations in varying degrees of enmity and alliance with one another. The 1940s subject, scattered and heterogeneous groups of people, lent itself uneasily to approaches Boasians had grown accustomed to using. To make these tools relevant the unit had to be bounded, made wieldy. "Pattern" became isomorphic with such a unit; a pattern implied limits and the arrangement of internal elements. At the same time, perception of pattern presumed as much as established the unit of study. Recognizing pattern assumed a preexisting "whole," an integrated unit. "For the study of national character a quasi-aesthetic ability to recognize pattern is probably a prerequisite; but this ability can be adequately exercised only within the framework of cultural anthropology and individual psychology."[17]

Ruth tried to avoid tautology, was well as a static view of culture, by concentrating on child-rearing. Child-rearing practices shared by a group at once revealed pattern to the observer and perpetuated pattern over time for the individuals who lived by it. According to Ruth Benedict, child-rearing practices cut across regional, economic, and ethnic differences; the "similarity of the basic assumptions about life in any nation" emerged in child-rearing practices.[18] This consistency in learning solved the "complexity" problem. People who learned the same set of assumptions and attitudes acquired a recognizable, and shared, "national character." Moreover, in the training of a new generation lay potential for change. Ruth tested, and validated, these ideas about child-rearing in her study of Japanese patterns of culture.

In 1946 Ruth Benedict published her clearest statement about national character and simultaneously about her discipline. She started *The Chrysanthemum and the Sword* in 1944, still in Washington and still officially connected to the OWI. Approach and content reflected the reports she had prepared during the war, the atmosphere of the government agency she worked for, and the current attitudes of social scientists toward scientific research on nations and complex societies. The book, begun as a description of Japanese patterns, ended up providing insight into American patterns of culture. Utilizing procedures developed for propaganda purposes, Ruth Benedict told as much about the United States as about its "most alien enemy."[19]

In chapter 1 of *The Chrysanthemum and the Sword*, Ruth outlined the premises and the methods of her study. "Assignment: Japan" showed the impact of OWI work on her anthropology, the influence of colleagues and co-workers, and the personal fascination she developed for Japanese culture. These nineteen pages epitomize her anthropology, with its roots in Boasian precepts, in her own writings of a lifetime, and in her sense of civic responsibility.

"In June, 1944, I was assigned to the study of Japan. I was asked to use all the techniques I could as a cultural anthropologist to spell out what the Japanese were like."[20] That was her assignment, made crucial by the war and by likely Japanese defeat and occupation by Western powers. "I had to try to use Japanese behaviors in war as an asset in understanding them, not as a liability."[21] Denied fieldwork, the "most important technique of the cultural anthropologist,"[22] Ruth evaluated techniques that were available. For *The Chrysanthemum and the Sword* she had to find ways of uncovering Japanese personality without seeing Japanese people, social arrangements, and cultural expressions on their home ground.

"I read, asking the ever-present question: What is 'wrong with this picture'? What would I need to know to understand it?"[23] The anthropologist read and went to the movies, and she talked to Japanese living in the United States. She had informants, key elements in national-character study. "There were plenty of Japanese in this country who had been reared in Japan and I could ask them about the concrete facts of their own experiences, find out how they judged them."[24] She did not question the reliability of memories, the value of reports given by a transplanted population, or the interference of translator and interpreter. Given her assumption that interviews provided native points of view, Ruth had no need to ask such questions. She interpreted interviews along with novels, films, dramas, and rituals—further pieces in the pattern.

Confronting a literate, self-conscious culture, Ruth in fact had better sources than ever before. "The vast literature on the Japanese and the great number of good Occidental observers who have lived in Japan gave me an advantage which no anthropologist has when he goes to the Amazon headwaters."[25] She especially appreciated the remarkable self-revelations: the Japanese "have a great impulse to write themselves out."[26] To reconstruct Japanese character, Ruth Benedict combined these voluntary descriptions with details not articulated and responses left unsaid. "Of course they did not present the whole picture. No people does."[27] She had learned as a biographer and again as an ethnographer the challenge of interpreting a self-portrayal. Deliberate statements about self demanded a special close scrutiny. Ruth met the challenge by rearranging statements, setting them one against another and in context. She also took pains to distinguish the anthropologist's approach from that of any sensitive interpreter. The crucial distinguishing marks of an anthropological perspective, she wrote, were comparison and a focus on the "commonplace," the daily habits of people.[28]

"I knew in these simpler cultures how these institutions worked and could get clues to Japanese life from the likeness or the difference I found."[29] The primitive versus the complex was one form of comparison; the contrast between similarly complex cultures was another. In *The Chrysanthemum and the Sword,* Ruth compared Pacific Island cultures to Japan; she also compared Japan to the United States. The contrast is "unbelievable" she had written about the Pueblo and Plains Indians, and could have about the two modern industrialized nations.

She had not made the point about the "commonplace" so explicitly before. The anthropologist studied and compared "homely matters" and "trivial details of daily intercourse,"[30] thus discovering how diversely peoples arranged their lives—and the pattern in every arrangement. *The Chrysanthemum and the Sword* contained Ruth Benedict's most eloquent statement of the significance of pattern, for the anthropologist and for the experiencing individual.

> As a cultural anthropologist also I started from the premise that the most isolated bits of behavior have some systematic

relation to each other. I took seriously the way hundreds of
details fall into over-all patterns. A human society must make
for itself some design for living. . . . Some degree of consistency is necessary or the whole scheme falls to pieces.[31]

A concept of pattern allowed Ruth to do this study of a distant,
inaccessible culture at all. Assuming "pattern," any piece of data might
be clue to the whole. "This volume therefore is not a book specifically
about Japanese religion or economic life or politics or the family. It ex-
amines Japanese assumptions about the conduct of life."[32] "Assumptions
about the conduct of life," like "dominant attitudes" in *Patterns of Culture*, represented the cohesive force of pattern. Assumptions about life
patterned the behavior of individuals and determined the learning of
culture.

Ruth further clarified her concept in "Assignment: Japan." The pattern by which ordinary men and women lived was usually taken for
granted; assumptions went unstated. "In any matter of spectacles, we do
not expect the man who wears them to know the formula for the lenses,
and neither can we expect nations to analyze their own outlook upon the
world."[33] At the same time, these were shared lenses, a common outlook
that, pointed out, would be recognizable to any man or woman in the
society. "This book, then, is about habits that are expected and taken
for granted in Japan. . . . The ideal authority for any statement in this
book would be the proverbial man in the street."[34] The social scientist
pointed out patterns, the interrelationships known to but not formulated
by those who lived by them.[35]

In the process of elucidating the pattern in another life, the observer
gained insight into her own. That completed Ruth Benedict's concept of
pattern: recognition of pattern elsewhere increased awareness of pattern
at home. And like everything else Ruth wrote, *The Chrysanthemum and
the Sword* preached the importance of increased awareness, the necessity of bringing to light the conditioning factors in any life. "It is hard
to be conscious of the eyes through which one looks," but a worthy
goal.[36]

Chapter 1 also announced Ruth's purpose in writing the book, a purpose that took her beyond the assignment to a general argument for
"understanding." "The study of comparative cultures too cannot flourish
when men are so defensive about their own way of life that it appears
to them to be by definition the sole solution in the world. Such men will
never know the added love of their own culture which comes from a
knowledge of other ways of life."[37] The argument for understanding was
both political and intensely personal for Ruth Benedict. Chapter 1 sum-

marized an anthropology that by 1946 carried a weight of responsibility, directed toward the improvement of conditions in the United States and in the world; Ruth had achieved her humanistic application of scientific inquiry. Chapter 1 of *The Chrysanthemum and the Sword* is also more personal than Ruth's other public writings; the author is present—a quality she praised in books she reviewed. Ruth ended the chapter on a quiet note. "I began to see how it was that the Japanese themselves saw certain violent swings of behavior as integral parts of a system consistent within itself. I can try to show why."[38]

The book is carefully structured, partly along the lines of her OWI reports. Between the problems of war ("The Japanese in the War") and of peace ("The Japanese Since V-J Day") Ruth delineated Japanese character and its unfolding. The OWI reports provided organization and the concept of pattern provided texture. In the manner of the OWI reports, *The Chrysanthemum and the Sword* moved from historical and cultural background, to interactions between individuals, to the feelings behind and the consequences of behavior, to the ways each individual learned to be Japanese.

Like Ruth's earlier writings, too, *The Chrysanthemum and the Sword* explored the sources of integrity and coherence in a culture. In chapter 3, "Taking One's Proper Station," the anthropologist suggested the dominant theme of Japanese culture. "So long as they stayed within known boundaries, and so long as they fulfilled known obligations, they could trust their world."[39] "Everything in its place"—Ruth took up the theme, showing its origins in culture context and its implications for personality development. She gave the impression, throughout, of a highly integrated culture, an intricate patterning. The intricacy she portrayed had more in common with the poet's "redundancy" than with the psychologist's "overdetermination" (a word Mead used), and Ruth portrayed Japanese intricacy with a poet's skill. Differently nuanced images demonstrated the unity of thought and feeling in Japanese culture.

In *The Chrysanthemum and the Sword*, Ruth recreated for readers the process of getting to know Japanese character and, at the same time, the process of becoming Japanese for each Japanese individual. Chapter by chapter she moved closer to Japanese personality, a personality dominated by debts to be paid, obligations to be assumed, pleasures to be enjoyed—all according to rule. "They see the 'whole duty of man' as if it were parceled out into separate provinces on a map."[40]

Circumspection and boundary-making ran through Japanese life, from government policies through philosophical principles and poetic novels to the planting of a garden. Everywhere extraordinary care was taken to maintain "circles" and distinct spheres: order must be kept, *on* repaid, people keep their proper station. The world thus controlled and rule-bound was matched by a personality of care and control. Ruth described, not without admiration, a culture with place for passion and place for principle, separate domains of pleasure and of duty, the balance strictly regulated. "The good player is the one who accepts the rules and plays within them."[41]

Individuals appeared in *The Chrysanthemum and the Sword*, people who learned and then taught these rules. Individuals are more present in *The Chrysanthemum and the Sword* than in *Patterns of Culture*, but still not as idiosyncratic personalities. In *The Chrysanthemum and the Sword*, individuals are typical actors in a likely drama; Ruth used people to illustrate pattern. Like the heroic figures in her sonnets, individuals are there to embody and convey a theme.

These individuals also, in her writings, preserved and transmitted the patterns of culture. People made the pattern work. submitting to sanctions and training a younger generation to do the same. Finally, too, sanctions and child-rearing became the most influential subjects of Ruth's last book.

Ruth considered child-rearing central to national-character study. She shared this view with Geoffrey Gorer, and it was from Gorer that she borrowed material on Japanese child-rearing practices.[42] Gorer more than Ruth favored psychoanalytic theories, but his general assumptions about the ramification of childhood training on adult personality resembled hers. Both avoided cause and effect, sometimes mainly by subterfuge and linguistic ploy. Dominant traits of Japanese personality, Ruth warily said, "are intelligible from their childrearing."[43] Chapter 12, "The Child Learns," is about *learning*—the process behind the behaviors and attitudes she described in chapters 3 through 11. In chapter 12 Ruth "explained" Japanese character, with references to child-rearing in the United States and to a strikingly contrasting American character.

Childhood training repeated and enforced the pattern of Japanese culture. Ruth included numerous details; data for her interpretations filled forty pages, the longest chapter in the book. Unity came from an emphasis on the discontinuity in Japanese child-rearing, an echo of her 1938 article, "Continuities and Discontinuities." For Japanese, the world of childhood was utterly distinct from the world of adulthood; in Ruth Benedict's account, the one was a world of freedom and indulgence, the other a world of restraint and self-discipline.[44] Yet her account was not fully consistent. The anthropologist showed how the Japanese child learned to be circumspect and self-observant, a learning that began early and crucially linked childhood to adulthood.

To call the child's feeling "embarrassment" and the adult's "shame" stretched a variation into a difference. Embarrassment and shame both indicated supreme sensitivity to the disapproval (actual or imagined) of others. "One striking continuity connects the earlier and the later period of the child's life: the great importance of being accepted by his fellows."[45] The continuity pointed out here made Japanese "discontinuity" quite different from the American discontinuity Ruth had described eight years earlier. A mode of response, a psychological trait, provided continuity between the world of childhood and the world of adulthood in Japan.

Childhood training involved learning shame, in defined stages. Shame provided the sanction for proper behavior and attitude. "But their extreme statements nevertheless point out correctly where the emphasis falls in Japan. It falls on the importance of shame rather than on the importance of guilt."[46] Ruth explained what she meant: "True shame cultures rely on external sanctions for good behavior, not, as true guilt cultures do, on an internalized conviction of sin."[47]

Shame, variously expressed, characterized Japanese culture. "Characterized" is important; Ruth did not psychoanalyze Japanese culture but brought together its outstanding traits. She used "shame" because the word captured the spirit of these traits taken together and, in addition, indicated the link between individual and culture. Shame characterized the fit of Japanese person and Japanese society, as well as suggesting how the "fit" lasted. Shame was a social process; Ruth did not psychoanalyze the Japanese individual either—she used a "psychic mechanism" to describe his relation to his culture. Shame explained Japanese character and suggested the pattern of future Japanese behaviors.

Ruth Benedict wrote *The Chrysanthemum and the Sword* for administrators and policymakers, as well as for colleagues and general readers. The book is political, arguing the necessity of understanding how and why the Japanese act as they do—how and why they might act after a crushing defeat. To complete her explanation, Ruth had to talk about the Emperor, especially in a book written for the American government after a victory over Japan. "The most famous question about Japanese attitudes concerned His Imperial Majesty, the Emperor. What was the hold of the Emperor on his subjects?"[48] For Ruth it was crucial to understand the relationship of the Japanese to the Emperor, not only to guide military policy but in order fully to understand Japanese personality. Ruth took on a classic problem and solved it in her own terms.

She did this by connecting loyalty to the Emperor to every aspect of Japanese culture. Loyalty to the Emperor was not an isolated factor in Japanese life but culmination and symbol of a whole culture. "*On* is always used in this sense of limitless devotion when it is used of one's first and greatest indebtedness, one's 'Imperial *on*.' This is one's debt to the Emperor, which one should receive with unfathomable gratitude."[49] The pattern of *on*, established in childhood and in the family, spread out, culminating in "limitless devotion" to the Emperor. *On* in its Imperial form was part of Japanese character, learned in childhood and practiced in adulthood.

The message of *The Chrysanthemum and the Sword* was too important to be left at description and indirection. Ruth Benedict also preached—the significance of differences and the need to respect differences. More insistently, she reminded her readers that differences in actions and in assumptions were *learned*; what was learned could be changed. "Under a new dispensation they [Japanese] will have to learn new sanctions."[50] In statements like this, scattered through the book but forcefully brought together in "The Child Learns" and "The Japanese Since V-J Day," Ruth took on a stern, moral tone. She also turned back to what she valued in American society: spontaneity and creativeness; a cautious adventurousness and enterprise; a respect for individuality.[51] On another level her list of values did not so much refer to American patterns as repeat her plea for extending individuality and the opportunities for "being natural" in any society. "So too the Japanese in Japan can, in a new era, set up a way of life which does not demand the old requirements of individual restraint. Chrysanthemums can be beautiful without wire racks and such drastic pruning."[52]

While suggesting better alternatives for Japan, Ruth Benedict did not forget the importance of existing customs, the age-old pattern of Japanese culture. She talked of change, using "sword" and "chrysanthemum" to represent dominant themes in the Japanese pattern. The point was to take advantage of existing values and mold these to a new era and a new alignment of nations. Her point was clear in the programmatic last chapter, "The Japanese Since V-J Day." The means for attaining peace "depend on the character of the people and upon the traditional social order."[53] Her book had described that character.

Ruth went a step further, with her audience in mind. Chapter 13 contained practical advice for government and military officials in Japan. Here, and elsewhere, her "idealism" became a brand of realism, a paradox she mentioned in "Pre-War Experts";[54] idealists "realistically" considered changed circumstances while realists clung to the past. Ruth wrote about changes in Japanese economy, schooling, local government —all to inform American military personnel. Her prescriptions would not have been persuasive extracted from her portrait of Japanese character.

The Chrysanthemum and the Sword is effectively written, drawing a portrait of a culture more persuasively than her earlier writings. In her book, Ruth remarkably matched style to argument; distinct phrases and repeated motifs embodied the sense of a paradoxical culture, providing nearly the "vicarious experience" she advocated. Here, as well, Ruth recreated the pattern in the process of describing "dominant attitudes," explaining the source and the persistence of values. *The Chrysanthemum and the Sword* was called literary and impressionistic; it was—and for a deliberate purpose. Ruth wrote to influence a political decision and to guide military policy toward peaceful interaction rather than future war. "The 160,000 American soldiers and 2000 citizens who staff the American military Government of Japan could do a better job if they studied Miss Benedict's suggestions," said reviewers.[55]

Simply, too, Ruth admired Japanese culture. She was attracted to the culture of paradox more than to the unmodulated Apollonian culture of the Pueblo Indian. The Japanese symbols of sword and of chrysanthemum, representing sides of their character, symbolized values that Ruth held: the sword stood for self-discipline and endurance; the flower for an aesthetically pleasing arrangement of naturally "wild" elements.

She emphasized the central paradox while portraying Japan as a highly integrated, complex culture. *The Chrysanthemum and the Sword* described a culture of carefully maintained integrity, an integrity at risk and continually redesigned. Unlike Zuñi integrity, Japanese integrity contained inconsistencies, splits, ambivalences—"contained" by conscious manipulation. Japan was a culture of controlled self-presentations, an elegantly and endlessly composed pattern. "So, too, chrysanthemums are grown in pots and arranged for the annual flower shows all over Japan with each perfect petal separately disposed by the grower's hand and often held in place by a tiny invisible wire rack inserted in the living flower."[56] Ruth hoped the elegance and the arrangement could survive without drastic pruning and a "wire rack." A perfect design might some day not require rigid scaffolding.

"The most important contemporary book yet written about Japan"

Publication of *The Chrysanthemum and the Sword* brought a flurry of reviews, and not only of Ruth Benedict's Japanese book. Her study of Japanese patterns of culture prompted an assessment of her work in general, her contribution to a discipline and to a twentieth-century frame of mind. Coincident with publication of *The Chrysanthemum and the Sword* a twenty-five-cent edition of *Patterns of Culture* appeared, making the 1934 book readily available to a range of readers. The year before, 1945, *Race* had been reissued with a new preface by Ruth Benedict. Her books reached millions of readers in America and, translated, all over the world.

Though different in content and in circumstances of composition, Ruth's three books elicited similar comments. (*Zuñi Mythology*, focusing exclusively on Pueblo materials, had a separate critical history.) Reviewers and essayists, anthropologists and nonanthropologists, commented on the evident pedagogical purpose in all her writings. The fact that Ruth directed her anthropology to current events and crises drew both negative and positive response; few failed to mention that she wrote, and practiced, an anthropology formed by contemporary problems and addressed to common readers.

Reviewers of *Patterns of Culture, Race,* and *The Chrysanthemum and the Sword* debated the virtues of popularizing—at least semi-popularizing—anthropology. The issue united otherwise differently motivated reviewers, who questioned the effect of literary techniques on scientific inquiry. Discussion revolved around the relationship of science and aesthetics, in research and in presentation. Ruth herself had been clear: She wrote to educate her readers in a science and used artistic devices to make the lessons not just palatable but meaningful in day-to-day experience.

Reviewers of her books ended up discussing the definition of a science and, specifically, the degree to which anthropology *was* a science. Again Ruth was clearer than many of her critics. Hers was a "humanistic science," she said, a science pursued and publicized for the purpose of improving human lives. She believed, too, that a well-constructed presentation of data would move men's passions and change men's minds; improvement would then be theirs to make.

"But that Dr. Benedict recognizes and condemns asocial traits which are destructive of human values is a tribute to her humanitarianism not to her anthropological theory."[57] This kind of remark was typical. Humanitarianism, while praiseworthy, was not scientific. Several World War II critics claimed Ruth Benedict could not be reliable as an ethnographer or student of society when she expressed opinions about the condition of mankind. From being dismissed for her cultural relativism, misunderstood as blind tolerance, Ruth found herself being dismissed for making judgments, misunderstood as bias and subjectivity. The importance of judging a whole culture, on its own terms, had always been part of her anthropology and was definitely implied in her cultural relativism. To view traits in context, take their measure, and display the unique combination of strengths and weaknesses, beauties and flaws, was part of an anthropology dependent on artistry along with science.

The critical response to Ruth's "scientific method" varied from book to book. *Race* was largely spared, gaining sympathy and unanimity of support from reviewers. Unabashedly propaganda, the book was not reviewed as anthropology. *The New Republic* set the tone, calling *Race* a "tract for the times, and a genuine contribution to sound popular knowledge."[58] *Patterns of Culture*, subtly propagandistic, in the postwar years was discussed in terms of the reliability of data and the accuracy of portraits designed to convert Americans. *The Chrysanthemum and the Sword* fell between, clearly propagandistic but for world peace not an altered American pattern and, simultaneously, an intensive ethnographic study. Responses to *The Chrysanthemum and the Sword* were echoed, deliberately or not, in World War II reappraisals of *Patterns of Culture*.

Most reviewers of *The Chrysanthemum and the Sword* agreed with Ruth's goals. "Miss Benedict's significant analysis of Japanese institutions and ways of life can aid us to understand the past for the sake of a better future."[59] Many reviewers praised her attempt to provide better understanding of "our most alien enemy," some referring to the challenges of postwar occupation. Several of those who praised her attempt also questioned how accurate her portrayal of the Japanese was. This brought up the matter of sources, of data and nonfieldwork, plus the usual wariness about her "abstract" portraits of whole societies. Had Ruth Benedict drawn a true Japanese character, or did *The Chrysanthemum and the Sword* present a picture alarmingly distant from reality? "Applied to present-day Japan, these abstractions of conduct are just as revelant as the prescriptions of Emily Post in an American Hooverville."[60] Similar comments on *Patterns of Culture* emerged during these years, though usually from anthropologists, not from journalists. It is "hopeless to characterize adequately a whole culture by a neat phrase," wrote Robert Lowie.[61] The complaint was the same: a doubt about Ruth's method of collecting data, a concern that she listened only to particular informants with special viewpoints, and—primarily—concern about her broad generalizing concepts and phrases: Apollonian and Dionysian, guilt and shame.

"While the stuff was beautiful and while it was most excellently tailored," a reviewer wrote about *The Chrysanthemum and the Sword*, "somehow there was a lack of true fit in the garment."[62] Ruth used her generalized words to evoke a culture; she did not intend the characterizations to be a perfect fit, tightly tailored representations of Pueblo or Japanese culture. Rather, she gave a sense, a strong impression, of the dominant "predispositions." "*Chrysanthemum and Sword*, like *Patterns of Culture*," said a sympathetic reviewer, "is concerned with the discovery of fundamental attitudes. . . ."[63]

Ruth's method of evoking and sweepingly characterizing a culture caused lasting distress to some readers. Her value-laden terms and generalizations implied lack of objectivity, anathema in the scientific 1940s. Ruth Benedict found a pattern, then summarily named it; the cavalier approach bothered critics. Yet the very idea of pattern allowed her to make the inclusive characterizations that distinguished her anthropology and established for future anthropologists a dynamic relationship between culture and personality. Pieces fell together, forming institution and individual temperament. Pattern unquestionably involved abstraction from structural, symbolic, and psychological details. Pattern also entailed a bold summation and an evocative presentation, a garment not precisely tailored to the model. Ruth did smooth over wrinkles, inconsistencies, and disturbances, but she equally indicated how and why disturbances and "nonconformity" arose—given pattern and dominant themes.

For Ruth an account of pattern was as close to the truth of a life as one could possibly come. The best testimony to the truth of her portrait of Japan lay in the shock of recognition on the part of Japanese readers.[64] They saw themselves "recreated."

That the truth of the portrait depended on the "eye" of the portraitist did not impugn its accuracy. A few World War II critics saw the importance of Ruth Benedict's subjectivity to her work, and to anthropology as a whole. Reviewing Pueblo materials in 1946 (the year of *The Chrysanthemum and the Sword*), John Bennett emphasized the need to confront not eliminate subjectivity; part of data was selection of that data.[65] And Alfred L. Kroeber, Ruth's longtime colleague, rival, and friend, paid a fine tribute by pointing out that passion intelligently informed Ruth's anthropological achievement.[66]

By 1946 Ruth Benedict was thoroughly in the public eye. Her books had been extraordinarily successful, acclaimed by professional and lay readers, used by administrators, the army, teachers, and psychiatrists. By 1946 her concepts and her perspective had become central to disciplinary development and part of the outlook of ordinary men and women—not only in the United States. Ruth seemed to have resolved her conflict between self-fulfillment and the need for a worthwhile, public achievement.

She did not record her responses to the acclaim given *The Chrysanthemum and the Sword*. She did reveal a sense of achievement and of satisfaction in the speeches she made and the articles she wrote about anthropology after World War II. The subjects were familiar: the importance of difference; the need for harmonious and willing cooperation; the potential in every individual to create (and recreate) the terms of his, and her, own living. The anthropologist repeated these ideas for diverse audiences, from the United Nations Secretariat, to the readers of the Vassar College *Alumnae Magazine,* to unseen radio listeners. Ruth's pieces were widely reprinted, and she wrote the accompanying biographical blurbs herself, with confidence, no longer sending an "S.O.S." to Margaret Mead asking, "Be a dear, and do this for me."

But the completion of a project and the finishing of a book could be crushing. With the war over and the disappearance of a consuming purpose, Ruth experienced her familiar dread. Unabsorbed, she faced the fact of growing older without the anchors she was used to. In 1947 she needed to chart a new course, make another choice, recognizing once again that "I can't exclude the knowledge of pain from my choices."[67]

"I knew she wanted most to be with you"

Ruth Benedict had been assigned Japan by the OWI and found herself caught up in the intricacies and inconsistencies, the paradox of Japanese culture. She never visited the country, and thus she missed the impact of landscape and the direct experience of Japanese "commonplaces." But this study of a place she never saw and a people she talked with only at a distance is in many ways Ruth's finest achievement. "This analysis of Japan is a book that makes one proud to be an anthropologist. It shows what can be done with orientation and discipline even without speaking knowledge of the language and residence in the country."[68] *The Chrysanthemum and the Sword* tied together ideas and commitments from a self-conscious life story. *The Chrysanthemum and the Sword* also sketched in the outline of Ruth Benedict's future course.

"In anthropological studies of different cultures the distinction between those which rely heavily on shame and those that rely heavily on guilt is an important one."[69] It seems clear that Ruth planned to elaborate the shame/guilt dichotomy. The dichotomy related to her 1930s interest in sanctions, the motivating force in learning a culture and simultaneously learning to be a type of person. Sanctions, the enforcement of behavior and attitudes, linked person to culture without diminishing the activity of the person or minimizing shared culture values. Ruth used "shame" and "guilt" to indicate the dynamic of individual participation in a culture and to characterize different cultural systems of reward and punishment. "In a culture where shame is a major sanction, people are chagrined about acts which we expect people to feel guilty about."[70] The statement fit her exploration of the links between acting individuals and a powerful culture pattern.

The Chrysanthemum and the Sword also pointed out the strains for an individual caused by each type of sanction. Repeatedly Ruth's admiration for Japanese character, for circumspection and self-consciousness, for even distribution of duty and of pleasure, came up against her awareness of the heavy burden a Japanese individual must bear. "Those who do respect themselves (*jicho*) chart their course, not between 'good' and 'evil' but between 'expected man' and 'unexpected man,' and sink their own personal demands in the collective 'expectation.' These are the good men who 'know shame (*haji*)' and are endlessly circumspect."[71] Ruth Benedict also knew the toll that guilt could take on people and on a culture: "All psychiatrists know what trouble contemporary Americans have with their consciences."[72] She had experienced and puzzled over her own inherited "guilt tradition."

By the end of *The Chrysanthemum and the Sword*, the guilt culture came out better than the shame culture with its infinite restrictions and constant monitoring of the individual. "The Japanese have paid a high price for their way of life. They have denied themselves simple freedoms which Americans count upon as unquestionably as the air they breathe."[73] From her first anthropology courses in 1919, through World War II, Ruth Benedict had been concerned about freedom; she understood the concept in terms of the scope given individuals to choose a course and to fit their culture while also finding self-fulfillment. As an individual learned a culture, he also learned the extent to which he could chart his way through cultural prescriptions and perhaps even experience happiness.

"No culture, except as it functions to decrease or increase the happiness of its members, can be ranged on a psychological scale of values."[74] This *was* judgment, but not an absolute definition of "happiness." Ruth added a clumsy significant footnote. "Because of the different goals for which people strive in different cultures and the different character structure induced, what happiness consists in differs in different societies."[75]

"What happiness consists in differs in different societies." Ruth's notion of happiness included freedom and dignity, the ability to recognize and to fulfill one's goals. Happiness varied, depending on the character of a culture and on the social institutions molding and responding to individual idiosyncrasies. Toward the end of her life Ruth concentrated on child-rearing, the practices and values surrounding a "natural" course of events and one faced by every society, necessarily and distinctively. How individuals acquired the potential for happiness had precipitated and continued to prompt Ruth's interest in primitive cultures, in complex societies like her own, and in national character.

After the war Ruth Benedict and Margaret Mead applied for a grant to carry national-character study into the postwar years. The Office of Naval Research provided funds, and the two women moved the project from Washington, D.C., to New York, first to Columbia University and then to the American Museum of Natural History (where Margaret had an office). They changed the name from "national character" to "cultures at a distance" or contemporary cultures, to include a wider array of "units" of study and, probably, to avoid association with the federal government propaganda office. Ruth did a good deal of the administrating, enjoying her supervision of graduate students, her contact with interviewers, and her access to variously gathered data. "It is no accident that this complex, sprawling, backbreaking project is headed up by Ruth Benedict. Few people would be so well able to organize the skills and orchestrate the special gifts of the 70-odd anthropologists and volunteer workers on such an intricate undertaking as this."[76]

The project provided distance and distraction from Columbia, activity to fill in the space left when war ended and her book appeared. The success of *The Chrysanthemum and the Sword* pleased Ruth, especially its reception in Japan. She had described a culture, illuminating and winning approval from that culture—a rare reward for an anthropologist, and one she had not had with the Pueblos. Teaching also took time and attention; in those years Ruth inspired and encouraged a group of students whose values and ethics had been substantially altered by a second world war. Her old progressive ideas persisted; learning had to be individual and fired by personal passion.

But Ruth seemed restless and discontent. She had been ill off and on during the war; overwork, overstimulation, and excessive concern about conditions in the world drained her energies while leading to some of her best anthropology. In 1947, in her sixtieth year, she questioned the course of a future whose lines had been drawn in the past. She had ideas and notes for another book and yet—there always seemed to be an "and yet," echo of Sapir's *cui bono* and reminder of her own persistent doubts about her purpose. That year Ruth went to Pasadena to live with her mother, Margery Freeman, and occasional nieces and nephews. Bertrice Fulton, at eighty-eight a contented grandmother, and Margery, with her career and household, both represented a pattern Ruth had missed in her own life.

Ruth continued to suspect that motherhood might finally have subdued her anxieties and restless strivings, put an end to her sense of futility. At home with the two women she had continually compared herself with, Ruth grew uncomfortable and doubtful. Eventually she moved into a house with Ruth Valentine, a psychologist and longtime

California friend. They lived near the Freeman's Constance Avenue house, and the arrangement suited each woman very well. Living with another woman had become Ruth Benedict's preferred domestic pattern, and Ruth Valentine enjoyed the company. Margery Freeman expressed her pleasure and optimism to her sister, saying about Ruth Valentine, "I knew she *wanted* most to be with you."[77]

The sisters had realized by then a solid and satisfying relationship, built on mutual respect and a shared, awed fondness for Bertrice Fulton. "Mother is much the same," Margery wrote after Bertrice had fallen and broken a hip. "Truly she is made of india-rubber!"[78] Margery also worried about her older sister, who was subject to depression and lassitude. Dizziness and weakness plagued Ruth, suggesting a not-quite-perfect happiness. "Have you had any more 'spells?'" Margery asked.[79] Ruth's answer does not exist, but sentences she wrote in 1934 might do: "But we, caught between the accident of birth and the desirability of death, how shall we set stars in heaven? We shall wither to our deaths as in a dream, knowing all things are folly, phantoms, shadows."[80] Yet she countered thoughts of death, summoning other old thoughts and returning to the issues of womanhood, children, and the bringing up of a new generation to be better content than her own.

12
The End of a Life

"My family are now all reunited, a fine healthy lot"

FOR NEARLY A DECADE, after "Continuities and Discontinuities" in 1938, Ruth Benedict devoted a good part of her anthropological energies to the study of child-rearing. The institutions for and attitudes toward bringing up a younger generation formed a central focus of national-character and, later, culture-at-a-distance research. Observations of child-rearing in primitive and complex societies provided data for culture-and-personality theory. For Ruth, how an individual learned a culture "explained" his personality.

She made the study of child-rearing central to anthropology by extending the implications of a classic subject in Boasian cultural anthropology. Child-rearing study had "legitimacy"; Ruth emphasized its potential for illuminating the links between culture and personality in any setting. In addition, her private speculations about motherhood, family, and love continued to parallel the broadening of her anthropological perspectives. Summers at the Norwich farm reminded Ruth of family and of a distinctly toned family constellation. In the Freeman household, too, she watched Margery Freeman mother her children; then those five children have their own babies. "My little grand-nephew who lives in the house is a constant delight, a sweet year and a half old baby. . . ."[1]

All the time Ruth lived in the Freeman house she was daughter as well as sister and aunt. Bertrice Fulton remained a significant and out-spoken member of the family, relinquishing little of her well-learned roles of mother and teacher. She continued, as she had years before, to voice strong opinions and display sudden emotion.[2] Ruth observed two different women being mothers and two generations of nieces and nephews growing up. She was "mothered" at the same time.

Children and learning, socialization and education, had become dominant concerns among Ruth's contemporaries. As in Ruth's case, these concerns often combined personal, professional, and political points of view. An assumption that education, and the creativeness in a new generation, would rescue America, the world, and the future unified several modes of thought. Children, properly taught, carried the burden for a lasting peace. "Education must face today a whole array of new and complicated problems, for upon the clear-sightedness of children now in school will depend the functioning of the post war world," Ruth wrote in 1942.[3]

World War II had justified anthropology for Ruth. She had realized a worthwhile endeavor and made publicly useful her private debate about the freedom and the compulsion in custom. The debate continued, however, and after the Second World War Ruth returned to her First World War issue. Women, the tension between self-fulfillment and social reward, between woman's "nature" and official achievement (the "world's coarse thumb and finger"), focused her speculations. The specific subject served as test, for how far any human being could stretch the givens of her or his life and for how receptive a culture could be to idiosyncratic, imaginative vision.

The consistency in Ruth's publications after World War II and *The Chrysanthemum and the Sword* reflected the closer merging of professional and private concerns. In 1948 Ruth published four pieces: a foreword to a book on women,[4] a review of the first *Kinsey Report*,[5] an article in the *National Association for Nursery Education Bulletin*,[6] and an article titled "Are Families Passé?" in the *Saturday Review of Literature*.[7] That same year she gave a speech to the annual meeting of the American Orthopsychiatric Association titled "Childrearing in Certain European Countries."[8]

Ruth discussed child-rearing in terms of one generation learning the habits and manners of the preceding generation—learning, in effect, the national character. "A whole nation of babies have to be brought up to replace their elders."[9] She was interested in *how* this worked, differently in different countries. "The cultural study of certain European nations on which I am reporting has taken as one of its basic problems the ways in which children are brought up to carry on in their turn their parents' manner of life."[10] That was Ruth's professional interest in child-rearing. Behind it lay her autobiographical story, a longtime concern with learning and with the realization of both an individuality and a place in the "whole."

Her purpose remained to find out how an individual learned to be a "self" without completely conforming or yet eliciting the brand "deviant." In the postwar years she began to consider more concentratedly than before the teachers and the mothers—the people responsible for rearing children. Ruth studied, then, the interpersonal relationships that underlay learning.

In the article for the Nursery Education Association, referring to her own country, Ruth made a distinction between mothers and teachers. The distinction carried an important point about the need both for emotional reassurance at home and for structured, formal training at school. This idea was new in her writings, perhaps a response to the growth of nursery school education during World War II and probably, as well, a reflection of her turning back to the significance of motherhood and a woman's nurturing qualities. The year before the article appeared, Ruth gave an interview to the *New York Times*; her speculations on the value of "lay education" (that is, mothers) and of professional education (that is, nursery school teachers) reached a wide audience.[11] What she said to the professional association of orthopsychiatrists in the spring of 1948 had similar implications. "Careful studies of mother-child relations in this country have abundantly shown the infant's sensitivity to the mother's tenseness or permissiveness, her pleasure or disgust, whether those are expressed in her elbows, her tone of voice, or her facial expression."[12]

Ruth Benedict talked to the American orthopsychiatrists primarily about child-rearing practices in Europe. She explained her national-character work and reminded her audience of the importance of culture-context for assessing any aspect of child-rearing. This was a warning geared to psychiatrists, a warning against assuming that the same trait had the same consequence in every setting. Ruth picked an instructive example, the well-researched and frequently misapplied "swaddling hypothesis" about the effect on adult personality of tightly binding an infant. But Ruth's real subject was communication—the different messages conveyed to an infant by different swaddling practices.

> Specifically I shall try to show that any such student of comparative cultures must press his investigations to the point where he can describe *what is communicated* [hers] by the particular variety of the widespread technique he is studying. In the case of swaddling, the object of investigation is the kind of communication which in different regions is set up between adults and the child by the procedures and sanctions used.[13]

A discussion of swaddling was a discussion not of wrapping a baby up but of the emotions and expectations accompanying the procedure.

The speech began with two general ideas: the importance of comparison within one area (the "culture-area approach"[14]) and the complexity of links between child-rearing and the adult personality. The culture-area approach, in fact, showed unmistakably the intricacy of connection between a practice and a personality. "When a great area shares a generalized trait, the particular slants each subarea has given to these customs is diagnostic of its special values, and the range of variation gives insight which could not be obtained from the study of one nation in isolation."[15]

Variations in adult personality from culture to culture were rooted in patterns of communication, the nuances of a particular practice. In her 1948 speech, Ruth talked about national character, about child-rearing, and about a context that included, markedly, interpersonal relationships. Contact between the teachers and those who were taught, the emotional tone of transmitting values, now became an important item in Ruth's anthropological inquiries.

Ruth brought these thoughts to interdisciplinary and international meetings—phenomena of the postwar era. In 1947, for instance, the education and cultural branch of the United Nations, UNESCO, made a series of resolutions authorizing

> [the] study of "Tensions Affecting International Understanding." The general purpose of the resolutions was to encourage social scientists to focus their attention and their research techniques on an understanding of the development and perpetuation of attitudes which make for national aggression and, on the basis of their findings, to recommend ways and means of promoting attitudes that would increase international understanding.[16]

Although Ruth Benedict had voiced some reservations in *The Chrysanthemum and the Sword*, she even became intrigued by the "possibility of adapting polling and surveys to investigations of national character."[17] She concentrated on the *transmission* of attitudes, the handing down of customs and "shibboleths" from one generation on to the next.

"The cultural patterns which men in each society invent and transmit down the generations have a considerable degree of consistency within themselves." Ruth made this, a familiar remark, for a UNESCO summer seminar organized to study certain educational problems. She reminded fellow discussants that education, bringing up infants and young children, fit a whole configuration, and again chose "swaddling" for her example. "Genetic study of different cultures is precisely this study of how the members of each generation are conditioned 'to become responsible participants' in the way of life which is traditional in the community into which they are born."[18]

At the seminar she talked about her discipline and its distinctive method, fieldwork. "The 'cultural surprise' he experiences [in the field] gives him an education in patterns of culture which it is hard to obtain in any other way"—adding her particular slant: "After he has finished his observations, he should be able to see the cultural arrangements of his own nation with clearer vision."[19] As if to emphasize her move from intensive study of single cultures to extensive comparative study, Ruth added to her seminar talk a detailed questionnaire. The format and length reflected her recent war-inspired insistence on gathering comparable data from a range of societies in order to design a reasonable postwar world. Taken together, the questions—on motherhood and attitudes toward children—reiterated Ruth's recognition of interpersonal relationships and the emotional bases for a national character. She conveyed once more her conviction that how the child learns and how the teacher teaches, the communication between the two, was of prime importance. What is striking is her emphasis on the mother, on learning at home and in the family. Ruth substantially shifted her attention from formal settings for transmitting values and norms to the informal, the fuzzier domain of emotion and sensual interaction—the woman's domain. In 1947 she told readers of the Vassar College *Alumnae Magazine* that women were especially qualified to study the details of domesticity. Women, she wrote, "are less inclined to label as trivia the details of the daily round of living. This is important because it is in small recurrent situations that any people learn their ways of acting and thinking."[20]

Ruth Benedict began to consider family, and a woman's role in the family, the core of social process, a source of stability and continuity and quality in a culture. She wrote about family and mothers from her position as "expert" anthropologist; at the same time she drew on her personal experience of various mothers—her own, Margery, friends.

By the end of World War II Ruth had become a public figure, "one of America's most distinguished anthropologists" the Vassar *Alumnae* said in 1947. The speeches she gave, accepting awards,[21] sounded confident.

> I had believed for a long time before the war that the same kind of research [as in primitive tribes] could help us to understand civilized nations. I believed that by serious study of learned cultural behavior we could achieve a better international understanding and make fewer mistakes in international communication.[22]

During those years, too, her statements were widely reprinted: "Let's Get Rid of Prejudice," from *Race,* in the *National Parent-Teacher,*[23] and "Japanese Are So Simple" and "The Puzzling Moral Code of the Japs," from *The Chrysanthemum and the Sword*[24] are typical examples. Ruth in effect sold anthropology and an anthropological point of view to diverse audiences.

In 1946, 1947, and 1948 Ruth's talks and articles were about children and family. Americans were fascinated by children and families and responded to a cross-cultural perspective that challenged accepted conventions. In 1948, for example, Ruth gave a speech to the U.N. Secretariat about children and child-rearing in America. "We [Americans] do not ask whether our little boy has the eye of an artist or the ear of a musician. We want to know whether he is as good as the next boy, whether he is like him,' whether he is 'normal.' "[25] For Ruth Benedict this competitiveness and denial of individuality was damning; American mothers had failed.

She did not suggest that "motherhood" or family had failed or were outmoded. "The anthropologist knows that the changes taking place in the home in any decade in any country do not mean that the family is now about to disintegrate under our eyes unless we do something about it," she wrote in "Are Families Passé?"[26] Ruth's criticisms of American women as mothers reflected a belief in the importance of motherhood and a worry about how being a mother fit with other roles available to women in American society, namely, wife and worker. Once more, as she had in 1915, Ruth wondered about the "mocking faith"[27] that permitted a woman to live vicariously, through her children. She wondered about the woman's life when children had grown up and, as ever, about the association of love, marriage, motherhood, and a conviction of self-worth.

"Are Families Passé?" brought her private issues to the general public. Ruth Benedict pointed out that women in American society suffered especially; their family and marital roles had not kept up with changes in society. "Mothers who are going through this period [child's "nursery years"] give remarkably little thought to the leisure that will come soon. . . . [In] part it is a result of the sentiment which selects this period, no matter how short, as the fulfillment of a woman's chief duty in life."[28] Women in American society, she argued, could no longer depend on children for satisfaction or, for that matter, on their husbands. An important goal in America is "the pursuit of happiness" and "the right to terminate an unhappy marriage is the other side of the coin of which the fair side is the right to choose one's spouse," Ruth wrote, perhaps with retrospective regret.[29]

Love remained woman's "supreme power."[30] Ruth argued for greater choice in the ways and means and timing of love. She had learned from her "primitive laboratory" the diverse arrangements of human intimacy, and she remarked on how severely Americans limited their arrangements. To expand choice in personal relationships suited American tradition; choice was a dominant culture-value and could be expanded without violating existing patterns. Changing the conditions under which women, and men, formed relationships would benefit the individual and the society—as long as the change meshed with the "whole way of life which is valued."[31]

"Full normal happiness only comes to men and women who give as well as take."[32] The preachy note on which the article ended may be attributed to her forum—the *Saturday Review*—and to an anxiety about her own "full normal happiness" in 1948. Erik Erikson saw her in June 1948, just after her sixty-first birthday. "Here was a person who was not vitally healthy any more. Yet she was not sick. . . . Here was a friend, who was deeply alone, who had, in fact, stopped fighting loneliness. . . . Here then, a consciously aging woman. . . ."[33]

This is sadder than need be. Ruth was debating as always her happiness and her "endeavor." She was not despairing. She had planned to write a textbook for a one-culture world;[34] in 1948 she listed as her current project "Contributions of psychocultural studies to international relations," for the Carnegie Foundation.[35] She had not stopped looking forward. Erikson accurately saw the vulnerable and retrospective side of Ruth's nature but underplayed the vigorous and resilient side. In contemplating her past Ruth found direction for the future. She reinterpreted her life story in the process of formulating new anthropological questions.

"The premise of man's creativity"

On an evening late in December 1947, Ruth Benedict gave a speech to the American Anthropological Association meeting at Albuquerque, New Mexico. She was retiring from the presidency, her term uncompleted, and she took the opportunity to outline her vision of anthropology. She had been in the discipline from a first world war to a second and had seen that discipline change in content, size, and sense of responsibility. She had had much to do with these changes over the past quarter-century, through teaching, writing, and participating in various professional organizations. Not only had Ruth influenced several generations of anthropologists, she had also opened the eyes of people outside her discipline: academics, nonacademics, politicians and psychiatrists, schoolchildren and the proverbial man-in-the-street. She had successfully shown Americans and the world the value of an anthropological perspective and had taught individuals to re-view the terms of their lives.

The year before, December 1946, her professional organization had elected Ruth Fulton Benedict president, an acclamation and testimony to her place in the discipline. She responded with mixed feelings to administrative duties, but presidency of the American Anthropological Association was an honor, and a forum, she could not refuse. This was not her first presidency; twenty years earlier she had been president of the American Ethnological Society (1927–29), a society so small that its meetings could be held in someone's New York City apartment.

The American Anthropological Association (AAA) was in a state of turmoil when Ruth Benedict took over the presidency from Ralph Linton. Greatly expanded in size and complexity, the AAA had a quite different character from its prewar familial one. Through World War II the discipline had grown not only in numbers but also in subject matter, so that the umbrella of one organization barely seemed adequate. Members argued, during the war years, about AAA structure and criteria for membership.[36] Some wanted a tighter structure and a controlled membership; Ruth, not surprisingly, argued for flexibility— a looser structure, allowing for distinct specializations and for differently trained anthropologists. Her projected AAA resembled her "joint stock company" vision of society: diverse members cooperating for the common good. Her position was defeated, and AAA members voted for tighter organization with strict membership requirements. Ruth presided over an association which had rejected her point of view, succeeding a president who harbored, and voiced, a strong dislike for her. The situation was not promising; the combination did not bode well for Ruth's presidency or her peace of mind.

The AAA decision reflected the discipline's effort to become a "science." The model for organization and membership was taken from the physical and biological science associations, the hard sciences that were well funded in the postwar years. The notion of becoming more scientific did not appeal to Ruth Benedict either. Anthropology, she believed, fell between science and humanities. Its virtue, not its defect, lay in an ability to straddle and to incorporate two perspectives at once. Thus in her definition of the discipline as well, the newly elected president went against what was the dominant grain of her professional association.

Ruth did not sympathize with the insistence on science and scientific objectivity, especially when the world evidently, and exigently, needed concerned inquiry and research frankly devoted to the improvement of human lives. She had announced her creed a year earlier, in a speech to the American Association of University Women.

> I have the faith of a scientist that behavior, no matter how unfamiliar to us, is understandable if the problem is stated so that it can be answered by investigation and if it is then studied by technically suitable methods. And I have the faith of a humanist in the advantages of mutual understanding among men.[37]

In the AAA, the task and the conflicts proved overwhelming, and Ruth Benedict resigned from the presidency she had assumed in January 1947. She resigned in June; six months later, with some sense of defeat and some relief, she stood up to address her fellow anthropologists. Subdued in manner and in dress, Ruth began hesitantly and then delivered one of the most stirring statements of her career.[38] The speech, "Anthropology and the Humanities," had a profound effect on anthropology in America.

Ruth Benedict had been preparing for the speech throughout her career. Presidency of the AAA testified to her position in the discipline, and the farewell speech revealed the intertwining of a professional achievement and a personal "adventure."[39] In the speech, "Anthropology and the Humanities," Ruth described anthropology as a way of seeing and a way of seeing man in the *whole* of his experience. She meant by "experience" not just what men did and formalized but also what men thought, broadly "man's emotions, his rationalizations, his symbolic structures."[40] A focus only on what men did, she said, resulted in abstracting trait from context and violating the holism of anthropology. With the "mind of man" as subject, an anthropologist necessarily grasped the whole culture, the dominant assumptions and deeply held values: "the consequences of his [man's] acts and thoughts in his own world."[41]

Ruth Benedict had outlined, in her words, "the humanist's approach —being holistic and always taking account of context in the mind of man. . . ."[42] The humanist's approach suited an anthropology that acknowledged that "man is a species which can create his way of life— his culture" and culture cut of whole cloth, an integrated pattern.[43] Ruth turned to the humanists to prove her point and became, for the moment, surprisingly autobiographical. "Long before I knew anything at all about anthropology, I had learned from Shakespearian criticism— and from Santayana—habits of mind which at length made me an anthropologist."[44] These "habits of mind" included sensitivity to context and an emphasis on creativity.

And like the humanists of her tradition, poet and philosopher, she proclaimed the absolute significance of the individual human being. The individual was important beyond the brief mention in her speech. Ruth had constructed an anthropological approach around individuality and, by extension, around imaginative creativity—the source of distinctive character in person and in culture. Her concept of culture included the individual who made, observed, and remade his world. Every person who was subject to the force of custom was equally able to re-view and redesign the conventions by which he lived.

An enormous respect for individuality and its corollary, creativeness, determined Ruth's ethical stance. Clear in the AAA speech and in everything she wrote was Ruth's respect for integrity and for the unique arrangement by which person and culture survived, and changed one another over time; these ideas also formed the basis for judgment. Ruth was simultaneously open-minded about other "designs for living" and firm about measuring the costs for human lives of different arrangements. Happiness and welfare replaced "efficiency" as she learned to assess a design in terms of its impact on the whole of individual experience.

In her AAA speech Ruth Benedict referred to life histories, getting to know the individuals in a society. "The unique value of life histories lies in that fraction of the material which shows what repercussions the experiences of a man's life—either shared or idiosyncratic—have upon him as a human being molded in that environment."[45] More, Ruth knew that only through close study of man, an individual, could one comprehend the values in a culture; individuals demonstrated the quality, impact, and inspiration of prevalent beliefs. The source of all values, she wrote, lay in the "hearts and minds" of men.[46] The anthropologist's job would not be complete without the addition of a humanist's approach, the inclusion of hearts and minds in the study of mankind.

The same year she gave the AAA speech, Ruth Benedict wrote an article for her college alumnae magazine. Not exactly a farewell, the piece—"Anthropology in Your Life"—did have a tone of summing up and retrospection. She described for her fellow Vassar graduates and for current students the major premises and principles of her discipline. In the process Ruth sketched another version of her life story.

"The anthropologist," she said, "becomes culture conscious." He recognizes, she explained (using the male pronoun throughout) that customs are not given or natural, but learned and changeable. "They are different ways in which man has tried to solve the problems of living together in a community." The anthropologist, startled by "strange" customs, gained insight into familiar customs. "The shock of recognizing basic differences in social arrangements made them [anthropologists] look back again at their own culture and define more particularly what peculiarities it had."[47] Above all Ruth stressed learning. Anthropology is the science of what and how men learn in a culture, what they absorb from and reconstruct in their surroundings.

In the article written for a virtually all-female audience, Ruth used the male pronoun and "man" for "human being." At the end she focused specifically on women and reminded her readers that women had special talents and skills. "Women are particularly fitted to further international and minority understanding by paying attention to *people*."[48] Women know the significance of the commonplace in daily lives. "It is in the home where every generation first learns the accepted ways of authoritarianism or of egalitarianism, and the sanctions that are used in that nation for ensuring proper behavior. This is a sphere where women have reason to be good judges. . . ."[49]

At last an acknowledgment of woman's "special power" did not mean denying a woman the capacity for contributing to her society and to the world. Ruth began to resolve the "woman issue" and to reconcile the two sides of her temperament, without violating "nature" or ignoring the customs she valued. She seemed in those years to achieve the understanding that dichotomy did not have to be eliminated but could in fact be productive, fruitful—the source of creativity in a discipline and a self.

"I am going to miss her more than I would have dreamed"

During the spring of 1948 Ruth Benedict once again lived at 448 Central Park West, on Manhattan's Upper West Side. Relieved of her AAA duties, she spent time in the Columbia department; William Duncan Strong was chairman, and Ralph Linton had gone to Yale. With Margaret Mead she also supervised the many people involved in culture-at-a-distance studies. Tired and a bit dispirited through the spring months—doctors' appointments are scrawled into her appointment books—Ruth yet managed to convey her commitment to anthropology and convert students to her way of seeing. In the midst of these assorted activities she at last received a full professorship in the department of anthropology. Ruth had been teaching for twenty-five years, much of that time virtually running the department.

Years of experience in the classroom, supplemented by public lectures and formal speeches, had bolstered Ruth's confidence but not substantially altered her manner of presenting herself and her anthropology. For official audiences like the U.N. Secretariat or the Columbia faculty, Ruth structured her talks carefully, combining vivid detail with a systematic argument. She usually began with a remark on the range of human behaviors, followed this with illustrative "proof," and concluded with a paean to the awesome differences in designs for living and the value of a cross-cultural perspective. Ruth repeated ideas and phrases, partly a timesaving strategy and partly a reflection of her steady devotion to certain articles of anthropological faith.

To people who met and knew Ruth in those years, she seemed calm and settled, if not totally content. She was satisfied with her achievement, and anthropological inquiry effectively contained the restless energies plaguing her younger years. She still spoke quietly and in a low voice, but with more certainty and fewer awkward pauses. She also dressed still according to pattern, in muted colors, in deep-grays, greens, and rose. People who liked her said "soft-spoken and poised"; people who did not like her said "aloof, cold, withdrawn." Yet even those who found Ruth aloof, vague, and impressionistic responded to her anthropology and to the visionary faith in her practice of a science.

Postwar students who came to work with Ruth Benedict at Columbia did not disagree about the impressionistic, or poetic, component in her anthropology. Her admirers accepted the importance of intuition and a humanistic perspective as crucial to anthropological inquiry, not to be subdued by logical analysis. "I don't know how to operationalize what she says, but over and over again I feel convinced that she is right. I don't know how to deal with that feeling, but it's one of the reasons I don't dwell on the distinction between the humanities and the sciences."[50] Students carried out the message in Ruth's AAA speech, reconciling science and humanities in distinct ways. An emphasis on individual creativity and consciously constructed "coherence," the premise of Ruth's anthropology, appealed to a generation just through World War II and before that a debilitating depression.

That spring, 1948, Ruth began planning her summer vacation, hoping to get away from New York City. She had not been feeling well, and Margaret Mead repeatedly urged her to keep the doctors' appointments she made then broke. During those months of "blossom in the front of summer,"[51] Ruth craved both rest and stimulation, family and work. She finally decided to divide her summer between a trip to Pasadena and attendance at a UNESCO seminar in Czechoslovakia. In her small appointment book she made a list of things to bring— "Briefcase. Dress. Stockings. White bag"—and, later, a reminder "To get Wallace Stevens."[52] It is the list of a professional, a poet, and a "civilized" woman.

In California, Ruth visited the Freemans and her mother; she also attended a Conference on International Affairs sponsored by the American Friends Committee. Sometime in June she met and talked with Erik Erikson. "When I saw Ruth last June, in California, I asked her to sit for a sketch. . . . She seemed so calm that to ask whether she was happy in any conversational sense would have seemed incongruous."[53] Ruth often was "calm" away from New York, near her family, and anticipating a professional event. Maybe, too, being sketched by Erikson induced a quiet demeanor, a placidity and self-control. Ruth did not enjoy being looked at and usually set herself to endure the prospect with a kind of stiffness and formality. Occasional spontaneous photos contrast with the posed portraits. At her ease, Ruth displayed the energy, humor, and liveliness perceptible to very close friends at some moments of her life. Erikson possessed a sharply acute vision: Ruth felt protected under her mask of calm.

She left Pasadena in early summer to travel through Europe. Before getting to Czechoslovakia, Ruth could finally see the landscapes of countries whose character she had described: Holland, Belgium, France, Germany. At the end of July she arrived in Podebrady, Czechoslovakia, to talk about children and child-rearing. She came armed with her anthropological awareness of the importance of child-rearing in culture-and-personality research and with her political awareness that a better future depended on the bringing up of the next generation. *"The way they* [children] *live their daily lives will add up to the only total there will be,"* she had written, emphatically, six years before.[54]

Ruth Benedict brought her anthropology to a seminar organized to promote peace and international welfare. She also brought the private experiences of a lifetime, her continuing reflections on the talent required for teaching, nurturing, and preparing individuals to meet the unexpected, and the expected, in their lives. At the UNESCO seminar on children, Ruth gathered together thoughts of the past several years and revealed the emotional underpinning of her career. She presented her intellectual position and hinted at its basis in her long-term concerns as a woman.

She came home from Europe in the late summer, tired and strained. She came back in time to prepare classes and arrange her apartment before the fall semester began at Columbia. Less than a week after her return, Ruth felt sick enough to go to a doctor, without her usual protests. Margaret oversaw the September doctor's visit; Ruth was hospitalized the second week of September, the diagnosis a coronary attack. She moved into a room at New York Hospital, a wing of the Cornell University medical building where years before Stanley Benedict had had his laboratory and taught biochemistry. Friends visited Ruth Benedict, traveling across town from Columbia and the West Side and in from suburbs. Margery Freeman wrote seven- to eight-page letters and Ruth Valentine left Pasadena as soon as she heard the news, to come east. Uncomfortable about flying, Ruth Valentine took the train from Los Angeles to New York City, a five-day trip.

Lying in a hospital, Ruth Benedict had time to think, to pick up the threads of her own life and other peoples' lives. She had time, too, to think about death, a subject never far from her mind.

> We weary of the earth, its madrigal
> Of still-renewing autumns, and the sky
> Spread as an azure curtain on the heavens,
> Marking our sight its confines. Earth is a child,
> Sings but one rondelay.[55]

Being "weary of the earth" was a persistent phrase in Ruth's life story. She had looked weary in the spring and summer of 1948; some saw a hard-won composure, others saw sheer exhaustion in the lines on her face. In the hospital she seemed quiet and restful, recovering from the past months, not uneasy about her condition. During those autumn days Ruth accepted the course of events:

> Bind breath no more in sheaves that melt as mist
> From sunrise river valleys. Breath's a wraith
> No cord shall bind, no dreamer twist
> To image of his love or any faith.[56]

She had once written in her diary, "If I can just live till I'm 50, I'll be peaceful."[57] That September she was sixty-one years old.

Fourteen years before, Ruth had begun the first draft of an autobiographical sketch with a paragraph on suicide. Characteristically, she treated a deeply troubling matter in a careful intellectual formulation, comparing Roman suicide to a nineteenth-century suicide of a neighbor in the Norwich area.[58] She began the final draft of her life story with her father's death. "The story of my life begins when I was twenty-one months old, at the time my father died."[59] For Ruth death represented a measure of life, a judgment of its value. A type of death—self-inflicted or natural, too soon or too late—commented on the life; a way of dying underlined a way of living. Similarly, responses to death by survivors commented on their living. Bertrice Fulton's outbursts in mourning expressed her life to the little girl as effectively as Frederick Fulton's calm and resigned face in the coffin expressed his life. Death and attitudes toward death carried an interpretation of life, for a person and for a culture. "The chief speaks to the people telling them that they shall not remember any more. 'It is now four years he is dead.' "[60]

Death preoccupied Ruth Benedict, but not a wish for death or an obsessive attraction to suicide. Death preoccupied Ruth as a measure and test of living, a balance for her "precious moments." When she thought about death she weighed the qualities of her life, even in childhood. Margery Fulton Freeman remembered:

> Those were the days [before Vassar] when she struggled over the problem of why we had to live, what was the purpose of it all—and when she frankly wished that she had never been called into existence. I wasn't much help to her, either. My natural euphoria filled me with such an instinctive love of life that I couldn't quite grasp the depths of her thinking.[61]

Ruth tried the balance constantly, weighing joys and pains against death, "the gift of sleep."[62] She drew the parameters of choice, wondering when choice was possible.

Suicide represented choice, a decision to act on one's measure of life. In this, their total ignorance of self-inflicted death, Ruth Benedict found the Zuñi at once dismaying and soothing: "It does not occur to them that he could have taken his own life. Their story is only of a man whose death occurred in the form he had been heard to wish for."[63] The Japanese recognized, and practiced, suicide. Ruth understood the act, though not entirely the psychological impulse, the enormous burden of debt-to-be-paid. "In modern times suicide is a choice to die. A man turns violence against himself . . . a chosen self-destruction."[64] Her exploration of other lives *was* a salvation of sorts, and her discipline a distraction from "blue devils."[65] At the same time in anthropology Ruth found new versions and new interpretations of death and mourning.

She also experienced, vicariously, two suicides during her anthropological career. In each case Ruth turned the experience back to life; she channeled her emotions toward the future. After Marie Bloomfield's suicide in 1923, Ruth confirmed her growing intimacy with Margaret Mead.[66] After Buell Quain's suicide in 1938, Ruth urged students to carry on his Amazon fieldwork and gave them portions of his legacy for the fieldtrips. She could view death as an ending that did not close off all "roads."[67]

Death was neither a "paramount affront" nor a "humiliation" in Ruth's eyes.[68] This was true in one way for self-inflicted death and in another for "natural" deaths—her father's, Stanley Benedict's, Sapir's, Franz Boas's. Of these, only Boas (like her grandparents and Auntie My) had died a timely death, by age; to none did Ruth respond with articulated horror or overwhelming grief. She viewed death as an event, an episode in life—perhaps a reward, not unwelcome although not deliberately chosen. In 1917 she said as much when she wrote about Mary Wollstonecraft, who died too young and in childbirth. She described Mary Wollstonecraft as "one who had come to her last resting bed, 'weary and content and undishonored.' So was she granted in the end the gift of sleep."[69] More horrible than death for Ruth was blank despair; at such moments life could be too dreadful to bear:

> . . . the echoing
> Of hours that are rust.[70]

In November 1948 Erik Erikson said about the woman he had seen six months earlier: "She had begun to befriend death, without in any way inviting it or being demanding of it."[71] And so she appeared during that week of September, quiet and at ease. "But the picture of Ruth lying there so utterly peaceful and serene, preparing herself for eternity —is one that I shall never forget."[72] Ruth Valentine's train arrived on Friday morning, September 17; the two women had a long afternoon conversation together. That evening Ruth Benedict died of heart failure. Her father had been born on September 17, ninety-one years before.

Margaret Mead was nearby when Ruth Benedict died, and she telephoned the news to Pasadena—to Margery and to Ruth's mother, then eighty-eight years old. "Never will I ever forget your unutterable great thoughtfulness in telephoning me as you did last night," Margery Freeman wrote to Margaret Mead on Saturday morning, September 18.[73] Writing an eight-page letter, Margery comforted herself as well as Margaret. The letter contained reassurance, shared grief, and fond appreciation for Ruth as a person and a worker. "One of the deepest satisfactions of her life has been the privilege of stirring up your interest," she told Mead, "—and then watching you carry the torch into fields where she could never go."

Many people wrote to comfort Margaret Mead, sending sympathy for her shock and loss. "The shock must be terrific for you," several said.[74] The letters often showed greater feeling for Margaret than for

Ruth, an insight into the two women's intimacy rather than into Ruth's personality. (At least this is true of letters available at Vassar College.) The letters give the impression of a woman not quite known to her friends and associates. "I met Ruth for the first time at your house," Helen Lynd wrote to Margaret Mead. "She wore a very simple deep rose dress. I'll never forget the impression that her beauty and serenity and quiet strength made on me."[75] To write thus about Ruth's peace, calm, and serenity was to recall her aloofness, her restrained and distant manner. Some people were drawn in and intrigued, others put off by what seemed an otherworldliness, a disdain in Ruth. She could be withdrawn, cooly indifferent; she could also be movingly, passionately enmeshed in the diverse patternings of lives. A few people saw Ruth as tragic. "There is tragedy here, we know. Ruth was too young to be completed and detached."[76] Fewer still saw the deeper side, an absolute lack of detachment and a full engagement with issues and events, the more energetic because inextricably intertwined with self-interpretations.

"Formal," "elegant," and "civilized" were words that came close to the truth of Ruth's personality and captured her sense of herself. Alfred Kroeber said it well, sympathetically, and officially for Columbia University. "She was in herself completely fine-grained; surcharged with feeling, yet irrevocably tolerant. Reserved as a person, restrained in expression, yet sympathetic and kindly, she was civilized utterly and without abatement, and dedicated to civilization."[77] Luther Cressman used words that are strangely similar, though written earlier and to a friend. "Ruth was, I believe genuinely, the most deeply vital, gentle, tolerant and civilized person I have ever known. Her understanding and wisdom were outstanding. Gentle and tolerant, she never compromised with cheapness or shoddy values. These are the qualities about Ruth among many others that have kept coming to my mind in the last 24 hours in its unwilling acceptance of the word of her death."[78] Erikson expressed the idea in Eriksonian terms: ". . . the near fulfillment of a life cycle which has found accord with the moral and esthetic realization of its community."[79] This, too, is to be "civilized."

Fulfillment was an important word for Ruth, one that relates to the question of whether she wished for death and welcomed the possibility of dying in autumn 1948. She was calm and serene during those days, but being calm did not mean she wished for death. In writings, under various rubrics—an ethnographic detail, a telling metaphor—Ruth wrote about wishing for death: an active choice, a "purposeful act,"[80] a leap out of ennui, boredom, despair. For her that was a coward's solution. "And my mood has nothing to do with suicide. It's a cheap way of attaining death, and death at least need not come cheap.

I shall come by it honestly, and I wish I could think that people would feel that same honor for me that I feel first at any news of death—the honor for anyone who has held out to the end."[81] Ruth valued bravery, a combination of endurance and adventurousness, and she demonstrated the courage she preached.

Always Ruth distinguished self-destruction from self-consciously noting the arrival of death. She wanted to be alert to this next experience in life. "Did I hear Ruth say this, a few years ago, or did one of you quote her as saying it? Anyway the thought was this. She said that she hoped she would not die unconscious but would *know* that it was happening (or about to happen)—because she did not want to miss any experience in life—and that was the last one."[82]

Being alert to death was an ideal, self-destruction an act of desperation. One cannot, of course, know Ruth's thoughts that September week; she was a steadfastly private woman who took to heart her dislike of confession and uncensored revelation. Certainly the recent years had been rewarding, distracting, and gratifying. Her colleagues and her "common man" recognized and adopted her distinctive anthropological perspective. By then, too, the constant fear of ennui and futility had a fair balance in a now-appreciated "power to love," in her writings, and in public acclaim for her contributions.

> She commented to me only this summer on how strange it was, that in her early days she had been completely out of step with her generation, unable to feel that instinctive joy of life that seemed well-nigh universal in youth—but that now, in late middle age, when so many of her generation had become disillusioned and cynical and bored with life—she was out of step with her generation by far outstripping most of them in her keen interest in living![83]

Ruth was alert and responsive to life in the 1940s, perhaps more than ever. In 1940 she wrote a poem to Margaret, expressing comfortable sensuality.

> Haws when they blossom in the front of summer,
> Snow-breasted to the sun, and odorous
> Of wind-dissolved honey, flaunt their bodies.
> Secret and quick, to eyes incurious.[84]

Ruth never shared Margery's cheerfulness, optimism, and contentment with life. She did, with struggle, attain a view of her life in which past patterns offered reasonable and desirable direction for the future.

In September 1948 Ruth had planned not death but a year of teaching, work, and friendships. Her handbag, near her bed when she died, its contents saved at Vassar College, showed a woman charting a distinct and demanding course. The handbag was jammed full: notes, lists, scraps of paper, in addition to usual handbag contents. Ruth had even managed to stuff into it a seven-page letter from Margery and part of an article by A. I. Hallowell, "Psycho-sexual Adjustments, Personality, and the Good Life in a Non-Literate Culture" (published in 1949). There are notes on guilt and shame—"France—(country) M [mother] for weaning shames child"—and a check for $64.80 for theater tickets. Similarly, Ruth's appointment book for the last months of her life looked ahead. She listed movies and plays, meetings, and the people who would receive her Christmas cards. "And so it was," Margery said perfectly, "that she could face the future undismayed. Her old accustomed love of death merged with her newfound love of life, and she could be utterly at peace—I am going to miss her more than I would have dreamed."

Notes

The following abbreviations are used throughout the Notes:

RFB Papers Ruth Fulton Benedict Papers, Special Collections, Vassar College Library, Poughkeepsie, N.Y.

FB Papers Franz Boas Papers, American Philosophical Society, Philadelphia, Pa.

Chapter 1

1. Ruth Benedict, Journal, December 3, 1930, RFB Papers.

2. Ruth Benedict, *The Chrysanthemum and the Sword* (Boston: Houghton Mifflin Co., 1946), p. 12.

3. Ibid.

4. In various versions of the "Mary Wollstonecraft" essay, Ruth Benedict wrote about a life without purpose, a life composed only of "episodes," without a clear chart or course. See Margaret Mead, *An Anthropologist at Work: The Writings of Ruth Benedict* (Boston: Houghton Mifflin Co., 1959), p. 500. In one draft, Ruth Benedict wrote, "And women have notoriously seen their life's navigation marked out for them in one or another of two broad, black lines traced across an inherited chart." RFB Papers, n.d.

5. Fifteen years after *An Anthropologist at Work*, Margaret Mead published another book about Ruth Benedict; in this one, too, she combined biographical accounts with a large selection of Ruth's papers and writings. *Ruth Benedict* is one of the Columbia University Press series on anthropologists. Margaret Mead, *Ruth Benedict* (New York: Columbia University Press, 1974).

6. Personal interviews.

7. *Anthropologist at Work*, p. xv.

8. Personal interviews.

9. Virginia Woolf, *Granite and Rainbow* (New York: Harcourt Brace, 1958), p. 208.

10. Benedict to Morris Opler, November 27, 1931, RFB Papers.

11. Woolf, *Granite and Rainbow*, p. 208.

12. "The Story of My Life" is an uncompleted autobiographical fragment, written by Ruth Benedict in 1935. Draft of manuscript is in RFB Papers; a version is printed in *Anthropologist at Work*, pp. 97–112.

13. J. W. N. Sullivan, *Beethoven: His Spiritual Development* (1927; New York: Vintage Books, 1960).

14. *Anthropologist at Work*, p. 324.

15. Ruth Benedict kept various drafts, notes, and outlines for her biographical studies of Mary Wollstonecraft, Margaret Fuller, and Olive Schreiner. Manuscript drafts of the "Mary Wollstonecraft" piece, and drafts of the preface to the whole book, are in RFB Papers. A version of "Mary Wollstonecraft" is printed in *Anthropologist at Work*, pp. 491–519.

16. *Anthropologist at Work*, p. 111.

17. Ibid., pp. 464–65.

18. Ibid., p. 506.

19. Ibid., p. 33.

20. Ruth Benedict, "Religion," in *General Anthropology*, ed. Franz Boas (Boston: D. C. Heath, 1938), p. 630.

21. *Anthropologist at Work*, p. 494.

22. Ibid., p. 540.

23. Ibid.

24. *The Chrysanthemum and the Sword*, p. 216.

25. *Anthropologist at Work*, p. 489.

26. Ibid., p. 102.

27. *The Chrysanthemum and the Sword*, p. 246.

28. Ruth Benedict, "Myth," in *Encyclopedia of the Social Sciences* 11–12 (1933): 173.

Chapter 2

1. In *Anthropologist at Work*, pp. 97–98.

2. Ibid., p. 98. 3. Ibid., p. 99.

4. Ibid., p. 98. 5. See RFB Papers.

6. James H. Smith, *History of Chenango and Madison Counties, N.Y. With Illustrations and Biographical Sketches* (Syracuse: D. Mason, 1880), pp. 567, 679.

7. Ibid., p. 308.

8. Ibid., p. 306.

9. *Anthropologist at Work*, p. 201.

10. Ibid., p. 98.

11. Ibid.

12. Ruth Benedict, "To My Mother," April 9, 1927, RFB Papers.

13. In the 1870s, some 0.7 percent of American women between the ages of eighteen and twenty-one attended college. Mabel Newcomer, *A Century of Higher Education for American Women* (New York: Harper & Row, 1959), p. 46.

14. *Baptist Quarterly Review* 11 (1889): 374–75.

15. *Anthropologist at Work*, p. 99.

16. Ibid., p. 98. 17. Ibid., p. 84.

18. Ibid., p. 102. 19. Ibid., p. 100.

20. Ibid., pp. 101–2.

21. Ibid., pp. 105–6.

22. Ibid., p. 100.

23. Ibid.

24. Ibid., p. 101.

25. Ibid., p. 103.

26. Ibid.

27. Brooks Hays and John E. Steely, *The Baptist Way of Life* (Englewood Cliffs, N.J.: Prentice-Hall, 1963), p. 101.

28. *Anthropologist at Work,* p. 109.

29. Maitland M. Lappin, *Baptists in the Protestant Tradition* (Toronto: Ryerson Press, 1947), p. 44.

30. *Anthropologist at Work,* p. 107.

31. Ibid., p. 109.

32. Ibid., p. 99.

33. Ibid.

34. Ibid., p. 83.

35. Ibid., p. 485.

36. Ibid., p. 105.

37. Ibid.

38. Ibid., p. 100.

39. One of the more moving accounts of a deaf child's childhood is in James P. and Thomas S. Spradley's *Deaf Like Me* (New York: Random House, 1978).

40. *Anthropologist at Work,* p. 100.

41. Spradley, *Deaf Like Me,* passim.

42. *Anthropologist at Work,* p. 100.

43. Ibid., p. 106.

44. Ibid.

45. Ibid., p. 108.

46. Ibid., p. 105.

47. Ibid.

48. Eugene Morrow Violette, *A History of Missouri* (Cape Girardeau, Mo.: Ramfire Press, 1951), pp. 451–52.

49. *Anthropologist at Work,* p. 107.

50. Ibid., p. 104.

51. Mabel Dodge Luhan, *Intimate Memoirs: Background* (New York: Harcourt, Brace & Co., 1933), p. 3.

52. Brenda K. Shelton, *Reformers in Search of Yesterday: Buffalo in the 1890s* (Albany: State University of New York Press, 1976), p. 2.

53. Luhan, *Intimate Memoirs,* p. 16.

54. Ibid., p. 3.

55. Shelton, *Reformers,* p. 101.

56. Luhan, *Intimate Memoirs,* pp. 212. 217. 222.

57. Haring to Margaret Mead, 1948, RFB Papers.

58. *Anthropologist at Work,* p. 110.

59. Ibid., pp. 110–11.

60. Ibid., p. 110.

61. Ibid., p. 111.

62. Ibid.

63. Ibid.

64. Ibid.

65. Ibid., p. 538.

66. Ibid.

Chapter 3

1. Anna C. Brackett, ed., *Woman and the Higher Education* (New York: Harper, 1893), p. 68.

2. H. N. MacCracken, *The Hickory Limb* (New York: Scribner's, 1950), p. 24.

3. Brackett, *Woman and the Higher Education,* p. 142.

4. Ibid., p. 88.

5. Agnes Rogers, *Vassar Women* (Poughkeepsie, N.Y.: Vassar College Press, 1940), p. 55.

6. Ibid., pp. 119–20.

7. Margaret Mead, *An Anthropologist at Work: The Writings of Ruth Benedict* (Boston: Houghton Mifflin Co., 1959), pp. 134–35.

8. Dale Mezzacappa, "Vassar College and the Suffrage Movement," *Vassar Quarterly* 69 (1973): 3.

9. D. Plum and G. B. Dowell, *The Magnificent Enterprise: A Chronicle of Vassar College* (Poughkeepsie, N.Y.: Vassar College, 1961), p. 43.

10. *Anthropologist at Work*, p. 107.

11. Ibid., p. 113.

12. Ruth Benedict, "Literature and Democracy," *Vassar Miscellany*, March 1909, RFB Papers.

13. *Anthropologist at Work*, p. 111.

14. Ibid.

15. Katherine G. Busbey, *Home Life in America* (London: Methuen & Co., 1910), p. 76.

16. *Anthropologist at Work*, pp. 201, 492.

17. Robert H. Bremner, *From the Depths: The Discovery of Poverty in the United States* (New York: New York University Press, 1956).

18. Brenda K. Shelton, *Reformers in Search of Yesterday: Buffalo in the 1890s* (Albany: State University of New York Press, 1976), p. 9.

19. Ibid., p. 10.

20. Ibid., p. 6.

21. John F. Barry and Robert Elmes, *Buffalo's Text Book* (Buffalo: Robert W. Elmes, 1924).

22. *Anthropologist at Work*, p. 100.

23. Ruth Benedict, typewritten manuscript of story, n.d., RFB Papers.

24. New York State, *Annual Report of the New York State Board of Charities* (Albany, 1911), p. 701.

25. *Anthropologist at Work*, p. 519.

26. Ibid., p. 84.

27. Carey McWilliams, *Southern California Country: An Island on the Land* (New York: Duell, Sloan & Pearce, 1946), p. 127.

28. Margery Freeman to Mead, September 18, 1948, RFB Papers.

29. McWilliams, *Southern California Country*, p. 205.

30. *Anthropologist at Work*, p. 161.

31. Ibid., p. 207.

32. Ibid., p. 217.

33. Ibid., p. 150.

34. McWilliams, *Southern California Country*, p. 129.

35. *Anthropologist at Work*, p. 121.

36. To Ruth Benedict, "Dear Friends of Miss Orton and Former Students in Her School," April 10, 1934, RFB Papers.

37. *Anthropologist at Work*, p. 161.

38. Ibid., p. 121.

39. Ibid., p. 485.

40. Ibid., p. 102.

41. Ibid., p. 119.

42. Ibid., pp. 118–19.

43. Ibid., p. 119.

44. Ibid.

45. Ibid.

46. Ibid., p. 122.
47. Ibid., p. 120.
48. Ibid.
49. Ibid., pp. 120–21.
50. Ibid., p. 122.
51. Ibid., pp. 121–22.
52. Ibid., p. 123.
53. Ibid., p. 121.
54. Ibid., p. 123.
55. Ruth Benedict, "The Woman-Christ," n.d., RFB Papers.
56. *Anthropologist at Work*, p. 123.
57. Ibid., p. 127.
58. Ibid., p. 124.
59. Ibid., p. 122.
60. Ibid., p. 127.
61. Ibid.
62. Ibid., p. 128.
63. Ibid.
64. Ibid.
65. Ibid., p. 539.
66. Ibid., p. 537.
67. Ibid., pp. 541, 537.
68. Ibid., p. 541.
69. Ruth Benedict, "To My Mother," April 9, 1927, RFB Papers.
70. *Anthropologist at Work*, p. 129.
71. Ibid., p. 126.
72. Ibid., p. 541.
73. Ibid., p. 540.
74. Ruth Benedict, "Awakening," n.d., RFB Papers.
75. *Anthropologist at Work*, p. 129.
76. Ibid., pp. 129–30.

Chapter 4

1. Margaret Mead, *An Anthropologist at Work: The Writings of Ruth Benedict* (Boston: Houghton Mifflin Co., 1959), p. 131.
2. Ibid.
3. Ibid., p. 477.
4. Ibid., p. 64.
5. Ibid., p. 537.
6. Ibid., p. 133 (November 1915).
7. Ibid., p. 121.
8. Ibid., p. 133.
9. Ibid., p. 132.
10. Ibid.
11. See RFB Papers.
12. *Anthropologist at Work*, p. 126.
13. Ibid.
14. Ibid., p. 133.
15. Ibid.
16. Ibid., p. 137.
17. Ibid., p. 484.
18. Ruth Benedict, Journal, n.d., RFB Papers.
19. *Anthropologist at Work*, p. 135.
20. Ibid., p. 130.
21. Ibid., p. 149.
22. Ruth Benedict, Journal, July 26, 1930, RFB Papers.
23. Ruth Benedict, Journal, n.d., RFB Papers.
24. Ibid.
25. Ruth Benedict, Journal, July 26, 1930, RFB Papers.
26. *Anthropologist at Work*, p. 136.
27. Personal interview.
28. Personal interviews.
29. *Anthropologist at Work*, p. 131.
30. Ruth Benedict, Journal, December 3, 1930, RFB Papers.

31. *Anthropologist at Work,* p. 143.

32. Ibid., p. 139.

33. Ibid., p. 488.

34. Ruth Benedict, Journal, n.d., RFB Papers.

35. Personal interview.

36. *Anthropologist at Work,* p. 138.

37. Ruth Benedict, Journal, n.d., RFB Papers.

38. *Anthropologist at Work,* p. 136.

39. Ibid., p. 133.

40. See George Santayana, *The Life of Reason* (New York: Scribner's Sons, 1905), p. 41.

41. *Anthropologist at Work,* p. 488.

42. Ruth Benedict, Journal, n.d., RFB Papers.

43. Ibid., July 26, 1930.

44. Ibid.

45. Ibid.

46. *Anthropologist at Work,* p. 136.

47. Ibid., p. 70.

49. Ibid., p. 136.

48. Ibid., p. 140.

50. Ibid., p. 147.

51. Ibid., p. 141.

52. Ruth Benedict, Journal, n.d., RFB Papers.

53. *Anthropologist at Work,* p. 141.

54. Ibid., p. 136.

55. Ibid., p. 142.

56. Ibid., pp. 138–39.

57. Ibid., p. 479.

58. Ibid., p. 139.

59. Ibid., p. 132.

60. Draft A of "Mary Wollstonecraft," RFB Papers.

61. *Anthropologist at Work,* p. 494.

62. Ibid., p. 492.

63. Ibid., p. 142.

64. Ibid., p. 141.

65. Benedict to Houghton Mifflin Co., 1917, RFB Papers.

66. Janet M. Todd, "The Biographies of Mary Wollstonecraft," *Signs* I (3) (1976): 725.

67. *Anthropologist at Work,* p. 519.

68. Draft of "Mary Wollstonecraft," n.d., RFB Papers.

69. *Anthropologist at Work,* p. 519.

70. Draft of "preface" to biographical essays, n.d., RFB Papers.

71. Draft A of "Mary Wollstonecraft," RFB Papers.

72. Ibid., Draft B.

74. Ibid., Draft B.

73. Ibid., Draft C.

75. Ibid.

76. Ibid., Draft C.

77. *Anthropologist at Work,* p. 491.

78. Ibid., pp. 513–14.

79. Draft of "preface" to biographical essays, n.d., RFB Papers.

80. *Anthropologist at Work,* p. 519.

81. Ibid.

Chapter 5

1. Margaret Mead, *An Anthropologist at Work: The Writings of Ruth Benedict* (Boston: Houghton Mifflin Co., 1959), p. 135.

2. Ibid., p. 501

3. Ibid., p. 142.

4. Speech to the American Association of University Women, June 1946, RFB Papers.

5. *New School Bulletin 1919*, p. 5.

6. Ibid., p. 7.

7. Ibid., pp. 6, 7.

8. Ibid., p. 14.

9. Ruth Benedict, Draft of obituary for Alexander A. Goldenweiser, 1940, RFB Papers.

10. *Anthropologist at Work*, p. 179.

11. Ibid., pp. 61–62.

12. Ibid., p. 67.

13. Ruth Benedict, review of *Pueblo Indian Religion* by Elsie Clews Parsons, *Review of Religion* 4 (1940): 438.

14. Nancy O. Lurie, "Women in Early American Anthropology," in *Pioneers of American Anthropology*, ed. June Helm (Seattle: University of Washington Press, 1966), pp. 29–81.

15. Ibid.

16. L. Spier, "Elsie Clews Parsons," *American Anthropologist* 45 (1943): 244.

17. Alfred L. Kroeber, "Elsie Clews Parsons," *American Anthropologist* 45 (1943): 255.

18. Ibid., p. 252.

19. Elsie Clews Parsons, *The Family* (New York: G. P. Putnam, 1906), preface.

20. Elsie Clews Parsons, *The Old-Fashioned Woman: Primitive Fancies About Sex* (New York: G. P. Putnam, 1913), p. 49.

21. Ibid., p. 24.

22. *Anthropologist at Work*, p. 146.

23. Ibid., p. 67.

24. Ibid., p. 476.

25. Ruth Benedict, "Monk of Ariège," 1928, RFB Papers.

26. *Anthropologist at Work*, p. 148.

27. Ibid., p. 145.

28. Ibid.

29. Ibid.

30. Ibid., p. 146.

31. Alexander A. Goldenweiser, *History, Psychology, and Culture* (1933; Magnolia, Mass.: Peter Smith, 1968), pp. 420–21. The article first appeared in *The Nation*, 1925.

32. *Anthropologist at Work*, p. 58.

33. Ibid., p. 120.

34. G. W. Stocking, *Race, Culture, and Evolution: Essays in the History of Anthropology* (New York: The Free Press, 1968), p. 273.

35. Adelin Linton and Charles Wagley, *Ralph Linton* (New York: Columbia University Press, 1971), p. 14.

36. Franz Boas, "Anthropology: A Lecture Delivered at Columbia Uni-

versity in the Series on Science, Philosophy, and Art, December 18, 1907," in *The Shaping of American Anthropology,* ed. George W. Stocking (New York: Basic Books, 1974), pp. 280–81.

37. *Anthropologist at Work,* p. 64.

38. Ibid., p. 61.   39. Ibid., p. 63.

40. Ibid., p. 57.   41. Ibid., p. 61.

42. Ruth Benedict, misc. notes, n.d., RFB Papers.

43. *Anthropologist at Work,* p. 63.

44. Ibid.

45. Franz Boas, "Anthropological Instruction in Columbia University," letter to N. M. Butler, November 15, 1902, in *The Shaping of American Anthropology,* pp. 290–93. In summarizing courses to be given at Columbia, Boas did not then stress the importance of "methods."

46. *Anthropologist at Work,* p. 60.

47. A. L. Kroeber, "Franz Boas: The Man," in *American Anthropological Association Memoir* 61 (1943): 22.

48. See, e.g., Stanley Benedict to F. P. Rous, October 17, 1929; V. C. Myers to Rous, April 22, 1930, F. P. Rous Papers (for the Society of Experimental Biology and Medicine), American Philosophical Society, Philadelphia, Pa.

49. See letters from Boas to Benedict and from Benedict to Boas, 1920s and 1930s, FB Papers.

50. *Anthropologist at Work,* p. 100.

51. Ibid., p. 103.

52. Boas usually dismissed inquiries about his health and well-being, and Ruth often took the occasion of his birthday to voice her concern and her affections; e.g., July 7, 1928, FB Papers.

53. *Anthropologist at Work,* pp. 500–501.

54. Ibid., p. 151.

55. Ruth Benedict, "The Vision in Plains Culture," *American Anthropologist* 24 (1922): 1–23.

56. Ruth Benedict, "Franz Boas as an Ethnologist," in *American Anthropological Association Memoir* 61 (1943): 33.

57. *Anthropologist at Work,* p. 59.

58. Ruth Benedict, "The Concept of the Guardian Spirit in North America" (Ph.D. diss., Columbia University, 1923). Published in *Memoirs of the American Anthropological Association* 29 (1923): 1–97.

59. Ibid., p. 84.

60. *Anthropologist at Work,* p. 67.

61. Kroeber, "Franz Boas: The Man," p. 14.

62. Ibid.

63. *Anthropologist at Work,* p. 67.

64. Ibid.   65. Ibid.

66. Ibid.   67. Ibid., p. 66.

68. Ibid.

69. Ruth Benedict, Journal, n.d., RFB Papers.

70. *Anthropologist at Work,* p. 151.

71. Ibid., p. 140.

72. Ruth Benedict, "Monk of Ariège," 1928, RFB Papers.

73. *Anthropologist at Work,* p. 144.

74. Ibid., p. 49.
75. Sapir reported his move to Boas, June 26, 1925, FB Papers.
76. *Anthropologist at Work*, p. 181.
77. E.g., Sapir to Boas, September and October, 1920, FB Papers.
78. *Anthropologist at Work*, p. 180.
79. Ibid., p. 132. 80. Ibid., p. 68.
81. Ibid. 82. Ibid., p. 6.
83. Ibid., p. 71. 84. Ibid., p. 87.
85. Ibid., p. 94. 86. Ibid., p. 143.
87. Ibid. 88. Ibid., p. 56.
89. Ibid., p. 53. 90. Ibid., p. 58.
91. Ibid., p. 141. 92. Ibid., p. 133.
93. Ibid., pp. 508–9. 94. Ibid., pp. 517–18.
95. Ibid., p. 508. 96. Ibid., p. 69.
97. Ibid., p. 159. 98. Ibid.
99. Ibid., p. 69.
100. Ruth Benedict, Journal, March 22, 1930, RFB Papers.
101. *Anthropologist at Work*, p. 161.
102. Ibid., p. 160. 103. Ibid., p. 148.
104. Ibid., p. 149. 105. Ibid.
106. Ibid., p. 59. 107. Ibid., pp. 70–71.
108. Ibid., p. 71. 109. Ibid., p. 50.
110. Sapir to Lowie, March 1925, Sapir-Lowie Letters, Library of the Museum of the University of Pennsylvania, Philadelphia, Pa.
111. *Anthropologist at Work*, p. 487.
112. Ibid., p. 164. 113. Ibid., p. 88.
114. Ibid., p. 484. 115. Ibid., p. 182.
116. Ibid., p. 183. 117. Ibid., p. 74.
118. Ibid., pp. 184–85. 119. Ibid., p. 185.
120. Ibid., p. 182.
121. Sapir to Lowie, March 1926, Sapir-Lowie Letters.
122. *Anthropologist at Work*, p. 181.
123. Ruth Benedict, untitled unpublished poem, March 25, 1919, RFB Papers.
124. *Anthropologist at Work*, p. 6.
125. Ibid., p. 169. 126. Ibid., p. 187.
127. Ibid., p. 180. 128. Ibid., p. 181.
129. Ibid., p. 94. 130. Ibid., p. 179.
131. Ibid., p. 183. 132. Ibid., p. 166.
133. Ibid., p. 185. 134. Ibid., pp. 166–67.
135. Ibid., p. 163. 136. Ibid., p. 162.
137. Edward Sapir, *Language* (New York: Harcourt, Brace & World, 1921), p. 182; Ruth Benedict, *Patterns of Culture* (Boston: Houghton Mifflin Co., 1934), chap. 1.
138. *Anthropologist at Work*, p. 171.
139. Ibid., p. 163. 140. Ibid., p. 487.
141. Ibid., p. 483. 142. Ibid., p. 180.
143. E.g., ibid., p. 175.
144. Harriet Monroe offered "women's poetry" issues of her journal; see *Poetry*, 1920s, passim.

145. *Anthropologist at Work*, p. 186.

146. Horace Gregory, *A History of American Poetry 1900–1940* (New York: Gordian Press, 1969), p. 68.

147. *Anthropologist at Work*, pp. 163, 175.

148. Ibid., p. 479.

149. Jeffers to Benedict, January 13, 1929, RFB Papers.

150. *Anthropologist at Work*, pp. 163, 165.

151. Ibid., p. 482.   152. Ibid., pp. 182–83.

153. Ibid., p. 172.   154. Ibid., p. 92.

155. Ibid., p. 193.

156. Edward Sapir, "Observations on the Sex Problem in America," *American Journal of Psychiatry* 8 (1928): 519–34.

157. *Anthropologist at Work*, p. 195 (April 1929).

158. Ibid., p. 475.

159. Ibid., p. 94.

Chapter 6

1. Margaret Mead, *Blackberry Winter* (New York: William Morrow & Co., 1972), pp. 111–12.

2. Ibid., pp. 112–13.   3. Ibid., p. 114.

4. Ibid., pp. 2–3.   5. Ibid., pp. 19–20.

6. Ibid., p. 164.

7. Margaret Mead, *An Anthropologist at Work: The Writings of Ruth Benedict* (Boston: Houghton Mifflin Co., 1959), p. 59.

8. Ibid., p. 68.

9. Ruth Benedict, "Tribute to Dr. Margaret Mead," *The Eleusis of Chi Omega* 42 (1940): 390.

10. *Anthropologist at Work*, p. 57.

11. Mead, *Blackberry Winter*, p. 113.

12. Personal interview.

13. *Anthropologist at Work*, p. 286.

14. Ibid., p. 92.

15. Ibid., p. 88.

16. Ibid., p. 486.

17. "Misericordia," in *Poetry* 35 (1930): 253.

18. *Anthropologist at Work*, p. 65.

19. Ibid.

20. Mead, *Blackberry Winter*, p. 115.

21. *Anthropologist at Work*, pp. 484–85.

22. Personal interviews.

23. See letters from Boas to Benedict and to Sapir, and letters from Benedict to Boas, 1925, FB Papers. Several of these, and related letters, are also in RFB Papers.

24. Reported by Boas to Benedict, July 16, 1925, FB Papers.

25. Ruth Benedict, engagement books, RFB Papers.

26. Benedict to Boas, June 1925, FB Papers.

27. Ibid.

28. Mead, *Blackberry Winter*, p. 124.

29. *Anthropologist at Work*, p. 491.

30. Mead, *Blackberry Winter*, p. 61.

31. *Anthropologist at Work*, p. 141.

32. Ibid., p. 301.

33. Ibid., p. 294.

34. Especially on the fieldtrips she made during the 1920s, Margaret Mead wrote long letters to Franz Boas, full of details about her work, questions about anthropological approaches, and general remarks about her state of being. See Mead to Boas and Boas to Mead, 1925, 1926, 1928, FB Papers.

35. *Anthropologist at Work*, p. 301.

36. Most of the letters from Ruth Benedict to Mead are reprinted in *Anthropologist at Work*, pp. 284–338. See also RFB Papers.

37. Mead, *Blackberry Winter*, p. 132.

38. *Anthropologist at Work*, p. 72.

39. Ibid., p. 67.

40. Ibid.

41. Ibid., p. 73.

42. Ibid., p. 74.

43. Ibid., p. 76.

44. Personal interview.

45. Mead, *Blackberry Winter*, p. 163.

46. *Anthropologist at Work*, p. 140.

47. Ibid., p. 496.

48. Ruth Benedict, Journal, July 26, 1930, RFB Papers.

49. *Anthropologist at Work*, p. 447.

50. Ruth Benedict, "To My Mother," April 9, 1927, RFB Papers.

51. Ruth Benedict, Journal, n.d., RFB Papers.

52. *Anthropologist at Work*, p. 491.

53. Ruth Benedict, "For Faithfulness," n.d., RFB Papers.

54. Ruth Benedict, "The Moon New Seen," n.d., RFB Papers.

55. Ruth Benedict, unpublished poem, handwritten on a valentine, n.d., RFB Papers.

56. *Anthropologist at Work*, p. 129.

57. Mead, *Blackberry Winter*, p. 113.

58. *Anthropologist at Work*, p. 73.

59. Ibid., p. 74.

60. Ibid.

61. Personal interviews.

62. Ibid.

63. Mead, *Blackberry Winter*, p. 114.

64. Personal interviews.

65. *Anthropologist at Work*, p. 135.

66. Ibid., p. 74.

67. Ibid., p. 76.

68. Ibid.

69. Personal interviews.

70. Benedict to Boas, July 12, 1929, FB Papers.

71. Benedict to Boas, September 5, 1930, FB Papers.

72. Benedict to Boas, August 24, 1937, FB Papers.

73. Personal interviews.

74. (Mary) Jean States to Benedict, June 27, 1930, RFB Papers.

75. Lucetta Harkness to Benedict, May 26, 1930, RFB Papers.

76. Personal interviews.

77. William Thomas, ed., *Yearbook of Anthropology* (New York: Wenner-Gren Foundation, 1955), pp. 703–4.

78. Benedict to Jesse Nusbaum (Santa Fe Laboratory), May 22, 1931, RFB Papers.

79. Personal interviews.

80. Benedict to "Mrs. Freeman," July 6, 1936, RFB Papers.

81. Personal interviews.

82. Benedict to Boas, June 31, 1931, FB Papers.

83. Personal interviews.

84. Reichard to Boas, November 26, 1922, FB Papers.

85. Personal interview.

86. *Ruth Fulton Benedict: A Memorial* (New York: The Viking Fund, 1949), p. 22.

87. Ruth Benedict to Boas, September 28, 1930, FB Papers.

88. Sullivan to Benedict, May 26, 1933, RFB Papers.

89. *Anthropologist at Work*, p. 133.

90. Personal interviews.

91. Benedict to Boas, August 24, 1931, FB Papers.

92. Benedict to Boas, August 1, 1932, FB Papers.

93. Personal interviews.

94. Clyde Kluckhohn, in *Ruth Fulton Benedict: A Memorial*, p. 18.

95. *Anthropologist at Work*, p. 66.

96. Bunzel to Boas, July 28, 1927, FB Papers.

97. Sapir to Boas, May 12, 1927, FB Papers.

98. Reichard to Boas, March 22, 1927, FB Papers.

99. Boas to Social Science Research Council, December 13, 1926, RFB Papers.

100. Board on National Research Fellowships in the Biological Sciences to Benedict, April 29, 1924, RFB Papers.

101. Social Science Research Council to Benedict, April 7, 1926; American Council of Learned Societies to Benedict, April 23, 1926, RFB Papers.

102. Sapir to Benedict, in *Anthropologist at Work*, p. 183.

103. White to Benedict, January 7, 1927 (or 1928?), RFB Papers.

104. Personal interviews.

105. *Anthropologist at Work*, p. 65.

106. Ruth Benedict, "Franz Boas as an Ethnologist," *American Anthropological Association Memoir* 61 (1943): 28.

107. *Anthropologist at Work*, p. 65.

108. Ibid.

109. Ibid., p. 342.

110. Ruth Benedict, "A Brief Sketch of Serrano Culture," *American Anthropologist* 26 (1924): 380–81.

111. Ibid., pp. 366–92.

112. *Anthropologist at Work*, p. 62.

113. Ibid., p. 39.

114. Ibid., p. 399.

115. Ibid., p. 400.

116. Mead, "Apprenticeship Under Boas," in *The Anthropology of Franz Boas*, ed. Walter Goldschmidt (American Anthropological Association Memoir 89, 1959), p. 34.

117. Bunzel to Boas, August 6, 1924, FB Papers.

118. RFB Papers.

119. Ruth Benedict, *Zuñi Mythology*, 2 vols., Columbia University Contributions to Anthropology 21 (New York: Columbia University Press, 1935).

120. *Anthropologist at Work,* p. 287.

121. Ibid., p. 485.

122. Ruth Benedict, untitled unpublished poem, 1928, RFB Papers.

123. *Anthropologist at Work,* p. 166.

124. Ibid., p. 178.

125. In her earliest fieldtrip letters Ruth Bunzel showed a point of view different from Ruth Benedict's, and she continued to be more sharply aware of conflicts and difficulties in the Pueblos than Benedict was; see, e.g., Bunzel to Boas, August 6, 1924, and August 14, 1924, FB Papers.

126. E.g., Bunzel to Boas, September 1927, FB Papers.

127. *Anthropologist at Work,* p. 291.

128. Ibid., p. 293.

129. Ibid., p. 291.

130. Ibid., p. 301.

131. Ibid., pp. 291–92.

132. Ibid., p. 299.

133. Ibid., p. 300.

134. Ibid.

135. Ibid., p. 292.

136. Ibid.

137. Bunzel to Boas, July 5, 1926, FB Papers.

138. Personal interview.

139. Elsie Clews Parsons, *Pueblo Indian Religion* (Chicago: University of Chicago Press, 1939), 1:65.

140. *Anthropologist at Work,* p. 300.

141. Benedict to Boas, 1932, FB Papers.

142. *Anthropologist at Work,* p. 301.

143. Ibid.

144. Ibid., p. 303.

145. Ibid., pp. 295, 298.

146. Ibid., p. 302.

147. Ruth Bunzel's and Ruth Benedict's fieldwork letters to Boas are in FB Papers (1924, 1925, 1928, and passim). Both women wrote to him from the field on every trip.

148. *Anthropologist at Work,* pp. 296–97.

149. Ibid., p. 298.

150. Ibid., pp. 296, 299.

151. Ibid., p. 295.

152. Benedict to Boas, August 17, 1927, FB Papers.

153. Ibid.

154. Personal interview.

155. Ibid.

156. Benedict to Opler, November 27, 1931, RFB Papers.

157. Personal interviews.

158. Benedict to Boas, June 28, 1931, FB Papers.

159. Ibid., June 30, 1931.

160. Ibid., August 24, 1931.

161. Ibid.

162. Benedict to Boas, July 12, 1939, FB Papers.

163. See, e.g., Boas to Benedict, July 28, 1931; August 24, 1931; December 26, 1931, FB Papers. Also, Benedict to Jesse Nusbaum, July 29, 1931; Nusbaum to Benedict, August 1, 1931; Benedict to Nusbaum, November 1931; Harry Carr to Benedict, February 27, 1933; and Benedict to Carr, March 9, 1933 (referring to Schmerler as a "brilliant graduate student"); and other letters in RFB Papers.

164. Thomas, *Yearbook of Anthropology,* p. 703.

165. Franz Boas, *Race, Language, and Culture* (New York: The Free Press, 1940), passim.

166. Benedict to Boas, July 28, 1931, FB Papers.

167. Benedict, engagement book, July 25, 1931, RFB Papers.

168. Letters concerning the Schmerler incident are in RFB Papers, 1931–33.

169. See Ruth Benedict's Preface to Quain's posthumously published *Fijian Village* (Chicago: University of Chicago Press, 1948).

170. See RFB Papers and FB Papers, 1939, for letters concerning the Quain matter.

171. Ruth Benedict, Journal, e.g., March 22, 1930, and July 26, 1930, RFB Papers.

Chapter 7

1. Margaret Mead, *An Anthropologist at Work: The Writings of Ruth Benedict* (Boston: Houghton Mifflin Co., 1959), p. 311.

2. Ibid., p. 139. 3. Ibid., p. 136.

4. Ibid., p. 528. 5. Ibid., p. 136.

6. Benedict to Boas, August 17, 1927, FB Papers.

7. *Anthropologist at Work*, p. 152.

8. Ibid., p. 93.

9. Ibid., pp. 480, 153.

10. Ruth Benedict, Journal, n.d., RFB Papers.

11. Ruth Benedict, "Gray Pavements," n.d., RFB Papers.

12. *Anthropologist at Work*, p. 319.

13. Ibid., p. 347.

14. Boas to Kroeber, March 9, 1931, FB Papers.

15. Personal interview.

16. See Theodora Kroeber, *Alfred L. Kroeber* (Berkeley: University of California Press, 1970).

17. Ruth Benedict, *Tales of the Cochiti Indians,* Bureau of American Ethnology Bulletin 98 (Washington, D.C.: Smithsonian Institution, 1931).

18. *Anthropologist at Work*, p. 319.

19. Ruth Benedict, Journal, n.d., RFB Papers.

20. Ibid., June 15, 1934.

21. *Anthropologist at Work*, p. 3.

22. See Esther Goldfrank, *Notes on an Undirected Life* (New York: Queens College, 1978).

23. Ruth Benedict, engagement book, 1931, RFB Papers.

24. Ruth Benedict, Journal, n.d., RFB Papers.

25. *Anthropologist at Work*, p. 496.

26. Ibid.

27. Ruth Benedict, Journal, n.d., RFB Papers.

28. Ibid.

29. Ruth Benedict, Journal, June 15, 1934, RFB Papers.

30. *Anthropologist at Work*, p. 497.

31. E.g., Benedict to Paul Frank, July 19, 1933, response to an inquiry about Nat, RFB Papers.

32. Boas to Benedict, August–September 1936, RFB Papers.

33. Ruth Benedict, engagement book, 1936, RFB Papers.

34. Copy of Ruth Benedict's will, July 16, 1937, RFB Papers.

35. *Anthropologist at Work*, p. 319.

36. *Patterns of Culture* (Boston: Houghton Mifflin Co., 1934), p. 58.

37. Ruth Benedict, "Parlor Car—Santa Fe," n.d., RFB Papers.

38. *Anthropologist at Work*, p. 206.

39. *Patterns of Culture*, p. 80.

40. *Anthropologist at Work*, p. 130.

41. Ibid., p. 548.   42. Ibid., p. 138.

43. Ibid.   44. Ibid.

45. Ruth Benedict, "Religion," in *General Anthropology*, ed. Franz Boas (Boston: D. C. Heath, 1938), p. 630.

46. *Anthropologist at Work*, p. 318.

47. Ibid., p. 311. Fortune was in the Admiralty Islands with Margaret Mead.

48. Ibid., p. 312.

49. Ibid., p. 321 (August 1932).

50. Ronald P. Rohner, "Franz Boas: Ethnographer on the Northwest Coast," in *Pioneers of American Anthropology*, ed. June Helm (Seattle: University of Washington, 1966), passim.

51. See Leslie White (leader in the attack), "The Ethnography and Ethnology of Franz Boas," Texas Memorial Museum Bulletin 6, 1963; and idem, *The Social Organization of Ethnological Theory*, Rice University Studies 52 (Houston: Rice University, 1966).

52. *Patterns of Culture*, pp. 173–74.

53. *Anthropologist at Work*, p. 324.

54. Ibid., p. 321.   55. Ibid.

56. Ibid., p. 338.   57. Ibid., p. 312.

58. *Patterns of Culture*, p. 7.

59. *Anthropologist at Work*, p. 322.

60. Ruth Benedict, "Psychological Types in the Cultures of the Southwest," in *Proceedings of the Twenty-Third International Congress of Americanists*, 1930, pp. 572–81; and "Configurations of Culture in North America," *American Anthropologist* 34 (1932): 1–27.

61. Ruth Benedict, "The Science of Custom," *Century* 117 (1929): 641–49.

62. *Anthropologist at Work*, p. 322.

63. *Patterns of Culture*, p. 55.

64. *Anthropologist at Work*, p. 322.

65. *Patterns of Culture*, p. 55.

66. Ibid., p. 56.

67. Ruth Benedict, publicity notes written for Houghton Mifflin Co., 1934, RFB Papers.

68. *Patterns of Culture*, p. 17.

69. Personal interviews.

70. Benedict, "Psychological Types," p. 527.

71. Benedict, "Configurations of Culture," p. 4.

72. See criticism of A. R. Radcliffe-Brown in *Anthropologist at Work*, p. 326.

73. *Patterns of Culture*, p. 47.   74. Ibid., p. 24.

75. Ibid., p. 46.   76. Ibid., p. 48.

77. *Anthropologist at Work*, p. 177.

78. Kurt Koffka, *The Growth of the Mind: An Introduction to Child Psychology*, trans. Robert M. Ogden (New York: Harcourt, Brace & Co., 1924).

79. "Culture, Genuine and Spurious" appeared in various forms, in *The Dial* (1919), *The Dalhousie Review* (1922), and the *American Journal of Sociology* (1924). Quotations in my text come from the article as reprinted in *Culture, Language, and Personality*, ed. David Mandelbaum (Berkeley: University of California Press, 1970).

80. First published in the *Journal of Abnormal and Social Psychology* (1932). Reprinted in Mandelbaum, *Culture, Language, and Personality*.

81. Mandelbaum, *Culture, Language, and Personality*, p. 104.

82. See George Santayana, *Character and Opinion in the United States* (New York: Scribner's, 1921); and idem, *Three Philosophical Poets: Lucretius Dante, and Goethe* (Cambridge: Harvard University Press, 1947), both delivered as lectures at Columbia in 1910.

83. See sources in *Patterns of Culture;* these demonstrate Ruth Benedict's familiarity with studies of the self, and constraints on the self, from philosophy, history, and other disciplines.

84. Ibid., p. 99.

85. Reo Fortune, *The Sorcerers of Dobu* (New York: Dutton, 1932), p. 176.

86. *Patterns of Culture*, p. 200.

87. Benedict, "Psychological Types."

88. Elsie Clews Parsons, *Pueblo Indian Religion* (Chicago: University of Chicago, 1939), 1:63–66.

89. *Patterns of Culture*, p. 252.

90. Ruth Benedict, "Animism," in *Encyclopedia of the Social Sciences* 2 (1930): 65–67. See also Ruth Benedict, review of *L'Âme Primitive* by Levy-Bruhl, *Journal of Philosophy* 25 (1928): 717–19.

91. *Patterns of Culture*, p. 109.   92. Ibid., pp. 62–63.

93. Ibid., p. 160.   94. Ibid., p. 216.

95. Ibid., p. 109.   96. Ibid., p. 117.

97. See, e.g., Li An-che, "Zuni: Some Observations and Queries," *American Anthropologist* 39 (1937): 62–76; Florence H. Ellis, "Patterns of Aggression and the War Cult in Southwestern Pueblos," *Southwestern Journal of Anthropology* 7 (1951): 177–201; E. A. Hoebel, "Major Contributions of Southwestern Studies to Anthropological Theory," *American Anthropologist* 56 (1954): 720–27; and Esther Goldfrank, "Socialization, Personality, and the Structure of Pueblo Society," *American Anthropologist* 47 (1945): 516–37.

98. *Patterns of Culture*, pp. 172, 220.

99. Ibid., p. 118.   100. Ibid., p. 113.

101. Ibid., p. 258.   102. Ibid., p. 259.

103. In *Journal of General Psychology* 10 (1934): 59–82.

104. *Patterns of Culture*, p. 253.

105. Ibid., p. 251.   106. Ibid., p. 265.

107. Ibid., p. 262.   108. Ibid., p. 265.

109. Ibid.

110. *Anthropologist at Work*, p. 149.

111. Virginia Woolf, *The Waves* (New York: Harcourt, Brace & Co., 1931), p. 257.

112. *Patterns of Culture,* p. 167.

113. *Anthropologist at Work,* p. 123.

114. Franz Boas, *General Anthropology* (Boston: D. C. Heath, 1938), pp. 681, 685.

115. Ruth Benedict, description sent to Houghton Mifflin Co., 1934, RFB Papers.

116. *Patterns of Culture,* pp. 272, 276.

117. Ibid., pp. 78–79.

118. Ruth Benedict, Journal, December 3, 1930, RFB Papers.

119. See the sources cited in *Patterns of Culture.*

120. I am not minimizing her extraction of appealing qualities. Nevertheless, Ruth's choice of emphases in Pueblo life on the basis of pedagogical principle and a deliberate plan was not equivalent to imposing personal values on the data. See John W. Bennett, "The Interpretation of Pueblo Culture," *Southwest Journal of Anthropology* 2 (1946): 361–74. Similar approaches have recently been brought forward as reasonable and ethically just ethnographic procedure.

121. *Anthropologist at Work,* p. 154.

122. Ibid., p. 321.

123. *Patterns of Culture,* p. 78.

124. Ibid., p. 253.

125. Benedict to Houghton Mifflin Co., 1934, RFB Papers.

126. Benedict to Ferris Greenslet, 1933–34, RFB Papers.

127. *Anthropologist at Work,* p. 14.

128. Benedict to Houghton Mifflin Co., 1933, RFB Papers.

129. *Anthropologist at Work,* p. 14.

130. *Patterns of Culture,* p. 46.

131. *Anthropologist at Work,* p. 202.

132. Sapir to Lowie, June 1917, Sapir-Lowie Letters, Library of the Museum of the University of Pennsylvania, Philadelphia, Pa.

133. Ruth Benedict, Journal, December 3, 1930, RFB Papers.

134. Benedict to Ferris Greenslet, June 21, 1934, RFB Papers.

135. Benedict to Houghton Mifflin Co., December 14, 1934, RFB Papers.

136. Benedict to Mr. Linscott, June 28, 1934, RFB Papers.

137. See Margaret Mead, "Preface," in *Patterns of Culture* (Boston: Houghton Mifflin Sentry Edition, 1959).

138. Alfred L. Kroeber, review of *Patterns of Culture* by Ruth Benedict, *American Anthropologist* 37 (1935): 690.

139. See Franz Boas, "Introduction," *Patterns of Culture* (Boston: Houghton Mifflin Co., 1934), p. xiii.

140. *Patterns of Culture,* p. 278.

141. Benedict to Jones, December 14, 1934, RFB Papers.

142. *Anthropologist at Work,* pp. 154–55.

143. Ruth Benedict, Journal, June 15, 1934, RFB Papers.

144. *Time,* March 20, 1933, p. 36.

145. Ruth Benedict, Journal, July 26, 1930, RFB Papers.

146. Ibid., June 15, 1934, RFB Papers.

147. Ibid.

Chapter 8

1. Ruth Benedict, *Zuñi Mythology*, 2 vols., Columbia University Contributions to Anthropology 21 (New York: Columbia University Press, 1935), 1:xvi.

2. Ruth Benedict, *Tales of the Cochiti Indians*, Bureau of American Ethnology Bulletin 98 (Washington, D.C.: Smithsonian Institution, 1931).

3. Ibid., pp. 201–2.

4. Ibid., p. x.

5. Ruth Benedict, "A Matter for the Field Worker in Folk-Lore," *Journal of American Folk-Lore* 36 (1923): 104.

6. Franz Boas, *Race, Language, and Culture* (New York: The Free Press, 1940), p. 455 (1914 essay).

7. Ruth Benedict, misc. notes, 1930, RFB Papers.

8. Benedict to "My dear Mrs. [Julia?] Hamilton, March 19, 1934, RFB Papers.

9. E.g., Franz Boas, *General Anthropology* (Boston: D. C. Heath, 1938), p. 609.

10. Margaret Mead, *An Anthropologist at Work: The Writings of Ruth Benedict* (Boston: Houghton Mifflin Co., 1959), p. 344.

11. Ruth Benedict, Journal, n.d., RFB Papers.

12. Personal interviews.

13. See *Journal of American Folk-Lore* Correspondence, Department of Folk-Lore and Folk-Life, University of Pennsylvania, Philadelphia, Pa., 1925–40.

14. *Anthropologist at Work*, p. 401.

15. George Herzog to Melville Herskovits, November 1940, University of Pennsylvania Archives.

16. Report of 1928 meeting, Folk-Lore Society, University of Pennsylvania Archives.

17. Ruth Benedict, "Folklore," in *Encyclopedia of the Social Sciences* 6 (1931): 288.

18. Beckwith to Reichard, April 1931, University of Pennsylvania Archives.

19. W. Thomas, ed., *Yearbook of Anthropology 1955* (New York: Wenner-Gren Foundation, 1955), p. 739.

20. Ibid., p. 704.

21. Herzog to Melville Herskovits, November 1940, University of Pennsylvania Archives.

22. Herzog to Gayton, January 31, 1940; Gayton to Herzog, February 5, 1940, University of Pennsylvania Archives.

23. Herzog to Gayton, February 18, 1940, University of Pennsylvania Archives.

24. Herzog to "Pete" [A. I. Hallowell], March 3, 1940, University of Pennsylvania Archives.

25. Benedict to Herzog, February 24, 1940, University of Pennsylvania Archives.

26. Ruth Benedict, "A Matter for the Field Worker," p. 104.

27. Ibid.

28. Ibid.

29. Ibid.

30. Franz Boas, *The Mind of Primitive Man* (1911; New York: The Free Press, 1963).

31. Ruth Benedict, "Myth," in *Encyclopedia of the Social Sciences* 11 (1933): 173.

32. Ruth Benedict, misc. notes, 1924, RFB Papers.

33. *Anthropologist at Work*, p. 113.

34. Ibid.

35. *Patterns of Culture*, p. 139.

36. *Anthropologist at Work*, p. 474.

37. *Zuñi Mythology*, 1:xxi.

38. Ibid., p. xvi.

39. *Anthropologist at Work*, p. 143.

40. Ruth Benedict, "Miser's Wisdom," n.d., RFB Papers.

41. See Boas, *Race, Language, and Culture*, p. 478, and passim (1914 essay).

42. Benedict, "Myth," p. 173.

43. Ibid., pp. 170–71.

44. Ibid., p. 173.

45. Ibid., p. 171.

46. Benedict, "Folklore," p. 289.

47. Benedict, "A Matter for the Field Worker," p. 104.

48. Benedict, "Folklore," p. 289.

49. *Anthropologist at Work*, p. 54.

50. Ibid., p. 49.

51. Ibid., p. 181.

52. Ibid., p. 151.

53. Sapir to Lowie, March 1926, Sapir-Lowie Letters, Library of the Museum of the University of Pennsylvania, Philadelphia, Pa.

54. *Anthropologist at Work*, p. 305.

55. B. Malinowski, *Myth in Primitive Psychology* (New York: W. W. Norton & Co., 1926), p. 30.

56. Ibid., p. 77.

57. *Anthropologist at Work*, p. 152.

58. Ibid., p. 188.

59. Ibid., p. 548.

60. George Santayana, *The Life of Reason* (New York: Scribner's, 1905), 2:101.

61. *Anthropologist at Work*, p. 548.

62. See ibid., p. 123.

63. Friedrich Nietzsche, *The Birth of Tragedy*, trans. W. Haussmann, vol. 3 of *The Complete Works*, ed. Oscar Levy (London: T. N. Fowlis, 1910), p. 62.

64. Ibid., p. 163.

65. *Anthropologist at Work*, p. 479, from "Eucharist."

66. Ibid., p. 478.

67. Georgia O'Keeffe, *Georgia O'Keeffe* (New York: Viking Press, 1976), p. 58.

68. *Anthropologist at Work*, p. 410.

69. Ruth Benedict, "Religion," in *General Anthropology*, ed. Franz Boas (Boston: D. C. Heath, 1938), pp. 627–65.

70. Ruth Benedict, "Ritual," in *Encyclopedia of the Social Sciences* 13 (1934): 396.

71. Ruth Benedict, "Magic," in *Encyclopedia of the Social Sciences* 10 (1933): 40.

72. *Patterns of Culture*, p. 127.

73. *Anthropologist at Work*, p. 331.

74. Ibid., p. 85.　　　　　　　　　75. Ibid., p. 188.

76. "Religion," passim.　　　　　　77. Benedict, "Myth," p. 179.

78. Ibid.

79. *Anthropologist at Work*, p. 154.

80. *Patterns of Culture*, p. 67 and passim.

81. Bunzel to Boas, July 28, 1927, FB Papers.

82. *Patterns of Culture*, p. 128.

83. *Anthropologist at Work*, p. 188.

84. Ruth Benedict, e.g., "Monk of Ariège," 1928, and "untitled," 1928, RFB Papers.

85. Ruth Benedict, "Too Great Has Been the Tension of My Cloud," n.d., RFB Papers.

86. See "Discourse on Prayer" (1924) in *Anthropologist at Work*, p. 160.

87. *Anthropologist at Work*, p. 407.

88. Ruth Benedict, "For Holy Days," n.d., RFB Papers.

89. *Anthropologist at Work*, p. 194.

90. Ibid., p. 479.　　　　　　　　　91. *Patterns of Culture*, p. 79.

92. Ibid., p. 93.　　　　　　　　　　93. Ibid., p. 97.

94. *Anthropologist at Work*, p. 476.

95. Ibid., p. 494.

96. *Zuñi Mythology*, passim.

97. *Anthropologist at Work*, p. 475.

98. Ruth Benedict, "The Woman-Christ," n.d., RFB Papers.

99. Sapir to Benedict, in *Anthropologist at Work*, p. 193.

100. Ibid., p. 194.

101. Ibid., p. 195.

102. Ibid., p. 477.

103. George Santayana, *Interpretations of Poetry and Religion* (1927; New York: Harper Torchbook, 1957), p. 89.

104. Ibid., pp. v, 26–27.

105. *Anthropologist at Work*, p. 100.

106. Ibid., p. 152.

107. T. S. Eliot, "Tradition and the Individual Talent," in *The Sacred Wood* (1920; New York: Barnes & Noble, 1960), p. x.

108. *Anthropologist at Work*, p. 478.

109. Ibid.　　　　　　　　　　　　110. Ibid.

111. Ibid., p. 488.　　　　　　　　112. Ibid., p. 162.

113. Ibid., p. 488.　　　　　　　　114. Ibid., pp. 164–65.

115. Ibid., p. 482.　　　　　　　　116. Ibid., p. 481.

117. Ibid., p. 188.

118. Elsie Clews Parsons, review of *Zuñi Mythology* by Ruth Benedict, *Journal of American Folk-Lore* 50 (1937): 108.

119. *Anthropologist at Work*, p. 411.

120. Ibid.

121. Chase to Benedict, December 15, 1945, RFB Papers.

122. Benedict to Chase, January 6, 1946, RFB Papers.

123. *Anthropologist at Work*, p. 464.

124. Chase to Benedict, n.d., RFB Papers.

125. Ibid.

126. Ibid.

127. Benedict to Chase, February 3, 1946, RFB Papers.

128. See *Anthropologist at Work*, pp. 467–68, on A. C. Bradley, the Shakespeare critic.

129. *Zuñi Mythology*, 1:xxix.

130. *Anthropologist at Work*, p. 155.

131. J. W. N. Sullivan, *Beethoven: His Spiritual Development* (1927; New York: Vintage Books, 1960), p. 154.

132. *Anthropologist at Work*, p. 141.

Chapter 9

1. Ruth Benedict, *Race: Science and Politics* (New York: Modern Age, 1940).

2. Margaret Mead, *An Anthropologist at Work: The Writings of Ruth Benedict* (Boston: Houghton Mifflin Co., 1959), p. 348.

3. Butler to Benedict, October 8, 1940, RFB Papers.

4. Reichard to Boas, October 30, 1938, FB Papers.

5. Boas to Benedict, December 20, 1939, FB Papers.

6. Cressman to Marian Smith, September 18, 1948, RFB Papers.

7. Ruth Benedict, review of *The Racial Myth* by Paul Radin, *Herald Tribune*, August 12, 1934, p. 6.

8. Benedict to Boas, July 3, 1938, RFB Papers.

9. Ibid.

10. To the Columbia University Research Council, RFB Papers.

11. Benedict to Boas, August 16, 1939, RFB Papers.

12. Archibald Gulick to Benedict, November 9, 1939; and Benedict to Gulick, December 13, 1939, RFB Papers.

13. Boas to Benedict, November 17, 1939, RFB Papers.

14. *Race*, p. 133. 15. Ibid., p. 148.

16. Ibid., p. 126. 17. Ibid., p. 150.

18. Ibid., pp. 156–57. 19. Ibid., p. 157.

20. Ruth Benedict, "Child Marriage," in *Encyclopedia of the Social Sciences* 3 (1930): 395–97; Ruth Benedict, "Marital Property Rights in Bilateral Society," *American Anthropologist* 38 (1936): 368–73.

21. Ruth Benedict, "Unemployment and Society," *Social Work Today* 4 (1937): 12.

22. *Race*, p. 162.

23. E.g., *The New Republic* 104 (1941): 62.

24. Ruth Benedict and Gene Weltfish, *Races of Mankind* (New York: Public Affairs Committee, 1943).

25. *Anthropologist at Work*, p. 88.

26. Sapir to Lowie, September 1917, Sapir-Lowie Letters, Library of the Museum of the University of Pennsylvania, Philadelphia, Pa.

27. Ruth Benedict, "Edward Sapir," *American Anthropologist* 41 (1939): 465–77.

28. In 1924; *Anthropologist at Work,* p. 164.
29. Sapir to Lowie, September 1917, Sapir-Lowie Letters.
30. Edward Sapir, *Dreams and Gibes* (Boston: Badger, 1917), p. 64.
31. *Anthropologist at Work,* p. 164.

Chapter 10

1. Benedict to R. Lynd, May 29, 1936, RFB Papers.
2. Ibid.
3. Adelin Linton and Charles Wagley, *Ralph Linton* (New York: Columbia University Press, 1971), pp. 48–49.
4. Benedict to Boas, October 24, 1939 (repeated on November 5, 1939), FB Papers.
5. Linton and Wagley, *Ralph Linton,* p. 50.
6. Personal interviews.
7. Linton and Wagley, *Ralph Linton,* p. 49.
8. Personal interviews.
9. Benedict to Boas, October 24, 1939, FB Papers.
10. Reichard to Boas, October 30, 1938, FB Papers.
11. Margaret Mead, *An Anthropologist at Work: The Writings of Ruth Benedict* (Boston: Houghton Mifflin Co., 1959), p. 350.
12. Benedict to Hallowell, April 3, 1939, RFB Papers.
13. Abram Kardiner, *The Individual and His Society* (New York: Columbia University Press, 1939), p. xxiii.
14. Ruth Benedict, *Patterns of Culture* (Boston: Houghton Mifflin Co., 1934), p. 271.
15. Margaret Mead, *Blackberry Winter* (New York: William Morrow & Co., 1972), p. 61.
16. Ruth Benedict, review of *Growing Up in New Guinea* by Margaret Mead, *Herald Tribune,* September 21, 1930, p. 5.
17. Ruth Benedict, "Continuities and Discontinuities in Cultural Conditioning," *Psychiatry* 1 (1938): 161–67.
18. Quotations are from "Continuities and Discontinuities," in *Personality in Nature, Society, and Culture,* ed. Clyde Kluckhohn and Henry Murray with David Schneider (New York: Alfred Knopf, 1953), p. 525.
19. Ibid., p. 526.   20. Ibid., p. 523.
21. Ibid., p. 524.   22. Ibid., p. 531.
23. Ruth Benedict, Journal, passim, RFB Papers.
24. The Benedict–de Laguna correspondence, January–February 1940, is in RFB Papers.
25. "Synergy: Some Notes of Ruth Benedict," selected by Abraham Maslow and John J. Honigmann, *American Anthropologist* 72 (1970): 320–33.
26. See the Benedict–de Laguna correspondence, January–February 1940.
27. "Synergy," pp. 322, 323.
28. Ruth Benedict, "Pre-War Experts," *The New Republic* 107 (1942): 410.
29. "Synergy," p. 326.
30. Ibid., p. 330.

31. Ibid., p. 331.

32. Ruth Benedict, review of *Sex and Temperament in Three Primitive Societies* by Margaret Mead, *Herald Tribune*, June 2, 1935.

33. Edward Sapir, "The Discipline of Sex," *American Mercury* 16 (1929): 413.

34. Ruth Benedict, review of *The Neurotic Personality of Our Time* by Karen Horney, *Journal of Social and Abnormal Psychology* 33 (1938): 133–35.

35. Ruth Benedict, typewritten manuscript "Crime Against Nature," for speech to the New York Academy of Medicine, April 11, 1939, RFB Papers.

36. Ruth Benedict, "The Kinsey Report," *Saturday Review* 30 (1948): 34–35.

37. Benedict to Murray, July 30, 1940, RFB Papers.

38. Editorial Statement, *Psychiatry* 1 (1938): n.p.

39. Mandelbaum to Benedict, April 29, 1941, RFB Papers.

40. Ruth Benedict, "Race Problems in America," *Annals of the American Academy of Political and Social Sciences* 216 (1941): 76.

41. Ibid., p. 77.

42. Ruth Benedict, "Transmitting Our Democratic Heritage in the Schools," *American Journal of Sociology* 48 (1943): 723.

43. Ruth Benedict, "Teachers and the Hatch Act," *Frontiers of Democracy* 8 (1942): 165.

44. Lee to Benedict, January 24, 1944, RFB Papers.

45. Personal interview.

46. Ruth Benedict, biographical blurb in *American Scholar* 12 (1942): 126.

47. Ruth Benedict, Letter to the Editor, *The New Republic*, September 1, 1941, pp. 279–80.

48. *Anthropologist at Work*, pp. 374, 376, 377.

49. See Boas to Benedict, December 20, 1939, RFB Papers.

50. Unpublished manuscript, "The Natural History of War," in *Anthropologist at Work*, p. 381.

51. Ruth Benedict, Position Description (OWI), 1943, RFB Papers.

52. Taylor to Benedict, July 2, 1943, RFB Papers.

53. Williamson to Benedict, January 10, 1944, RFB Papers.

54. "Background for a Basic Plan for Burma," September 13, 1943, pp. 1, 3, RFB Papers.

55. Ibid., pp. 9, 11.

56. Ruth Benedict, "Thai Culture and Behavior" (1944), Data Paper 4, Southeast Asia Program, Cornell University, Ithaca, N.Y., 1952, pp. 37, 44.

57. Ibid., p. ii.

58. Ibid., pp. 28, 34.

59. Ibid., p. 31.

60. Ruth Benedict, *Rumanian Culture and Behavior*, Occasional Papers in Anthropology 1 (1943; Fort Collins, Colo.: Colorado State University, 1972).

61. Leonard Doob, "The Utilization of Social Scientists in the Overseas Branch of the Office of War Information," *American Political Science Review* 41 (1947): 649–67.

62. See Mead, *Anthropologist at Work*, p. 355.

63. Boas to Benedict, December 20, 1939, RFB Papers.

64. Ruth Benedict, "Professor Franz Boas, President of the American Association for the Advancement of Science," *Scientific Monthly* 32 (1931): 279–80.

65. Ruth Benedict, "Franz Boas," *Science* 97 (n.s.) (1943): 60.

66. Ibid., p. 61.

67. Ruth Benedict, "Franz Boas as an Ethnologist," *Memoirs of the American Anthropological Association* 61 (1943): 31.

68. In *Anthropologist at Work,* p. 420.

69. Ibid., p. 422.

Chapter 11

1. Ruth Benedict, "Recognition of Cultural Diversities in the Postwar World" (1943), in Margaret Mead, *An Anthropologist at Work: The Writings of Ruth Benedict* (Boston: Houghton Mifflin Co., 1959), p. 448.

2. Ibid., p. 440.

3. *Science, Philosophy, and Religion,* ed. Lyman Bryson and L. Finkelstein (New York: Conference on Science, Philosophy, and Religion, 1941), 1:1.

4. Ibid., 2 (1942): 69.

5. Ibid., p. 70.

6. Ruth Benedict, review of *Ethical Relativity* by Edward Westermarck, *Herald Tribune,* June 26, 1932, p. 3.

7. *Anthropologist at Work,* p. 441.

8. Ruth Benedict, "Pre-War Experts," *The New Republic* 107 (1942): 411.

9. Editorial in *American Scholar* 12 (1942): 4.

10. *Science, Philosophy, and Religion* 3 (1943): 154.

11. Ruth Benedict, "Victory over Discrimination and Hate: Differences Versus Superiorities," *Frontiers of Democracy* 9 (1942): 82.

12. In 1943; *Anthropologist at Work,* p. 442.

13. Ruth Benedict, "The Study of Cultural Patterns in European Nations," *Transactions of the New York Academy of Science* 8 (1946): 274.

14. Ibid., pp. 275, 276.

15. Ibid., p. 274.

16. Ibid.

17. Geoffrey Gorer, "National Character: Theory and Practice," in *The Study of Culture at a Distance,* ed. M. Mead and R. Métraux (Chicago: University of Chicago Press, 1953), p. 62.

18. Benedict, "The Study of Cultural Patterns," p. 277.

19. Ruth Benedict, *The Chrysanthemum and the Sword* (Boston: Houghton Mifflin Co., 1946), p. 1.

20. Ibid., p. 3.

21. Ibid., p. 5.

22. Ibid.

23. Ibid., p. 7.

24. Ibid., p. 6.

25. Ibid.

26. Ibid., p. 7.

27. Ibid.

28. Ibid., pp. 9, 11.

29. Ibid., p. 9.

30. Ibid., p. 11.

31. Ibid., pp. 11–12.

32. Ibid., p. 13. 33. Ibid., p. 14.
34. Ibid., p. 16. 35. Ibid., p. 17.
36. Ibid., p. 14. 37. Ibid., pp. 15–16.
38. Ibid., p. 19. 39. Ibid., p. 70.
40. Ibid., p. 195. 41. Ibid., p. 219.
42. Geoffrey Gorer, "Themes in Japanese Culture" (1943), in *Personal Character and Cultural Milieu,* ed. Douglas Haring (Syracuse: Syracuse University Press, 1949).
43. Benedict, *The Chrysanthemum and the Sword,* p. 286.
44. Ibid. 45. Ibid., p. 287.
46. Ibid., p. 222. 47. Ibid., p. 223.
48. Ibid., p. 29. 49. Ibid., p. 101.
50. Ibid., p. 295. 51. Ibid., pp. 294–96.
52. Ibid., pp. 295–96. 53. Ibid., p. 300.
54. Benedict, "Pre-War Experts," p. 410.
55. Mark Starr, review of *The Chrysanthemum and the Sword* by Ruth Benedict, *Saturday Review* 29 (1946): 11.
56. Benedict, *The Chrysanthemum and the Sword,* p. 295.
57. Elgin Williams, "Anthropology for the Common Man," *American Anthropologist* 49 (1947): 84–89.
58. Review of *Race* by Ruth Benedict, *The New Republic* 104 (1941): 62.
59. Starr, review of *The Chrysanthemum and the Sword,* p. 11.
60. Harold Strauss, review of *The Chrysanthemum and the Sword* by Ruth Benedict, *New York Times,* November 24, 1946, pt. 4, p. 3.
61. Robert Lowie, *Ethnologist: A Personal Record* (Berkeley: University of California, 1959), p. 114.
62. Gordon Bowles, review of *The Chrysanthemum and the Sword* by Ruth Benedict, *Harvard Journal of Asiatic Studies* 10 (1947): 241.
63. Peter Lawrence, review of *The Chrysanthemum and the Sword,* by Ruth Benedict, *Nature* 161 (1948): 78.
64. John W. Bennett and M. Nagai, "The Japanese Critique of the Methodology of Benedict's *Chrysanthemum and Sword,*" *American Anthropologist* 55 (1953): 404–11.
65. John W. Bennett, "The Interpretation of Pueblo Culture," *Southwestern Journal of Anthropology* 2 (1946): 373.
66. Alfred L. Kroeber, review of *The Chrysanthemum and the Sword* by Ruth Benedict, *American Anthropologist* 49 (1947): 469.
67. In *Anthropologist at Work,* p. 67.
68. Kroeber, review of *The Chrysanthemum and the Sword,* p. 469.
69. Benedict, *The Chrysanthemum and the Sword,* p. 222.
70. Ibid. 71. Ibid., p. 293.
72. Ibid., p. 223. 73. Ibid., p. 294.
74. "Recognition of Cultural Diversities," in *Anthropologist at Work,* p. 441.
75. Ibid., p. 562.
76. Anon., "A Lady of Culture," *Science Illustrated* 3 (1948): 25.
77. Freeman to Benedict, September 7, 1948, RFB Papers.
78. Ibid. 79. Ibid.
80. *Anthropologist at Work,* p. 154.

Chapter 12

1. Benedict to Loeb, October 27, 1939, RFB Papers.
2. Personal interviews.
3. Ruth Benedict, "Victory over Discrimination and Hate: Differences Versus Superiorities," *Frontiers of Democracy* 9 (1942): 81.
4. Rebecca Reyher, *Zulu Women,* foreword by Ruth Benedict (New York: Columbia University Press, 1948). Reyher had been a Columbia student.
5. Ruth Benedict, "The Kinsey Report," *Saturday Review* 30 (1948): 34–35.
6. Ruth Benedict, "What Are We Educating For?" *National Association for Nursery Education Bulletin* 3 (1948): 5–9.
7. Ruth Benedict, "Are Families Passé?" *Saturday Review of Literature* 31 (1948): 5.
8. Ruth Benedict, "Child Rearing in Certain European Countries" (1949), in Margaret Mead, *An Anthropologist at Work: The Writings of Ruth Benedict* (Boston: Houghton Mifflin Co., 1959), pp. 449–58.
9. In 1948; ibid., p. 449.
10. Ibid.
11. *New York Times,* September 2, 1947, pt. 6, p. 36.
12. "Child Rearing in Certain European Countries," p. 451.
13. Ibid., p. 450.
14. Ibid.
15. Ibid.
16. Hadley Cantril, ed., *Tensions That Cause Wars* (Urbana: University of Illinois, 1950), p. 7.
17. From statement submitted by Ruth Benedict to *International Directory of Opinion and Attitude Research,* ed. Laszlo Radvanyi (Mexico: The Social Sciences, 1948), p. 18.
18. Ruth Benedict, "The Study of Cultural Continuities" and "An Outline for Research on Child Training in Different Cultures," in *The Influence of Home and Community on Children Under Thirteen Years of Age,* vol. 6: *Towards World Understanding* (Paris: UNESCO), pp. 7, 3, 10.
19. Ibid., p. 9.
20. Ruth Benedict, typewritten manuscript, "Anthropology in Your Life," 1947, RFB Papers.
21. In 1946, the American Design Award for War Service and the American Association of University Women Achievement Award. For others, see *Anthropologist at Work,* p. 525.
22. Remarks on receiving the Achievement Award from the American Association of University Women, June 1946, RFB Papers.
23. Ruth Benedict, "Let's Get Rid of Prejudice," *National Parent-Teacher* 40 (1946): 7–9.
24. "Japanese Are So Simple," *Asia and the Americas* 46 (1946): 500–505; and "The Puzzling Moral Code of the Japs," *Science Digest* 21 (1947): 89–92.
25. Speech to International House at Columbia University, 1948, RFB Papers.
26. Benedict, "Are Families Passé?" p. 5.
27. *Anthropologist at Work,* p. 136.

28. Benedict, "Are Families Passé?" p. 27.

29. Ibid., p. 6.

30. *Anthropologist at Work*, p. 130.

31. Benedict, "Are Families Passé?" p. 5.

32. Ibid., p. 29.

33. Erik Erikson, in *Ruth Fulton Benedict: A Memorial* (New York: The Viking Fund, 1949), p. 15.

34. Benedict to Charles Anderson, The Macmillan Co., March 7, 1944, RFB Papers.

35. Radvanyi, ed., *International Directory of Opinion and Attitude Research*, p. 18.

36. American Anthropological Association Papers, Smithsonian Institution, Washington, D.C. See George W. Stocking, "Ideas and Institutions in American Anthropology," in *Selected Papers from the American Anthropologist*, ed. G. W. Stocking (Washington, D.C.: American Anthropological Association, 1976), pp. 1–49.

37. Speech to the American Association of University Women, June 1946, RFB Papers.

38. Personal interviews.

39. See "Mary Wollstonecraft" drafts, RFB Papers.

40. In 1949; *Anthropologist at Work*, p. 463.

41. Ibid., p. 464.   42. Ibid., p. 467.

43. Ibid., p. 464, 468.   44. Ibid., p. 467.

45. Ibid., p. 469.

46. R. Benedict, review of *Search for a Social Philosophy* by Frederic W. Eggleston, *The Christian Century*, October 1, 1941, p. 1210.

47. Benedict, "Anthropology in Your Life," p. 3.

48. Ibid., p. 5.

49. Ibid., p. 6.

50. Sidney Mintz, "Ruth Benedict," in *Totems and Teachers*, ed. Sydel Silverman (New York: Columbia University Press, 1981), p. 166.

51. *Anthropologist at Work*, p. 473.

52. Ruth Benedict. engagement book, 1948, RFB Papers.

53. Erikson, in *Ruth Fulton Benedict*, p. 15.

54. Benedict, "Victory over Discrimination and Hate," p. 81; Benedict's italics.

55. *Anthropologist at Work*, pp. 484–85.

56. Ibid., p. 474.

57. Ruth Benedict, Journal, n.d., RFB Papers.

58. Ruth Benedict, draft of "The Story of My Life," 1935, RFB Papers.

59. *Anthropologist at Work*, p. 97.

60. Ruth Benedict, *Patterns of Culture* (Boston: Houghton Mifflin Co., 1934), p. 110.

61. Freeman to Mead, September 18, 1948, RFB Papers.

62. *Anthropologist at Work*, p. 519.

63. Benedict, *Patterns of Culture*, p. 118.

64. Ruth Benedict, *The Chrysanthemum and the Sword* (Boston: Houghton Mifflin Co., 1946), pp. 167-68.

65. Freeman to Mead, September 18, 1948, RFB Papers.

66. *Anthropologist at Work*, p. 65.

67. Benedict, *Patterns of Culture,* p. 109.

68. See Ruth Benedict on the Kwakiutl (ibid., p. 216) and on the Dobu (ibid., p. 172).

69. *Anthropologist at Work,* p. 519.

70. Ibid., p. 485.

71. Erikson, *Ruth Fulton Benedict,* p. 15.

72. Freeman to Mead, September 18, 1948, RFB Papers.

73. Ibid.

74. RFB Papers.

75. Lynd to Mead, September 18, 1948, RFB Papers.

76. Erikson, in *Ruth Fulton Benedict,* p. 16.

77. Alfred L. Kroeber, in *Ruth Fulton Benedict,* p. 11.

78. Cressman to Smith, September 19, 1948, RFB Papers.

79. Erikson, in *Ruth Fulton Benedict,* p. 16.

80. Benedict, *The Chrysanthemum and the Sword,* p. 166.

81. *Anthropologist at Work,* p. 154.

82. "Pelham" (nickname for Eleanor Pelham Kortheuer) to Mead, September 17, 1948, RFB Papers.

83. Freeman to Mead, September 18, 1948, RFB Papers.

84. For a volume of her poems, which she gave Mead that year; *Anthropologist at Work,* p. 473.

Bibliography

The following abbreviations are used in the Bibliography:

AA *American Anthropologist*
BAE *Bureau of American Ethnology*
JAFL *Journal of American Folk-Lore*
SWJA *Southwestern Journal of Anthropology*

Anderson, Sherwood. *Many Marriages.* New York: B. W. Huebsch, 1923.

Baptist Quarterly Review, vols. 11, 12, 14 (1889, 1890, 1892). New York: The Baptist Review Association.

Barnouw, Victor. "The Amiable Side of 'Patterns of Culture.'" *AA* 59 (1957): 532–36.

―――. "Ruth Benedict." *American Scholar* 49 (1980): 504–9.

Barry, John F., and Elmes, Robert. *Buffalo's Text Book.* Buffalo: Robert W. Elmes, 1924.

Bateson, Gregory. "Morale and National Character." In *Civilian Morale,* edited by Goodwin Watson, pp. 71–91. New York: Reynal and Hitchcock, 1942.

Bennett, John W. "The Interpretation of Pueblo Culture." *SWJA* 2 (1946): 361–74.

Bennett, John W., and Nagai, M. "The Japanese Critique of the Methodology of Benedict's Chrysanthemum and Sword." *AA* 55 (1953): 404–11.

Boas, Franz. *Anthropology and Modern Life.* New York: W. W. Norton, 1928.

―――. "Current Beliefs of the Kwakiutl Indians." *JAFL* 45 (1932): 177–250.

―――. *General Anthropology.* Boston: D. C. Heath, 1938.

―――. *Kwakiutl Ethnography,* edited by Helen Codere. Chicago: University of Chicago Press, 1966.

―――. *The Mind of Primitive Man.* New York: Free Press, 1963. Originally published in 1911.

―――. *Race, Language, and Culture.* New York: Free Press, 1940.

Brackett, Anna C., ed. *Woman and the Higher Education.* New York: Harper, 1893.

Bremner, Robert H. *From the Depths: The Discovery of Poverty in the U.S.* New York: New York University Press, 1956.

Bryson, Lyman, and Finkelstein, L., eds. *Science, Philosophy, and Religion.*

New York: Conference on Science, Philosophy, and Religion, 1941, 1942, 1943.

Busbey, Katherine G. *Home Life in America*. London: Methuen & Co., 1910.

Calverton, V. F., and Schmalhausen, S. D., eds. *Sex in Civilization*. New York: Macaulay Co., 1929.

Cantril, Hadley, ed. *Tensions That Cause Wars*. Urbana: University of Illinois Press, 1950.

Chase, Richard. *The Quest for Myth*. Baton Rouge: Louisiana State University Press, 1949.

———. "Ruth Benedict: The Woman as Anthropologist." *Columbia University Forum* 2 (1959): 19–22.

Columbia University. *The Rise of a University*. New York: Columbia University Press, 1937.

Dewey, John. *Democracy and Education: An Introduction to the Philosophy of Education*. New York: The Free Press, 1916.

———. *Human Nature and Conduct: An Introduction to Social Psychology*. New York: Henry Holt & Co., 1922.

———. "Racial Prejudice and Friction." *Chinese Social and Political Science Review* 6 (1921): 1–17.

Doob, Leonard. "The Utilization of Social Scientists in the Overseas Branch of the Office of War Information." *American Political Science Review* 41 (1947): 649–67.

Eliot, T. S. "Tradition and the Individual Talent." In *The Sacred Wood*. New York: Barnes & Noble, 1960. Originally published in 1920.

Endleman, Robert. "The Study of Man." *Commentary* 8 (1949): 284–91.

Fleming, Donald. "Ruth Fulton Benedict." *Harvard Encyclopedia of Notable American Women* (1971), pp. 128–31.

Fortune, Reo. *The Sorcerers of Dobu*. New York: Dutton, 1932.

Gilman, Charlotte Perkins. *Women and Economics*. Boston: Small, Maynard, & Co., 1900.

Goldenweiser, Alexander A. *History, Psychology, and Culture*. Magnolia, Mass.: Peter Smith, 1968. Originally published in 1933.

Goldfrank, Esther. *Notes on an Undirected Life*. New York: Queens College Press, 1978.

Goldman, Irving. "The Zuñi of New Mexico." In *Cooperation and Competition Among Primitive Peoples*, edited by Margaret Mead, pp. 313–53. New York: McGraw-Hill Book Co., 1937.

Gorer, Geoffrey. "National Character: Theory and Practice." In *The Study of Culture at a Distance*, edited by Margaret Mead and R. Metraux, pp. 57–82. Chicago: University of Chicago Press, 1953.

———. "Themes in Japanese Culture." In *Personal Character and Cultural Milieu*, edited by Douglas Haring, pp. 273–90. Syracuse: Syracuse University Press, 1949. Originally published in 1943.

Gregory, Horace. *A History of American Poetry 1900–1940*. New York: Gordian Press, 1976.

Hallowell, A. Irving. "Psychological Leads for Ethnological Field Workers." In *Personal Character and Cultural Milieu*, edited by Douglas Haring, pp. 341–88. Syracuse: Syracuse University Press, 1956. Originally published in 1937.

Hays, Brooks, and Steely, John E. *The Baptist Way of Life*. Englewood Cliffs, N.J.: Prentice-Hall, 1963.

Herskovits, Melville. *Franz Boas: The Science of Man in the Making.* New York: Scribner's, 1953.

Hoebel, E. A. "Major Contributions of Southwestern Studies to Anthropological Theory," *AA* 56 (1954): 720–27.

Horney, Karen. "Culture and Neurosis." *American Sociological Review* 1 (1936): 221–30. Comment by Walter Beck, pp. 230–35.

———. *Feminine Psychology,* edited by Harold Kelman. New York: W. W. Norton & Co., 1967.

Kardiner, Abram. *The Individual and His Society.* New York: Columbia University Press, 1939.

Key, Ellen. *Love and Marriage.* New York: G. P. Putnam's Sons, 1911.

Kirchwey, Freda, ed. *Our Changing Morality: A Symposium.* London: Kegan, Paul, Trench, Trubner & Co., 1925.

Kirkendall, Richard S. *Social Scientists and Farm Politics in the Age of Roosevelt.* Columbia: University of Missouri Press, 1966.

Kluckhohn, Clyde; Murray, Henry; and Schneider, David, eds. *Personality in Nature, Society, and Culture.* New York: Alfred Knopf, 1953.

Koffka, Kurt. *The Growth of the Mind: An Introduction to Child Psychology,* translated by Robert M. Ogden. New York: Harcourt. Brace & Co., 1924.

Kroeber, Alfred L. "Elsie Clews Parsons." *AA* 45 (1943): 252–55.

———. "Franz Boas: The Man." *Memoirs of the American Anthropological Association* 61 (1943): 5–26.

———. "The Place of Boas in Anthropology." *AA* 58 (1956): 151–59.

Kroeber, Theodora. *Alfred L. Kroeber.* Berkeley: University of California Press, 1970.

"A Lady of Culture." *Science Illustrated* 3 (1948): 24–27.

Lappin, Maitland M. *Baptists in the Protestant Tradition.* Toronto: Ryerson Press, 1947.

Linton, A., and Wagley, Charles. *Ralph Linton.* New York: Columbia University Press, 1971.

Lowie, Robert H. *Ethnologist: A Personal Record.* Berkeley: University of California Press, 1959.

Luhan, Mabel Dodge. *Intimate Memoirs: Background.* New York: Harcourt, Brace & Co., 1933.

Lurie, Nancy O. "Women in Early American Anthropology." In *Pioneers of American Anthropology,* edited by June Helm, pp. 29–81. Seattle: University of Washington Press, 1966.

Lynd, Robert. *Knowledge for What?* Princeton: Princeton University Press, 1939.

MacCracken, Henry Noble. *The Hickory Limb.* New York: Scribner's, 1950.

Malinowski, B. *Myth in Primitive Psychology.* New York: W. W. Norton & Co., 1926.

McWilliams, Carey. *Southern California Country: An Island on the Land.* New York: Duell, Sloan & Pearce, 1946.

Mead, Margaret. *An Anthropologist at Work: The Writings of Ruth Benedict.* Boston: Houghton Mifflin Co., 1959.

———. "Apprenticeship Under Boas." In *The Anthropology of Franz Boas,* edited by Walter Goldschmidt, pp. 29–45. American Anthropological Association Memoir 89. 1959.

———. *Blackberry Winter.* New York: William Morrow & Co., 1972.

———. "More Comprehensive Field Methods." *AA* 35 (1933): 1–15.

———. "National Character." In *Anthropology Today,* edited by A. L. Kroeber, pp. 642–67. Chicago: University of Chicago Press, 1953.

———. *Ruth Benedict.* New York: Columbia University Press, 1974.

———. "Ruth Fulton Benedict." In *Encyclopedia of the Social Sciences.* New York: Macmillan Co., 1968.

Mead, Margaret, ed. *Cooperation and Competition Among Primitive Peoples.* New York: McGraw-Hill, 1937.

Mead, Margaret, and Metraux, Rhoda, eds. *The Study of Culture at a Distance.* Chicago: University of Chicago Press, 1953.

Mezzacappa, Dale. "Vassar College and the Suffrage Movement." *Vassar Quarterly* 69 (1973): 2–9.

Mintz, Sidney. "Ruth Benedict." In *Totems and Teachers,* edited by Sydel Silverman, pp. 141–68. New York: Columbia University Press, 1981.

Modell, Judith. "A Biographical Study of Ruth Fulton Benedict." Ph.D. diss., University of Minnesota, 1978.

Murray, Henry A. *Explorations in Personality.* New York: Oxford University Press, 1938.

Newcomer, Mabel. *A Century of Higher Education for American Women.* New York: Harper & Row, 1959.

Newsom, G. E. *The New Morality.* London: Ivor Nicholson & Watson, 1932.

New York State. *Annual Report of the New York State Board of Charities for the Year 1910.* Albany, 1911.

Nietzsche, Friedrich. *The Birth of Tragedy,* translated by William A. Haussmann, vol. 3 of *The Complete Works,* edited by Oscar Levy. London: T. N. Fowlis, 1910.

O'Keeffe, Georgia. *Georgia O'Keeffe.* New York: Viking Press, 1976.

Pandey, Triloki. "Anthropologists at Zuñi." *Proceedings of the American Philosophical Society* 116 (1972): 321–37.

Parsons, Elsie Clews. *The Family.* New York: G. P. Putnam, 1906.

———. *The Old-Fashioned Woman: Primitive Fancies About the Sex.* New York: G. P. Putnam, 1913.

———. "Notes on Zuñi. Part I." American Anthropological Association Memoir 4. 1917.

———. *Pueblo Indian Religion.* 2 vols. Chicago: University of Chicago Press, 1939.

———. Review of *Zuñi Mythology* by Ruth Benedict. *Journal of American Folk-Lore* 50 (1937): 107–9.

Pells, Richard H. *Radical Visions and American Dreams: Cultural and Social Thought in the Depression Years.* New York: Harper & Row, 1973.

Piers, Gerhart, and Singer, Milton. *Shame and Guilt. A Psychoanalytic and a Cultural Study.* New York: W. W. Norton & Co., 1971. Originally published in 1953.

Plum, Dorothy A., and Dowell, George B. *The Magnificent Enterprise: A Chronicle of Vassar College.* Poughkeepsie, N.Y.: Vassar College, 1961.

Preston, Richard J. "Edward Sapir's Anthropology: Style, Structure, and Method." *AA* 68 (1966): 1105–28.

Radvanyi, Laszlo, ed. *International Directory of Opinion and Attitude Research.* Mexico: The Social Sciences, 1948.

Redfield, Robert. "Relations of Anthropology to the Social Sciences and to the

Humanities." In *Anthropology Today,* edited by A. L. Kroeber, pp. 728–38. Chicago: University of Chicago Press, 1953.

Rogers, Agnes. *Vassar Women.* Poughkeepsie, N.Y.: Vassar College Press, 1940.

Rohner, Ronald P. *The Ethnography of Franz Boas,* introduction by Ronald P. and Evelyn C. Rohner, translated by Hedy Parker. Chicago: University of Chicago Press, 1969.

———. "Franz Boas: Ethnographer on the Northwest Coast." In *Pioneers of American Anthropology.* Edited by June Helm. Seattle: University of Washington Press, 1966.

Santayana, George. *Character and Opinion in the United States.* New York: Scribner's, 1921.

———. *The Life of Reason.* New York: Scribner's, 1905.

———. *Three Philosophical Poets: Lucretius, Dante, and Goethe.* Cambridge: Harvard University Press, 1947. Originally published in 1910.

———. "The Elements and Function of Poetry," and "Mythology." In *Essays in Literary Criticism,* edited by Irving Singer. New York: Scribner's, 1956. Originally published in 1905.

———. *Interpretations of Poetry and Religion.* New York: Harper Torchbook, 1957. Originally published in 1927.

Sapir, Edward. *Culture, Language and Personality,* edited by David Mandelbaum. Berkeley: University of California Press, 1970.

———. "The Discipline of Sex." *American Mercury* 16 (1929): 413–20.

———. *Language.* New York: Harcourt, Brace & World, 1921.

———. "Observations on the Sex Problem in America." *American Journal of of Psychiatry* 8 (1928): 519–34.

Schneider, David, and Deutsch, Albert. *The History of Public Welfare in New York State 1867–1940.* Chicago: University of Chicago Press, 1941.

Shelton, Brenda K. *Reformers in Search of Yesterday: Buffalo in the 1890s.* Albany: State University of New York Press, 1976.

Smith, James H. *History of Chenango and Madison Counties, N.Y. With Illustrations and Biographical Sketches.* Syracuse: D. Mason, 1880.

Spier, L. "Elsie Clews Parsons." *AA* 45 (1943): 244–51.

Spradley, Thomas S., and James P. *Deaf Like Me.* New York: Random House, 1978.

Stocking, George W. "Franz Boas and the Culture Concept in Historical Perspective." *AA* 68 (1966): 867–82.

———. "Franz Boaz and the Founding of the American Anthropological Association." *AA* 62 (1960): 1–17.

———. "Ideas and Institutions in American Anthropology." In *Selected Papers from the American Anthropologist,* edited by G. W. Stocking. Washington, D.C.: American Anthropological Association, 1976.

———. *Race, Culture and Evolution: Essays in the History of Anthropology.* New York: The Free Press, 1968.

———. Review of *Ruth Benedict* by Margaret Mead. *Times Literary Supplement,* March 12, 1976, p. 288.

———. *The Shaping of American Anthropology, 1883–1911: A Franz Boas Reader.* New York: Basic Books, 1974.

Sullivan, Harry Stack. *The Fusion of Psychiatry and Social Science,* edited by H. S. Perry. New York: W. W. Norton, 1964.

Sullivan, J. W. N. *Beethoven: His Spiritual Development.* New York: Vintage Books, 1960. Originally published in 1927.

Thomas, William L., ed. *Yearbook of Anthropology 1955.* New York: Wenner-Gren Foundation, 1955.

Todd, Janet M. "The Biographies of Mary Wollstonecraft." *Signs* 1 (1976): 721–34.

Violette, Eugene Morrow. *A History of Missouri.* Cape Girardeau, Mo.: Ramfire Press, 1951.

White, Leslie A. "The Ethnography and Ethnology of Franz Boas." *Texas Memorial Museum Bulletin* 6. 1963.

———. "The Social Organization of Ethnological Theory." Rice University Studies 52. Houston, 1966.

Williams, Elgin. "Anthropology for the Common Man." *AA* 49 (1947): 84–89.

Wollstonecraft, Mary. *Mary: A Fiction.* New York: Garland Publishing, 1974. Originally published in 1788.

Woman's Centennial Congress. *100th Anniversary.* New York: Seneca Falls, 1940.

Woolf, Virginia. *Granite and Rainbow.* New York: Harcourt Brace, 1958.

———. *The Waves.* New York: Harcourt, Brace & Co., 1931.

Published Works of Ruth Benedict

1922 "The Vision in Plains Culture." *AA* 24:1–23.

1923 "The Concept of the Guardian Spirit in North America." Ph.D. diss., Columbia University. *Memoirs of the American Anthropological Association* 29:1–97.

1923 "A Matter for the Fieldworker in Folklore." *JAFL* 36:104.

1924 "A Brief Sketch of Serrano Culture" *AA* 26:366–92.

1925 Review of *The North American Indian, vol. 12: The Hopi* by Edward S. Curtis. *AA* 27:458–60.

1925 Review of *Shoshone Folk-Lore* by Sarah Emilia Olden. *AA* 27:461.

1925 Review of *Seneca Myths and Folk-Tales* by Arthur Parker. *JAFL* 38: 419–20.

1926 "Serrano Tales." *JAFL* 39:1–17.

1927 Review of *Actes des Congres International d'Histoire des Religions. Journal of Philosophy* 24:608–12.

1927 Review of *How Natives Think* by L. Levy-Bruhl. *Memphis Commercial Appeal,* January 16.

1928 Review of *Environment and Race* by Griffith Taylor. *Herald Tribune,* January 22.

1928 Review of *L'Ame Primitive* by L. Levy-Bruhl. *Journal of Philosophy* 25:717–19.

1928 Review of *The Story of the American Indian* by Paul Radin. *The Nation* 126:456.

1929 Review of *The Sexual Life of Savages* by Bronislaw Malinowski. *Herald Tribune,* July 28.

1929 Review of *I Saw the Congo* by G. Flandrau. *Herald Tribune,* September 22.

1929 "The Science of Custom." *The Century Magazine* 117:641–49.
1930 "Animism." *Encyclopedia of the Social Sciences* 2:65–67.
1930 "Child Marriage." *Encyclopedia of the Social Sciences.* 3:395–97.
1930 "Eight Stories from Acoma." *JAFL* 43:59–87.
1930 "Psychological Types in the Cultures of the Southwest." In *Proceedings of the Twenty-Third International Congress of Americanists*, pp. 572-81.
1930 Review of *Growing Up in New Guinea* by Margaret Mead. *Herald Tribune*, September 21.
1930 Review of *Tepotzlan, A Mexican Village* by Robert Redfield. *Herald Tribune*, November 2.
1930 Review of *Witchcraft in Old and New England* by George L. Kittredge. *JAFL* 43:120–21.
1930 Review of *Der Ursprung der Gottesidee* by P. Wilhelm Schmidt. *JAFL* 43:444–45.
1931 "Dress." *Encyclopedia of the Social Sciences* 5:235–37.
1931 "Folklore." *Encyclopedia of the Social Sciences* 6:288–93.
1931 "Professor Franz Boas, President of the American Association for the Advancement of Science." *Scientific Monthly* 32:278–80.
1931 Review of *California Indian Nights Entertainments* by Edward W. Gifford and Gwendoline Harris Block. *AA* 33:432–33.
1931 *Tales of the Cochiti Indians.* BAE Bulletin 98. Washington, D.C.: Smithsonian Institution.
1932 "Configurations of Culture in North America." *AA* 34:1–27.
1932 Review of *Dancing Gods: Indian Ceremonials of New Mexico and Arizona* by Edna Fergusson. *AA* 34:719–20.
1932 Review of *Ethical Relativity* by Edward Westermarck. *Herald Tribune*, August 6.
1932 Review of *Eskimo* by Peter Freuchen. *AA* 34:720–21.
1933 "Magic." *Encyclopedia of the Social Sciences* 10:39–44.
1933 "Myth." *Encyclopedia of the Social Sciences* 11:170–73.
1933 Review of *Life in Lesu* by Hortense Powdermaker. *Herald Tribune*, July 30.
1934 *Patterns of Culture.* Boston: Houghton Mifflin Co.
1934 "Anthropology and the Abnormal." *Journal of General Psychology* 10: 59–82.
1934 Review of *The Dawn of Conscience* by James H. Breasted. *Herald Tribune*, January 21.
1934 Review of *The Racial Myth* by Paul Radin. *Herald Tribune*, August 12.
1934 Review of *Rebel Destiny: Among the Bush Negroes of Dutch Guinea* by Melville J. and Frances S. Herskovits. *Herald Tribune*, June 10.
1934 "Ritual." *Encyclopedia of the Social Sciences* 13:396–98.
1935 *Zuñi Mythology.* 2 vols. Columbia University Contributions to Anthropology. New York: Columbia University Press.
1935 Review of *Sex and Temperament in Three Primitive Societies* by Margaret Mead. *Herald Tribune*, June 2.
1935 Review of *Are We Civilized?* by Robert Lowie. *Herald Tribune*, September 15.
1935 Review of *Sex and Culture* by J. D. Unwin. *AA* 37:691–92.
1936 "Marital Property Rights in Bilateral Society." *AA* 38:368–73.

1936 Review of *Manus Religion* by R. F. Fortune. *Review of Religion* 1:48–50.

1937 "Unemployment and Society." *Social Work Today* 4:11–12.

1937 "Anthropology and the Coronation." *Time and Tide*, May 8.

1937 Review of *Chan Kom: A Maya Village* by Robert Redfield and Alfonso Villa R. *AA* 39:340–42.

1937 Review of *Naven: A Survey of Problems Suggested by a Comparative Picture of a New Guinea Tribe Drawn from Three Points of View* by Gregory Bateson. *Review of Religion* 2:63–66.

1937 Review of *Life in a Haitian Valley* by Melville J. Herskovits. *Herald Tribune*, April 16.

1937 Review of *Savage Civilization* by Tom Harrison. *Herald Tribune*, October 10.

1937 Review of *Primitive Intelligence and Environment* by S. D. Porteus. *Herald Tribune*, October 10.

1937 Review of *Primitive Religion* by Paul Radin. *Herald Tribune*, October 17.

1938 "Religion." In *General Anthropology*, edited by Franz Boas. Boston: D. C. Heath.

1938 "Continuities and Discontinuities in Cultural Conditioning." *Psychiatry* 1:161–67.

1938 Review of *Die Frau in Offentlichen Leben in Melanesien* by Joachim Henning. *AA* 40:163.

1938 Review of *The Neurotic Personality of Our Time* by Karen Horney. *Journal of Social and Abnormal Psychology* 33:133–35.

1939 "Edward Sapir." *AA* 41:465–77.

1939 "A Reply to Dr. Aginsky." *Character and Personality* 7:344–45.

1940 *Race: Science and Politics.* New York: Modern Age.

1940 "Alexander Goldenweiser." *Modern Quarterly* 11:32–33.

1940 "Tribute to Dr. Margaret Mead." *The Eleusis of Chi Omega* 42:390–96.

1940 "Women and Anthropology." In *The Education of Women in a Democracy*, edited by The Institution of Professional Relations for the Women's Centennial Congress. New York: The Institution.

1940 Review of *Pueblo Indian Religion* by Elsie Clews Parsons. *Review of Religion* 4:438–40.

1941 "Foreword." In *Jungle People* by Jules Henry. New York: J. J. Augustin.

1941 "Letter." *New Republic* 105:279–80.

1941 "Our Last Minority: Youth." *New Republic* 104:271–72.

1941 "Privileged Classes: An Anthropological Problem." *Frontiers of Democracy* 7:110–12.

1941 "Race Problems in America." *Annals of the American Academy of Political and Social Sciences* 216:73–78.

1941 Review of *Search for a Social Philosophy* by Frederic William Eggleston. *Christian Century*, October 1.

1941 *Review of Pascua: A Yaqui Village in Arizona* by Edward H. Spicer. *American Historical Review* 47:170–71.

1942 "Anthropology and Cultural Change." *American Scholar* 11:243–48.

1942 "Editorial." *American Scholar* 12:3–4.

1942 "Nature Builds No Barriers." *Asia and the Americas.* 42:697–99.

1942 "Pre-War Experts." *New Republic* 107:410–11.

1942 "Primitive Freedom." *Atlantic Monthly* 169:756–63.
1942 "Teachers and the Hatch Act." *Frontiers of Democracy* 8:1965–66.
1942 "Victory over Discrimination and Hate: Differences Versus Superiorities." *Frontiers of Democracy* 9:81–82.
1942 "We Can't Afford Race Prejudice." *Frontiers of Democracy* 9:2.
1942 Review of *An Apache Life Way* by Morris E. Opler. *AA* 44:692–93.
1942 Review of *Becoming a Kwoma: Teaching and Learning in a New Guinea Tribe* by John M. Whiting. *Journal of Social and Abnormal Psychology* 37:409–10.
1942 Review of *The Crisis of Our Age* and *Social Cultural Dynamics* by P. Sorokin. *New Republic* 106:154.
1942 Review of *Escape from Freedom* by Erich Fromm. *Psychiatry* 5:111–13.
1942 Review of *Principles of Anthropology* by E. D. Chapple and C. S. Coon. *Psychiatry* 5:450–51.
1942 Review of *Propaganda for Democracy Through Public Opinion* by Harold D. Lasswell. *Saturday Review of Literature*, March 7.
1942 Review of *When People Meet* by Alain Locke and Bernhard Stern. *Herald Tribune*, February 8.
1942 Review of *Indians of South America* by Paul Radin. *Herald Tribune*, April 26.
1942 Review of *Men Before Adam* by Anne Terry White. *Herald Tribune*, December 27.
1943 "Franz Boas." *American Sociological Review* 8:223.
1943 "Franz Boas." *The Nation* 156:15–16.
1943 "Franz Boas." *Science* 97 (n.s.):60–62.
1943 "Franz Boas as an Ethnologist." *Memoirs of the American Anthropological Association* 61, pp. 27–34.
1943 "Human Nature Is Not a Trap." *Partisan Review* 10:159–64.
1943 "Recognition of Cultural Diversities in the Postwar World." *Annals of the American Academy of Political and Social Sciences* 228:101–7.
1943 "Two Patterns of Indian Acculturation." *AA* 45:207–12.
1943 "Transmitting Our Democratic Heritage in the Schools." *American Journal of Sociology* 48:722–27.
1944 Review of *A Scientific Theory of Culture and Other Essays* by Bronislaw Malinowski. *Herald Tribune*, November 5.
1946 *The Chrysanthemum and the Sword: Patterns of Japanese Culture.* Boston: Houghton Mifflin Co.
1946 "Anthropology in Your Life." *Vassar Alumnae* 32:10–11.
1946 "The Future of Race Prejudice." *American Scholar* 15:455–61.
1946 "Japanese Are so Simple." *Asia and the Americas* 46:500–505.
1946 "Let's Get Rid of Prejudice." *National Parent-Teacher* 40:7–9.
1946 "Racism Is Vulnerable." *English Journal* 35:299–303.
1946 "The Study of Cultural Patterns in European Nations." *Transactions of the New York Academy of Science* 8 (ser. 11): 274–79.
1946 Review of *Prehistoric Cave Paintings* by Max Raphael. *Herald Tribune*, January 27.
1946 Review of *Hiroshima* by John Hersey. *The Nation* 163:656–58.
1946 Review of *Meeting of East and West: An Inquiry Concerning World Understanding* by F. C. S. Northrop. *New Republic* 115:299–300.
1947 Interview, *New York Times*, September 2.

1947 "The Puzzling Moral Code of the Japs." *Science Digest* 21:89–92.
1947 "The Viking Fund." *AA* 49:527–30.
1947 Review of *Richer by Asia* by Edmond Taylor. *Saturday Review of Literature*, July 26, p. 13.
1947 Review of *Evolution and Ethics* by Sir Arthur Kieth. *New York Times Book Section*, August 3.
1947 Review of *The Road of Life and Death* by Paul Radin. *AA* 49:282–83.
1948 "Anthropology and the Humanities." *AA* 50:585–93.
1948 "Foreword." In *Zulu Woman* by Rebecca Reyher. New York: Columbia University Press.
1948 "The Kinsey Report." *Saturday Review of Literature* 30:34–35.
1948 "What Are We Educating For?" *National Association for Nursery Education Bulletin* 3:5–9.
1948 "Are Families Passé?" *Saturday Review of Literature* 31:5.

Posthumously Published Works of Ruth Benedict

1949 "Child Rearing in Certain European Countries." *American Journal of Orthopsychiatry* 19:342–48.
1949 "The Study of Cultural Continuities" and "An Outline for Research on Child Training in Different Cultures." In *The Influence of Home and Community on Children Under Thirteen Years of Age*. Vol. 6: *Towards World Understanding*. Pp. 5–13 and 15–25. Paris: UNESCO.
1952 "Thai Culture and Behavior." Data Paper no. 4, Southeast Asia Program. Ithaca: Cornell University.
1958 "Fragments of a Journal." *American Scholar* 28:33–36.
1970 "Synergy: Some Notes of Ruth Benedict." Selected by Abraham Maslow and John J. Honigmann. *AA* 72:320–33.

Archival Sources

American Anthropological Association Papers. Smithsonian Institution, Washington, D.C.
Ruth Fulton Benedict Papers. Special Collections, Vassar College Library, Poughkeepsie, N.Y.
Franz Boas Papers. American Philosophical Society, Philadelphia, Pa.
Columbiana. University Archives, Columbia University, New York, N.Y.
Rachel Davis DuBois Papers. Immigrant Archives, University of Minnesota, Minneapolis, Minn.
Journal of American Folk-Lore and American Folklore Society Correspondence. Department of Folk-Lore and Folk-Life, University of Pennsylvania, Philadelphia, Pa.
Alfred Kroeber Papers. Bancroft Library, University of California, Berkeley, Calif.
Robert Lowie Papers. Bancroft Library, University of California, Berkeley, Calif.
Elsie Clews Parsons Papers. American Philosophical Society, Philadelphia, Pa.

F. P. Rous Papers (for the Society for Experimental Biology and Medicine), American Philosophical Society, Philadelphia, Pa.

Edward Sapir–Robert Lowie Letters. Library, Museum of the University of Pennsylvania, Philadelphia, Pa.

Signed Reviews of Ruth Benedict's Books Cited in Text

An-Che, Li. Discussion of Patterns of Culture. *AA* 39 (1938): 62–76.

Bowles, Gordon. Review of *The Chrysanthemum and the Sword. Harvard Journal of Asiatic Studies* 10 (1947): 237–41.

Kroeber, Alfred L. Review of *Patterns of Culture. AA* 37 (1935): 689–90.

Kroeber, Alfred L. Review of *The Chrysanthemum and the Sword. AA* 49 (1947): 469–72.

Lawrence, Peter. Review of *The Chrysanthemum and the Sword. Nature* 161 (1948): 77–78.

Mead, Margaret. Review of *Patterns of Culture. The Nation* 139 (1934): 686.

Morris, John. Review of *The Chrysanthemum and the Sword. New Statesman* 33 (1947): 436.

Morris, John. Review of *The Chrysanthemum and the Sword. Pacific Affairs* 20 (1947): 208–10.

Parsons, Elsie Clews. Review of *Zuñi Mythology. JAFL* 50 (1937): 107.

Starr, Mark. Review of *The Chrysanthemum and the Sword. Saturday Review of Literature* 29 (1946): 11.

Strauss, Harold. Review of *The Chrysanthemum and the Sword. New York Times,* November 24, pt. 4.

Unsigned Reviews of Ruth Benedict's Books Cited in Text

Review of *Patterns of Culture. New York Times,* October 21, 1934.

Review of *Race. The New Republic* 104 (1941): 62.

Signed Obituaries of Ruth Fulton Benedict Cited in Text

Barnouw, Victor. "Ruth Benedict: Apollonian and Dionysian." *University of Toronto Quarterly* 18 (1949): 241–53.

Ruth Fulton Benedict: A Memorial. New York: The Viking Fund, 1949.
    Includes testimonies by:
        Alfred L. Kroeber, pp. 10–11.
        Cora duBois, pp. 12–13.
        Erik Erikson, pp. 14–17.
        Clyde Kluckhohn, pp. 18–21.
        Robert Lynd, pp. 22–24.
        Margaret Mead, pp. 25–27.
        Minutes Presented at Columbia University, pp. 31–33 (Horace Friess, W. Duncan Strong, Alfred Kroeber, Robert Lynd).

Lee, Dorothy. "Ruth Fulton Benedict." *JAFL* 62 (1949): 345–47.

Mead, Margaret. "Ruth Fulton Benedict 1887–1948." *AA* 51 (1949): 457–69
Richards, A. I. "Prof. Ruth Benedict." *Nature* 162 (1948): 725.
Sullivan, Harry Stack. "Ruth Fulton Benedict, Ph.D., D.Sc." *Psychiatry*
(1948): 402–3.

Unsigned Obituaries of Ruth Fulton Benedict Cited in Text

American Sociological Review 13 (1948): 775.
Newsweek 32 (1948): 56.
New York Herald Tribune, September 18, 1948.
New York Times, September 18, 1948.
Publishers Weekly 154 (1948): 1607.
School and Society 68 (1948): 206.
Science 108 (1948): 352.
Wilson Library Bulletin 23 (1948): 231.

Index